LAID LOW

LAID LOW

INSIDE THE CRISIS THAT OVERWHELMED EUROPE AND THE IMF

PAUL BLUST€IN

ISBN 978-1-928096-33-7 (cloth)
ISBN 978-1-928096-25-2 (paper)
ISBN 978-1-928096-24-5 (ePUB)
ISBN 978-1-928096-34-4 (ePDF)

Published by the Centre for International Governance Innovation.

Printed and bound in Canada.

Centre for International Governance Innovation
67 Erb Street West
Waterloo, ON Canada N2L 6C2

www.cigionline.org

CONTENTS

ACRONYMS AND ABBREVIATIONS

BRICS	Brazil, Russia, India, China and South Africa
CACs	collective action clauses
CDS	credit default swaps
CIGI	Centre for International Governance Innovation
CRA	Contingency Reserve Arrangement
ECB	European Central Bank
EFSF	European Financial Stability Facility
ESM	European Stability Mechanism
DEKOs	state-owned enterprises in Greece
FSAP	Financial Sector Assessment Program
G7	Group of Seven
G20	Group of Twenty
GDP	gross domestic product
HIPC	Heavily Indebted Poor Countries (debt relief initiative)
IEO	Independent Evaluation Office
IIF	Institute of International Finance
IMF	International Monetary Fund
IMFC	International Monetary and Financial Committee
ISDA	International Swaps and Derivatives Association
LSE	London School of Economics
LTRO	Long-term Refinancing Operations
OMT	Outright Monetary Transactions
OSI	official sector involvement
PASOK	Panhellenic Socialist Movement

PCL	precautionary credit line
PSI	private sector involvement
S&P	Standard and Poor's
SDAF	Sovereign Debt Adjustment Facility
SDRs	special drawing rights
SDRM	Sovereign Debt Restructuring Mechanism
SMP	Securities Market Programme
SPR	Strategy, Policy and Review Department
WEO	World Economic Outlook
WTO	World Trade Organization

To my parents
(Yes, of course that includes you, Charles!)

AUTHOR'S NOTE AND ACKNOWLEDGEMENTS

The person who first excited me about the idea of doing this book shall remain anonymous, because he is still a staff member at the International Monetary Fund (IMF) and might get into trouble. Suffice to say that the conversation took place in the spring of 2013, as the crisis in the euro zone was simmering, and this fellow was well aware that I had previously authored books about financial crises in which the IMF played a key role. "There's a great story to be told, and given all your experience writing about the Fund, you're the guy to do it," he told me. As appreciative as I was to hear that, my regretful reply was that I was in no position to do such a book, as I currently live in Japan (for family reasons — my wife is Japanese). Who would provide support to a resident of Japan for the research and writing of a book about the role played by a Washington-based institution in a European crisis?

Imagine my delight, therefore, when a few weeks later I got a call offering exactly that kind of sponsorship. The caller was Domenico Lombardi, who had just become director of the Global Economy Program at the Centre for International Governance Innovation, where I am a senior fellow. Domenico knew that I live in Japan, but he also knew that few, if any, journalists are interested in delving into the arcana of IMF policy. (It's an acquired taste, I must admit.) And although I would obviously have to travel to conduct interviews, that would be true even if I lived somewhere in Europe or the United States. I was therefore immensely pleased and grateful when, following some back-and-forth about the plan for the book, Domenico and the rest of CIGI's leadership gave the go-ahead for me to proceed.

I travelled to nine countries, where I interviewed more than 100 people, some upwards of 10 times. (Follow-ups were sometimes conducted by phone, Skype or email.) They included current and former officials of the IMF, European governments, European institutions, central banks and the private finance industry, with ranks ranging from heads of governments, finance ministers, central bank governors and managing directors to department heads and junior-level staffers. For their generosity with their time in helping to enlighten me, these people have my profound thanks. Nearly all interviews were conducted on a "deep background" basis, meaning I could use the information but the interviewee could not be quoted, even anonymously, without granting permission — the purpose being to elicit the maximum amount of candour. In some cases, interviewees granted access to memos, notes of meetings and other confidential documents in response to my request for assistance in achieving the greatest possible level of historical accuracy. I especially appreciate those peoples' willingness to share such documents; they recognized that, given a decent interval between the events in question and publication of the book, little harm would result from their disclosure, and my book would be less prone to error if I could rely on contemporaneous records, rather than the hazy and sometimes selective memories of interested parties. Of course, I also relied heavily on material that was not confidential, including newspaper articles, transcripts and documents in the public record. To the extent that I rely on public documents, I have inserted footnotes into the text, but in many parts of the narrative no footnotes have been included because I am relying on either confidential documents or information provided on deep background. I can only ask readers to trust that I have been scrupulously careful to check and double-check assertions by interviewees, especially concerning what people said during closed-door meetings.

Books, articles and reports by numerous people were of invaluable importance in helping me piece together the tale. Footnotes citing these sources are liberally sprinkled throughout the book, but special mention here is merited for Peter Ludlow's EuroComment publications, which were a goldmine of detail and insight about events involving meetings of European leaders and finance ministers. Books on the crisis (or with chapters relating to it) that I found especially useful in providing perspective and information included volumes by Jean Pisani-Ferry, Yannis Palaiologos, Martin Sandbu, Martin Wolf, Matt Cooper, Simon Carswell, Neil Irwin, Carlo Bastasin, Peter Spiegel, Barry Eichengreen, Alan Friedman, James Angelos, John Peet and Anton La Guardia, and Alan Crawford and Tony Czuczka. The tremendous influence on me of analyses and articles by Susan Schadler, Nicolas Véron and Barry Eichengreen will be obvious to anyone familiar with their work. As for newspaper reporting, it would be impossible for me to mention all the colleagues whose work I admired as I sifted through thousands of articles. I can only say this book would be a lot poorer if it had not been for the scoops, "tick-tocks" and other revelatory pieces produced by the likes of Peter Spiegel, Marcus Walker, Charles Forelle, Landon Thomas Jr., Yannis Palaiologos, Ian Talley, Andrew Mayeda, Simon Kennedy and Matthew Karnitschnig; and the analyses written by the likes of Alan Beattie, Stephen Fidler, Martin Wolf, Tony Barber and Wolfgang Munchau.

In addition to interviewing people involved in decision making, I gained immeasurably from conversations with experts and fellow journalists and authors. Among those whose brains provided especially rich pickings were Rob Kahn, James Boughton, Liaquat Ahamed, Nick Malkoutzis, Arvind Subramanian, Miranda Xafa, Thomas Bernes, Mark Allen, Morris Goldstein and Alan Friedman. I would be remiss if I failed to note that until January 2016 I was a nonresident fellow at the Brookings Institution, where colleagues warmly welcomed me during my visits to Washington.

The book, though, remained a CIGI project throughout, overseen by Domenico as well as Alisha Clancy, CIGI's Global Economy program manager, with Heather McNorgan assisting in administrative matters. Once I had written a draft manuscript, two anonymous experts selected by CIGI reviewed the book and provided countless comments that helped me improve the final product, not least by saving me from several embarrassing errors and omissions. (I am of course solely responsible for any that remain.) Then the manuscript came under the expert editorial guidance of Carol Bonnett, CIGI's publisher, who was ably assisted by Sara Moore, Melodie Wakefield and Jennifer Goyder.

One disclosure I feel obliged to make is that several key players at the IMF declined to speak with me, or were not permitted to do so. This was because of a voluminous number of confidential IMF documents that I cited in a previous book, *Off Balance: The Travails of Institutions That Govern the Global Financial System,* published by CIGI in 2013. The revelation of these documents upset some people at the Fund so much that the Communications Department decided I should be treated much more guardedly than I had been when researching my previous books on the Fund (even though those books also included material from confidential documents). I found this approach perplexing, and tried to convince the Communications Department that it would be in the institution's interest to be as forthcoming as possible in granting interviews, simply because I would glean better insight into the reasons for its policy choices and the actions of its leading figures. I am pleased to report that, in the end, I was able to arrange interviews with most of the people whom I most needed to see, but regret that Christine Lagarde was not among them. I can assure readers that the judgments I reach in the book were unaffected by any denial of access. Critics may complain that the book is either too harsh or too complimentary toward the IMF and Madame Lagarde, but I want to make clear that the willingness or lack thereof to grant interviews didn't cause me to tilt my findings in either a positive or negative direction. I wrote the narrative based on what I genuinely believe occurred, letting chips fall where they may. And fortunately, many of the confidential documents that I would have most wished to obtain were already published by intrepid reporters like the *Financial Times's* Peter Spiegel, anyway!

The extensive travel involved in my research necessitated a number of lengthy absences from home, during which my wife, Yoshie, had to cope without me amid her own heavy work demands. So, I would like to thank my sons Dan (15) and Jack (13), who dutifully rousted themselves in the morning without any prompting, prepared their own breakfasts, dashed off to school early, cooked many exquisite Japanese meals for their mother, laundered their dirty clothes, tidied up our house, finished their homework without the slightest nagging and retired in the evening exactly when bedtime arrived. Yeah, right — as if the previous sentence bore the slightest resemblance to reality! You get the picture. As is the case for many authors, I owe a tremendous debt to my spouse, who — in typical Japanese fashion — prefers that I avoid any elaborate references to my deep and tender feelings for her. And, like their little brothers, my two adult offspring provided many frequent reminders of what is truly important in my life — the highlight being Nina's wedding in July 2015, an occasion that was all the more fulfilling owing to Nathan's service as Man of Honour, and the sterling qualities of the groom, my new son-in-law Steven. Finally, regarding the people to whom this book is dedicated: it is difficult to express, without resorting to the most hackneyed cliches, how much inspiration I have drawn from my parents. So I won't try, but I think my father could tell, even though he died when I was just 19. I hope he could. Mom knows.

Paul Blustein
Kamakura, Japan
August 2016

1

AN ARRESTING DEVELOPMENT

Noon of May 14, 2011, was the deadline for a small team of economists at the International Monetary Fund (IMF) to complete a highly sensitive briefing paper that would be transmitted electronically to IMF Managing Director Dominique Strauss-Kahn, before his departure later that day for Europe. That morning, a Saturday, the economists made some last-minute adjustments to the figures and wording in the briefing paper before sending it off. They were keenly aware that a lot was riding on the success of Strauss-Kahn's mission, the most important event of which was a meeting scheduled for Sunday afternoon with German Chancellor Angela Merkel, to be followed by another meeting Monday with European finance ministers.

The topic of these meetings was the financial crisis that had erupted a year and a half earlier in Greece and had spread elsewhere in the 17-nation zone[1] that used the euro as its common currency. The crisis was taking ominous turns for the worse in the spring of 2011; an international bailout for Greece was failing to work as planned, and with financial lifelines also extended to Ireland and Portugal, speculation was rife that Spain, a much bigger economy, might be the next to need rescuing. The hope of the staffers working on the briefing

1 The euro area currently has 19 members, but at the time of the events of this chapter Latvia and Lithuania were not members.

paper was that it would give their boss — a savvy political operator with a strong command of economics — compelling material to use in persuading Merkel, the most powerful leader in Europe, of the need for a more aggressive approach to the crisis.

But the managing director never made it across the Atlantic.

As the IMF staffers in Washington were putting the finishing touches on the briefing paper, the 62-year-old Strauss-Kahn was eating his breakfast, delivered at 9:30 a.m. to his four-room suite at the New York branch of the Sofitel, a French hotel chain. His plan for the day was to have lunch with his 26-year-old daughter, Camille, who wanted to introduce him to her new boyfriend, and then head to John F. Kennedy Airport for a 4:40 p.m. Air France flight to Paris, where he would catch a connecting flight to Berlin in time for his meeting with Merkel. Shortly after noon, he emerged from the shower just as a hotel maid, a 32-year-old immigrant from Guinea, entered the suite and, as the world was soon to learn, a sexual encounter ensued. Whether it was forcible, as she alleged, or consensual, as he maintained, is beyond the scope of this book. Whatever took place, it was over quickly; Strauss-Kahn left the Sofitel before 12:30 p.m., had lunch with his daughter and her boyfriend, and took a taxi to Kennedy. Police, who had been summoned to the Sofitel in response to a complaint of sexual assault, were able to track him down because he called the hotel in search of a missing BlackBerry (he habitually carried several electronic devices) and provided information about his flight. When detectives boarded the first class cabin at 4:45 p.m., just minutes before takeoff, and escorted him off the plane for questioning, he demanded, "What is this about?"[2]

News that the IMF managing director was being held on suspicion of rape, which broke on the *New York Post* website in the early evening, spread so rapidly that it is impossible to determine who at the Fund first rang the alarm. William Murray, the IMF's deputy spokesman,

2 See Edward Jay Epstein, 2012, *Three Days in May: Sex, Surveillance, and DSK*, Brooklyn, NY: Melville House, for a detailed account of events regarding the alleged assault.

was just sitting down to dinner at his home in the Virginia suburbs of Washington when a reporter from Bloomberg News called asking about *The Post* report. Struggling to contain his incredulity, Murray replied that he would call the reporter back and immediately contacted the Fund's head of security, who provided the distressing information that the managing director had brought nobody from his usual security detail with him to New York; Murray then sent urgent emails to a number of top staff members. Around the same time, Douglas Rediker, the alternate director for the United States on the IMF executive board, was attending a bookstore event in northwest Washington for a close friend's book. Just as he neared the front of the line to get his copy signed, a headline about Strauss-Kahn's detainment flashed on his phone, prompting Rediker to rush away from his puzzled author friend to the front of the bookstore, where he began firing off text messages and emails.

Among the most flabbergasted — because he had just exchanged emails on IMF-related business with Strauss-Kahn earlier in the afternoon — was Olivier Blanchard, the Fund's chief economic counsellor (who, like Strauss-Kahn, is French). During a wedding reception he was attending in the Red Hook section of Brooklyn, Blanchard's phone started going off, first with a call from a friend informing him of Strauss-Kahn's arrest, then another from one of his children, who knew that a high-ranking IMF official in New York was being charged with rape and had drawn the conclusion that it had to be her father. After calming his offspring on that score, Blanchard rushed out of the reception with the aim of getting to his hotel as quickly as possible, in the hope of providing any help he could. Finding no taxis in the vicinity, he flagged down a passing car, whose driver, presumably impressed by Blanchard's aristocratic appearance and manner of speech, accepted his story about the seriousness of his boss's predicament and its possible bearing on world events. But they got lost in Brooklyn's back streets, and Blanchard was in any event unable to be much use that evening.

Some of the most urgent messages were going to John Lipsky, whose position as the IMF's first deputy managing director made him second-in-command to Strauss-Kahn. Lipsky also happened to be in Brooklyn, at a home he maintains there, and first heard about the day's developments in a phone call from his daughter. Like many at the Fund that day, Lipsky initially assumed that the news reports couldn't possibly be true, but he was soon rushing to catch the last train back to Washington. A similar experience occurred to Siddharth Tiwari, the secretary of the Fund's executive board, who was at a graduation party in Philadelphia. His daughter, having seen the news on Twitter, called to convey it to her father, who scoffed that it was too crazy to be believed. Only after his daughter called back did Tiwari realize there was no hoax, and he quickly retreated from the party to a quiet corner, where he spent the remainder of the evening on the phone.

Caroline Atkinson, the IMF's head of external relations, at first ignored the insistent ringing of phones at her Washington townhouse. She and her partner, Geoffrey Lamb, were getting ready to go to a party, and more importantly, she was in the midst of providing motherly guidance to their daughter regarding a boyfriend issue. Only when Lamb pointed out that someone was trying extremely hard to reach her did Atkinson answer her phone. Upon grasping what was going on, she was immediately embroiled in myriad conversations — with the French representative on the IMF's board, with the French embassy, with Lipsky, with the head of the IMF's governing council in Singapore, and other staffers. Finally, she realized it would be necessary to impose some order on the chaos that was enveloping the staff, and she arranged for a conference call to be organized. Lipsky participated on the call from the train he was on, and a second conference call followed at around 2:00 a.m.

Who would get hold of Strauss-Kahn? Did he have diplomatic immunity? Was he on IMF business? Those were just some of the questions that arose on that night's conference calls, and definitive answers were scarce. One of the few issues on which clarity did exist was that Lipsky would be acting managing director in Strauss-Kahn's absence, as was customary. Given her responsibility for the Fund's messages to the public, Atkinson directed everybody to show above all that the Fund was continuing to function normally. Members of the executive board, a 24-member body that represented the Fund's 187 member countries,[3] were summoned the following day to the Fund's headquarters, located on 19th Street three blocks west of the White House, although the board almost never meets on Sundays. Atkinson instructed everybody on how they should act upon arriving: Smile. Look calm. Don't talk to reporters.

In Europe, where it was past midnight on Sunday as these events were developing, a few key officials were awakened with the news, among them Xavier Musca, the chief of staff to French President Nicolas Sarkozy, who had to decide whether Sarkozy should be rousted too. Looking at his watch — it was well before 5:00 a.m. — Musca knew the only action Sarkozy could take at that point was to offer Strauss-Kahn the support of the French consulate in New York. When Musca finally got in touch with Sarkozy a couple of hours later, the president had already learned the news from one of his sons, and Musca advised him to avoid making any statement beyond offering the consulate's assistance. The blogosphere was predictably alive with theories that Sarkozy operatives had orchestrated events at the Sofitel; Strauss-Kahn had been widely expected to announce in coming weeks that he would seek the Socialist Party nomination for president, and some polls showed that he stood an excellent chance of unseating Sarkozy. (Those theories are also beyond the scope of this book.)[4]

At around 3:00 a.m. in Berlin, Jörg Asmussen, the German deputy finance minister, also awoke to a special alarm in the phone he kept at his bedside, and, like the others, was thunderstruck to hear what had happened. Asmussen, who was supposed to join Merkel and

3 As of this writing, the IMF has 189 member countries. South Sudan (2012) and Nauru (2016) are the newest.

4 Epstein, 2012, *Three Days in May* (see footnote 2 in this chapter), offers some interesting evidence regarding these theories.

other German officials at the meeting with Strauss-Kahn, got a call in the morning from his boss, Finance Minister Wolfgang Schäuble. "I suppose we have a free afternoon," Asmussen recalled saying ruefully.[5]

What would have happened if the IMF chief had made it to that meeting is, of course, unknowable. In an interview, Strauss-Kahn told me he was planning to make an urgent case for a change in strategy, toward what the Fund called a "comprehensive approach," to replace the pattern of rushing to the rescue of individual countries — first Greece, then Ireland, then Portugal — when their financial travails posed existential threats to the euro. "My point to Merkel was going to be, 'Don't go case by case,'" Strauss-Kahn said. "We can't do this over and over with every country. We need to solve the problem globally. To do that, the European Central Bank would have to do certain things; there would have to be changes in the whole European banking sector; and so on."

What can be ascertained is the content of the briefing paper that Strauss-Kahn would have brought with him. According to people familiar with the paper, it spelled out, in chilling detail, the possible consequences if a "disruptive event" caused the crisis to spiral out of control. The most obvious and worrisome such event was a disorderly default by Greece — that is, a failure by the Greek government to make a payment due on its bonds, without any agreement in advance between Athens and its creditors on revised payment terms. Another disruptive event, the paper noted, might be a sudden intensification of fears that Greece or some other country was on the verge of abandoning the euro; still another, a major misstep by European officials that shattered confidence in their ability to handle the crisis. The most vulnerable countries under such circumstances, according to the paper, would be Spain, Italy and Belgium. Two other countries that use the euro —

5 Like nearly all the interviews conducted for this book, the one with Asmussen was on a deep background basis, meaning interviewees were assured of confidentiality unless they gave permission to be quoted. See the author's note and acknowledgements for more information regarding use of interview information. In cases where permission for quotation was requested and granted, interviewees will be identified to the extent they have permitted, but source information about other material obtained from interviews will not be disclosed.

Ireland and Portugal — would also be affected, but whereas they had already secured rescue loans from the IMF and European institutions, the resources available to rescue the others were insufficient. The combined debts of Spain, Italy and Belgium totalled around €3 trillion, which dwarfed the amounts at the disposal of the IMF and a special euro-area lending institution. A disruptive event could thus lead to a "run" on those countries, in which financial markets would become so skittish that the three governments would be unable to raise the necessary amount of money from private sources to pay obligations coming due, and banks in the three countries might lose a significant portion of their deposits as people moved cash to safer havens. Interconnections between government debts and banks in Europe would severely exacerbate the resulting strains; 50 percent of Italy's debt, 45 percent of Spain's debt, and 65 percent of Belgium's debt was owed to creditors outside of those countries. Most heavily exposed were French banks, whose holdings of Spanish, Italian and Belgian debt totaled about €1 trillion, so around half of French banks' capital (that is, the narrow margin between their assets and liabilities) was at risk of being wiped out, according to the briefing paper. German banks were much less exposed — their losses might total only about 10 percent of capital. But this only accounted for the first-order effects; the severity of the problems for French banks would cause difficulties for the German banks with which they were closely intertwined, so trust among major financial institutions would likely evaporate, leading to the sort of "freezing" of global markets that ensued after the bankruptcy of Lehman Brothers in 2008.[6]

Given all these dire possibilities, the managing director's arrest had obviously come at an unpropitious time. That thought was weighing heavily on members of the IMF's executive board as they arrived on May 15 for their hastily called Sunday meeting. Entering the Fund's underground parking lot that day, the directors underwent the surreal

6 This memo is one of many confidential documents, not available in the public record, from which information will be quoted in this book. See the author's note and acknowledgements for an explanation of these documents, which also include emails and notes of meetings. Henceforth, such documents will be cited without footnotes, but for documents that are public, or which were leaked to the news media, footnotes will be provided.

experience of having questions shouted at them by TV crews as they waited for the garage door to slide open. Then, after they had gotten to their offices, events took a farcical turn: the fire alarm sounded, so the directors trudged outside, milling on the street within easy range of the camera crews. Feeling awkward, the directors tried to get into the World Bank building across the street, but the door was locked, so they circled the World Bank a couple of times before finally being allowed back into their own building. In the end, they found very little to discuss that day, because the facts surrounding Strauss-Kahn's circumstances remained so unclear.

Meanwhile, in New York, where Strauss-Kahn had spent the night in a police holding cell in East Harlem, Benjamin Brafman, a lawyer he had retained, was spending much of that Sunday trying to find out what charges the Manhattan District Attorney's office was going to bring and how to arrange bail. Another of the managing director's lawyers, Washington-based William Taylor, had rushed to New York in the morning and was in touch with the IMF's general counsel's office, which had retained its own attorney in New York to help with issues such as how to make sure that Strauss-Kahn's work papers and electronic devices would be kept secure and private. A bail hearing was set for Monday at noon, where Brafman and Taylor were hopeful of gaining Strauss-Kahn's swift release from jail pending trial, provided he put up a substantial amount of financial collateral and surrendered his passport; the lawyers contended that he obviously wouldn't try to become a fugitive, given his prominence. But the prosecutors, under the supervision of Manhattan District Attorney Cyrus Vance Jr., were coming to a different view, namely that Strauss-Kahn might become another Roman Polanski — that is, he might escape justice by somehow getting to France, which could refuse to extradite him, as was the case of the famous film director who eluded imprisonment for having sex with a 13-year-old girl in the 1970s.

The next day, Monday, European finance ministers who had been scheduled to meet Strauss-Kahn convened in Brussels, where instead of the Frenchman they heard from Nemat Shafik, one of the IMF's two deputy managing directors. A 49-year-old native of Egypt, Shafik was pressed to stand in simply because she happened to be in London with her family, preparing to move to Washington; she had just joined the IMF a few weeks earlier after spending much of her career at the World Bank and the British government's foreign aid agency. Having received a briefing from IMF staffers who had flown from Washington to meet her, she delivered her talking points in Brussels competently, but without the élan and forcefulness that would have presumably characterized a Strauss-Kahn performance. That same morning, in Washington, hundreds of IMF staffers gathered in the sunlit gallery of their headquarters to hear a morale-boosting address by Lipsky, their acting head. Strauss-Kahn was popular with most of the staff, and overcoming their shock and sadness posed a major challenge, but by all accounts, Lipsky rose to the occasion in delivering a message that the institution must press ahead with its enormously important work. While acknowledging how upset everyone was, Lipsky exhorted his audience to bear in mind that the Fund depended not on one person but on the depths and talents of a large group, and as evidence that business would proceed as usual he said he was about to go chair a board meeting where the Irish economy was on the agenda.

In fact, the big issue for the board that day was of course the managing director's arrest, with the main speaker being Sean Hagan, the IMF's general counsel. "It's a rapidly evolving situation. New information may possibly emerge," Hagan told the board members, according to notes of the meeting taken by participants. Hagan, who is a US citizen, carefully noted that he was "no expert in New York law," but explained that if convicted of the charges against him, the managing director could be sentenced to prison for terms ranging between five and 25 years. The board members received copies of the police report outlining the accusations against Strauss-Kahn — a shocking departure from their usual reading fare of dense, technical documents about economic matters. "The defendant engaged in oral sexual conduct and anal sexual conduct with another person by forcible compulsion," said the report, which was replete with graphic references to genitalia and underclothing in its account of the maid's version of the episode.

Hagan then explained what had happened at the bail hearing in New York that day: Strauss-Kahn did not have an opportunity to enter a plea, but "made it clear that he denies all charges." The judge had sided with the prosecutors in denying bail — and although that decision might be reconsidered, it was obviously a serious problem for anyone trying to function in an important job. Responding to questions from directors about the managing director's immunity from prosecution, Hagan said such immunity would apply only to actions taken in his official capacity. But the IMF should have the right to speak with Strauss-Kahn, Hagan said — although at that point, nobody from the Fund had been able to do so.

Next came a subject of utmost delicacy: what about Strauss-Kahn's continuation as managing director? Under his contract — which was governed by IMF rules — the board technically had the right to fire Strauss-Kahn without cause, and as Hagan explained, the contract stated that he was expected to obey local laws, just as ordinary Fund staffers were. A staff member accused of violating local law would ordinarily be put on administrative leave; the problem was that no provision for such leave existed in the managing director's contract. This aspect of the discussion didn't get very far, however, before it was cut short by Shakour Shaalan, the director representing Egypt and 12 other Middle Eastern countries, who had served longer than any other director and thus, by tradition, had been elected "dean" of the board. "This meeting is not to discuss how this affects his status as MD," Shaalan declared. "We don't really have to discuss his employment framework. This meeting is really to nail down the facts." Before the board could take action, he added, it needed to hear from Strauss-Kahn — who that day was being transferred to Rikers Island, New York's infamous jail complex in the middle of the East River.

As the furor intensified over the next 48 hours, an agonizing dilemma confronted the IMF about what, if anything, it should do about its incarcerated chief. The news media was full of reports about Strauss-Kahn's history of womanizing, including allegations of aggressive and offensive sexual overtures, and questions were raised about why the Fund hadn't taken tougher action against him following a 2008 scandal involving his affair with an attractive staff economist. Yet board members were understandably loath to act in the absence of proof that he had in fact committed the crimes of which he stood accused. Outrage was running high, especially in France, over Strauss-Kahn's treatment by the New York authorities, who forced him to undergo a "perp walk," with his hands cuffed behind his back and police officers standing on either side of him, in full view of the cameras as he went to his bail hearing. The presumption of guilt conveyed by this scene made it equivalent to "a horrible global lynching," as Pierre Chevenement, a French senator and former government minister, put it in a blog post.[7] Nobody knew at that point, of course, about all the problems, inconsistencies and downright falsehoods that would emerge in the story told by Strauss-Kahn's accuser, the most damning being her invention of details about having been raped by soldiers in her native country. Although this evidence of the maid's capacity for lying hardly meant that Strauss-Kahn deserved exoneration for the events at the Sofitel, it would later oblige prosecutors to drop the charges against him. (The maid still brought a lawsuit against Strauss-Kahn, which he settled out of court.)[8]

Still, for IMF board members, and their political overseers in world capitals, the question remained: even if Strauss-Kahn was eventually found innocent, how could he possibly run the Fund from jail — or, if granted bail, from house arrest in New York pending trial, with his passport confiscated? To the immense relief of the IMF directors and staff, who had been fretting that the institution's leadership might be left in limbo for months, Strauss-Kahn took the initiative.

In mid-afternoon on Wednesday, May 18, a Rikers Island corrections officer escorted the managing director and one of his lawyers to a sparely-furnished office with a desk and a phone. Wearing an orange jail jumpsuit, Strauss-Kahn picked up the phone and, in a call lasting about five or 10 minutes, spoke with Hagan and Tiwari, who told him that the board was seeking his direction about his intentions. The managing director replied that he recognized he couldn't conceivably head the IMF under the circumstances, so with regret he would step down from his post. He then transmitted a letter, which the IMF released within hours. "It is with infinite sadness that I feel compelled

7 *The Economist,* 2011, "That Guilty Look," July 7, www.economist.com/node/18929399.

8 Epstein, 2012, *Three Days in May* (see footnote 2 in this chapter).

today to present to the executive board my resignation," the letter said. "I think at this time first of my wife — whom I love more than anything....I think also of my colleagues at the Fund; together we have accomplished such great things over the last three years and more.... I want to devote all my strength, all my time, and all my energy to proving my innocence."[9]

Upon hearing word of Strauss-Kahn's decision, board members — who usually confine their meetings to normal daytime hours — insisted that they should convene that evening, rather than wait another day. So, at 10:22 p.m., their meeting opened with Hagan's formal report of the phone conversation, which, according to notes of the gathering, went as follows: "The interest and effectiveness of the IMF are [Strauss-Kahn's] paramount concern. He recognizes that the circumstances risk tarnishing the IMF, and he won't allow that to happen." A lengthy discussion followed about whether the board should express some sort of appreciation for Strauss-Kahn's service; in the end, the decision was made to avoid saying anything that might be construed as defending his alleged conduct. The IMF press release issued that evening simply reported the text of the resignation letter, noted that Lipsky's role as acting managing director would continue, and concluded: "The Fund will communicate in the near future on the executive board's process of selecting a new Managing Director."[10]

Four days had elapsed since Strauss-Kahn's detainment. For the IMF, this particular nightmare was over. The worst days of its most formidable challenge — the euro-zone crisis — still lay ahead.

9 IMF, 2011, "IMF Managing Director Dominique Strauss-Kahn Resigns," Press Release No. 11/187, May 18, www.imf.org/external/np/sec/pr/2011/pr11187.htm.

10 Ibid.

2

A SAGA WORTHY OF BROAD PUBLIC CONCERN

Globalization is a many-splendoured thing, infusing the capitalist system with dynamism that fuels economic growth and raises living standards around the world. It can also be a treacherous thing, especially with regard to international movements of money; countries may flourish amid torrents of inflowing capital, then suddenly go bust when investors flee. Never was the treacherous side more glaringly evident than during the crisis in the euro zone. The phenomenon of countries laid so low as to require international bailouts was once thought confined to the emerging world — Mexico, Thailand and Indonesia, for example. The euro-zone crisis showed that advanced economies may be equally susceptible to the vagaries of globalized finance. This has exposed a heightened degree of danger in a system where capital freely flows across international borders while government power still rests primarily at the level of the nation-state.

The importance of a muscular IMF, wielding power and authority commensurate with the strength of world markets, is thus greater than ever. The Fund is chief guardian of global financial stability, a role it fulfills mainly by seeking to prevent financial crises from occurring and managing them when they erupt, deploying the expertise of its staff and the monetary resources at its disposal. For all of its flaws, the Fund thereby provides what academics call a "global public good," from which all nations broadly benefit and which no single nation can deliver alone.

In the past, the IMF's crisis-prevention and crisis-fighting capacities were often found wanting when it came to emerging-market countries, as I chronicled in previous books on the crises that struck Asia, Russia and Brazil in the late 1990s and Argentina in 2001-2002.[1] Events in Europe during 2010–2015 taxed the Fund's resources and tested its crisis-fighting mettle in ways that were inconceivable a few years earlier. The sums the Fund lent in the euro zone were of unprecedented magnitudes, both in absolute terms and relative to the size of the countries it was aiding. Also unprecedented was the scale of risk and complexity of forces that the Fund was confronting as it laboured to keep a financial conflagration from engulfing a regional economy comprising nearly one-fifth of global output as measured by gross domestic product (GDP).

The international community is now on notice that it needs an institution with the potency to rescue countries much richer than those afflicted by market volatility and reckless policies in past years. Yet the Fund's involvement in the euro zone left it bruised and enfeebled. The implications for the management of future crises are disheartening.

The sudden departure of Strauss-Kahn in May 2011 was the most sensational setback in the IMF's efforts to quell financial turmoil in Europe. Quite apart from the embarrassment involved, it deprived the Fund of strong leadership during a crucial period when the Greek crisis was nearing a major decision point and bigger euro-area economies were about to come under intense speculative attack. But the weakening of the Fund can be attributed to much more fundamental factors than this sordid episode.

Under pressure from powerful European policy makers, who maintained heavy influence over the Fund's levers of control, the IMF joined in rescues of euro-zone countries despite grave misgivings among many of its top officials about the key features and terms.

1 Paul Blustein, 2001, *The Chastening: Inside the Crisis That Rocked the Global Financial System and Humbled the IMF*, New York, NY: PublicAffairs; and Blustein, 2005, *And the Money Kept Rolling In (And Out): Wall Street, the IMF, and the Bankrupting of Argentina*, New York, NY: PublicAffairs.

Some of these emergency loan packages worked out reasonably well in the end, but all too often they piled debt atop existing debt, extracted crushingly high interest charges and imposed excessively harsh conditions on the countries that were borrowing the money. This approach, taken in conjunction with the Europeans, suited nations such as Germany and France, whose banks were anxious to stave off losses and whose voters were incensed at paying to bail out countries they perceived as irresponsible. It also suited the European Central Bank (ECB), because it helped preserve the international status of the euro and the ECB's own independence — principles on which the central bank's leaders attached supreme importance. Although the approach taken was based in large part on fear that the crisis might otherwise spread more widely in Europe and even beyond, the legitimate interests of crisis-stricken nations were sacrificed in the process. Bound though these countries were to undergo economic misery, they suffered substantially more than was necessary. And the crisis was a much more prolonged, painful and near-catastrophic affair than it ought to have been.

The IMF's complicity in this lamentable situation stemmed from a Faustian bargain of sorts. When the crisis started, the Fund was eager to play a part; it was recovering from a long period of inactivity on the crisis-fighting front, during which extensive doubt arose about the need for an institution like the Fund to continue operating as it was. To become involved in the euro zone, the Fund had to overcome strenuous opposition from European officials who felt that their region ought to handle its own problems without international help. As a condition of participation, the Fund accepted that it would work cooperatively with the European Commission and the ECB in a tripartite arrangement that came to be known as the "Troika," with the Fund effectively taking a role as junior partner.[2] Even though IMF economists saw, to their credit, that Troika bailout packages were based on unrealistic projections and unwarranted stringency, the Fund often yielded to the

2 The term "junior partner" is controversial; among those disputing its use to characterize the IMF's role is the Fund's Independent Evaluation Office. But I believe the term is apt, and that the evidence presented in this book will amply support its use. For further elaboration, see chapter 20, footnote 8.

clout of policy makers in Berlin, Frankfurt, Brussels and Paris. The result sapped the institution of its most precious asset — its credibility as an independent, neutral arbiter of how to fix economic and financial problems that beset countries, regions and the world as a whole.

These criticisms are hardly novel. Many experts in academic and policy circles were making similar arguments as the crisis unfolded.[3] But this book will examine the IMF's role in far greater detail than has heretofore been available, chronicling key decisions and turning points. Controversy continues to rage, not only about the appropriateness of the policies that were implemented, but the truth about what actually happened during the decision-making process. One important aim of this book is to shed new light on those questions, including some revelations about previously undisclosed events.

Other books about the crisis, as well as articles in newspapers and magazines, have reported at length on the actions taken by European policy makers such as Merkel, Sarkozy, their counterparts in the crisis-torn countries and top officials of European institutions including the ECB, European Commission, European Council and European Stability Mechanism. The inner workings of European policy making merit close scrutiny, especially for readers living in the euro area; they need to understand how their leaders have performed and how the crisis has changed the nature of governance on the continent. This book, by contrast, focuses on the IMF's role, because doing so imparts a more global perspective on events, and because people everywhere — not just Europeans — have an enormous stake in fostering a healthy multilateral financial institution capable of fulfilling the lofty missions entrusted to it.

The IMF's Articles of Agreement, forged in 1944 at a historic conference of Allied nations in Bretton Woods, New Hampshire, enjoin countries to refrain from "measures destructive of national or international prosperity." That phrase encapsulates the original inspiration for

3 See, for example, Mohamed A. El-Erian, 2011, "It's Time for the IMF to Stand Up to the European Bullies," December 29, www.greekcrisis.net/2011/12/its-time-for-imf-to-stand-up-to.html.

creating the Fund — namely, ensuring that the world would never again witness the epidemic of mutually deleterious actions of the 1920s and 1930s that made the Depression as great as it was. During the interwar period, countries dragged each other down with "beggar-thy-neighbour" policies that boosted their economies or protected their industries at the expense of economies elsewhere. Governments sharply lowered their foreign exchange rates to spur exports and curb imports, for example; in other cases, they erected high tariff walls and even engaged in outright trade wars. Replacing that chaos with a rule-based, cooperative institution was the vision of the two men primarily responsible for shaping the Fund — John Maynard Keynes of the British Treasury and Harry Dexter White of the US Treasury. The institution that emerged, after much debate across the Atlantic and three weeks of conferring at Bretton Woods, was endowed with monetary resources that it could make temporarily available to countries in difficulty — the hope and expectation being that they would eschew those "measures destructive of national or international prosperity."

In its efforts to fulfill the Keynes-White vision, the IMF has assumed various responsibilities in the decades after World War II. During the first postwar quarter century, the Fund policed a system of fixed exchange rates, with most countries (those in the Communist bloc being a major exception) pegging their currencies to gold or to the US dollar. Later, when that system broke down and financial flows became increasingly globalized, the Fund's primary purpose became that of crisis preventer and manager, helping countries that fall into financial distress with loans aimed at keeping their economies functioning while they make the tough adjustments necessary for getting back on a sound economic footing. This role is well-suited to the Fund's structure as a sort of credit union for countries, in which each member country contributes funds to a central kitty from which loans can be made — the loans being in the form of "hard currency" such as US dollars, Japanese yen, euros and British pound sterling. (Hard currency is almost always necessary for conducting international transactions; without it, countries are often unable to import goods essential to running a modern economy or pay their foreign obligations.) By providing this sort of aid, the Fund can help minimize the hardship that a crisis causes — not entirely, of course; the policy adjustments that the Fund requires as a condition of its loans are often painful to citizens of the recipient country, but when the assistance is properly designed such pain should be less than it would be otherwise. And at its best, Fund aid serves not only the directly targeted countries, but the wider world as well. If successful, a Fund loan keeps crisis-stricken nations from dragging others down, which they might otherwise do by taking "measures destructive of national or international prosperity" or via contagion — that is, the spread of crisis conditions from one country to another.

Given such weighty duties, the IMF has consistently strived to maintain an image as a technocratic institution, free of gross political interference. Although it has often fallen short, there are sound reasons for hewing as close as possible to the ideal. The Fund stands the best chance of success when, in both appearance and reality, it represents the interests of the world community writ large rather than any single power or region. In the case of financial emergencies, for example, one of the Fund's primary goals is to help a country that has lost the confidence of investors regain access to financial markets. The money the Fund lends is only a part, and perhaps a relatively unimportant part, of its value. Equally crucial, if not more so, is its seal of approval — its signification that the country is adopting policies conducive to economic fitness. If the Fund's seal of approval is severely tarnished, especially by the perception of manipulation by forces from on high, its effectiveness at restoring market confidence will be eroded. Cynicism among market players about the Fund's susceptibility to political meddling makes its job much harder — an unwelcome development at a time when financial crises have become so pervasive.

For those reasons, the IMF's travails in the euro zone — in particular, its submission to European political exigencies — comprise a saga worthy of broad public concern. The most salient and widely debated case is that of Greece, where, in retrospect, the country was saddled with an excessively high debt and should have gotten relief from its indebtedness much earlier than it eventually did. Greece's first bailout in May 2010 is the subject of chapters 5, 6 and 7, and as shall be seen, secret discussions took place in which IMF economists, acting at the behest of Strauss-Kahn, made the argument to officials from the German and French finance ministries that Greece's debt was unsustainable and would need to be restructured. Most of European officialdom remained vehemently opposed until late the following year to any major reduction in Athens' debt obligations; during that time, many investors who had foolishly bought Greek bonds got paid in full. It is now widely accepted that the European view prevailed for too long.

Another example is the rescue of Ireland, which is recounted in chapters 8 and 9. The most contentious issue there was whether the Irish government should continue ensuring full payment by Irish banks to their senior bondholders, many of which were based in continental Europe. IMF officials argued that using the country's tax resources to bail out all of these bondholders would impose an unreasonable and unjust burden on the Irish people. But under enormous pressure from the ECB, Dublin buckled and fully paid off those bondholders.

It would be wildly misleading to suggest that everybody working at IMF headquarters was of one mind in viewing the rescue strategies undertaken in Europe as wrongheaded, or that the Fund as an institution was dragged kicking and screaming into going along with every major decision that was taken. As with any complex, rapidly evolving financial crisis, opinions were sharply divided within the IMF about both the diagnosis of the euro zone's woes and the best course of action to pursue. Economic policy making does not generate single, clear prescriptions of undisputed technocratic merit; it entails tough judgment calls among forecasts, risks, trade-offs and priorities, about which seasoned experts often differ. But the evidence presented in forthcoming chapters points to the conclusion that the Fund would probably have handled the crisis much differently if it had enjoyed full independence — that is, if the decisions had been up to the management, staff and non-euro-zone directors, free from intervention by European policy makers. Not only would the IMF have taken different approaches in individual country cases, it would have insisted on swift, aggressive adoption of broader measures in Europe aimed at containing the turmoil, especially by the ECB, which waited until mid-2012 before pledging to do "whatever it takes" to stand behind imperiled countries and save the euro. One clear example of a step the IMF had long recommended was banking union (the transfer of power for banking policy from national governments to the EU level), a breakthrough that Europe took only belatedly, as shall be seen in chapter 15. The Fund was hamstrung in its efforts to obtain broad policy change in Europe, in part because, as a member of the Troika, it was sitting on the same side of the negotiating table as the ECB and European Commission.

In a number of prior crises, the IMF has joined forces with other institutions and donors, such as the World Bank, regional development banks and individual governments, to maximize the amount of rescue money available. But by convention, the Fund has played the dominant role in designing terms and conditions, in recognition of its expertise, experience and status as agent of the international community. Had that precedent been applied in Europe, the Fund would have been entitled to a "senior partner" role relative to the European institutions, in which it would be the ultimate arbiter of terms for rescues. Indeed, had that precedent been carried to its logical conclusion, the IMF's senior partner status would have applied to the entire region, with the Fund having the right to demand the adoption of euro-zone-wide policies by the ECB and the member states of the monetary union. Politically unrealistic as that may sound, the case has been advanced by Edwin "Ted" Truman of the Peterson Institute for International Economics, one of the most battle-hardened veterans of financial diplomacy (from his decades at the Federal Reserve and US Treasury) whom I have ever encountered. "The IMF should have insisted as part of the first program for Greece that the other members of the euro area adopt a complementary strategy as a condition for its approval of the Greek program," Truman wrote in 2013. "The IMF was too timid, paralyzed or conflicted to require such steps." In Truman's trenchant words, "The members of the euro area wanted to preserve the euro, but they were not prepared to accept conditionality applied to the euro area as a single entity. The rest of the world, to its regret, allowed the Europeans to have it both ways — save the euro but by imposing all the policy conditions only on the countries in crisis."[4]

4 Edwin M. Truman, 2013, "Evolution of the Asian and European Financial Crises: Role of the International Monetary Fund," in *Responding to Financial Crisis: Lessons from Asia Then, the United States and Europe Now,"* edited by Changyong Rhee and Adam S. Posen, Washington, DC: PIIE Press.

At times during the crisis the IMF was not only overruled, it was left completely out of the loop. One revealing example, which will be chronicled in chapter 11, is the ECB's effort to impose discipline on Italy and Spain in August 2011, when those countries' governments were facing difficulty borrowing money in the markets. Private letters sent by the central bank's leadership to the Italian and Spanish prime ministers spelled out actions the two governments must take, with the implication that these actions were required for ECB purchases of the countries' bonds. The IMF was not consulted, nor even informed, about those letters sent by its Troika partner until news of them leaked to the press.

In certain respects, it is perfectly appropriate for major countries to exert influence over Fund policy; indeed, it is incumbent on them to do so. The Fund is a political institution at the end of the day, with a management and staff accountable to the board that represents the member countries. The governments of those countries put up the money that the Fund lends, which legitimizes their expectation that the Fund will use that money in a manner they support. In every big decision or action that it has taken in recent decades, the Fund has coordinated closely with the Group of Seven major industrial countries together with other important players in the international community. And the euro-zone crisis was by no means the first time that powerful countries exercised disproportionate control; the US government often did so in previous instances. A classic illustration of this phenomenon was a February 1999 *Time Magazine* cover, titled "The Committee to Save the World," during a period when IMF loans were being used to quell the financial turbulence that was ravaging Asia's emerging economies, along with Russia and Brazil. The cover displayed Robert Rubin, the secretary of the US Treasury, his deputy (and eventual successor) Lawrence Summers and Federal Reserve Chairman Alan Greenspan, posing amid the marbled splendour of the Treasury, with arms folded and faces cheerfully composed. Although the impression created by the photo and accompanying article overstated the degree to which American officials were dictating IMF policy — the Fund's top management and staff, together with officials of other major industrialized nations, maintained considerable power as well — the "Committee to Save the World" underscored America's hegemonic position at that time.[5]

But, in the euro-zone crisis, the line separating legitimate influence from harmful interference was not only crossed, it was trampled on. From the standpoint of the Fund's integrity, the control that Europeans exerted in the euro-zone crisis posed a different and much more damaging threat than that of US officials during previous crises. Unlike the United States, European nations were borrowing from the Fund. Even the rich European countries that never needed IMF aid were in many respects supplicants, using the Fund — both its seal of approval and its money — to save their terribly flawed system of monetary union and their banks. Not only were policy makers from these rich European countries desperate to protect the euro, they were aiming at the same time to ensure their political survival; they were concerned about placating angry, fed-up electorates. For Europeans to be pushing the Fund around under such circumstances was an affront to robust multilateralism.

Moreover, the approach taken during the crisis exacerbated the IMF's long-standing governance problem, a vestige of the post-World War II economic power structure. Relative to its economic size, Europe has enjoyed over-representation on the IMF's board and a disproportionate share of the voting power — a source of resentment to rising powers of the emerging world that festered for years, until it was remedied, at least partially, in 2015. Europe's over-representation came at the expense of the BRICS (Brazil, Russia, India, China and South Africa), who held about 11 percent of the voting power, even though their economies account for more than 20 percent of world GDP.[6] Mistrust of the IMF in the Global South has been especially pronounced since the crises of the late 1990s, when some of Asia's economic dynamos were forced into rescues on terms that required them to embrace practices prevalent in the West. Whatever their merits or shortcomings, the conditions that were imposed on countries such as Indonesia and South Korea

5 Joshua Cooper Ramo, 1999, "The Three Marketeers," *Time*, February 15.

6 The GDP of the BRICS is about 28 percent of the world total, as measured by purchasing power parity, and their population is 42 percent of the world total.

reinforced the perception that the Fund is a "handmaiden" of the North Atlantic powers. It is all the more galling, then, that Europeans got to call so many of the shots when their region was the one in trouble.

A notorious manifestation of the IMF's Euro-centrism is the hoary "gentlemen's agreement" between Europe and the United States to divvy up the top jobs at the Fund and the World Bank. Under this arrangement, the Fund's managing directorship has always been under European control, while the president of the World Bank and the first deputy managing director at the IMF have always been Americans, chosen by the White House. The IMF is a strictly hierarchical organization, with the managing director holding hiring and firing powers over nearly the entire staff, so the ability of one region to choose the Fund's top executive is no small matter. The selection of Christine Lagarde, chronicled in chapter 10, was the most egregious instance ever of Europe maintaining control over the managing directorship. Even though European leaders had vowed that Strauss-Kahn would be the last IMF chief appointed under the gentlemen's agreement (as noted in chapter 3), they insisted on keeping their hammerlock on the job when it became vacant in mid-2011, on the grounds that only a European could properly understand the woes afflicting the euro zone. This running roughshod over good governance will not soon be forgotten.

To be sure, Lagarde deserves considerable credit for restoring luster to the IMF. Following Strauss-Kahn's downfall, she not only repaired the Fund's tattered image, but also infused it with glamour and grace; her pronouncements on all manner of issues routinely receive worldwide attention. Much more substantive and important was the Fund's increasing willingness to stand up to Europe, starting in the latter months of 2011, when a new management team led by Lagarde and First Deputy Managing Director David Lipton took over. In part due to IMF insistence, Greece finally got major debt relief from its private creditors in the spring of 2012, a development recounted in chapter 14, and after initial missteps, the bailout of Cyprus was resolved in a manner the Fund favoured (although, as shall be seen in chapter 16, not with the Fund's most-preferred approach). The IMF's ability to get its way during this period was probably traceable less to stiffer backbones in its top leadership ranks than to changes in attitudes by the German government and other factors that enhanced the Fund's leverage. But the Fund's status was indisputably on the rise from its previous subordinate level. In 2012, Lagarde also mobilized a major boost in the IMF's financial resources from member countries. Most commendable of all, from the standpoint of the IMF's independence, were the events of 2015, when Lagarde and other Fund officials, notably chief economist Olivier Blanchard, publicly broke with Europe on the need for Athens to receive further debt relief along with the adoption of tough reforms, thereby winning accolades for the Fund as an "honest broker" and "truth teller." That series of episodes is the subject of chapters 18 and 19.

Even so, tremendous damage had already been inflicted — on the Greek economy in particular (which has undergone a depression roughly comparable to that of the United States during the 1930s), as well as the IMF as an institution. And well after the Lagarde era began, the Fund suffered yet another blow that could threaten its long-term viability as a crisis lender. This issue has gotten little attention considering its seriousness.

The IMF always gets its money back, on time — or at least that's how things are supposed to work. In IMF-speak, the Fund enjoys "preferred creditor status," which means that when a country has received international bailout loans, the Fund must be repaid ahead of all other creditors, whether those creditors are official (for example, the German government) or private (for example, a commercial bank). Although not enshrined in any law or treaty, the Fund's preferred creditor status is a near-sacred principle in international finance, because the Fund is the closest thing the world has to an international lender of last resort. In other words, the Fund's readiness to lend in situations where all other sources of credit have dried up — metaphorically, to enter a burning building that others are fleeing — means that its claims get top priority and countries that fail to repay their IMF loans can expect to be treated like international financial pariahs. Only with such assurances in place can the IMF's member countries feel comfortable providing the resources for such risky lending. US Treasury officials routinely invoke preferred creditor status when they seek to persuade members of Congress to vote for handing Washington's money to the Fund; the American taxpayer has never lost a dime on the IMF, whose loans are ultimately the safest in the world, as Treasury secretaries tirelessly remind lawmakers.

In mid-2015, the IMF's gold-plated financial standing was badly impaired when Greece's radical left-wing government ran perilously short of cash, raising the prospect that the Fund would suffer severe losses on the biggest loans it had ever extended to any country. Athens failed to make a couple of sizable payments to the Fund when the amounts came due, and negotiations over the terms for a new Greek bailout came within a whisker of ending in a total breakdown that would have resulted in Greece abandoning the euro — which, in turn, would have surely meant even larger and more consequential defaults on IMF loans. Although Greece finally accepted a deal allowing it to stay in the euro zone, and repaid its overdue obligations to the Fund, this episode (recounted in chapter 19) has cast into unprecedented doubt the whole surety of the Fund's ability to recover the money it lends. This could well make it much more difficult for the Fund to raise money in the future from its member countries; if that happened, the world would be deprived of an institution with the capacity to serve as international lender of last resort. At the very least, the IMF will be much more hesitant to lend aggressively the next time a big crisis erupts.

The euro-zone crisis abated in 2013, and although the situations in Greece, Italy and Portugal remain unsettled in mid-2016, no individual countries that use the euro are facing financial emergencies as this book goes to press. Indeed, with the exception of Greece, all of the countries that received rescue packages — Ireland, Portugal, Spain and Cyprus — staged healthy enough recoveries to have exited from their programs. In part due to sensible IMF prodding, Europe has taken strides toward fixing some of the gravest defects in its monetary union, such as the lack of an integrated banking system with shared responsibility for bank supervision and resolution.

Still, these successes have come at a stiff price to the IMF, given the subservient position that it took on so many occasions during some of the worst phases of the crisis. Even if the Fund never has problems obtaining financial resources, the impact on its reputation is indelible. When future crises arise, the affected countries or regions may point to decisions taken in 2010–2015 and argue that their influence over Fund policy in their part of the world ought to be commensurate with that exercised by Europeans in the euro zone. The Fund's ability to manage financial turmoil satisfactorily is in deeper doubt as a result.

This is all the more true because of the way in which the IMF and its Troika partners handled one of the thorniest problems in the global financial system — how to treat private investors and lenders in crisis situations, especially when the country involved has incurred more debt than it can reasonably afford. Highly undesirable consequences may result in the future from the actions taken during the euro-zone crisis, which departed in certain key respects from rules and principles the Fund had developed over many years of trial and error. Most notably, the Fund circumvented what for simplicity's sake can be called the "No More Argentinas" rule, which was adopted following the Fund's most spectacularly abortive rescue effort. This rule, and other approaches that preceded it, merit a brief review, along with the trials and errors that gave rise to them.

Should banks and bondholders be bailed out? Or should they be bailed *in*? This is the dilemma that confronts the IMF often when a country seeks a Fund rescue. A big loan package may ensure that the stricken country gets enough cash to avoid defaulting on any of its obligations as they come due — that's a bailout. Alternatively, the terms may require private creditors to accept losses on their loans, or perhaps stretched out repayment of their claims, thereby giving the debtor more realistic prospects for recovery — that's a bail-in.

The IMF did not have to concern itself much with private creditors during the first quarter century or so after its creation, because the rules of the original Bretton Woods system stringently limited the movement of private capital around the world. But in the 1970s and 1980s, when regulations were loosened and international flows of private funds burgeoned, countries began undergoing the boom-bust syndrome characteristic of financial markets, and the dilemma arose.

The first major test case was Mexico, at the dawn of the "Third World debt crisis" (also known as the "Latin debt crisis"). As with many other developing countries, the Mexican government had borrowed heavily from commercial banks during the inflationary 1970s, when bankers were falling over themselves offering credit to commodity-exporting nations. But by the summer of 1982, as a global recession sapped Mexico's financial resources, the banks were demanding repayment on loans coming due, and the government's reserves of US dollars dwindled to dangerously low levels. Mexican officials flew to Washington seeking help from the IMF and US Treasury.

The banks got an ultimatum from the IMF on November 16, 1982, when Managing Director Jacques de Larosière, an owlish man with wire spectacles, summoned a group of the world's most powerful financiers to the gilded boardroom of the New York Federal Reserve Bank. Present were CEOs and other top brass from Citibank, Chase, Morgan Guaranty, Lloyds, Deutsche Bank, Société Générale, Swiss Bank Corp., the Bank of Tokyo, the Bank of Montreal and several other major banks. The Mexican authorities had signed a letter of intent with the Fund agreeing to a number of austerity measures, and rather than simply handing over a loan to Mexico that would enable the banks to pull their money out, de Larosière wanted the banks to contribute their fair share to keeping the country afloat. His implicit threat: if the banks didn't go along, Mexico would default, with ruinous consequences for their solvency. According to an account by the journalist Joseph Kraft, the scene unfolded as follows:

> The Managing Director stepped to the rostrum, and sprung the trap.
>
> He started with a detailed account of the events leading to the signing of the Letter of Intent by Mexico....He then presented an analysis of Mexico's financial requirements for 1983 [which totaled about $8.3 billion]....In meeting that deficit, de Larosière was prepared to offer $1.3 billion

> from the IMF. He thought another $2 billion could be advanced by the U.S. and other governments. He expected the banks to put up the remaining $5 billion.
>
> Moreover, he wasn't just asking. He was telling. Unless the banks came up with the money, the Managing Director would not recommend acceptance of the Mexican program by the directors of the IMF. Since his board was meeting on December 23, de Larosière told the bankers he wanted their written commitments for that amount of new money a week in advance. The deadline was December 15.[7]

Thus were the banks bailed in; although they hated being ordered to lend, they grudgingly bowed to de Larosière's demand. This approach — also dubbed "private sector involvement," a term that will come up later in this book — was applied in several other Latin American countries when they followed Mexico into crisis.

Considerable doubt soon arose about whether the banks had been bailed in enough — whether, in other words, Mexico and other debtor countries needed outright relief from their debts rather than new loans. This is analogous to the quandaries that arise often in the corporate world, when lenders must decide whether a struggling company can survive over the long haul. Maybe the company just has a liquidity problem — a shortage of cash, which if addressed would put the firm on the road to profitability. But maybe the problem is one of solvency — an insurmountable surfeit of liabilities over assets, which an emergency loan would alleviate only temporarily. For countries, like companies, insolvency can be a trap from which there is no path to recovery. Lenders and investors will shy away from providing new funds once the chances of repayment start looking dim, and the economy will wither for lack of capital, making the debt all the harder to service.

Later in the 1980s, the answer became a matter of consensus: Latin nations were unable to grow out of their debts; they were effectively

7 Joseph Kraft, 1984, "The Mexican Rescue," New York: Group of Thirty.

insolvent. To give the debtors an escape route from economic stagnation and deepening poverty, a new approach emerged, called the "Brady Plan," named for US Treasury Secretary Nicholas Brady, aimed at significantly reducing the amounts of the debtor countries' burdens. The banks were induced to accept the terms by offering them new bonds that were partially guaranteed by the US Treasury.

It is one thing to corral a few hundred bankers into a series of meetings and boss them around, especially given their awareness that if they don't comply they may encounter difficulties with their government regulators. It is quite another when a country's creditors number in the many thousands, and that is the problem that often arose in the 1990s, when more countries turned to borrowing money by issuing bonds that were purchased by banks, pension funds, insurance companies, mutual funds, hedge funds and even small individual investors. As a result, bail-ins became more difficult to effectuate. In some of the crises that erupted in emerging markets during the 1990s, international rescues involved organized, coordinated sacrifice by private creditors; that seemed both fair and appropriate, since the creditors were often guilty of having provided funds with scant regard for the potential risk. But in some cases, the complexity involved in this type of operation proved too great.

The stage was now set for the IMF's greatest debacle. Throughout much of the 1990s, Argentina had been the darling of Wall Street — and of the IMF, thanks to its seemingly disciplined macroeconomic policies and devotion to free markets, which contrasted with crisis-riddled emerging economies elsewhere. But, by the turn of the century, a number of factors that had once worked in Argentina's favour (commodity prices, for one) were turning against it, and the $100 billion[8] that the government owed to bondholders was putting an unbearable strain on the recession-bound Argentine economy. With once-bullish investors deserting the country in droves, Horst Kohler, the IMF's managing director, flew back to Fund headquarters from a Maine vacation in the second week of

8 All dollar figures are in US dollars unless otherwise noted.

August 2001 to preside over emergency meetings in a conference room down the hall from his office. At issue was whether to lend the government in Buenos Aires an additional $8 billion on top of a $14 billion rescue the IMF had approved the previous year. Three days of debate pitted economists who argued that the extra loan offered Argentina its only hope to avert economic disaster, against those who argued that the nation's economy and political system simply didn't have the wherewithal to continue paying such a large debt. The loan was approved.[9]

To say that this rescue failed would be a colossal understatement. The Argentine default that came four and a half months later was the biggest ever at that time, and the collapse of the nation's economy the following year — GDP shrank 11 percent, leaving nearly one-quarter of the workforce unemployed — matched the default's historic dimensions. Argentina descended into near-anarchy in late 2001 and early 2002, with one president after another forced from office as mobs looted shops and stormed government buildings. Clearly vindicated were those on the IMF staff who had opposed lending Argentina any additional money on the grounds that the country's debt was unsustainable. The Fund's loan had provided no benefit for the Argentine people; indeed, it had done them a major disservice. The money had gone to pay off some of Argentina's private creditors who wanted to pull out of the country, and now the nation's taxpayers had to pay back the loan from the Fund, given its preferred creditor status. Criticism was heaped on the Fund from all quarters, eventually including its own internal evaluators.[10]

One thing the IMF does pretty well is studying its mistakes and drawing lessons from them. Knowing that it isn't supposed to lend to countries with unsustainable debts, but recognizing that the dilemmas in such

9 Blustein, *And the Money Kept Rolling In (And Out),* chapter 7 (see footnote 1 in this chapter).

10 Michael Mussa, 2002, *Argentina and the Fund: From Triumph to Tragedy,* Washington, DC: The Institute for International Economics; and IMF Independent Evaluation Office, 2004, "Report on the Evaluation of the Role of the IMF in Argentina, 1991-2001," www.imf.org/External/NP/ieo/2004/arg/eng/.

cases are often agonizing, the Fund looked for ways of better managing these situations in the future.

First, the IMF's leadership proposed a far-reaching scheme with a name and acronym that only the wonkiest of international finance experts could love — the Sovereign Debt Restructuring Mechanism, or SDRM. In the words of Anne Krueger, the senior Fund official who spearheaded the initiative in late 2001, "Our model is one of a domestic bankruptcy court," although there would be some important differences.[11] That was music to the ears of many experts who had been arguing for years that countries burdened with excessive debt — just like companies and individuals — need a system of legal procedures enabling them to obtain realistic terms for repaying the amounts they owe. Whereas a firm facing financial ruin can go to court and negotiate new debt-payment terms that all creditors may be obliged to accept, no such court exists at the international level for countries. As a result, countries that need to restructure their debts may be hounded by "holdouts" — also known by the less-flattering label of "vultures" — who buy the bonds of distressed debtors, reject settlements accepted by other creditors and file lawsuits demanding full payment of their claims. The SDRM was aimed partly at giving countries legal protection from the holdouts and vultures, thereby making debt restructuring more feasible.

The SDRM went nowhere, thanks to opposition from a host of critics, notably the George W. Bush administration, which saw the plan as an excessive intrusion in the prerogatives of private markets. In early 2003, the SDRM lost out to a watered-down approach with an equally wonky name — "collective action clauses," or CACs, which involved voluntary action by governments to issue bonds with provisions aimed at limiting the power of holdouts. CACs will come up in later chapters.

Notwithstanding the defeat on the SDRM, the IMF undertook another initiative, which is where the No More Argentinas rule comes in. It too

11 Anne Krueger, 2001, "A New Approach to Sovereign Debt Restructuring," speech given at the National Economists' Club Annual Members' Dinner, Washington, DC, November 26, www.imf.org/external/np/speeches/2001/112601.htm.

had a wonky label, reflecting its wider objectives,[12] but to spare readers' eyes any unnecessary glazing, the No More Argentinas rule will do for purposes of this book.

With the aim of restraining itself from repeating the kind of mistake it had made in Argentina, the IMF toughened its limitations on lending large amounts of money. Under a new set of lending criteria approved by the board in 2003, the Fund could give an exceptionally large loan to a country only if rigorous analysis showed that the country's debt had a "high probability" of being sustainable. If this standard (together with several others) could not be met, the Fund would provide aid only on condition that the country's debt was restructured.

The first case in which this rule arose was Greece. Instead of abiding by its rule, the IMF hastily concocted a loophole so that its loan could go forward. Instead of preventing another Argentina-style mistake, the Fund let it happen again. But that is getting ahead of the story.

Even to well-informed laypeople, the IMF is mystifying, as is the tortured history of the euro, as are financial crises in general, as is the issue of sovereign debt. To comprehend them, the tale that unfolds in chapters to come affords a dramatic backdrop. This is not to suggest that forthcoming pages are abounding with more sex scandals and perp walks. On the contrary, the narrative plunges often into thickets involving complexities such as the distinctions between orderly and disorderly debt restructuring, the intertwining of monetary union and banking union and the relative merits of various types of anti-contagion "firewalls," which in turn entails the use of myriad acronyms — EFSF, ESM, SDR, and so on.[13] But these are the sort of complexities

12 See IMF, 2003, "IMF Concludes Discussion on Access Policy in the Context of Capital Account Crises," Public Information Notice (PIN) No. 03/37, March 21, www.imf.org/external/np/sec/pn/2003/pn0337.htm.

13 See the glossary of acronyms on page vii. There is also a reference guide of people whose names appear in more than two different parts of the book on page 477.

on which millions of livelihoods depend, and there are few better ways of fathoming them than the crucible of crisis. As the biggest and most risk-laden crisis the IMF has ever faced, the Fund's exploits in the euro zone are replete with highs and lows of significant amplitude, laying bare both the strengths and weaknesses of an institution whose success may determine whether economic globalization proceeds in a benign or malign fashion.

To all outward appearances the IMF is a monolithic organization. News reports of its activities and positions typically refer to it simply as "the IMF," and although Christine Lagarde has imparted a humanizing touch, the Fund generally comes across in public as drone-like, uniform in its adherence to economic orthodoxy as it promotes policies it deems well advised. To some extent, the IMF intentionally cultivates this countenance, which helps serve the purpose of conveying omniscience, detachment and a near-scientific righteousness to its opinions. Its jargon-laced, data-filled documents and press statements seem almost deliberately designed to intimidate lay people, and when its staff members make public appearances, they tend to adopt sober demeanors as if to suggest membership in a high priesthood endowed with wisdom of exclusive profundity. Aiding further in this regard is the national diversity of the 2,580-strong staff, about half of whom are economists — at last count, 14.4 percent of those economists were citizens of the United States or Canada, 4.6 percent were British, 39.3 percent came from other European countries, 12.2 percent were Latin American, 11.6 percent were East Asian, 6.7 percent were African, 4.6 percent were Middle Eastern and 3.5 percent were Indian.[14] The wide variety of accents with which they speak English (fluency is a requirement for all staff) lends authority to their utterances; it underscores that wherever in the world economists come from, their views on certain fundamental issues are thoroughly informed by a common set of principles about the way economies work, especially if — as is true for most Fund Ph.D.s — they have gotten their degrees at top-flight universities.

14 IMF, "Diversity & Inclusion Annual Report 2014," 34, www.imf.org/external/np/div/2014/index.pdf.

Like my previous books on the IMF, this one will show the Fund as decidedly non-uniform in its thinking, and far from omniscient. Having said this, I would emphasize that the Fund's mistakes, bad as they often are, do not stem from stupidity or venality on the part of the people who work there, who include some of the smartest and most public-spirited policy makers I have ever met. To be sure, considerations about career advancement and the desire to please higher-ups sometimes colour their judgment, as does "groupthink." But their policy errors are usually traceable to systemic forces, both financial and political, that are beyond the control or comprehension of civil servants working for an international institution in a world of sovereign nations and globalized capital. This is what makes the IMF's failures so worrisome; improving its record at reducing and mitigating financial crises is not a simple matter of replacing its economists with more competent ones. And if, as this book argues, the events of 2010 to 2015 bode even more ill for the Fund's efficacy, the international community had better consider corrective action, ideas for which are discussed in the final chapter.

Before delving into the early stages of the euro-zone crisis in 2010, some historical background is in order about developments at the IMF in the period spanning roughly 2005 to 2009. In the course of researching this book, I have been struck by the profound ramifications of these events. This period includes years when the world of finance seemed blissfully tranquil, so much so that the IMF's very reason for existence was questioned. It also includes the arrival of dynamic new leadership at the Fund in the person of Dominique Strauss-Kahn, the eruption of the global crisis triggered by the bankruptcy of Lehman Brothers, and the rescues of European countries outside the euro zone, which gave the Fund a new lease on life. Understanding these events is essential to providing proper context for what came later in the monetary bloc, so they are the subjects of chapters 3 and 4.

Also covered in these chapters is the issue of the IMF's farsightedness, or lack thereof, about the risk of financial turbulence in Europe. Not all of the Fund's failings regarding the euro-zone crisis can be laid at the doorstep of powerful European policy makers. For being overly sanguine in the period before the crisis, the Fund has only itself to blame.

3

EXISTENTIAL CRISIS

In the early spring of 2006, an IMF staff member named Bas Bakker gave a presentation to colleagues that was a rare example of foresight in policy-making circles prior to the global financial crisis. Bakker, a sandy-haired economist from the Netherlands, argued that Eastern Europe was a hotbed of financial vulnerability, with many countries becoming dangerously dependent on inflows of capital from abroad that could reverse abruptly with devastating consequences. His presentation — "Asia 1996 and Eastern Europe 2006 — Déjà vu all over again?" — was kept strictly within the confines of the IMF, since its message might have sparked market perturbations. It was based on data showing that many countries in the former Communist bloc bore alarming similarities to the economies of East and Southeast Asia in the mid-1990s, prior to their financial crises.

It is now clear that Bakker was right; crises battered a number of Eastern European countries in 2008 and 2009. If anything, he was understating the case, because his presentation did not include any of the more advanced European economies that used the euro. At the time his analysis was produced, it drew a sharply negative retort from members of the IMF's European Department, which had chief responsibility for overseeing the economies of the countries involved. European Department economists contended that Bakker was exaggerating the peril in Eastern Europe, and although a couple of countries might be at risk, he was misconstruing the situation in the region. As for the possibility of crises in the euro zone, the Fund missed the boat completely.

This was a peculiar period in the IMF's history. The Fund was struggling to define its role in a seemingly crisis-free world, even as trouble was brewing in countries it would later help to rescue. Based on the widespread assumption that the kinds of crises it had fought in the past were unlikely to recur, the Fund underwent a crisis of its own — an existential crisis — in which its staff would be shrunk and its resources limited. As a result, it would be less prepared than it ought to have been when, in the fall of 2008, the panic that struck global financial markets spooked investors into pulling money out of any country that looked vulnerable. And the legacy of this period would continue to weigh heavily on the Fund at the onset of the euro-zone crisis.

For the staff, the experiences they had during this pre-crisis period depended on which of two broad categories they belonged to — "grunts" or "eggheads." Grunts have expertise in programs — that is, mobilizing loans for troubled member countries. These staffers pride themselves on their skill at performing under pressure as currencies crash and markets swoon, jetting off on missions to stricken capitals to negotiate the terms of rescue aid. Eggheads prefer surveillance — that is, appraising the economic and financial policies and prospects of individual nations, regions and even entire global systems. These men and women get their greatest professional satisfaction from producing reports that shed new light on key economic issues, with the aim of helping to move policy in a favourable direction.

The middle years of the twenty-first century's first decade were a busy time for the Fund's eggheads. Starting around 2005, the number of working papers increased sharply, with titles such as "Testing the Transparency Benefits of Inflation Targeting: Evidence from Private Sector Forecasts," published in December 2006; and "British Influence on Commonwealth Budget Systems: The Case of the United Republic of Tanzania," published in April 2007. The reason for the increase was simple: there were no crises to fight, and with a lack of programs to work on, Fund economists — seeing surveillance as the surest path to career advancement — were generating a voluminous body of analytical work.

By the same token, severe ennui was afflicting the IMF's grunts during this period. Not since 2002 had a major crisis materialized that demanded the Fund's attention, and most typical recipients of Fund loans showed no signs of needing such help in the foreseeable future. Countries throughout Latin America, emerging Asia and the Middle East were flush with cash — that is, hard currency of the sort the Fund doles out in emergencies. One of the Fund's department heads, Mohsin Khan, acknowledged in a story I wrote for *The Washington Post* in 2006 that although the dearth of financial turmoil was obviously desirable, tedium was taking a toll on staff morale. "Firefighters don't like to sit in the firehouse," Khan said. "If you're in this organization and you've been caught up in the excitement of rushing around to countries helping them fight crises — well, if there are no crises, you're sitting around wondering what to do."[1]

A vexing problem thus confronted Rodrigo de Rato, the IMF managing director — how to justify the Fund's existence. A Spaniard who had served as his country's finance minister before gaining appointment to the managing directorship in mid-2004, de Rato was admired by the staff for his intelligence, but he lacked inspirational spark and struck some of his underlings as disengaged at times. And a few months into his term, he was besieged by criticism that the Fund needed to find new ways of making itself relevant in a world where so few countries appeared to need its money. New loans in the financial year ended April 30, 2005, were just $2.5 billion, the lowest since the late 1970s. Moreover, countries that had borrowed large amounts in previous years — Brazil, Argentina and Indonesia — decided to pay back their loans ahead of schedule. If the Fund did not find a productive new role

1 Blustein, 2006, "IMF Has No Crisis to Manage," *The Washington Post*, September 15.

for itself now that crisis lending was becoming passé, it would "slip into obscurity," Bank of England Governor Mervyn King warned in a widely cited 2006 speech.[2]

A flurry of media articles and op-eds highlighted questions about the IMF's usefulness. "Not Even a Cat to Rescue," was the mocking headline of an April 2006 article in *The Economist*. Conferences were held, learned articles written, eminent-persons groups convened and reports published regarding how the Fund might reorient its priorities to provide value.[3]

In previous years, countries in the emerging world had been rife with imbalances of the sort that give the IMF its raison d'être. Time and again, these countries had encountered trouble because of large deficits in their current accounts, the broadest measure of the balance of trade, which essentially implied that they were living beyond their means. Over long periods, in other words, these countries were importing significantly more goods and services from abroad than they were exporting, and to pay for that extra amount of foreign goods and services, they were using funds coming from abroad in the form of loans and investments. Like individuals who max out on their credit cards and can no longer obtain the funds needed to maintain their lifestyles, these countries sometimes found themselves cut off from sources of hard currency — which, as noted previously, is necessary to conduct international transactions, including the importation of essential goods. When this happens, a loan from the Fund's pool of hard currency can help tide a country over, with the money forthcoming on condition that the government makes the policy changes necessary for restoring reasonable balance between the country's income and outgo. The Fund's diagnosis and prescriptions are sometimes off the mark,

2 Mervyn King, 2006, "Reform of the International Monetary Fund," speech given at the Indian Council for Research on International Economic Relations, New Delhi, February 20.

3 One of the most influential sources of input was the report by a committee chaired by Andrew Crockett, president of JPMorgan Chase International and former general manager of the Bank for International Settlements. See IMF, 2007, "Panel Seeks More Stable Income for IMF," *IMF Survey*, February 12, www.imf.org/external/pubs/ft/survey/so/2007/INT051B.htm.

and its job has gotten more difficult as global flows of money have grown bigger and more overwhelming. But an IMF loan is sometimes the only way for a country to avoid total economic collapse.

In the mid "noughties," most countries in the emerging world were running large current account *surpluses*, thanks in part to the high prices of commodities that they exported. And the dollars, euros and yen they were earning on those exports were filling the coffers of their central banks. That was a source of delight to national leaders who could relax in the knowledge that these reserves of foreign exchange were helping to insure against ever having to seek IMF help.

The one area of the emerging world that didn't fit the general pattern at the time was Eastern Europe. That is why it was the focus of the presentation by Bakker, who worked in a unit that conducted "vulnerability exercises" on emerging economies. His central point was that Eastern European countries such as Bulgaria, Latvia, Hungary and Estonia were running large current account deficits, just as Thailand, South Korea, Malaysia and other Asian countries were doing in 1996. Current account deficits were well over 10 percent of GDP in a few of the Eastern European countries, even bigger than the one a decade earlier in Thailand, where the Asian crisis started. Although it was no secret that current account deficits of such dimensions existed in Eastern Europe, Bakker cited other striking parallels with pre-crisis Asia, notably the existence of booms fuelled by rapid expansion of bank lending.

To be sure, a large current account deficit does not lead inexorably to crisis, and economists in the European Department took strong exception to Bakker's conclusion that the current account deficits in Eastern Europe were symptomatic of financial fragility. The poorer countries of Eastern Europe weren't overheating, according to the European Department staff; they were slowly but surely developing more like their wealthy neighbours to the west, a phenomenon significantly attributable to the capital that was flowing from west to east.[4] A memo from one European Department economist huffily urged an end to further discussions likening Eastern Europe to pre-crisis Asia.

The dispute was a typical example of a clash between one of the Fund's area departments, which are responsible for major regions (for example, Europe, Africa, the Asia-Pacific), and one of its "functional departments," which have global responsibilities. This tension is both natural and healthy; the area departments regard themselves as possessing specialized knowledge about the economic forces and political realities in the countries they oversee, while the functional departments regard themselves as repositories of expertise about how economic policies work best around the world. The most powerful department, and the one usually involved in the most consequential fights, is the Strategy, Policy and Review Department (SPR), some of whose members will feature prominently in this book. SPR, to which Bakker belonged in 2006,[5] is sometimes mocked as the "thought police," or "defenders of the faith," because the department's mission includes ensuring that the Fund's rescue programs, monitoring and advice are applied consistently and in accord with the institution's standards. For their part, the area departments stand accused of being prone to "clientitis" — excessive sympathy for the authorities in national capitals with whom area department staffers closely interact while on missions. When economists in one department can't agree with their colleagues in another, the department heads may first try to reach a compromise, but if they can't, the issue may have to be bucked "upstairs" (both figuratively and literally, since top management's offices are on upper floors) to the managing director or a deputy managing director for resolution. Once judgment is rendered, staffers

4 For an example of the European Department's thinking at the time, see Abdul Abiad, Daniel Leigh and Ashoka Mody, 2007, "International Finance and Income Convergence: Europe is Different," IMF Working Paper WP/07/64, March, www.imf.org/external/pubs/ft/wp/2007/wp0764.pdf.

5 This department's title at the time was Policy Development and Review, but for simplicity's sake the current name and acronym will be used throughout this book.

are expected to toe the line, regardless of whether they privately agree, lest the Fund send mixed messages that might convey doubt or irresolution to the outside world.

In the battle between Bakker and the European Department, the latter's position essentially prevailed. A number of public statements and documents published by the IMF during this period depicted Eastern Europe's breakneck growth in relatively benign terms.

Perhaps the most remarkable fact about this episode is that Eastern Europe was the only region where anyone in the IMF was ringing alarm bells, even in private.

On June 28, 2007, the obscurity-bound IMF pulsed with a frisson of excitement. To widespread astonishment, de Rato announced that he was quitting as managing director, well before his five-year term was due to end. A divorced father, de Rato said he needed to fulfill his obligations to his two teenage children, who lived in Spain. Speculation immediately turned to the question of who would succeed him, and whether Europe would once again exercise control over the decision.

A logic of sorts pertained at one time to the mutual-backscratching deal that divides the top positions at the IMF and World Bank between Europe and the United States. As a rookie economics reporter in the 1980s, I heard the following explanation from an IMF spokesman: the Americans and Europeans are the biggest contributors to the Fund and the Bank, while developing countries are most likely to be borrowing the institutions' money. Thus, rich countries have a legitimate claim on a majority of the votes on the institutions' boards, and they could hardly be expected to hand over control of the management to the borrowers.

Even some European governments — the British in particular — saw this arrangement as increasingly untenable as the BRICS and other middle-income nations had grown in economic size and importance. There were good, self-interested reasons for wanting to liberate the

Fund and the Bank from the perception of North Atlantic domination, because the emerging powers would otherwise become more likely to ignore the institutions' advice and dismiss their authority.

Soon after de Rato's announcement, word came from London that the British government wanted to make the selection process orderly and transparent, so that candidates might be considered regardless of nationality. But from Paris came word that the French government had different ideas. French officials had a favourite in mind to be named Europe's candidate, and thus the presumptive choice: Strauss-Kahn, a former French finance minister and Socialist Party presidential candidate.

Round one in the contest for the IMF managing directorship went easily to the forces supporting Strauss-Kahn. On July 10, 2007, at a meeting of European finance ministers in Brussels, Alistair Darling, the UK Chancellor of the Exchequer, was briefing British journalists on London's position when he received a text message informing him that his fellow ministers had officially endorsed the Frenchman.[6] The Europeans argued that they were perfectly within their rights; only a few weeks earlier, when Paul Wolfowitz had resigned as president of the World Bank, the Bush administration had exercised the US monopoly over that post by choosing Robert Zoellick, another American, and making it clear that it expected other countries to go along.

Still, the battle was not quite over. In mid-August, even as Strauss-Kahn was several weeks into a tour of major world capitals aimed at showing developing countries that he felt obliged to campaign for the job, a rival candidate emerged — Josef Tosovsky, a former central bank governor and caretaker prime minister of the Czech Republic. Behind his candidacy was Russia's finance ministry, which wanted, at a minimum, to register its disgust with the selection process, and harboured hopes that perhaps the neoconservative Bush White House would help block a French Socialist from heading the Fund even if he was Europe's nominee.

6 George Parker, 2007, "Strauss-Kahn gets IMF nomination," *Financial Times*, July 10.

The Russians knew that their gambit was a long shot, given the way voting power was apportioned among the 24 executive directors who represented the IMF's member countries. Countries with the biggest "quotas" — which depend broadly on economic size, and determine the amount each country contributes to the Fund — hold the biggest percentage of votes. The US director, of course, held the biggest single vote, with 16.83 percent of the total. (The United States is one of eight countries with its own director;[7] other directors represent constituencies of countries, and their voting power is based on those countries' quotas.) Directors from Germany, the United Kingdom, France, Italy, Belgium and the Netherlands controlled another 29.69 percent, and the Europeans could presumably count on the votes of other directors (the one representing the Nordic countries, for example) to pad their total by a few extra percentage points. The exact numbers don't matter much, because formal votes are extremely rare; the board adopts as many decisions as possible by consensus, in keeping with the institution's ethos of projecting authority. But the math is simple: if the Americans and Europeans join forces, they can dominate.[8] In this consensus-oriented body, the pressure to go along with the majority is intense.

To the Russians' delight — and the Europeans' consternation — an editorial headlined "Not Strauss-Kahn" appeared in the *Financial Times* a few days after Tosovsky entered the race. The newspaper belittled the Frenchman's qualifications and thundered that even if he were the best candidate:

7 The others are Japan, Germany, France, the United Kingdom, China, Russia and Saudi Arabia.

8 This is especially true when it comes to the managing directorship. The selection procedure traditionally works as follows: First the board meets informally and takes a straw vote, using secret ballots, so that if, say, three candidates are in the running, the secretary of the board takes the ballots outside the boardroom and returns to announce the elimination of the candidate with the least votes (without disclosing the actual figures). Then another straw vote, in similar fashion, decides the contest among the two remaining candidates. Finally, the board meets in formal session to bestow a unanimous vote on the winner.

> Emerging countries no longer understand why Europeans should determine who might dictate to them in any crisis, as if their old empires still existed. The IMF is either a global institution with a head chosen by the world, or it is an expression of Europe's will to cling on to every scrap of its prestige and power. In this latter guise, the Fund will be shorn of all legitimacy.[9]

Anxious to head off a serious rebellion against their man, Europe's economic leadership hastily offered assurances that the days of the "gentlemen's agreement" were numbered. "The next director will certainly not be European," stated Jean-Claude Juncker, Luxembourg's prime minister, who presided over the Eurogroup, the high-powered forum consisting of euro area finance ministers plus the ECB president and European economic affairs commissioner. "In the Eurogroup and among EU finance ministers, everyone is aware that Strauss-Kahn will probably be the last European to become director of the IMF in the foreseeable future."[10]

The Russians had to be content with receiving such promises and scoring propaganda points against this stacked system. Their scheme to divide the Americans and Europeans might have worked if the European candidate had really been objectionable to Washington, but that wasn't the case. This French Socialist was a breed apart.

In June 1997, when Strauss-Kahn became finance minister of France, he was still an unknown quantity, certainly outside of his own country. Pretty much the only thing that the conservative German leadership knew about him was that he was part of a "plural left" government consisting of Socialists, Communists and Greens. And in Berlin's view, this newly elected coalition posed a serious threat — probably a fatal one — to plans for European Monetary Union. With its much-

9 *Financial Times* (2007), "Not Strauss-Kahn," August 28.

10 Wolfgang Proissi (2007), "European control of IMF 'to end,'" *Financial Times*, August 29.

ballyhooed promise to institute a 35-hour workweek, the new French regime appeared unlikely to maintain the economic discipline required for making the euro project successful. Only when Theo Waigel, the German finance minister, held a get-acquainted session with his French counterpart on the eve of a regional meeting did Berlin's perspective change. "Strauss-Kahn charmed everyone from the first minute," Klaus Regling, who was then one of the German finance ministry's top officials, recalled in an interview.

For starters, Strauss-Kahn stunned Waigel and his colleagues by speaking German with such fluency that the entire meeting was conducted in their language; the interpreter the Germans had brought was needed only for one member of the French team. Moreover, Strauss-Kahn convincingly assured Waigel that France's economic policies would not be incompatible with euro-zone membership. "It was impressive," Regling said. "Monetary union was back on track after that evening."

This was vintage Strauss-Kahn. Dubbed "Le Grand Séducteur" by a French weekly, he earned the title not only because of his amorous adventures. His ability to command rooms, influence debate and forge consensus was a gift that he deployed with extraordinary effectiveness in almost any professional setting in which he operated.[11]

Born in an upmarket Paris suburb in 1949 to a family of progressive, secular Jews — his father was a successful attorney, his mother a journalist — Strauss-Kahn earned a law degree and Ph.D. in economics from the University of Paris, and worked first as a professor at that university, gaining tenure in 1978. He then began pursuing a career in government and politics, winning election to the French National Assembly and serving in various Socialist Party and government bodies.

11 Information about Strauss-Kahn can be found in George Parker, 2007, "The resurgent charmer," *Financial Times,* July 14; David Gauthier-Villars and Bob Davis (2008), "Strauss-Kahn's Road to IMF Chief Led from Local Politics to Global," *The Wall Street Journal,* October 18; Apolline de Malherbe, 2011, "The Invisible Man," *Washingtonian,* June; Brian Love, 2011, "The two faces of DSK," Reuters, May 19; and Landon Thomas Jr. and Steven Erlanger, 2011, "Atop I.M.F., Contradiction and Energy," *The New York Times*, May 17.

In 1991, Strauss-Kahn secured his first cabinet position, Minister of Industry and International Trade; around the same time, he married Anne Sinclair, one of France's foremost television journalists (his third wife). Elevation to the top ranks of economic policy — the finance minister's post — came with the left's victory of 1997. Delicately sidestepping his party's election manifesto, Strauss-Kahn promoted pragmatic, stability- and market-oriented policies in a number of areas, just as he had promised the Germans. He oversaw the privatization of state-owned enterprises, notably the giant bank Crédit Lyonnais, and with the aim of ensuring that France would meet one of the major criteria for adopting the euro, he also laboured to shrink the government budget deficit to below three percent of GDP. It helped that he was working closely with a credible embodiment of economic orthodoxy — Jean-Claude Trichet, the governor of the Banque de France. The two men represented France at meetings of Group of Seven (G7) finance ministers and central bank governors, and together they promoted the *franc fort* policy of strengthening the French currency, another essential element of France's euro-zone entry. Their efforts were rewarded when, on January 1, 1999, they basked in the birth of the euro — never imagining, of course, that a little more than a decade later they would be playing major roles in trying to save it.

Strauss-Kahn's star faded when accusations of financial irregularities led to his resignation from the finance ministry, even though he was later cleared, and his career took another downturn following an unsuccessful run in 2006 to become the Socialist nominee for president. But the unexpected vacancy at the IMF in mid-2007 afforded a golden opportunity for a comeback.

The French government enthusiastically backed Strauss-Kahn for the managing directorship, in part because Nicolas Sarkozy, the president whom Strauss-Kahn had hoped to defeat in the 2006 election, was glad to get a formidable rival out of Paris. In Europe, where memories of Strauss-Kahn's record as finance minister were fond, few reservations were voiced aside from a blog post by Jean Quatremer of the newspaper *Libération*, who wrote: "Strauss-Kahn's only real problem is his behavior with women...This fault of his is well-known by the media, but no one speaks about it." As for Bush administration officials, their qualms abated when Treasury Secretary Henry Paulson spoke by phone with Robert Rubin, his predecessor from the Clinton administration, who had worked with Strauss-Kahn in the 1990s. Strauss-Kahn was no radical; indeed, he was extremely capable, Rubin assured Paulson.

The clincher was the first face-to-face encounter between Strauss-Kahn and Paulson. Beforehand, Strauss-Kahn asked aides what sort of man the Treasury secretary was; informed that Paulson hated long meetings — his attention span is notoriously short — the Frenchman made sure to keep his remarks confined to three points that he could rattle off in about 30 seconds. "That's all I have to say," he concluded, according to one attendee at the meeting — much to the delight of Paulson, who had regarded de Rato as a waffler and swiftly concluded that Strauss-Kahn was a man of action.

It was another virtuoso performance, just like the one in 1997 that had led the Germans to put aside their reservations about proceeding with European Monetary Union. In retrospect, reasons abounded to be worried about the euro experiment — both in 1997, and even more so at the time Strauss-Kahn was taking over at the IMF. Some people, in fact, were expressing such concerns in 2007. But they were not at the Fund.

"As the euro rides high, an unhealthy sense of complacency pervades European capitals about the currency's long-run viability...[C]racks in the euro's very foundations are widening....European policymakers' pride in their currency today might be yet another example of pride before a fall."[12]

Those assertions appeared in an op-ed published in the *Financial Times* on February 28, 2007. The author was Desmond Lachman, a South Africa-born scholar at the American Enterprise Institute who had worked at the IMF in the 1980s and 1990s. Lachman has

12 Desmond Lachman, 2007, "The Real Reforms Needed to Secure the Euro's Future," *Financial Times*, February 28.

a reputation as an economic Cassandra, but excessive though his gloomy prognostications sometimes are, they generally merit careful consideration. Some of his direst forecasts have proven perspicacious, and have come well ahead of the pack, most notably his warnings (while working at the Wall Street firm of Salomon Brothers) that Argentina was almost certain to default on its debt and abandon the peg of its currency, the peso, to the US dollar.

Lachman was hardly the first to discern weaknesses in the system underpinning the euro. During the 1990s, when European officials were moving forward in earnest toward their goal of monetary union, US and UK economists were particularly vocal in questioning whether a common currency for such a disparate group of countries made sense. Among them were some of the biggest names in the field, including Milton Friedman, Martin Feldstein, Rüdiger Dornbursch and Paul Krugman, as well as some lesser-known specialists such as Bernard Connolly, Wynne Godley and Charles Calomiris. Beneficial as it might be in fostering trade and other economic exchanges within the European Union, and noble as it might be to bind former wartime enemies more closely together, joining a currency union requires a sovereign government to relinquish control over some enormously important tools for influencing the health of the national economy, notably the money supply, interest rates and the currency exchange rate — all of which would now become the responsibility of the ECB. So Friedman, Feldstein and others warned that countries in the euro zone would risk serious trouble by embracing a unified monetary policy when so many other aspects of their economies and societies — their fiscal and regulatory policies, their financial systems, the competitiveness of their industries and of course their languages — were so different. The obvious comparison was the United States, where a common currency and monetary policy are practical in part because of labour mobility; if one region of the country is suffering from high unemployment, the jobless can move to more prosperous areas, better enabling the central bank (the Federal Reserve) to decide on money supply expansion and interest rate levels based on the aim of keeping the overall economy on a stable, low-inflation path. In Europe, by contrast, people are much more loath to seek work by moving many hundreds of miles away, where they may not be able to communicate with their neighbours or relate culturally to them. If one European country (or group of countries) underwent a severe slump while others boomed, the slumpers — lacking control over their own money supply and exchange rate — would have very limited ways of generating recovery, the euro skeptics pointed out.

Their concerns were not assuaged by the Maastricht Treaty, signed in February 1992, when the euro zone's prospective members agreed to a number of "convergence criteria" that would be required for membership, most importantly including low inflation, low interest rates and budget deficits below three percent of GDP. Nor did euro skepticism abate much following the "Stability and Growth Pact," agreed in 1997 to boost enforcement of the rules by threatening sanctions against violators. The rules didn't cover enough crucial areas, naysayers said, and wouldn't be enforced anyway.

Pessimism about the euro receded, though, along with memories of francs, deutsche marks, lira, pesetas and guilders, which disappeared from circulation in 2002. The most striking sign of confidence in the currency was the way financial markets increasingly treated member countries of the euro zone as if their creditworthiness was almost identical. Now that investors no longer had to worry about, say, a Spanish bond falling in value because of a decline in the peseta, they were more eager to buy. Accordingly, even for a country such as Greece, where in the early 1990s borrowers had had to pay roughly three times as much in interest as German borrowers did, funds could be raised in 2007 at wafer-thin "spreads" — 4.29 percent for Greek government 10-year bonds, versus 4.02 percent for the German equivalent.[13]

Lachman, characteristically, saw highly worrisome trends underlying the market buoyancy. As he wrote in his February 2007 op-ed:

13 Neil Irwin, 2013, *The Alchemists: Three Central Bankers and a World on Fire,* New York, NY: Penguin Press, chapter 13.

> [D]evelopments in the individual countries comprising the eurozone have hardly evolved in the direction that the euro's founders had envisaged. Nor have they evolved in the direction necessary for the currency's survival....
>
> Looking at the continued wayward wage and price performance of Greece, Italy, Portugal and Spain since 1999, one might be forgiven for thinking that little has changed in these countries in spite of their having joined the euro. In the short space of seven years, these countries have managed to lose between 30 and 45 per cent of international competitiveness to Germany. This is already exerting a serious toll on Italian growth performance, and it does not bode well for growth prospects in Mediterranean Europe, especially if Spain's housing market bubble bursts.[14]

Lachman then shone a spotlight on "a further symptom that something is amiss in the working of the single currency system" — namely, divergent trade imbalances among member countries. Whereas Germany had run a current account surplus of 6.1 percent of GDP the previous year, and the Netherlands' surplus was even bigger, at 8.2 percent of GDP, current account deficits were running between 8 percent and 11 percent of GDP in Greece, Spain and Portugal. "It would be a grave mistake for European policymakers to assume that... supportive conditions will persist indefinitely," Lachman concluded.

The imbalances problem is now widely identified as one of the major factors driving the crisis.[15] The surplus countries of northern Europe were helping to finance a binge of consumption and housing purchases in deficit countries such as Spain and Ireland, as well as a binge of government spending in Greece. Capital was pouring from the thrifty, ultra-competitive north into the peripheral countries of the zone; among the most enthusiastic funders were Germany's Landesbanken,

14 See footnote 12 in this chapter.

15 Richard Baldwin et al., 2015, "Rebooting the Eurozone: Step 1—Agreeing a Crisis narrative," voxEU.org, November 20.

public-sector regional institutions with close connections to local politicians. This flood of money made it much easier for governments, businesses and individuals in the periphery to borrow — and in many cases, to borrow excessively, as the world would eventually learn to its sorrow.

So how did the IMF perceive the situation around the time of Lachman's op-ed? Rather differently, as indicated by the conclusion of the so-called Article IV report for the euro area that year. Article IV reports are produced by missions that visit capitals for a couple of weeks — usually once annually — to conduct economic checkups, and the first sentence of the 2007 euro-zone report summarized conditions there as follows: "[T]he outlook is the best in years. The economy is poised for a sustained upswing, partly because of cyclical considerations, but also because of policies."[16]

The Fund was especially blasé — before the crisis, at least — about imbalances within the euro zone. The surpluses pretty much cancelled out the deficits, putting the zone overall in rough balance, so there was little point in raising the issue, as far as the Fund was concerned. Michael Deppler, the director of the European Department, was one of the staunchest and most influential advocates of this view, which European policy makers widely shared.

A US citizen who spoke fluent French, Deppler was popular in European officialdom, not only for his manner — he manifested none of the cockiness that Europeans associated with Americans — but for his depth of knowledge about the euro zone and belief in its virtues. When challenged by other Fund economists about the imbalances issue, Deppler often noted that nobody pays attention to the large trade surpluses run by some US states and the large trade deficits run by others, because US states are part of a nation with a single currency. Likewise, he contended, the creation of the euro zone, with its own central bank, had essentially eliminated the risk that member countries

16 IMF, 2007, "Euro Area Policies: Staff Report for the 2007 Article IV Consultation with Member Countries," July 10, www.imf.org/external/pubs/ft/scr/2007/cr07260.pdf.

might suffer "sudden stops" in which they would lose access to the currency needed for their economies to function. Greece or Portugal could no more undergo that type of crisis than, say, Oregon, in other words.

This nonchalance about intra-European imbalances was especially striking because the IMF was striving mightily at the time to take a leading role in encouraging other major countries, notably the United States and China, to shrink current account deficits and surpluses. IMF reports on global trends, such as its flagship *World Economic Outlook*, repeatedly sought to raise the alarm about this issue, the mantra being that a "disorderly adjustment" (which essentially meant a large-scale flight from the US dollar) "could impose heavy costs on the global economy." But Europe, being in overall balance, was spared any pressure in this regard.[17]

It would be unfair to suggest that the IMF saw no problems in the euro zone, or that it believed a crisis there would somehow violate the laws of physics. Although its reports on the countries that underwent crises look rosy in hindsight, they pointed out vulnerabilities and urged sensible reforms. (Surveillance of those countries will be covered in later chapters.) But there is no gainsaying how blind the IMF was to the forces building within Europe that would eventually menace the entire globe. In a review that the Fund commissioned in 2011 of its surveillance of the euro zone, the authors, who worked at Bruegel, the

17 In one high-profile initiative, dubbed the Multilateral Consultations, the Fund convened discussions in 2006-2007 among representatives of five big economies, the hope being that they would reach an agreement or at least accelerate efforts to reduce overspending and excessive borrowing in deficit countries while inducing surplus countries to rely less on exports for economic growth. The five economies naturally included the country with the most gaping deficit — the United States — and the biggest surplus generators, namely China, Japan and Saudi Arabia. The euro zone was the fifth economy represented, because of its size. But the IMF's concern regarding Europe had nothing to do with the surpluses in the north and deficits in the south. Confidential records of the discussions that took place, and the IMF's own internal memos preparing the initiative, include no mention of those internal imbalances. Rather, the Fund exhorted Europe to boost overall productivity and growth, thereby helping at least a little in absorbing goods produced elsewhere and sustaining global economic expansion.

Brussels-based think tank, found the Fund guilty of a fundamental error: its surveillance, they wrote, "failed to take account of the implications of being in a monetary union." As this report also stated:

> The Fund was the institution best placed to recognize that credit booms, large current account deficits and large external indebtedness are eventually associated with significant turbulence. It had a clear comparative advantage with respect to the institutions responsible for EU surveillance. However the Fund fell victim to the mindset that "Europe is different."[18]

And in another report, the Bruegel authors elaborated on this point:

> [Balance-of-payment] crises are the bread-and-butter of IMF assistance. However, even the Fund was unprepared for the possibility of BOP crises in the euro area. In their surveillance work during the period 1999-2009, IMF staff never raised the possibility of major sovereign or balance-of-payment crises in the euro area despite their intimate knowledge of crises elsewhere and potential parallels with the euro area that should have drawn their attention, in particular consumption booms...and large current account deficits, which are typical in countries before a BOP crisis.[19]

An unflattering assessment, and it is well deserved.

In the fall of 2007, Strauss-Kahn and his wife settled in a five-bedroom home in the tony Georgetown section of Washington (the couple also owned two luxurious apartments in France and a house in Marrakesh,

18 Jean Pisani-Ferry, André Sapir and Guntram B. Wolff, 2011, "An Evaluation of IMF Surveillance of the Euro Area," *Bruegel Blueprint* 14.

19 Pisani-Ferry, Sapir and Wolff, 2013, "EU-IMF Assistance to Euro-area Countries: An Early Assessment," *Bruegel Blueprint* 19.

Morocco). Despite his "caviar socialist" lifestyle, Strauss-Kahn's work ethic favourably impressed his new IMF colleagues, who often saw him on weekends at headquarters, clad in jeans. He typically arrived at meetings with small pages of bullet points he wanted to discuss, handling most subjects with command of detail.

But he came under orders from shareholders to downsize the institution, given the doubts that had arisen about the need for a sizable crisis lender as well as the Fund's inability to generate sufficient income from loans to cover its expenses. Those orders, initiated by Dutch and Swiss officials with backing from the G7 major industrial nations, included a significant reduction in personnel, which would be the first in the Fund's history. Previous efforts to cut the Fund's operating budget had made limited headway, because of resistance among the board and staff to cuts in expensive perks such as education allowances and relocation grants. Now complaints were coming from members of the US Congress in particular about the size of an international bureaucracy that appeared to be doing a lot less than before while continuing to receive handsome compensation. (Entry-level Ph.D.'s at the IMF were earning salaries between $79,600 and $119,400, tax free.) And the US authorities had leverage, because in order to obtain part of the income necessary for financing its budget the Fund was planning to sell some of its gold reserves, for which Congress had required its approval.[20]

In early December, Strauss-Kahn announced plans to cut staff by as much as 15 percent — 300 to 400 positions. With his usual aplomb, he managed to explain the necessity of this move in ways that appealed to the staff's logic as economists: it would not be credible for the Fund, an institution that often preached budgetary frugality, to shore up its revenue through gold sales without taking commensurate action on the expenditure side, he argued. The lavish pay and bonuses that Wall Street firms were offering ex-IMF economists, to be sure, helped

20 Information about the downsizing can be found at IMF Independent Evaluation Office, 2014, "IMF Response to the Financial and Economic Crisis: An IEO Assessment," October 8, annex 2, www.ieo-imf.org/ieo/files/completedevaluations/Full%20Text%20of%20the%20Main%20Report.pdf.

dampen the distress with which the news was received. Still, it was a demoralizing period. "It was the low point of my career. My worst experience in the Fund was managing that process in my department," said Teresa Ter-Minassian, who was director of the Fiscal Affairs Department.

The downsizing can be seen as the ultimate symbol of cluelessness among the world's top economic policy makers about impending developments in financial markets; it was akin to a fire department laying off its hook-and-ladder crew for lack of recent blazes even as smoke was wafting around the firehouse. By that time, early signs of the global crisis were manifest in the near-collapse of two hedge funds that had invested heavily in securities backed by US mortgages, with similar woes at the mid-sized German lender IKB; in the shocking run by depositors to withdraw money from the British bank Northern Rock; and in a seize-up in markets in August 2007 that required emergency injections of vast amounts of cash by the Fed and ECB.

Strauss-Kahn was plenty uneasy about the ramifications of those market developments on economies around the globe, and he demonstrated readiness to scrap the IMF's traditional ways of thinking about such issues. At the World Economic Forum in Davos in January 2008, the managing director asserted that major countries should pursue more expansionary fiscal policies to help stimulate demand — a surprising shift coming from an institution commonly associated with recommendations for painful spending cuts and tax hikes.[21] As the crisis in the United States began to unfold in the middle months of 2008, the Fund tried to lend its expertise to the Bush administration, as witnessed by a speech delivered in March 2008 by First Deputy Managing Director John Lipsky, who exhorted policy makers to "think the unthinkable" and "keep all options on the table, including the potential use of public funds to safeguard the financial system."[22] But the United States has no need of the IMF's hard currency loans, and it paid little heed to Fund admonitions.

21 Chris Giles and Gillian Tett, 2008, "IMF head in shock fiscal appeal," January 28.

22 IMF, 2008, "Dealing with the Financial Turmoil," speech by John Lipsky at the Peterson Institute, March 12, www.imf.org/external/np/speeches/2008/031208.htm.

All the while, Strauss-Kahn forged ahead energetically with the downsizing, showing remarkable grasp at "town hall" meetings of the minutiae regarding the retirement plan, medical benefits and other aspects of the package for departees. The idea was to avoid forced departures if possible, by offering generous inducements (up to two years of pay) for people to quit voluntarily. In the end, this undertaking exceeded expectations. Nearly 600 members of the staff — about 20 percent of the workforce — accepted the buyout offer, which was more than intended, and the Fund told more than 100 staffers who wanted to take the package that they would have to stay. By some accounts, this process rid the IMF of a fair amount of deadwood — staffers, especially senior managers, who had worked at the institution too long and were slow to adapt to new ways of functioning.

But in the words of the Fund's own Independent Evaluation Office, "the IMF lost some of its most experienced staff" — especially those well-practiced in designing and running programs — "just when it was needed."[23] Indeed, within months the Fund would reverse course and launch a recruitment drive resulting in the hiring of more than 100 economists by end-April 2009. These warm bodies would be required, much sooner than anybody at the Fund realized in mid-2008, amid the hell that was about to break loose in global financial markets.

Not only the IMF's human resources, but its financial resources too, were allowed to dwindle in 2008, with scant recognition of the imminent need for more.

The money that the IMF lends to countries comes from two major sources. The first is quotas, which as previously noted are based broadly on member countries' economic size and determine the amount they contribute to the Fund. The second is borrowing arrangements with advanced and middle-income countries, the main one being the "New Arrangements to Borrow," under which a number of governments

23 IMF Independent Evaluation Office, 2014, annex 2 (see footnote 20 in this chapter).

pledge to lend hard currency to the IMF if necessary. The IMF operates on the tenet that quotas — being more permanent and reliable — are its best source of financing, and should be used first, with borrowing providing a supplement if and when quotas run low.

On October 8, as the IMF prepared to host officials from around the world for its joint annual meetings with the World Bank, a confidential staff paper, titled "The Fund's Liquidity Position: Review and Outlook," provided an assessment of whether the Fund had enough money to lend to member countries that might undergo financial emergencies. At that point, the IMF's war chest of lendable funds — from quotas and borrowing arrangements — totalled about $250 billion, which although a substantial amount in absolute terms was at record lows relative to world GDP and other relevant metrics such as global trade and flows of capital across international borders.

The paper deemed the Fund's financial situation "satisfactory." It noted the need to closely monitor global developments, citing uncertainties that had arisen in the wake of the Lehman Brothers bankruptcy on September 15. But it maintained the long-standing complacent view about the desirability of a modest-sized IMF. Given the money available, the Fund was "well-placed to meet the near-term external financing needs of its members," the paper concluded.[24]

Different words would have been chosen if the authors could have foreseen the extent of forthcoming demands for IMF aid, the first of which would materialize the very next day.

24 Excerpts from this paper, which is still confidential, can be found in Eduard Brau and Louellen Stedman, 2014, "IMF Efforts to Increase the Resources Available to Support Member Countries," IMF Independent Evaluation Office Background Paper BP/14/10, October 8.

4

EGG ON MANY ILLUSTRIOUS FACES

A momentous call from Budapest came for James Morsink, the IMF's mission chief for Hungary, shortly after returning to his desk from lunch on October 9, 2008. Less than a month had passed since the bankruptcy of Lehman Brothers, and financial markets the world over were undergoing staggeringly large gyrations that week, with some of the biggest banks and securities firms in New York and London on the brink of going under as credit virtually ceased flowing. Although attention was riveted on developments in major financial centres, Hungary too was a Lehman-shock victim; indeed, a Hungarian government bond auction that day had failed for lack of buyers. So it came as little surprise to Morsink to hear from András Simor, Hungary's central bank governor, that his country was requesting assistance from the Fund. But the call for help was the first of its kind that the Fund had gotten in years — and the alacrity with which the institution responded reflected its determination to play a substantial part in the worldwide effort to forestall a systemic financial breakdown.

Morsink immediately put the governor in touch with John Lipsky, whose duties as first deputy managing director included management oversight for Hungary. Approval was promptly forthcoming that day, a Thursday, for "emergency procedures," enabling a mission to depart as soon as the executive board was notified and a briefing paper could be drafted. In non-emergency cases, missions commonly take a month or more to go through this process, so that all relevant departments get a chance to reflect and comment on how programs should be designed; the go-ahead for this mission came on Friday evening. Morsink managed to attend his son's soccer game on Saturday before rushing to the airport to join colleagues flying to Budapest.

At last, the world's firefighters were no longer condemned to sit around their firehouse! Within days of the Hungarian mission's departure, negotiations were under way on more programs — for Ukraine, Iceland and Pakistan; others would follow in late 2008 and early 2009 for Latvia, Serbia, Belarus and Romania. Not that anyone at the IMF took pleasure in the privations that were being visited upon ordinary people in crisis-torn countries. But the new sense of institutional purpose was obviously welcome, especially since it sparked widespread commentary that the world needed a bigger IMF rather than a smaller one.

Unfortunately, the IMF was not fully ready for springing into action. The timing was especially inopportune for the European Department, whose purview included nearly all of the countries outside of the United States that were hardest hit in the weeks and months following the Lehman shock. The department suffered from a serious dearth of "grunts" with experience negotiating programs (Morsink, who had worked on the Thai crisis, was an exception), and the downsizing exacerbated the staffing problem. To make matters worse, both the department director, Michael Deppler, and his deputy, Susan Schadler, had left the Fund (Deppler in the spring of 2008, Schadler the previous year), with replacements for neither position having arrived at that point. An acting director, who was himself on the verge of leaving, was handling the department's administrative functions pending the arrival of a new director, Marek Belka, an economist and former Polish prime minister.[1]

On the other hand, the Eastern European crisis afforded valuable experience for both IMF and European officials. It was a dress rehearsal for the euro-zone crisis; it obliged the Fund and European authorities in Brussels to learn how to work together — something they would have to do under much higher-pressure circumstances later.

1 Belka's appointment had been announced in July, but he had not yet arrived in Washington.

The need for such experience became painfully clear at the outset. Word of the IMF's Hungary mission aroused a tempest in Brussels, where the European Commission was jealously guarding its role as the executive body of the European Union and it had no intention of allowing the IMF to run the whole show in Hungary. The European Union had its own loan facility for member countries undergoing balance-of-payments difficulties (available only for countries that did not use the euro, such as Hungary, which has its own currency, the forint). The point was established: the Europeans would have to be at the table, even if they would not be exerting detailed control over the terms, when one of their own was in trouble. And more of their own were clearly in trouble.

Up until just a few weeks earlier, Wall Street's tribulations had generated only modest effects abroad. But as the shockwaves from Lehman reverberated around the globe, they buffeted Eastern Europe with particular intensity. Not only did the region's exports fall precipitously, as they did elsewhere in the world, but the Western banks that had previously been shifting large amounts of capital to their Eastern European subsidiaries abruptly ceased doing so because of their own needs to husband capital and cash at home — the upshot being a massive contraction of lending in the region. The failed bond auction in Hungary reflected a similar phenomenon; the Hungarian government had been selling a large chunk of its bonds to foreigners, who no longer had either the ready cash nor the inclination to fund the country's large budget deficit.

Even though most of the region's economies were small relative to the advanced nations of Western Europe, the possibility of a financial collapse in one or more Eastern European countries was frightening. For one thing, Austrian, Swedish and Italian banks were heavily exposed to Eastern European borrowers, and in Lehman's immediate aftermath the global financial system was in no condition to absorb the losses that would result from widespread defaults on those loans. Equally important, especially given the European Union's eastward expansion, were the political risks of an economic catastrophe giving rise to populist or nationalist movements in countries where the institutions of capitalism and democracy were still relatively young and underdeveloped.

As the crisis spread, the inexperience of some of the IMF missions became apparent in their difficulties drafting technical memoranda and other documents such as the letters of intent that top economic policy makers must sign for their governments to receive Fund loans. To compensate, a group of crisis veterans from other departments was formed, helping the teams in European capitals formulate positions and explaining how to draft the necessary documents — in some cases, by speaking late at night over the phone or in video conferences.

This did not prevent the IMF from deploying a distinct approach in these rescues, which differed in important respects from the stereotypically stringent programs of past years. Noting Strauss-Kahn's Socialist Party background, pundits called the new approach a "charm offensive," requiring less fiscal and monetary belt-tightening than the Fund had demanded in Asia. Also noteworthy was the more relaxed approach to conditions that the Fund used. The Serbian program did not require Belgrade to privatize its state-owned industries, for instance, and the Hungarian program didn't include an overhaul of the country's generous pension system, somewhat to the surprise of Fund watchers. To be sure, the IMF was hardly adopting a no-strings policy to its lending; Iceland had to endure a steep rise in interest rates, and Ukraine had to pass new banking legislation.[2] But even long-time critics of the Fund credited it with learning from past mistakes. "The IMF seems to be modestly improving its flexibility and conditionality, compared to its dreadful practices in previous decades," said a July 2009 report by the Bretton Woods Project, an organization that had frequently accused the Fund of disregarding the needs of the poor.[3]

Although the terms obviously differed according to national circumstances, they generally followed a pattern: the Fund mobilized rapid responses and provided sizable, fast-disbursing loans — "shock and awe," Lipsky liked to call it, to the discomfort of some on the staff

2 Alan Beattie, 2008, "IMF rescue does not mean cash without strings," *Financial Times,* October 29; Bob Davis, 2009, "An Empowered IMF Faces Pivotal Test," *The Wall Street Journal,* March 31.

3 Bretton Woods Project, 2009, *Hungary and the IMF: Indebted Future,* July 10, www.brettonwoodsproject.org/2009/07/art-564876/.

— aimed at impressing the markets that the countries had ample cash on hand to meet all claims coming from abroad. IMF rules limit the amount a country can normally borrow based on the size of its quota; in 2008, countries were entitled to borrow up to 100 percent of quota annually and 300 percent of quota cumulatively. The loans to Eastern European countries, granted under rules covering "exceptional circumstances," were often well in excess of the limits, even after the limits were doubled in March 2009. In Hungary, for example, the €12.3 billion ($15.7 billion) that the IMF lent was 1,015 percent, or 11 times the country's quota.[4]

In EU countries, where IMF missions had to work alongside staffers from the European Commission, the Fund was clearly calling the shots in two cases — Hungary and Romania. The IMF's superiority in program design was beyond dispute, and its loans going to those countries were bigger than the loans coming from Brussels.

However, in a third Eastern European country — Latvia — the IMF and Europe would undergo a role switch. Despite involving a tiny nation of just 2.2 million people, the Latvian case would haunt the Fund during the still-unseen crisis in the euro zone.

The IMF mission that travelled in mid-November 2008 to the Latvian capital of Riga encountered numerous logistical problems. The hotel where the team first checked in, although conveniently close to both the finance ministry and central bank, had poor Internet connectivity, and staffers sometimes had to crouch in the hallways near routers to send and receive emails. They also felt compelled to evacuate to Warsaw at one point, because of fears that their lives might be at risk from vengeful financial executives who were suffering major losses

4 One additional and important feature of these programs was that they included an internationally coordinated effort, known as the Vienna Initiative, for foreign banks to maintain the lending exposures of their subsidiaries in Eastern Europe.

due to government actions. At mission meetings in the bar of another hotel where they later stayed, they had to cope with the distraction of a couple of prostitutes who regularly sat at a nearby table, soliciting drunken tourists.

Apart from those inconveniences, however, the biggest difficulty the mission faced was in pitched battles over Latvia's policy concerning its currency, the lat, which was tightly pegged to the euro at an exchange rate of about 0.7 lats per euro. (The lat could rise or fall as much as one percent, but not more, from the pegged rate.) Most IMF economists dealing with Latvia believed the currency was grossly overvalued and should decline substantially. But Latvian policy makers, backed by European officials in Brussels and elsewhere, rejected the idea of abandoning the peg, insisting that it would deprive the economy of an essential stabilizing force. So sensitive was the issue that members of the Fund mission used code words, thus making sure that if they were overheard in public places — a restaurant, for example — outsiders wouldn't be able to decipher the conversation. "Obama" referred to a change in currency policy, since the newly elected US president had campaigned on a promise of change. "McCain" was the code word for Ilmars Rimsevics, the governor of the Bank of Latvia, the country's central bank, because of his ironclad opposition to "Obama." And "Palin" referred to Parex Bank, one of Latvia's biggest, not only because of the identity in the first letters of their names, but because the troubled bank was a liability to Latvia just as the Republican vice presidential nominee had appeared to be for the Republican ticket.

The IMF's reasoning was based on textbook economics. Latvia's current account deficit had swelled to 25 percent of GDP in 2007, the result of a boom fuelled by Swedish banks that enthusiastically provided credit to Latvian businesses and homeowners based on the economic progress this former Soviet satellite was making. A country with a large current account deficit needs foreign creditors and investors to pour money in to keep the economy moving, but in 2008 foreigners were doing the opposite in Latvia. Thus the country would have to shrink that deficit in a hurry — and using the exchange rate offered the most obvious way of doing so. The IMF's Research Department estimated that the lat was overvalued by 23 percent to 37 percent, depending on the methodology used, meaning that a decline in the exchange rate of that order of magnitude would be required to reduce imports and increase exports sufficiently to bring the current account to something approaching reasonable balance.[5]

An email sent on November 17 by Christoph Rosenberg, the IMF mission chief, conveyed the depth of Latvian antipathy toward the idea of altering the peg: "The governor [Rimsevics, of the central bank] is emphatic that any change...is completely out of the question... When I asked him if he still wanted to proceed with his request for Fund assistance under this premise, he accused me of 'issuing an ultimatum.'...[The governor said a devaluation] would 'completely destroy the economy.' In fact, he said that suggesting such a thing was unprofessional and immoral (I will spare you his more graphic language used in this context.)"

The central banker was not alone. From the prime minister on down, Latvian officials contended that the currency peg was a linchpin of the economy's progress. It enjoyed enormous popular support, not least because the public understood that it would help Latvia gain euro membership sooner rather than later — and euro membership would mean moving permanently away from the despised orbit of Moscow. Moreover, Latvian policy makers feared that a decline in the lat exchange rate would lead to widespread bankruptcies, as it would inflate the debt burdens of businesses that had borrowed in hard currencies from abroad. Officials at the European Commission and ECB vigorously concurred, and cited other reasons for why any rescue program should be based on keeping the peg. The most important was the danger of contagion: modifying Latvia's exchange rate system would lead to heavy assaults on the similar currency arrangements

5 Highly informative retrospective analyses of the Latvian crisis include Anders Aslund, 2011, *How Latvia Came Through the Financial Crisis,* Washington: Peterson Institute for International Economics; and Olivier Blanchard, Mark Griffths and Bertrand Gruss, 2013, "Boom, Bust, Recovery: Forensics of the Latvia Crisis," Brookings Papers on Economic Activity, Fall.

of neighbouring countries, Estonia and Lithuania, and since Swedish banks were exposed throughout the Baltic region, a much broader crisis would likely result that might spread to the rest of Europe.[6]

Although IMF economists understood those objections, they believed the fallout from a major decline in the currency was manageable, and they contended that the alternative would be worse — an "internal devaluation," in which the economy gains competitiveness by drastically lowering wage costs and living standards. Sooner or later, they warned, the pain involved in an internal devaluation would force the government to surrender, the likely result being a disorderly, uncontrolled crash in the lat. Among those sharing this perspective was Strauss-Kahn, who according to one IMF email said at a meeting: "I don't believe for one second it will be possible to maintain the peg."

Irritated with what they considered the IMF's high-handedness, European officials vowed to proceed, with the IMF playing at most a minor part. On December 2, Marco Buti, the director-general for economic and financial affairs at the European Commission, told Lipsky in a phone call that the Europeans were contemplating a "reverse Hungary," according to an email from Lipsky to his colleagues. In other words, instead of the IMF ponying up the bulk of the loans and dictating the key terms, with the European Commission as junior partner (as had happened in Hungary), Brussels would take the senior partner role.

This idea affronted principles on which the IMF is supposed to operate, as Reza Moghadam, the director of SPR, observed in an email to Lipsky and other senior Fund officials. In taking the position he did, Moghadam was fulfilling his department's role as protector of Fund standards. His words merit quotation at length, because they are highly relevant to criticisms of the way the Fund would handle itself later in the euro-zone crisis:

6 Yet another argument was that in a small open economy such as Latvia's, where so many goods are imported, a cheaper currency would cause prices to rise, leaving the country still facing a severe competitiveness problem.

> We need to explain to the Europeans that we cannot delegate responsibility for use of Fund resources [Moghadam wrote]. This applies whether we put in one cent or the entire financing of the program. The Fund needs to be able to have...underlying policies that enable us to support the program...EU can always put in place its own program and financing without the Fund if that is what they and the Latvians want but our support, and by implication that of the international community, requires a normal Fund program which can of course be done jointly with the Europeans.

Notwithstanding these high-minded sentiments, the IMF backed down, at least on the issue of the peg. A few days after Moghadam's email was written, the Fund agreed to join the European Commission and the governments of several Nordic countries in a program that would allow Latvia to keep its currency system. How did this happen? In a nutshell, the Europeans insisted, and they were in a position to get their way, given their voting power on the IMF board. To be sure, the Fund also insisted that in exchange for its support, Latvia would have to agree to extremely tough conditions, with the aim of generating an internal devaluation. The Latvian authorities had to slash the number of public employees by 15 percent, cut public wages by a similar percentage, raise the value-added tax by three percentage points and boost other taxes on goods such as fuel and alcohol.

The IMF also accepted the proposal that it should play a junior partner role, providing less than one quarter of a €7.5 billion ($10 billion) loan to Latvia. An important precedent was thus set: the Fund might take a subordinate position in a program in Europe, and European policy makers could prevail over the best technocratic judgment of the Fund's management and staff if Europe was putting up the majority of the funding. Approval by the IMF board came on December 23.

Seen from a certain perspective, this outcome was right and proper. The IMF, after all, does not consist solely of the managing director and the staff; it belongs to its shareholders, and a large segment of the shareholders held adamant views about the type of program they wanted their institution to support. Moreover, nobody could claim with certainty that the program would fail. Judgments about economic policies are always a matter of probabilities and risks, so even if the chances of the Latvian peg surviving appeared slim to just about everyone working in the IMF headquarters building, they had to admit that they might be wrong.

And they *were* wrong, at least on that very crucial issue. Long after the European-IMF program was agreed, Latvia continued to defy loud predictions by prominent economists (with whom many at the IMF privately agreed) that its peg was doomed. The resolve of the Latvian body politic to continue down the path of full marriage with Europe, and lasting divorce from Moscow, proved stronger than any economic force that technocrats with spreadsheets could imagine. To attain this national goal, Latvia underwent one of the most wrenching economic contractions in history, a fall in GDP of 25 percent from its peak in the fourth quarter of 2007 to its trough in the third quarter of 2009. Unemployment, which had been as low as 5.3 percent in the months before the crisis, soared above 20 percent. But in the process, Latvia achieved enough of an internal devaluation that, amazingly, it was running a current account surplus in 2009. This was due mainly to the fact that demand for imports had dried up, but the economy soon began to enjoy an increase in exports thanks in part to a major reduction in unit labour costs (the expense of paying workers to produce a given amount of output), which stemmed from both lower wages and higher productivity.

Champions of austerity would later brandish Latvia's example as "Exhibit A" for their belief that crisis-stricken countries in the euro zone could likewise manage internal devaluations if only they could discipline themselves to do so. The rebuttals by those opposed to austerity — that Latvia is a small, heavily trade-oriented economy different from those of the Mediterranean, and that the Latvian people might have suffered a lot less without the peg — would not impress the disciplinarians much. In this regard, too, the Latvian case had important precedental impact.

The IMF thus ended up with egg on its face in Latvia, in addition to accepting a junior partner role. But on the bigger issue of where the crisis was headed, there is plenty of egg to be wiped off of many illustrious faces.

Anglo Saxon-style finance was to blame. Continental Europe's system had been vindicated. So went the mantra of euro-zone policy makers in the weeks and months following the Lehman bankruptcy. Whereas the United States and the United Kingdom were getting their comeuppance for having allowed the buccaneers of Wall Street and the City of London to run amok, the countries using the euro would reap rewards for the virtuous restraint they had imposed on their financial sectors, according to predictions emanating from European capitals.

Encapsulating the prevailing view on the continent was an op-ed article published a month after the Lehman shock by Klaus Regling, who had just left the European Commission after serving as director general for Economic and Financial Affairs. "These are difficult economic times for the world. But there are good reasons for Europe to be optimistic about its prospects in the medium to long term," Regling wrote, adding that although some knock-on effects from the US downturn were inevitable, "Europe can be expected to be a pole of stability in the international financial system during these difficult times."[7]

Regling cited a number of factors to justify his sanguine perspective, including the fiscal soundness of most European government budgets, the stabilizing effects of a common currency, and the credibility of the ECB in keeping inflation low. But one reason loomed above all: "Firstly, the financial sector in most member states of the EU (with the exception of Britain) is organised differently from the US," he wrote.

7 Klaus Regling, 2008, "Reasons for optimism," *The Straits Times* (Singapore), October 16. In fairness to Regling, he was among the most vigilant European policy makers at detecting financial vulnerabilities in the region and taking action to counter them, one important example being excessively rapid credit growth in Baltic countries.

"Commercial banks play a much more important role in the European economy than they do in the US," where the process of mobilizing and channelling capital is heavily based on securitized financial products traded on markets.

Continental Europe's financial system differed from America's all right. But not all the differences were of the sort that would enhance stability in Europe. On the contrary, some of the most fundamental features of the European financial landscape were leaving the region exposed to forces that could blow the currency union apart.

For all of Europe's vaunted unity, which included a commitment to establish an integrated financial market with capital flowing freely across European borders, governance of finance was remarkably fragmented. Not only did euro-zone member states maintain their own central banks (the Bank of Ireland, the Banca d'Italia, the Bundesbank, for example) that function as branch-like extensions of the ECB, the member states also insisted on maintaining regulatory control over their commercial banks at the national level. Monetary union; in other words, was not matched by anything comparable for banking. This arrangement stemmed in large part from an ingrained penchant for economic nationalism; a number of the member states wished to foster and defend national banking "champions" — Deutsche Bank for Germany, BNP Paribas for France, Fortis for Belgium, and so on. Knowing that a wave of mergers and consolidations was likely to materialize in the European banking sector as the continent's financial markets grew more integrated, these member states were anxious to ensure that their champions emerged with their national identities intact from the battles between predators and prey. This in turn made national bank regulators more indulgent toward their champions' efforts to grow larger, and less inclined to crack down on risky loans for fear that doing so might put their champions at a competitive disadvantage vis-à-vis banks elsewhere in Europe.

The fractured nature of European banking would prove to matter a lot in 2010–2012, once doubts arose about the financial strength of individual European governments and the banks under their control, because doubts would also arise about those governments' capacity for ensuring that their banks were soundly capitalized. The US system, for all its faults, has no such weakness, being both a monetary and a banking union. If a giant bank headquartered in, say, North Carolina gets into trouble, responsibility for propping it up (or closing it and paying the insurance that is owed to depositors) does not rest with North Carolina's taxpayers; it rests with the federal government. In 2008, such responsibilities in Europe belonged with national authorities.

On this score, the IMF deserves credit for prodding Europe in the right direction. Well before crisis struck the euro zone, the Fund was warning European policy makers about their financial system's inadequacies and exhorting them to move toward more coordinated regulatory control. For example, in its 2007 Article IV report on the euro area (the same one that proclaimed "The outlook is the best in years"), the Fund said it had urged "imparting to the system a greater sense of joint responsibility and accountability, considering it essential to meaningful progress in the prevention and the efficient and effective handling of (large bank) solvency crises."[8] A working paper by two Fund staffers published around the same time proposed the creation of a "European Banking Charter" aimed at overseeing large financial institutions with substantial pan-European operations. "While a cross-border [large bank] crisis may have a low probability, the need for effective coordinated arrangements to deal with it is pressing," the authors wrote.[9]

Disparities between American and Continental European financial policies widened in the months after the Lehman shock — again, in a manner that would eventually prove detrimental to stability in Europe. The US approach was bolder by far; to counter panicky withdrawals of cash from major banks and securities firms, the US Treasury and Federal Reserve essentially forced those institutions — even healthy ones — to accept billions of dollars in government funds in exchange

8 IMF, 2007, "Euro Area Policies" (see footnote 16 in chapter 3).

9 Martin Čihák and Jörg Decressin, 2007, "The Case for a European Banking Charter," IMF Working Paper WP/07/173, July, www.imf.org/external/pubs/ft/wp/2007/wp07173.pdf.

for stock, thereby bolstering their capital. (Although often confused with cash reserves, "capital" refers to a bank's net worth, the difference between assets and liabilities — in other words, its cushion in bad times against insolvency.) Later, in the spring of 2009, US authorities subjected banks to rigorous "stress tests" in order to determine whether they had enough capital to survive another severe shock, and ordered banks that were capital-deficient to raise more. By contrast, Continental European governments did little of this sort of nettle-grasping. Instead, regulators in European capitals let banks defer recognizing losses — of which they had plenty, including investments in toxic US mortgage-backed securities — in the hope that balance sheets would recover and strengthen with the passage of time. Here too, the IMF was appropriately raising concern that European banks as a whole were hiding losses and lacked adequate capital to sail through another crisis, even as European officials insisted that their banks were perfectly sound. In the fall of 2009, the Fund published estimates indicating that capital levels in euro-zone banks were about $310 billion short of levels that prudence would dictate.[10]

But both at the IMF, and in Europe, policy makers were very slow to perceive how dire these sorts of problems might become, and how soon.

It was time to atone for the woefully misguided October 2008 paper that had deemed the IMF's financial position to be "satisfactory." On January 12, 2009, the Fund staff produced another paper aimed at assessing the adequacy of Fund resources based on recent developments. In a section titled "The Worst Global Crisis in 75 years," the paper noted that during the three months since the previous assessment, "the global

10 Chris Giles, 2009, "IMF warns on further institutional losses," *Financial Times*, September 30; also IMF, 2009, *Global Financial Stability Report*, October.

economy has been hit by an unprecedented shock," and accordingly, "a doubling of the Fund's pre-crisis lending capacity [of about $250 billion] would be justified, at least on a temporary basis."[11]

Rarely has an institution like the IMF adjusted its view of its appropriate size so rapidly. Even then, the Fund was failing to fully comprehend the dimensions of the likely demands on its resources.

Worry had been steadily mounting in the final months of 2008 about whether the Fund had sufficient financial firepower to cope with all plausible eventualities. Throughout the emerging world, the Lehman shock was exerting malign effects, causing money to flee and currencies to dive in countries such as Brazil, South Korea, Turkey, Mexico, Poland and South Africa. Instead of "slipping into obscurity," the Fund was suddenly in such demand for its loans and expertise that it was in danger of being overwhelmed. In addition to lending Hungary, Ukraine, Latvia and others much more than normal limits, the Fund announced a new "precautionary" loan program in late October 2008, with up to $100 billion available promptly with no conditions, for countries whose policies could be deemed sound. As a result, the IMF's pool of hard currency was starting to look uncomfortably small relative to the potential for further financial trouble, even though the Japanese government took the initiative to lend $100 billion of its own for the Fund to use.

The January 2009 paper contained several scenarios to bolster its conclusion about the need for the IMF's pool of lendable cash to be doubled. It cautioned that the scenarios "should be viewed only as a rough gauge of the potential orders of magnitude for potential financing needs." But under the worst scenario, 16 countries would require Fund loans of significant size, and if such a scenario materialized, the amounts required would total about $300 billion, "substantially exceeding the resources available," the paper said.

11 IMF, 2009, "Review of the Adequacy of and Options for Supplementing Fund Resources," January 12, www.imf.org/external/np/pp/eng/2009/011209.pdf.

Which countries were these? They weren't specifically named, presumably for fear of attracting unwelcome investor attention. Yet all were emerging markets, according to the paper, meaning that none was in the euro zone. Just one brief passage in the paper even acknowledged the possibility that a rescue might be necessary for countries other than emerging markets. "The scenario analysis... does not take into account potential demand by advanced countries beyond Iceland," it said. "While such a development appears unlikely, the unprecedented nature of the current crisis suggests that it may be imprudent to rule it out."

Based on this bottom-up analysis, Strauss-Kahn and other IMF officials began spreading the word about the urgency of the Fund's need to get twice as much lendable resources as it then had. This turned out to be a surprisingly easy sell — indeed, it required almost no sales job at all, because the impetus was coming from major capitals. *Mirabile dictu;* having been compelled to downsize the institution's staff, Strauss-Kahn was going to preside over an unexpectedly large financial upsizing.

The managing director received this news in a phone call while attending a conference in Dar es Salaam, the capital of Tanzania, on March 10, 2009. The caller was Timothy Geithner, the boyish-faced 48-year-old who was in his first months as US Treasury secretary. Geithner's message both stunned and delighted Strauss-Kahn: the IMF would get a tripling of its resources instead of a mere doubling.

Motivating this move was the desire to make a splash of the sort that only numbers in the 12- or 13-digit range could produce. The Group of Twenty (G20) major economies, which was establishing itself as the global economy's new steering committee, wanted to show that it was taking bold and decisive action against the crisis that was continuing to menace the world in the first quarter of 2009. G20 leaders were preparing to hold a summit in London on April 2, and the host, UK Prime Minister Gordon Brown, was eager to orchestrate a package of crisis-fighting measures backed by enormous monetary commitments — a goal shared by the Obama administration, in particular Geithner and Larry Summers, who was then chairman of the White House National Economic Council. Brown was envisioning headlines about total summit pledges in the trillions, not hundreds of billions, and the Obama team agreed: at times like these, the bigger, the better; the more shock, the more awe. Hence a tripling of IMF resources was deemed in order, based on purely "top-down" decision making — not because the amount was carefully calibrated, but because it was an order of magnitude more than a doubling.

The half-trillion dollars was to come in part from the world's rising powers — the BRICs as well as richer industrialized nations. It didn't involve direct quota contributions into the IMF's pool of funds, which would have entailed a time-consuming process, but rather pledges of specific amounts that the IMF could tap in a hurry if necessary, under the terms of the New Arrangements to Borrow. Although the BRICs didn't get any additional voting shares (a modest rejigging of votes had been agreed in principle the year before), they made sure to put the world on notice that they expected to gain more clout in the future from an institution that needed their financial backing. And to puff up the summit headline figure even further, the G20 also agreed that the IMF would give all of its member countries a one-time distribution, worth about $250 billion, of its own quasi-currency, special drawing rights (SDRs), which were made up from a basket consisting of US dollars, euros, Japanese yen and British pounds. (At that point, one SDR was worth about $1.50.) The impact of this move was limited — SDRs aren't like real money; ordinary people don't use them to buy goods and services. But it expanded the amount of reserves held by central banks, since SDRs count toward reserve totals, so it helped a bit in easing global cash shortages.[12]

"The IMF is back. Today you get the proof," Strauss-Kahn proclaimed at a press conference in London after the summit.[13]

12 G20, 2009, "London Summit—Leaders' Statement," April 2, www.imf.org/external/np/sec/pr/2009/pdf/g20_040209.pdf.

13 IMF, 2009, "Transcript of a Press Conference by IMF Managing Director Dominique Strauss-Kahn at the G-20 Summit," April 2, www.imf.org/external/np/tr/2009/tr040209.htm.

Astonishingly, the people involved in showering money on the IMF at the G20 summit gave no consideration to the idea that these funds might be needed for rescuing countries in the euro zone. Just as in the case of the IMF's January paper, policy makers from the Obama administration, the British government and the IMF who played key roles at the summit recalled that they were concerned solely with ensuring that the Fund had the resources it needed to aid emerging economies. They were surely aware that gloomy prophecies about Europe were starting to circulate; as early as January 2009, Desmond Lachman wrote an article in the *Australian Financial Review* stating: "The potential unraveling of the Euro in its present form constitutes a major risk not only for the Mediterranean member countries but rather for the Eurozone as a whole."[14]

It was not as if market signals were absent. In the weeks before the summit, a bout of financial turmoil had struck the weakest euro-zone countries, notably Greece and Ireland, as a sell-off in the government bonds of those countries caused a sharp rise in the yields demanded by investors — with a commensurate rise in the interest rates those governments would have to pay on new borrowing. Yields on 10-year bonds of the Greek government, for example, spiked above six percent at one point in early 2009, and the spread on those bonds — that is, the difference in yield with German bonds, which are regarded as the safest European investment — widened to above 300 basis points, or three percentage points. (A basis point is one one-hundredth of a percentage point.) As recently as mid-2008, spreads on the government bonds of all euro-zone countries, including Greece, had been below 50 basis points, but in early 2009 the spread on Ireland's bonds swelled to about 250 basis points, Italy and Portugal's to about 150 basis points, and Spain's to about 125 basis points.

14 Lachman, 2009, "Prolonged Recession Could Shake Euro to Its Core," *Australian Financial Review*, January 9.

Nevertheless, the reasoning behind the action at the G20 summit reflected concern about emerging markets; those involved do not recall anyone anticipating that a country using the euro would need IMF assistance. The summiteers did something that proved beneficial — for reasons of luck, not foresight.

"By tripling the IMF's resources in response to the 2009 crisis, we built up a buffer that would turn out to be quite important for the subsequent crisis in Europe," said Michael Froman, who was Obama's Sherpa (chief negotiator) at the summit.

The eruption of the crisis in Greece was less than a year away.

5

STRIKING THE FAUSTIAN BARGAIN

Every financial crisis has its "what were they thinking?" moments — points when policy choices are made that, in retrospect, were obviously unwise. In the case of Greece, one such moment was the country's entry into the euro zone, which took place on January 1, 2001. Many among Europe's policy elites rue the decision, taken in a flush of pan-European exuberance, to extend the common currency to a country that they now see as having been poorly suited for it. In Athens as well, regrets are widespread that the costs of fettering the economy to a monetary union were poorly understood.

In early November 2000, a few weeks before the official switch from drachmas to euros, a mission of four IMF economists arrived in Athens to conduct discussions — Article IV consultations, in Fund parlance — with the country's economic policy makers, as the Fund does annually with most of its members. If the Fund staffers on that mission had been able to peer into a crystal ball, they would have recoiled in horror at the fate awaiting Greece after just a few years' experience with the euro. They would have seen that Greece was going to become the first victim of a crisis that would bring the monetary union — a supposedly inviolable currency bloc, with no provision for exit — to the brink of fragmentation, menacing the entire global economy in the process. They would have seen, moreover, that the Greek economy was going to contract by more than one-quarter between 2008 and 2015, driving the nation's unemployment rate above 26 percent. That look into the future also would have shown that central Athens was going to undergo repeated bouts of disruptive, often violent, unrest, and that marginal parties on the extreme left and right were going to make major political inroads amid popular fury against the governing establishment, with a far-left coalition ultimately winning power in a national election. Perhaps most disturbing of all for Fund staffers, they would have seen that these adverse economic and political developments were going to occur despite the receipt by Greece of the largest international bailout in history, and the largest sovereign debt reduction in history.

So looking back on the period of that Article IV mission, perhaps the IMF team, and the ones preceding it, should have firmly and publicly urged the Greeks to turn back before it was too late, lest the country embark on a course that might well end in tears. The mission did no such thing; its report depicted Greece as being on the cusp of economic triumph. The talks, which lasted 12 days, "took place amid a well-deserved sense of accomplishment," the report said.[1]

The IMF's deference toward Greek adoption of the euro was partly a matter of convention, because the Fund's articles of agreement give each member country the prerogative to choose its own currency regime. This has been true since the 1970s, when the post-World War II system of fixed exchange rates collapsed. Instead of policing rules that obliged countries to fix their currencies against gold or the US dollar, the Fund now oversees a system in which the rules allow exchange rates to float freely according to forces of supply and demand, or to be loosely pegged against other currencies, or to be rigidly fixed, or to be included in a currency union. Pretty much all the Fund can do, if a country's exchange rate appears likely to create problems, is to warn against inconsistencies between the country's domestic policies — fiscal and monetary policy, in particular — and its exchange rate.

Moreover, at the time of that Article IV mission to Athens, euro espousal was showing every sign of being a boon to the Greek economy. The IMF report included a chart showing dramatically improved economic

1 IMF, 2001, "Greece: 2000 Article IV Consultation—Staff Report," Country Report No. 01/52, March, www.imf.org/external/pubs/cat/longres.aspx?sk=4005.0.

data in the second half of the 1990s, when the Greek government had initiated an intense effort to qualify for euro membership. Whereas the economy had grown at an anemic 1.2 percent annual rate during the years 1991–1995, with yearly inflation averaging nearly 14 percent, a turnaround had occurred in the five-year period starting in 1996, when GDP expanded at a 3.3 percent annual clip, reaching four percent in 2000.[2] Although aiming for the euro entailed imposing discipline over the budget deficit and money supply, which incurred short-term political costs, the result was "a transformation of Greece's macroeconomic landscape" in which "inflation and interest rates have declined to historically low levels," the Fund's report observed. "Given the starting conditions, the authorities are to be commended for the road traveled."

Greece had indeed made enormous strides from the days when it was perennially plagued by inflation, stagnation, high interest rates and repeated sinking spells of the drachma. Yet beneath the surface, the economic and social system retained many features of Balkan backwardness even in the era following the 1974 overthrow of the military junta. As journalist Yannis Palaiologos writes in his deservedly acclaimed book *The 13th Labour of Hercules,* "family and local affiliations in Greece have remained unusually strong by European standards," the result being a form of politics in which voters "continue to behave and to be treated by politicians as clients — to be kept loyal with public sector jobs, government contracts or targeted tax breaks — rather than citizens." The two major parties, the centre-right New Democracy and the centre-left Panhellenic Socialist Movement (PASOK), "fanatically opposed each other, but as time passed it became clear that their clash was not ideological. It was a naked conflict for the spoils of the state."[3]

2 The contrast between the Greek economy's performance in the first and second half of the 1990s is somewhat misleading, because the reform effort started under the government of Constantine Mitsotakis (1990–1993), which privatized and closed down some public enterprises and eliminated price controls. Also, Greek growth was adversely affected in the earlier period by sluggish growth in Europe, and helped in the latter period by the region's economic recovery.

3 Yannis Palaiologos, 2014, *The 13th Labour of Hercules: Inside the Greek Crisis*, London: Portobello Books.

For ordinary Greeks, one of the most prized forms of largesse was a job with a DEKO — state-owned enterprises in sectors such as railways, electricity, water and air travel. The DEKOs offered substantially more generous pay, job security and retirement benefits than did most private sector employers, and they were by no means the only enterprises where large segments of the population enjoyed the fruits of political connections. In a range of sectors and professions — trucking, pharmacy, legal services, beer and milk being prime examples — government regulations and bureaucratic obstacles sharply restricted competition to a favoured few, who reaped the rewards of high profitability while the general public suffered from exorbitant costs and inefficiency. Perhaps most insidious of all was the rampant tax evasion that Greeks had come to regard as an accepted way of doing business, especially among the large number of tiny family-run firms that couldn't be bothered to keep proper books. As noted by Palaiologos, it was routine for Greek doctors, tutors, plumbers and gardeners to take payment without giving receipts, and standard practice for purchasers of homes to sign documents (in the presence of lawyers and notaries) massively understating the value of the property so as to minimize tax bills. Collection and enforcement was in the hands of a stultified, technologically laggard bureaucracy, whose staff was far from incorruptible. The upshot was a personal income tax system that, in the first decade of the twenty-first century, generated revenues totalling a mere 4.6 percent of GDP, compared with an average of 8.7 percent of GDP in other euro area countries.[4]

Sensibly, the IMF's Article IV team coupled its congratulatory language in 2000 with admonitions that Athens must hew to a strict reform path, since the government would no longer be able to guide the economy using its own monetary control over interest rates or the foreign exchange rate. "Monetary union provide[s] a formidable challenge but also a welcome spur to policies in Greece," said the report, which cited a number of areas where advancement was necessary. Revamping government spending policy would be crucial, the report said, adding that the rapid growth of wages and jobs among Greek

4 Ibid.

civil servants "underscored, in the view of the [IMF] staff, the need for more decisive steps — not least the need to address widespread inefficiencies in the sector." Similar warnings were issued for Greece's "overly complicated and inefficient" tax system. To help reduce the relatively high unemployment rate, the government should dismantle unnecessarily stiff entry requirements for many professions such as law and accountancy, and it could also encourage employers to hire more by easing burdensome restrictions against the firing of workers. Provided Athens addressed such deficiencies with sufficient resolve, the Fund concluded, "euro entry provided a unique opportunity for a more rapid advance of living standards in Greece."

In the years that followed, as Greece went on a debt-fuelled boom made possible by its membership in the euro zone, the IMF continued to issue cautionary reports[5] — although not nearly alarmist enough to match the severity of the dangers that would ultimately materialize, nor blunt and sustained enough to have a beneficial impact on Greek policy.

The basic dynamics behind Greece's borrowing spree — and the accompanying growth spurt — were much in evidence when I visited the country in mid-2002 on assignment from *The Washington Post* to report on the euro's early impact. One of the business executives I interviewed, Dimitri Papalexopoulos, drew a vivid contrast between the situation then and the pre-euro Greece he encountered when he returned home from the United States in the early 1990s to help run his family's building-materials company. He recalled asking people at the company what "hurdle rate" — acceptable borrowing cost — they used to evaluate investments, "and they asked me, 'what do you mean?'" That was because with inflation in double digits and the exchange rate in constant flux, "there were no long-term fixed interest rates at that point — just one-year rates. So it was very difficult to fund any sort of long-term projects in Greek drachma." But now that Greeks were borrowing in a currency controlled from Frankfurt — just as Germans, Dutch and Belgians did — "as unbelievable as it sounds to Greek ears, we

5 It should be noted that the European Commission and the ECB also issued such reports.

have a cost of capital roughly equal to that of the US," Papalexopoulos told me, adding that "this has made a tremendous difference" to his company's ability to finance expansion as well as sparking demand for cement and other products the firm made. For similar reasons, a market for mortgages and consumer lending, which barely existed in the country before, had burgeoned and was generating an explosion in home buying.[6]

What wasn't known at that point, of course, was how the Greek government would also take advantage of low interest rates, and borrow its way into deeper and deeper trouble — more than €300 billion of debt by the end of the decade — without acknowledging its profligacy. Thanks to the relatively easy terms on which creditors were lending to Athens, interest payments on the government's debt, which in the mid-1990s were a costly 11.5 percent of GDP, declined to five percent of GDP in the mid-2000s. Instead of using these savings to bolster its fiscal position, the government increased spending on civil service wages and pensions by an even greater amount.[7]

Worse yet, the Greek authorities skewed statistics to give a misleadingly favourable picture of the government's fiscal health, mostly by shifting various expenditure items off-budget — and the country's European partners looked the other way.[8] When Athens came under the threat of EU disciplinary proceedings for running a budget deficit that peaked at 6.2 percent of GDP in 2004 (more than twice the euro zone's agreed ceiling), the European Union's Luxembourg-based auditors investigated allegations that Greek data were deliberately fudged and that the country had never properly met the terms for euro entry. But the appetite in Europe for cracking down on Greece was limited. Germany and France, the bloc's biggest members, had themselves breached the deficit caps

6 Paul Blustein, 2002, "Capitalizing on the Euro," *The Washington Post,* July 4.

7 IMF, 2013, "Greece: Ex Post Evaluation of Exceptional Access under the 2010 Stand-By Arrangement," Country Report No. 13/156, June, www.imf.org/external/pubs/ft/scr/2013/cr13156.pdf.

8 Some of this began even before Greece's euro accession, involving, for example, the way the government started in the late 1990s to account for transfers to loss-making public enterprises such as railways and urban transport, which should have been included in expenditure but were shifted to other budgetary categories.

in 2003, largely because of recessions, and although they reasonably argued that the rules ought to be applied less rigidly during economic downturns, their exercise of raw power to block sanctions undermined the credibility of the system. Later efforts by the EU auditors to gain enhanced powers ran into resistance from member states, so Athens' claims in 2006 and 2007 to have shrunk its deficit within allowable limits went essentially unscrutinized and unchallenged.[9]

In its own examinations of Greek data promulgation, the IMF did not cover itself in glory. A 2003 report stated that "Statistics-producing agencies in the main have a legal and institutional environment that supports statistical quality....All agencies demonstrate professionalism."[10] Later, after suspicions of book-cooking had come to light, a 2006 report took a more negative view, asserting that "Greece has not modernized its fiscal institutions and systems...major reforms are still necessary in...advancing more open budget preparation, execution and reporting."[11] Still, the Fund's focus on the issue was ephemeral. As noted in the aforementioned evaluation of Fund surveillance by the think tank Bruegel, "The important 2006 findings about public accounting did not find their way into the subsequent Article IV reports and did therefore not have the effect they could and should have had." One reason, according to the Bruegel authors, was that IMF missions "did not want to make policy discussions overly repetitive and instead aimed to bring in fresh ideas."[12]

Only in mid-2009 did the IMF's assessments of Greece evince significantly greater worry, in the aftermath of the turbulence (mentioned in the previous chapter) that struck in the spring of that year and temporarily drove spreads on the yields on Greek 10-year bonds to 300

9 Dan Bilefsky, 2010, "Greece's Stumble Follows a Headlong Rush Into the Euro," *The New York Times,* May 4.

10 IMF, 2003, "Greece: Report on the Observance of Standards and Codes," Country Report 03/318, October, www.imf.org/external/pubs/ft/scr/2003/cr03318.pdf.

11 IMF, 2006, "Greece: Report on the Observance of Standards and Codes (ROSC), Fiscal Transparency Module," Country Report 06/49, February, www.imf.org/external/pubs/ft/scr/2006/cr0649.pdf.

12 Pisani-Ferry, Sapir and Wolff, 2011, chapter 3 (see footnote 18 in chapter 3).

basis points above German bonds. In the Article IV report dated June 30, 2009, the Fund mission exhorted Athens to adopt "more urgency for stronger policies, which are needed to shore up confidence and avoid a replay of the spike in spreads in an already weakened real/financial environment." With the budget deficit projected to swell to 7.5 percent of GDP in 2010, and the government's total debt headed above 100 percent of GDP, "Greece cannot postpone fiscal consolidation," warned the report, which recommended that Athens adopt politically painful spending cuts and tax-revenue-raising measures sufficient to narrow the deficit by about 1.5 percent of GDP starting in 2010. To boost growth and lower costs in product, service and labour markets, a host of structural reforms were advised; as in previous reports, these included eliminating laws and regulations that protected politically powerful industries, professions and unions. "Greece can ill-afford a new spike in spreads" that might occur if such actions weren't taken, the IMF concluded.[13]

Even with this degree of alarm, the IMF's report did not fully reflect the gravity of the problems that Greece would soon encounter. This insufficient pessimism was partially excusable, because the Fund did not realize that the Greek government's budget figures had gone from misleading to outlandishly false, especially for 2009, an election year in which politicians had dispensed even more than the usual amount of largesse to constituents. The report at least took a more critical line than before on that issue: "Improving economic statistics deserves high priority," the authors said.

In October 2009, three months after the issuance of that report, the shocking revelation came: Greece's budget deficit for that year would be upward of 12.5 percent of GDP, more than triple previous estimates.[14] With that, the country began its slide toward the financial abyss.

13 IMF, 2009, "Greece: 2009 Article IV Consultation—Staff Report," Country Report 09/244, August, www.imf.org/external/pubs/ft/scr/2009/cr09244.pdf.

14 IMF, 2013, "Greece: Ex Post Evaluation of Exceptional Access under the 2010 Stand-By Arrangement" (see footnote 7 in this chapter).

Scion of a famous family of Greek Socialist politicians — both his father and grandfather had served as prime ministers, and his father had founded PASOK — George Papandreou had a natural affinity with Strauss-Kahn, whom he had met several times in gatherings of left-leaning European leaders. Besides having a friendly relationship with the IMF managing director, Papandreou also knew of Strauss-Kahn's efforts to move the Fund in some non-traditional directions, such as the "charm offensive" during the Eastern Europe crisis. So in late 2009, after ascending to the prime ministership himself, Papandreou began a series of conversations with Strauss-Kahn, mostly by phone, about the challenges Greece was facing.

It was Papandreou's newly elected government that had disclosed the gross understatement of Greece's budget deficit and national indebtedness. Although this revelation suited the Socialists' political interests — they could point fingers at the previous centre-right regime for dishonesty — it also squared with the background and personality of Papandreou, who had been raised mainly in the United States and Canada and held degrees from Amherst College and the London School of Economics (LSE). High on his list of most-cherished values were transparency and good governance; the same was true of the man he appointed finance minister, George Papaconstantinou, an economist with a technocratic demeanor and a Ph.D. from LSE to match. They got kudos from their European colleagues for candour when, at a meeting in Luxembourg on October 18, Papaconstantinou told his fellow finance ministers of the drastically revised deficit estimates, and Papandreou admitted soon thereafter to his fellow prime ministers that his country was rife with corruption.[15] But having come clean, they had to deal with the consequences. The newly disclosed data was sparking nervousness in financial markets that Greece's debt could swell beyond the government's capacity to pay it.

Since 2003, the ratio of Greek government debt as a proportion of GDP had hovered in the 95 to 99 percent range — high compared to most euro area partners, but stable. Suddenly, the ratio was being

15 Carlo Bastasin, 2012, *Saving Europe: How National Politics Nearly Destroyed the Euro*, Washington, DC: Brookings Institution Press, chapter 9.

adjusted upward to 115 percent of GDP for the end of 2009,[16] and there was no telling how much higher it might go in the future. With Greece obliged to pay much steeper interest rates on new bonds than it had during its economic heyday, and the economy hobbled by recession (thereby diminishing tax revenue), the ratio was bound to rise, which might cause markets to get even more jittery and raise the country's borrowing costs still further. At the extreme, the country could get caught in a vicious cycle, called "exploding debt dynamics," which refers to an ever-increasing debt-to-GDP ratio, as higher interest rates, a sluggish economy and chronic deficits drive the ratio inexorably upward with the passage of time. This phenomenon is analogous to an individual who, having borrowed an excessive amount from credit-card companies, gets hit with much higher interest rates at the same time as his or her income stagnates, and keeps trying to borrow more until eventually being overwhelmed by mushrooming demands for interest and principal.

The obvious first step for an over-indebted country, just as for an over-indebted individual, is to cut spending and raise income. That was exactly what Papandreou repeatedly vowed in late 2009 to do — specifically, to shrink the budget deficit below the agreed euro-zone ceiling of three percent of GDP by 2013. Despite his pledges to freeze public sector wages and raise substantial new tax revenue, however, markets were unconvinced about the government's ability to achieve sufficient deficit-reduction measures to get the debt under control; for one thing, Papandreou himself had won office in a populist campaign featuring promises of increased welfare spending and denunciation of the previous government's efforts to reform pensions. In December, the three major credit rating agencies (Moody's, Standard & Poor's and Fitch) all downgraded their ratings on Greek debt. Investors who had once happily snatched up Greek bonds were refusing to continue holding them unless compensated for the risk with higher yields. The result was a steady climb in interest rates that by the end of January 2010 reached the seven percent range on Greek 10-year bonds. That

16 The ratio for year-end 2009 was adjusted again later, after additional scrutiny of government spending and revenue data, to 130 percent of GDP. In later years, the ratio rose much further, but because of new borrowing rather than data revisions.

was roughly twice the yield on equivalent German bonds, and a level of borrowing costs that Athens could not afford for long.

Previously unthinkable outcomes for Greece became the subject of speculation in market analyses and media reports — one grim but all-too-plausible scenario being a default on interest and/or principal payments. In the market for credit default swaps, a kind of insurance that investors can buy to protect themselves against default loss, the cost of buying insurance against a Greek default soared by late January to record levels, requiring the payment of about $400,000 to insure $10 million worth of bonds, roughly four times the level six months earlier.

But the endgame that inspired the most dread was abandonment by Athens of the euro, because of the hellish chaos that would ensue both for Greece and economies elsewhere. Although a handful of economic commentators argued that Athens ought to leave the monetary union and bring back the drachma to gain competitive advantages from a cheaper currency, the overwhelming consensus was that however foolish a marriage Greece may have entered by adopting the euro, the costs of divorce would far outweigh the benefits.[17] Whereas a long period of meticulous planning had preceded euro adoption — with computers being reprogrammed, coin-operated machines modified and so on — there would be no way to establish an orderly process for reversion to a currency that would obviously have a much lower value. Contracts and other financial obligations would have to be redenominated in drachma, triggering fierce and convoluted disputes, especially for those involving relationships between Greek companies and firms elsewhere in the common currency area. Were the Greek parties still obliged to make payments in euros (which might bankrupt them) or could they legally pay in drachma (which might entail huge losses for their European counterparties)? Whose courts would decide, and what basis would they use for rendering judgment, since no laws had been written to cover such an eventuality? Even more nightmarish was

17 Miranda Xafa, 2013, "Greece's exit from the Eurozone would be all pain, no gain," VoxEU, March 18, www.voxeu.org/article/greece-s-exit-eurozone-would-be-all-pain-no-gain.

the prospect that Greeks, desperate to preserve the value of their savings, would rush to transfer money abroad (presumably to banks in safer havens such as Germany), with potentially catastrophic consequences for the Greek banking system. And once the taboo of quitting the monetary union was broken, other vulnerable countries might be forced to revert to their original currencies too, as terrified citizens also shipped their money to safe havens. A full-blown economic crack-up in Europe, far-fetched though it might seem, no longer seemed beyond the realm of possibility.[18]

As the yields on Greek bonds continued to ascend, the quandary confronting Papandreou and Papaconstantinou was what to do if market sentiment turned so negative that fresh funds became unavailable at any reasonable cost. The government needed to borrow more than €50 billion in 2010 to pay off maturing bonds and keep paying salaries and pensions; suppose Athens couldn't get the money from private sources? The most obvious place to turn first was the country's European partners, but among policy makers in dominant euro-zone capitals during the early days of the crisis, emergency aid was deemed to be out of the question. The Maastricht Treaty contains a provision popularly dubbed the "no bailout clause," which states that neither the European Union nor its member states shall "be liable for or assume the commitments of" other governments. In the view of German officials in particular, the only viable option for overcoming Greece's financial strains was resolute action in Athens.

Papacontantinou received that message in unvarnished terms from Wolfgang Schäuble, his German counterpart, who had also become finance minister of his country in the fall of 2009. Wheelchair-bound — he had been shot in 1990 by a deranged would-be assassin — the crusty Schäuble commanded veneration throughout the continent for his perseverance over physical hardship as well as his role in negotiating the creation of the euro. Although Papaconstantinou was publicly averring that Greece needed no help from external sources, he privately beseeched

18 The argument that joining the euro was "effectively irreversible" was cogently spelled out in Barry Eichengreen, 2007, "Eurozone break-up would trigger the mother of all financial crises," VoxEU.org, November 19.

Schäuble on a trip to Berlin in December 2009 to start preparing a contingency plan for European aid. But Schäuble refused, telling Papaconstantinou: "Markets will respond if you show you can reduce the deficit."[19]

All this was the backdrop for Papandreou's conversations with Strauss-Kahn. The prime minister and his advisers knew that the government of almost any country would pay a terrible price for throwing itself on the mercy of the IMF — perhaps even more so in Greece, with its antipathy to foreign overlords having been nurtured by centuries of Ottoman Turkish rule and Nazi invasion during World War II. (The country's passionately celebrated Independence Day, October 28, is also known as Oxi Day — "oxi" meaning "no," referring to Athens' defiance in the face of Axis demands for military occupation in 1940.) But the Greek leaders felt obliged to explore all options, and they thought the IMF managing director might at least have a sympathetic approach.

The talks quickly led to the IMF's Fiscal Affairs Department sending technical assistance missions to help Athens improve its revenue collection and public management policies. But Papandreou and Papaconstantinou had a separate, much more pressing concern: Who, if anyone, would lend Greece money in a pinch, and calm the markets by showing that there was no reason to fear default? Since prospects for European aid appeared dim, the Greeks wanted to know whether Fund assistance might be available if worse came to worst.

The answer wasn't as comforting as they had hoped. It came at a meeting in a Davos kitchen, during the January 2010 World Economic Forum, because that was the one of the few places where Papandreou and Papconstantinou could parley with the IMF managing director away from the prying eyes of the numerous journalists attending the conference. Waiters bearing trays laden with dishes and glasses were bustling in and out, and security guards were keeping a watchful eye for unwelcome intruders as the three men stood and talked — as

19 George Papaconstantinou, 2016, *Game Over: The Inside Story of the Greek Crisis*, CreateSpace Independent Publishing Platform, chapter 5.

there was no place to sit, according to Papaconstantinou's account in his 2016 memoir, which continues:

> [Strauss-Kahn] was clear: lending money to countries which had lost access to markets was the Fund's mission; if Greece asked, it would have to help. But as long as other EU countries did not want the IMF involved in the Eurozone, they could block such a decision at the IMF board of directors. Nothing could be done without the agreement of the other European states and of the ECB. In any case, the IMF by itself would not be able to put up all the money needed for Greece.[20]

An IMF role in the Eastern European crises was one thing. Inviting the Washington-based institution to help rescue a euro-zone country was another. The idea was opposed by some extremely powerful Europeans — in particular, one man whom even Strauss-Kahn held in a measure of awe.

Central bank heads, being entrusted with the sacred responsibility of keeping money sound, are renowned for their rectitude, and few, if any, surpassed ECB President Jean-Claude Trichet in that regard. The son of a professor of Greek and Latin, Trichet was born in Lyons in 1942 and graduated fifth in his class from the Ecole Nationale d'Administration, the elite university where many of France's most distinguished policy makers have been educated. He rose swiftly to the pinnacle of the French civil service as director of the Treasury and spent more than a half-decade in that post before being appointed in 1993 to the governorship of the Banque de France, serving as the last central bank chief to exercise control over the French franc. (As previously noted, part of his tenure at the Banque de France overlapped with Strauss-Kahn's term as finance minister, so the two became well-acquainted, professionally at least.)

20 Ibid.

Having represented his country in one capacity or another at nearly all of the major conferences that led to monetary union, Trichet viewed the project with almost spiritual reverence. The capstone of his career came with his ascension to the ECB presidency in 2003; visitors to his office in the Eurotower, the central bank's 40-story headquarters in downtown Frankfurt, were often shown a seventeenth-century map of Europe on his wall, which he used to highlight the continent's progress from its fragmented past. As a Frenchman, he remained keenly aware that the central bank he headed had been established, and enshrined in treaty, on the model of Germany's revered Bundesbank — that is, with primacy on price stability, independence from political pressure and a ban on using money-creation powers to finance government borrowing — all of which Germany had demanded as the price for surrendering the Deutschmark. On those issues, the German public received frequent reassurances that Trichet was as Teutonic as anyone. In a 2007 interview with *Die Zeit*, the German daily, he proudly recalled how, shortly after becoming ECB president, he had spurned public calls for lower interest rates issued by three European heads of government. "The ECB demonstrated its independence," he said. "We did not comply."[21]

Accentuating his cultivated manner, Trichet sprinkles his conversational English with gentlemanly phrases ("I draw your attention to this particular point...Not to be neglected is the element that...") and his formal speeches are replete with references to poets and philosophers. But beneath his courtly exterior lies a capacity for wrath, sometimes expressed at high-decibel levels, especially when denouncing opinions that he perceives as threatening the principles and institutions he has spent his life building and defending. And IMF involvement in the rescue of a euro-zone country, he believed, could pose just such a danger.

21 Information on Trichet can be found in Irwin, *The Alchemists* (see footnote 13 in chapter 3); Ralph Atkins, 2010, "Man in the News: Jean-Claude Trichet," *Financial Times,* May 14; and James G. Neuter and Simon Kennedy, 2010, "Trichet Life Compass Points to Euro at Center of European Unity," Bloomberg News, June 7.

His allies on this issue included nearly all of the leading players in the European establishment. Also determined to keep the IMF at arm's-length were French President Sarkozy, European Commission President José Manuel Barroso, Economic and Monetary Affairs Commissioner Olli Rehn, and Luxembourg Prime Minister Jean-Claude Juncker, who chaired the committee of top euro-zone policy makers known as the Eurogroup.

In Berlin, opinion was divided. Schäuble was looking for ways to maintain full European control over the crisis, but Merkel was more inclined to view IMF help as a necessary evil. European institutions — specifically, the European Commission — were nowhere near up to the challenge, she believed. For all the professionalism of the Eurocrats who toiled in Brussels' high-rise offices, the commission lacked the program-designing skills of the IMF; more importantly, Merkel considered the commission to be too cozy with European politicians and too timid about offending them, as witnessed by its subpar monitoring of Greece. Still, Merkel was ambivalent about welcoming the IMF in the early weeks of 2010, as was Christine Lagarde, then French finance minister, although Lagarde loyally followed Sarkozy's lead, saying publicly at one point that the Fund had no more business lending money to Greece than it did to California, since each belonged to a single-currency area.[22]

In many ways, this aversion among European chieftains to the idea of IMF intervention resembled the denial syndrome that afflicts leaders of pretty much any government facing the need for an international bailout. They believed that Europe could — and should — handle its own internal problems, and that seeking help from the Fund would be tantamount to admitting that their monetary union was too

22 Tony Barber, 2010, "IMF's Role in Rescue Finally Wins Backing of Reluctant States," *Financial Times,* May 4. Explaining her initial view years later, after she had become IMF managing director, Lagarde said it was "predicated on the hope that the Europeans could put together enough of a package, enough ring-fencing, enough of a backstop so as to show that Europe could sort out its own affairs." See Lesley Wroughton, Howard Schneider and Dina Kyriakidou, 2015, "Special Report-How the IMF's Greek misadventure is changing the fund," Reuters, August 28.

weak and ineffectual to sustain itself. "Forget the IMF," Sarkozy told Papaconstantinou in a meeting at the Elysée Palace in Paris. "The IMF is not for Europe. It's for Africa — it's for Burkina Faso!"[23]

Trichet and his ECB colleagues had their own, supplementary reasons for resisting IMF involvement. Trichet feared that if European governments saw the Fund riding to the rescue of Greece, that would diminish their own willingness to take responsibility for what needed to be done to overcome the crisis. Also of concern to the ECB was the possibility that its independence might be compromised. IMF programs almost invariably come with conditions requiring the affected nation's central bank to change policy in one way or another — raising interest rates, for example. In an interview, Trichet maintained that he wasn't worried about ECB independence — which, as he archly noted, "is so fiercely guaranteed by treaty." But other European policy makers who participated in the debate about the IMF recall detecting a high degree of anxiety among ECB leaders about safeguarding their institution's prerogatives.

The forces opposing IMF involvement were winning the day at first, as Europe struggled in early 2010 to formulate a response to the markets' unrelenting assault on Greece. The first big test was a European leaders' summit on February 11 in Brussels, which came days after a scary market sell-off indicating that Greece's ills were infecting economies elsewhere; the cost of insuring the Spanish and Portuguese governments against default surged to record levels. European decision making is inherently unwieldy, especially at the summit level with so many heads of governments determined to score rhetorical points and preen for cameras. At this stage, Europe had the added problem of being riven by fundamental differences between Paris and Berlin that would continue long thereafter to colour the debate about how to handle the crisis.

The French vision, championed by Sarkozy with characteristic impetuousness and melodrama, put primacy on "solidarity" among euro-zone countries. In Sarkozy's view, plenty of money should be

23 Papaconstantinou, *Game Over,* chapter 8 (see footnote 19 in this chapter).

forthcoming from European institutions to assure markets that Greece had the necessary backing to avoid disaster, and Greek reform efforts should be overseen by those European institutions as well. It was not that the French president and his team held warm, fraternal feelings for Greece. They cared much less about what happened to the Balkan nation than they did about the implications of the Greek crisis for bigger countries in the euro zone, specifically Italy; if markets perceived that the bloc lacked the solidarity to keep one of its own member states financially afloat, Italy might be the next victim, and the euro would be in mortal peril. A logical corollary to this line of thinking was that the IMF had no substantial role to play; indeed, its involvement would be inimical to the concept that euro-zone membership conferred privileged solidarity.

German leaders had almost diametrically opposite ideas, stemming from their long-standing wariness about European unity leading to a "transfer union" in which taxpayers of big, rich countries would subsidize less-prosperous member states. The Germans, together with like-minded policy makers from northern European countries such as Finland and the Netherlands, wanted the no-bailout clause taken seriously. This was not a matter of petty stinginess. Writing Athens a fat cheque, in Berlin's view, would lead to the worst sort of moral hazard — that is, it would reward bad behaviour, create incentives for more and reduce or even eliminate incentives for reform. And since no European cheque of any size was conceivable without German backing, Merkel easily rebuffed Sarkozy's fervid demands at the February 11 summit to put a large sum on the table. In an effort to soothe market jitters, the leaders' statement declared that member states "will take determined and coordinated action, if necessary, to safeguard financial stability in the euro area as a whole."[24]

24 European Council, 2010, "Statement by the Heads of State or Government of the European Union," February 11.

Although this language marked a step toward providing a rationale for a possible rescue, investors were unimpressed, seeing little sign of any agreement about how bailout funds might be mobilized.

But on the IMF issue, the Sarkozy-backed view prevailed. The leaders implied they would relegate the Fund to a sort of advisory role, in which its "expertise" would be sought. Under their agreement, Greece's economic and budgetary policies would be subject to unprecedented oversight from Brussels, and the Fund would help European Commission economists in conducting the monitoring. This news evoked gloom at IMF headquarters; staffers wondered whether their institution, having only recently regained relevance, might be heading back to its bad old days of "slipping into obscurity."

In public, IMF officials assiduously avoided pressing for a big role in Greece or giving any hint that they were yearning for an invitation to provide major assistance. Strauss-Kahn was frequently asked by reporters about possible Fund involvement in a Greek rescue; he routinely responded, in diplomatic terms well attuned to the mentality of European leaders, that although the IMF always stands ready to consider a request from a member country, it had received no request from Athens, and he understood the desire in Europe to sort out the region's problems without outside interference.[25]

Behind the scenes, however, Strauss-Kahn was doing whatever he could do assuage the Europeans' worst worries and objections to IMF involvement. Anxious to avoid exclusion from participation in the crisis-fighting effort, lest doubts arise anew about the Fund's raison

25 See an interview (in French) with Strauss-Kahn, "Dominique Strauss-Kahn sur RTL: "La crise économique n'est pas finie!" February 4, 2010, www.youtube.com/watch?v=ghO6cgyJKOk.

d'être, he made it clear that the Fund would accept junior partner status, as it had in Latvia.[26]

The managing director's reasoning was as follows: The IMF would bring expertise and credibility to the task of managing the crisis that no European institution could match, and to ensure that its views were taken seriously, the Fund would have to make some financial contribution — something less than 50 percent of a rescue loan, perhaps, but well above zero. At the same time, the Fund could not expect to exercise the sort of total control over economic policy that it does in most countries because, in this case, it could not realistically demand policy action by the central bank. The ECB, the second-most powerful central bank in the world, conducts monetary policy for more than 300 million people, only 11 million of whom are Greek. So, although Europe had to accept an IMF role, the Fund had to play second fiddle.

Strauss-Kahn told me about a meeting he had at the European Commission with its president, Barroso, together with Marco Buti, the chief civil servant in Brussels for economic and monetary affairs. "I said, 'We have to be in, but you will be the leader,'" Strauss-Kahn recalled. "I told them, 'I want to be the leader myself. I cannot, because for political and logical reasons, I cannot take over the ECB. We will give technical assistance, and some financial resources, but you are leading.'"

26 One oft-heard theory is that, as a leading potential candidate of the Socialist Party for the French presidency, Strauss-Kahn was using his IMF position to further his political ambitions. He surely laboured under an implicit conflict of interest, because he would have been loath to take actions at the Fund that might have upset French voters. But this book offers no support for suspicions that he allowed his personal interests to cloud his judgment; no one provided me with a shred of convincing evidence that ethical dilemmas of that sort arose. If anything, the evidence strongly suggests that Strauss-Kahn was motivated by a desire to do what he thought best for the institution he led — that is, to ensure that it did not revert to its earlier crisis of irrelevancy.

Sarkozy also had an implicit conflict of interest that was a mirror image of Strauss-Kahn's, because IMF involvement could transform his political rival into Europe's saviour. But people who were advising Sarkozy at the time maintain that this was not an important motivating factor for him, at least not by comparison with the other reasons that Paris wanted to keep the Fund out.

Ultimately, the decision about the IMF came down to one person — Merkel. The German chancellor is famously cautious and deliberative. The daughter of a Protestant pastor, raised in East Germany during Communist rule (where, as she once put it, "one learned to keep quiet"), she was trained as a scientist, earning a doctorate in chemistry, which makes her determined to master subjects until she is sure she understands what makes things tick. But once that process is completed, she tends to be immovable. And in the weeks after the February 11 summit, as she weighed both economic and domestic political considerations regarding the IMF, her position hardened to the point where she deemed it imperative to overrule her fellow European leaders.

The German public, which was overwhelmingly negative toward rescuing a country that had clearly gotten itself into a mess, would never accept an emergency loan unless it came with severe conditions, enforced by arbiters with recognized neutrality and competence — and the IMF was the only institution that came close to that description, Merkel concluded. Furthermore, the powers of a German chancellor are limited (the Allies had made sure of that after World War II), so Merkel knew she would face enormous difficulties in getting approval for controversial measures in the Bundestag, where she led a fractious coalition. All in all, involving the Fund in the rescue of Greece was not just desirable from Merkel's perspective; it was essential if Berlin was to provide support.

Even so, weeks passed, financial agitation intensified, and Greece's predicament worsened before a concrete plan of action emerged. The anti-IMF forces finally had to yield at a European summit on March 25, where Merkel made it clear that excluding the Fund was untenable. The leaders' statement contained a pledge that if necessary, Greece would get a "package involving substantial International Monetary Fund financing and a majority of European financing."[27] This didn't mean that actual money was being disbursed; the leaders were clinging desperately to the hope that Athens, through its own budget-cutting

27 European Council, 2010, "Statement by the Heads of State and Government of the Euro Area," March 25.

efforts, would win back the confidence of investors. To avoid violating the spirit of the no-bailout rule, a number of conditions were attached: aid would be given only to protect the stability of the whole euro zone (not, in other words, as a favour to Greece); the European portion would be in the form of bilateral loans extended by individual member states, all of whom would have to approve; and interest rates on the European funding would be "non-concessional" — these were loans, not gifts.

At last, the IMF was in, albeit on junior partner terms. The precise ways in which the financial burden would be apportioned were left unstated; that would have to wait for later meetings, where it was agreed that the Fund's contribution would be roughly one-third of the total requirement.

Welcome as it was for the IMF to be included, the statement also contained language that deeply distressed Fund staffers. Support for Greece, the leaders said, "has to be considered *ultima ratio*" — a Latin phrase meaning "last resort." Specifically, Athens would get international loans only if markets wouldn't provide financing. This was another political necessity for Merkel; she had to show the political class in Berlin, and the German public more broadly, that every alternative would have been exhausted before bailout funds would be forthcoming. The *ultima ratio* approach exemplified Berlin's long-standing concern — which sometimes seems baked into German DNA — about moral hazard. Unorthodox measures to rescue countries could be justified, and gain German support, only in extreme circumstances (such as an imminent threat to the euro), the theory being that imprudence would otherwise proliferate.

As later chapters will show, the IMF shares some of the Germans' angst about moral hazard, but not nearly to the same degree. And *ultima ratio* went against the IMF's fundamental approach to crisis fighting. In ideal circumstances, the Fund intervenes early in a crisis, providing a loan that serves a "catalytic" purpose by encouraging markets to lend too, on reasonable terms. By contrast, giving an emergency loan *ultima ratio* means having to withhold the money until the country is on the very brink of default, unable to pay interest or principal on its debt

— which in turn means either allowing default or providing enough money to ensure that all creditors who want payment can receive it. Many Fund staffers were aghast at the illogic of this strategy.

That's how it goes for junior partners. The IMF was going to have to get accustomed to its new status, and fast. Fateful decisions were impending in the spring of 2010.

6

A DIFFERENT EPISODE AT A DIFFERENT SOFITEL

Normally, when an IMF mission chief arrives in a country to negotiate a rescue program, he or she can start meeting with the country's top economic policy makers almost immediately upon landing in the capital. Not so for Poul Thomsen, the IMF's mission chief for Greece. A Danish economist who was one of the European Department's few staffers with extensive program experience, Thomsen was facing a challenge unlike any of the previous programs he had worked on. For the Greek program, he first had to reach a common position with representatives from the European Commission and the ECB, before negotiating with Greek officials; that was the condition set by European leaders for the Fund's inclusion. And to make matters worse, when he arrived in Athens on the weekend of April 17-18, 2010, Thomsen learned that his counterparts from the European Commission were stuck more than 2,000 km away. A volcanic eruption in Iceland was spreading so much ash over northern Europe that it was forcing the closure of airports all over the region, making it impossible for the half-dozen members of the Commission team to fly out of Brussels.

By that time, dithering over Greece was no longer a luxury in which policy makers could indulge. A deadline loomed: the Greek government was obliged to pay its creditors €8.5 billion on May 19, and emergency funding was clearly needed to ensure against default. Before receiving that financing, the Greeks had to negotiate the terms of their program, which would involve countless details for how to put their nation's economy on a long-term sustainable path. The Commission team's inability to fly, therefore, came at a particularly inconvenient moment.

Frantically seeking alternatives to air travel, the Commission team procured a van, with the intention of driving to Athens, even though they learned that the trip requires about 24 hours on the road. The team left Brussels early on Monday, April 19, and drove all the way past Vienna before hearing that, with special intervention from the Austrian government, they could get on an Athens-bound flight in Vienna. So they turned around to catch that flight, arriving in the Greek capital early on Tuesday.

With that inauspicious beginning, the Troika convened for the first time. The leaders of the teams from the three institutions involved were soon to become household names, or at least household faces, in Greece, where the local population saw them as the country's new overlords. They included Servaas Deroose, a Belgian economist who headed the Commission team, and Klaus Masuch, a German from the ECB. And then there was Thomsen, who grew up in Aabenraa, a small town in southern Denmark so close to the German border that it had once been part of Prussia — a factoid deemed relevant by some IMF colleagues in accounting for the rigour with which he approached his job. He joined the Fund in 1982, considering himself lucky to land the job because his Ph.D. (for which he was studying at the University of Copenhagen) remained unearned.[1] In contrast to the eggheads who constituted most of his colleagues in the European department, Thomsen's strong suit was his diligence and zest for going to the aid of troubled countries rather than his intellect or analytical skills; he was renowned for spending long hours at his desk, whether in Washington or on missions. He was also unreserved in expressing himself in heated terms when aroused; as one former colleague joked, "For a northern European he could be somewhat Mediterranean."

1 Information about Thomsen can be found in Andrew Mayeda, 2015, "Meet One of the Most Hated Men in Greece," Bloomberg News, May 27.

So often did these three men appear on newspaper front pages, and on TV, that their personal safety became of major concern as protests gripped Athens. They and their teams first stayed at the Grande Bretagne, a landmark hotel close to Parliament and key government buildings, but on several occasions strikers blocked them from leaving and the police couldn't, or wouldn't, intervene. A move to the Hilton made their lives more convenient; it was further away and had a parking garage, enabling negotiators to travel back and forth from government buildings by car.

The tardiness of the Commission team's arrival in Athens symbolized a deeper problem. Endless squabbling within Europe over lending conditions and the legality of bailouts had already consumed substantial amounts of time, during which yields on Greek bonds had risen to 7.4 percent by April 16. And the Commission's slowness in matters of substance was going to continue. The Commission was designated to act as the agent of the Eurogroup, which meant it had to constantly consult with the finance ministers from euro area countries who comprised that body — and those ministers, in turn, were obliged to consult with key politicians in their capitals. So the process of reaching a common position within the Troika, which was hardly simple to begin with, was further complicated by the Commission's need to make sure it was properly responsive to its various political masters.

For the IMF, this arrangement was more than unusual. It was highly irregular. Not only was the Fund playing junior partner to the Commission — which it had done just one time before, in Latvia — it was also sitting alongside the ECB at the negotiating table, facing the Greek team. In typical negotiations with a country seeking an IMF loan, the Fund's negotiators sit opposite from the central bank and finance ministry, in the expectation that the conditions of the loan will oblige the central bank to adopt certain policies. In the Greek case, by contrast, the Fund had to acclimate itself to being the ECB's confederate. As noted above, the Fund had no intention of making demands on the central bank regarding Greece, and there were other grounds for cooperation between the two institutions. They could pool resources and expertise at a time when the crisis was still confined to one of the euro area's smallest economies, rather than being a systemic crisis for the whole region.

But qualms abounded about the Fund's status in the Troika as its first meetings got under way. "This has the makings of a strange dog's breakfast," Morris Goldstein, a former deputy director of the IMF's research department, told the *Financial Times*. "If a regional grouping can set IMF conditionality, what is the point of the Fund anyway? This could set a very dangerous precedent."[2]

Good crisis management involves contemplating fallback positions — "Plan Bs" — in case the primary approach comes to grief. Within the IMF, a sense of foreboding about "Plan A" for Greece was on the rise, and Strauss-Kahn, wily fox that he is, launched secret channels of discussion about alternative strategies, which will be covered later in this chapter. At the same time, however, he felt obliged to support Plan A as far as possible. He was anxious to keep the IMF at the table and exerting influence, which meant he had to avoid arousing any suspicion of harbouring an agenda for usurping European prerogatives. As frustrating as this was to some of his subordinates, he believed he had little choice, both because of European political realities and the danger of adverse market reaction to signs of dissension.

"The IMF can be a strong institution, but it has a huge limitation: Its duty, especially the duty of the MD, is to avoid creating a mess," Strauss-Kahn told me. "We were totally convinced that one of the strengths of the Troika was to appear united. So we couldn't take the risk of showing any kind of disagreement. Even if we believed something was wrong, I wasn't going to go to the media and make a statement like, 'What the hell are they doing!' In those cases, my institution just shut up." Citing a favourite phrase of Keynes, he added: "The idea that the Fund ought to be a 'ruthless truth-teller' is fine when it comes to the member countries. But not the public."

A policy of *pas devant les enfants* (not in front of the children) regarding internal arguments was also applied by the Troika in their relations with the Greek government. When Thomsen, Deroose and Masuch

2 *Financial Times*, 2010, "Greek rescue fills in bail-out blanks," April 13.

met with Greek officials, they sought to hide their differences to maintain a coherent stance. But try as they might, the Troika members did not always succeed, especially when it came to the issue that most sharply divided them — namely, how fast Greece should be required to implement measures aimed at changing its profligate ways.

"They would sometimes be open about their disagreements," recalled Papaconstantinou, who as finance minister was lead negotiator for Greece. "The Commission would say, 'We're not on the same page here as the IMF; we need to talk about it and get back to you.' And we would sometimes talk with them unofficially, on a bilateral basis."

Conversations with Thomsen, the IMF mission chief, left little doubt in Papaconstantinou's mind that the Fund was often the Troika's odd man out, favouring a more gradual approach than the others to austerity — just as the Greeks had hoped, given the less-traditional views that Strauss-Kahn brought to the institution. "But once a decision was taken, the IMF would not second-guess," Papaconstantinou added. "Poul might say to me on certain occasions, 'It's not exactly what I would have wanted, but that's the decision.'"

Papaconstantinou had an extraordinary vantage point. Not only was he dealing with the Troika in Athens, he was a member of the Eurogroup, which enabled him to see how his fellow finance ministers were exerting influence over the Commission. Pressure from Germany, he concluded, was the most important factor by far in determining the European position. The Germans enjoyed support from other northern European countries, while other members of the Eurogroup were, in Papaconstantinou's words, "often hiding under the table," as they feared their policies would come under assault too.

It was understandable that Germany's political class and public opinion would insist on the Troika taking an extremely tough line in demanding stringency from Athens. Examples of Greece's economic irresponsibility were both abundant and flagrant. The Greek pension system was far more generous than the country could afford, with an official retirement age of 60 and the average pension close to that received by a typical German retiree after a full life of work.[3] Powerful unions had made it possible for their members — comprising nearly 14 percent of the workforce — to start collecting government-funded retirement benefits early (age 50 for women, 55 for men) — another example of clientelism run amok.[4] Horror stories about Greek professionals declaring just a few thousand euros in taxable income, despite owning luxuries such as swimming pools and yachts, became staples of the German media. And it wasn't as if Greek society had earned the right to lavish lifestyles; the country's economy ranked among the least competitive in Europe, as witnessed by a trade deficit of nearly eight percent of GDP. All the more galling to Germans was the contrast with their own country's manifestation of thrift, hard work and other virtues. The German economy had undergone a painful adjustment during the decade from 1998 to 2008, with wages and purchasing power creeping upward at a sluggish pace even as consumption booms and property bubbles were materializing elsewhere. German industry, which had lost its edge during the 1990s following unification between East and West, regenerated itself to world-beating form in the 2000s, and by 2007 the government had brought its budget into balance. Requiring Greeks to embrace a similar regimen struck Germans as only fair — and as a necessity for Greece's long-term staying power in the euro zone.

The trouble was that proponents of austerity — whose most zealous adherents also included ECB officials — anticipated that budgetary rectitude would generate near-magical benefits. Whereas conventional Keynesian economic theory holds that slashing government outlays and hiking taxes will worsen a country's recession by reducing the spending power of ordinary citizens, the extreme pro-austerity view was that if Greece adopted a credibly abstemious fiscal policy, the "confidence effects" would lead to an economic expansion. An almost laughable illustration of this ideology was an agreement the European Commission had struck with Greece earlier in the year, under which

3 IMF, 2013, "Greece: Ex Post Evaluation of Exceptional Access under the 2010 Stand-By Arrangement" (see footnote 7 in chapter 5).

4 Landon Thomas Jr., 2010, "Patchwork Pension Plan Adds to Greek Debt Woes," *The New York Times*, March 11.

Athens pledged a brutally rapid shrinkage in its budget deficit to below three percent of GDP by 2012. The deal envisioned the Greek economy undergoing only a mild contraction in 2010 of 0.3 percent of GDP, followed by three years of steady growth.[5]

Notwithstanding its image, the IMF put little stock in such hard-core versions of economic puritanism, especially now that Strauss-Kahn was in charge and its chief economist was Olivier Blanchard, the former chairman of the Massachusetts Institute of Technology's star-studded economics department, who was earning a deserved reputation as a challenger of hidebound orthodoxies. Fund economists were concerned that too much austerity would be self-defeating, at least concerning the objective of restoring Greece's ability to pay its obligations. Although a tighter fiscal policy was essential, an overly severe approach would undoubtedly deepen the country's slump, thereby lowering tax revenue, which would lead to a wider deficit, higher debt and more worries about default. This was especially problematic because European officials, led by Germany, were demanding that Greece pay relatively high interest rates on the money it would borrow from European governments. Charging high borrowing costs was a way to show that loans to Athens weren't subsidies, and were therefore consistent with the no-bailout rule. But the result would make it all the harder for Greece to keep its debt-to-GDP ratio from exploding.

So instead of the European preference for setting 2012 as the goal for reducing the Greek budget deficit to below three percent of GDP, Fund economists argued for allowing Athens to wait until 2014 — and the other Troika members yielded on that point. Even then, however, the program was going to oblige Greece to undertake one of the biggest changes in budget and tax policy in history, with an indisputably negative impact on economic growth overall. Government outlays would be cut by seven percent of GDP — and to put that in more understandable dimensions, it is a greater amount, as a percentage of the American economy, than the US government spends on social

5 European Commission, 2010, "Commission Assesses Stability Program of Greece," Press Release IP/10/116, February 3, http://europa.eu/rapid/press-release_IP-10-116_en.htm.

security, Medicaid (which provides medical care to lower-income people), military retirement and unemployment insurance combined. Tax revenues would increase by four percent of GDP — which is equivalent to an increase of $8,600 in the taxes paid by an average American family of four.

Plainly, Greece would require measures to counter the recessionary impact of a tight fiscal policy, or it would never escape its debt trap. Because of its membership in the euro zone, the country was precluded from the policies that most governments adopt under such circumstances — that is, pumping up the money supply and devaluing the currency. That left one option, namely "structural" reforms aimed at enhancing the productivity, efficiency and flexibility of the economy.

The Fund had long been exhorting Greece to embrace such reforms, as will be recalled from the Article IV reports cited above. In 2009, an analysis by Delia Velculescu, an economist in the European Department, pressed the argument further, spelling out numerous measures in product and labour markets that, she argued, were essential for Greece "to restore competitiveness and boost long-run growth."[6] The European Commission had its own list of directives concerning these problems that Athens was supposed to follow. And now that Greece was on its knees, Thomsen and his colleagues in the Troika could insist on their institutions' advice being followed, by making their aid conditional on Greek implementation. The list was long. Policies giving advantages to unions in wage bargaining would be revised, as would laws protecting workers from layoffs. (The approval of the labour minister was legally required for a company to dismiss large numbers of staff — and virtually no approval had been given since 1982.)[7] Professions and trades that for decades had enjoyed restrictions from competition — law, auditing, pharmacy, engineering, architecture, road haulage — would be opened up. Licensing and

6 IMF, 2009, "Greece: Selected Issues," Country Report No. 09/245, August, www.imf.org/external/pubs/ft/scr/2009/cr09245.pdf.

7 IMF, 2014, "Fifth Review under the Extended Arrangement under the Extended Fund Facility," Country Report. No. 14/151, June, p. 18, www.imf.org/external/pubs/ft/scr/2014/cr14151.pdf.

other regulations inhibiting business formation would be scrapped. The bloated DEKOs, such as the national railway and other public transportation companies, would be streamlined.

It was far from certain that these policy changes, if adopted, would rekindle growth anytime soon. Arguably, the chances were nil; as Velculescu's analysis had observed, the gains from structural reform "predominantly materialize in the long run, while in the short term the estimated output responses are small or even negative. Time frames for strong reforms are measured by a decade, not by a few months or years." But their economic merit was hard to dispute, and they could also help Greece achieve another essential goal — an internal devaluation, of the sort that Latvia was undergoing, in which production costs decline absent any move in the exchange rate. If the Latvians could knuckle down, accept lower incomes and attain a miraculous turnaround in the process, maybe the Greeks could too — or so went the logic of the Troika-mandated reforms.

Recognizing that he was negotiating a wholesale makeover of his country, Papaconstantinou decided he ought to speak directly with higher-ups, to make sure Greece was going to get what it needed for such far-reaching concessions. With a promise to return promptly to the negotiating table in Athens, the Greek finance minister flew to Washington, landing at Andrews Air Force Base at 2:00 a.m. on April 24, barely in time to get ready for a 7:00 a.m. breakfast in Strauss-Kahn's office. The spring meetings of the IMF and World Bank were under way, affording the opportunity to meet with all of the Troika bosses in one place. As Papaconstaninou left Athens, a sell-off in Greek bonds was intensifying, with the yield on 10-year bonds reaching 8.83 percent — a level unseen since the 1990s — and union strikes were stopping hospitals and ferries from operating.

Joining Strauss-Kahn at breakfast were the ECB's Trichet and the Commission's Rehn. "It was a very good meeting, in that the three of them — and me — were all champions of a bailout taking shape quickly," Papaconstantinou recalled, adding that the meeting focused on the amount of funding Greece would get as well as the procedure for completing a deal.

One message was emphatically conveyed: there would be no restructuring of Greece's debt. A growing number of independent analysts were predicting that Athens would eventually have to obtain relief from its obligations one way or another,[8] but the Troika bosses wanted the Greek leadership to entertain no such thoughts.

"It was in the most clear terms, aimed at me: 'George, do not open this issue,'" Papaconstantinou told me. "I was not a fool. I would never have opened this issue unilaterally, and then be told, in the media, that it is not an option, and have all the investors running for cover in 24 hours. It was a very delicate situation."

Unbeknownst to Papaconstantinou — and everyone else in the room, except Strauss-Kahn — this option was being actively explored at the IMF, although in the most *sotto voce* way imaginable.

So clandestine was the scheme hatched by an IMF coterie in the spring of 2010 that years later, people who were intimately involved in working on Greece expressed surprise upon hearing about it. Extracting details was difficult; one interviewee whom I asked about it replied, "That is a subject I will not discuss until I die." This much I can confirm, from multiple sources on both the IMF and European side: with Strauss-Kahn's encouragement, top Fund staffers met officials from the German and French finance ministries at a hotel in Washington during mid-April 2010 to make the case for a restructuring of Greece's debt. The hotel was the Washington branch of the Sofitel — a coincidence, of course, since no one at the time could have dreamed what would happen later at the chain's New York location.

The IMF was divided, as is clear from a confidential March 24, 2010 memo by European Department Director Marek Belka. In a paragraph discussing the idea of a debt restructuring for Greece involving a

8 See Alan Beattie, 2010, "Athens faces big taboo on debt," *Financial Times*, April 28; and Desmond Lachman, 2010, "Greece's Long Road to Default," *The Wall Street Journal*, February 1.

"haircut," the memo said that the European Department believed a haircut "should not even be considered at this juncture," but "several departments" favoured it.

A haircut refers to a reduction in the amount that a debtor owes to its creditors — a typical method being a negotiated deal to swap new bonds for old ones, with the new ones paying lower principal and interest payments. Such a step is supposed to be taken, of course, only when there is scant reason to expect that the debtor can make full repayment, because important principles are at stake in ensuring that contracts to borrow money are honoured. But it is also a well-established financial truth that serious debt problems, left unaddressed, almost invariably burgeon, so if losses are inevitable it is better to take them sooner rather than later. This was one of the lessons of Argentina, where the impact of default was all the worse because of the costly efforts to stave it off. Another well-established truth is that if losses are inevitable, it is best to take them in an "orderly" fashion — that is, with creditors well-prepared for reduced payment, and hopefully willing to accept it voluntarily — than in a "disorderly" manner — a chaotic failure or refusal to make payments when they are due. Although the term "default" is often applied to any reduction in the amount paid to any creditor, the distinction between orderly and disorderly events is important, and default is more appropriately used in disorderly cases.

Two IMF fiefdoms were in the vanguard of the forces working behind the scenes for a haircut on Greek debt. One was the general counsel's office, headed by Sean Hagan, who had been one of the crusaders for an international sovereign debt system after the Argentine default. The other was the SPR department, whose director, Reza Moghadam, wielded more power than anyone at IMF headquarters except for Strauss-Kahn, according to commonly received staff wisdom. A Briton of Iranian descent — he was raised in Tehran, and sent by his parents to complete his education in London in 1979 when revolution engulfed the country — Moghadam had overcome an initial lack of fluency in English to earn degrees from Oxford, the LSE and the

University of Warwick, then joined the IMF soon thereafter, in 1992.[9] His influence stemmed partly from the authority his department held as passer of judgment over programs and policies to ensure conformity with Fund principles, and partly from his closeness with Strauss-Kahn, whom he had served (until the fall of 2008) as chief of staff. He was disliked and mistrusted by some on the staff for his adeptness at bureaucratic infighting; he surrounded himself with loyal allies by ensuring the promotion of those who supported him, while those who opposed him often seemed to find their careers stifled. But his admirers, of whom there were plenty, held his leadership talents in awe and viewed the criticism as attributable to a combination of jealousy and ethnic stereotyping. Nobody doubted his intellectual firepower or resourcefulness.

The chief IMF representative at the hotel meetings was Lorenzo Giorgianni, an SPR deputy director who was one of Moghadam's top lieutenants, backed by Hagan, the general counsel. The concern of Giorgianni's department was a logical extension of its "defender of the faith" responsibilities. An IMF loan to Greece must not go simply for payments to bondholders, as it had in Argentina's case. If Greece, like Argentina, had an unsustainable debt, a big IMF loan could be granted only on condition that the debt was restructured — so said the "No More Argentinas" rule. Imposing a haircut promptly would ensure that the burden of loss would fall on the private creditors who had lent all that money to Greece in the first place. Giving Athens a big international rescue loan, with no haircut, would shift the burden to taxpayers.

At the same time, secrecy was of the essence, because if word leaked that plans were afoot to inflict losses on Greek bondholders, investors might stampede. The official position in capitals was to dismiss talk of debt restructuring as absurd. The purpose of the secret talks was to see if support might be forthcoming from two key governments, before moving on to other players.

9 Information about Moghadam can be found in Tim Jones, 2013, "Reza Moghadam — The third man's man," *Politico,* October 9.

The idea of "involving" private lenders in a rescue — bailing them in, instead of bailing them out — was nothing new; as noted in chapter 2, during the Latin debt crisis of the 1980s the IMF had corralled banks into ponying up for new loans or accepting delayed payment on old ones. But deciding whether a haircut is appropriate for a country's debt entails tricky considerations. The biggest is how to determine whether the country is truly insolvent — that is, whether its debt dynamics will become explosive under almost any reasonable set of assumptions. Making such an assessment about a private company is often difficult; when the debtor in question is a country, the judgment is more an art than a science, because much depends on the political question of how willing the government and the public are to embrace fiscal austerity.

Greece's place on the spectrum was on the insolvency end, according to the data Giorgianni presented at the hotel meetings, which is called a "debt sustainability analysis." The details of this one remain secret, but like any debt sustainability analysis — concrete examples will come up in later chapters — it projected what would happen to Greece's debt-to-GDP ratio under various assumptions regarding key variables, the most important being economic growth, interest rates and the primary budget surplus (that is, the surplus of government revenue over government spending, excluding interest payments). The wider a primary budget surplus Greece could manage to run, the more money the government would have available to pay down its debt. On the other hand, running a big surplus entails the government extracting much more in taxes than it provides in benefits, which in turn requires political discipline and can depress the economy. The simulations shown by Giorgianni indicated that to keep its debt from soaring, Athens would have to run far more stringent primary surpluses than the economy and political system seemed capable of bearing, especially considering the magnitude of the adjustment that would be required from the deficit the government was running at that point. Only if economic growth and interest rates took almost inconceivably favourable paths would such surpluses prove unnecessary. Thus, Greece's chances of falling into explosive debt dynamics were uncomfortably high, implying that it was time to consider restructuring the country's debt.

Such a conclusion simply wasn't tolerable to Europe's senior-most leaders, the most implacable of whom was the ECB's Trichet. The issue arose at an ECB meeting in the spring of 2010, when Jürgen Stark, a member of the six-person executive board, argued that Greece's debt was unsustainable and therefore the solution should include losses for private creditors.

The ECB president "blew up," according to one attendee. "Trichet said, 'We are an economic and monetary union, and there must be no debt restructuring!'" this person recalled. "He was shouting."

Debt restructuring might be acceptable for emerging-market countries, in Trichet's view, but not for advanced countries, whose sovereign signatures were supposed to be above mistrust, and certainly not for the euro area. Once faith in the creditworthiness of one euro-zone country was shattered, he feared, confidence in the bonds issued by other European governments would be destroyed as well, the almost certain result being a Lehman-like event in which investors pulled money out of markets all over the continent. This anxiety over financial contagion was widely shared in Europe, and it was based on perfectly legitimate reasoning, starting with the condition of the region's banks.

Banks in continental Europe were, in all too many cases, insufficiently fortified with capital, as noted in chapter 4. Moreover, their portfolios were heavily laden with government bonds — the bonds of their own countries in particular, as well as the bonds of nations elsewhere in Europe — which their regulators had directed them to buy in massive quantities in 2009 as part of a recession-fighting initiative. Although such bonds were thought at the time to be risk free, the validity of that assumption no longer held in 2010, especially when it came to the bonds of Greece and the rest of the euro-zone periphery.

The exposure of French banks to Greece was €60 billion and German banks had €35 billion worth.[10] That was only a fraction of the banks' capital, but if the banks were obliged to take steep losses on their Greek paper — and if that caused a plunge in the value of their other government bondholdings as well — the financial system's viability would come under a huge cloud. Within

10 Bastasin, 2012, *Saving Europe*, chapter 12 (see chapter 5, footnote 15).

the IMF, many agreed that this problem trumped concerns about what was right for Greece, taken in isolation. The reason for the European Department's rejection of a restructuring was "the large risk of contagion to other vulnerable advanced countries in the euro area," according to Belka's memo.

Contagion worries were not lost on the SPR economists and others at the IMF who favoured a haircut for Greece. They had healthy respect for the tendency of panic to spread. Their answer, though, was that mitigating market unease about Europe depended first of all on a decisive and permanent resolution to Greece's problems; calm could not be restored as long as the danger of chaotic default continued to loom. And when it came to the impact that a Greek restructuring would have on investor worries about other countries, they argued, the ECB held the key. As a central bank, the ECB has the power to create unlimited numbers of euros and buy whatever it wants with them — that, after all, was pretty much how the Fed, with its determination to do "whatever it takes," had overcome the Lehman shock in US markets. If the ECB dealt with a Greek restructuring by sending a clear message that it stood behind the bonds of all other endangered euro-zone countries, and investors holding those bonds took comfort from the knowledge that they could always sell to the ECB, market hysteria would abate, perhaps even disappear.

Something pretty much like that eventually materialized, as anyone familiar with the history of the euro-zone crisis knows. Greek bonds were haircut and the ECB implemented a whatever-it-takes policy — but not until 2012, under Trichet's successor, Mario Draghi. In the spring of 2010, Trichet steadfastly opposed both moves. In fairness to him, he was operating under severe constraints regarding the creation of euros because the ECB, as the central bank for a monetary union of sovereign member countries, must abide by treaty provisions that don't apply to other central banks. As previously noted, the ECB's mandate prohibits it from "monetizing" the debt of governments, since doing so could spark inflation and could also be construed as a backdoor way of getting around the no-bailout clause. And Trichet knew his every move was undergoing scrutiny by the most purist of monetary institutions, the Bundesbank, which enjoys a status unlike those of other euro area national central banks because of its popularity among the German public for having safeguarded stability during the country's postwar boom. Although Trichet would show, at critical moments, that he was prepared to go further than Bundesbank representatives at the ECB thought appropriate, he would take such steps with extreme reluctance.

The hotel meetings ended inconclusively. The French government participants reacted badly to the case for a Greek restructuring, in keeping with their fears about the prospect of contagion reaching Italy. The response from the German government participants was much more positive. That was in keeping with the Germans' moral-hazard strictures: it was wrong to let irresponsible governments off the hook, and it was also wrong to let irresponsible lenders off the hook. The idea of penalizing bondholders for their folly, rather than using taxpayer money to save them, appealed to the German sense of discipline — as well it might.

Still, there was no time to implement Plan B, even if all the parties represented in the hotel meetings had agreed on its merit. Negotiations over terms for a debt restructuring typically take months, and Greece had only a matter of weeks to get the emergency funding it needed to avoid default on the May 19 payment that was coming due. For its part, the Papandreou government showed no inclination to pursue the idea. Top Greek officials, Papaconstantinou in particular, shared Trichet's aversion to the dishonouring of debt obligations, if not for quite the same moralistic reasons, then because of practical fears about the country's ability to borrow in the future. Moreover, until Greece had made a concerted effort to cut government spending, obtaining European backing for debt relief appeared politically inconceivable, and for Athens to attempt a debt restructuring without securing broad support would be risky in the extreme. Trichet's attitude alone was reason enough for the Greeks to recoil from pursuing the idea; his institution, as the euro area's lender of last resort, had the power to keep Greece's cash-strapped banks afloat with emergency loans of euros or cut them off if circumstances warranted. The ECB president's position was that such aid would be discontinued if Athens defaulted on its bonds, which were used by the banks as collateral in exchange for the emergency loans.

So it was back to Plan A.

The day after his breakfast meeting in Strauss-Kahn's office, Papaconstantinou flew back to Athens, resuming talks with the Troika the following morning, April 26. Knowing that whatever deal they struck would have to win approval in numerous parliaments and other official bodies, the negotiators worked around the clock every day that week, reaching a pact on May 1. The terms were spelled out in a 15-page "Memorandum of Economic and Financial Policies" for the IMF, and a separate, 26-page "Memorandum of Understanding on Specific Economic Policy Conditionality" for the European institutions. Thus did the word "memorandum" become an epithet for many Greeks.

Included in those pages were agreements on significant cuts to the wages and bonuses of public servants, a rise in the normal retirement age to 65, restrictions on early retirement, hikes in cigarette and alcohol taxes as well as the value-added tax, "presumptive" taxation of professionals such as doctors who might be evading taxes, and the aforementioned structural reforms, with the most controversial changes in policies protecting workers and unions. For agreeing to this, Greece was promised loans totalling €110 billion over three years, with €30 billion coming from the IMF and the rest from European governments. The money would not be disbursed all at once, of course; in keeping with customary practice, it would be doled out on a quarterly basis in "tranches" of a few billion euros, subject to approval of the Troika, whose officials would come to Athens each quarter to see whether Greece had complied with the conditions or needed to take further action. But so long as everything went according to plan, Athens could continue paying interest and principal on its existing debt, cover its salary and pension obligations, and set up a special fund to protect Greek banks against collapse.[11]

The length of the memoranda — and number of conditions imposed on the Greek government — ran contrary to a policy the IMF had adopted earlier in the decade aimed at reducing the degree of structural conditionality to the minimum necessary. This policy was the result of criticism heaped on the Fund during the Asian crisis for having applied

11 IMF, 2010, "Greece: Staff Report on Request for Stand-By Arrangement," Country Report No. 10/111, May, www.imf.org/external/pubs/ft/scr/2010/cr10111.pdf.

an "everything but the kitchen sink" approach in trying to remold the region's economies. One important reason for limiting conditionality is that excessive amounts can undermine a country's "ownership" of its program — that is, the willingness of its leaders and parliaments to pass laws and faithfully implement the terms. Ownership, as the IMF had learned over the years, often proves to be a make-or-break factor in determining whether a program succeeds or fails. In Greece's case, the unusually large number of conditions could be justified on the grounds that a complex combination of measures was needed for the sake of achieving an internal devaluation; there was no other way, given the fixed exchange rate, to improve competitiveness. But to some extent, the kitchen-sink conditionality reflected the desire of the Germans and other European policy makers to ensure that the rescue would be perceived as unpleasant for the borrowing country.[12] In that respect, the program succeeded brilliantly, as witnessed by the size and fury of the crowds that poured into the streets of Athens and other Greek cities in the early days of May as the nation's Parliament began deliberating the initial set of legislation.

The big question about the rescue package was not whether Greeks should suffer. They would suffer even more in its absence, since the government would have no way of obtaining the euros needed to pay its bills, including amounts owed to civil servants and pensioners. The question was whether the package stood a fair chance of restoring the country's economic and financial health. The combined hit from spending cuts and tax increases, on an economy already contracting at a rate of four percent in 2010, was equivalent to more than one-tenth of economic output over the next three years. How, then, was the economy going to fare as well as the Troika projected — namely, a downturn of just 2.6 percent in 2011, followed by a resumption of

12 Technically, the IMF did follow its policy regarding limiting structural conditions, because the Fund's own program in 2010 was more focused and streamlined than the European one. But since the rescue involved a joint IMF-EU program, this didn't matter; Athens was expected to implement conditions attached to both programs. Also, the IMF's own conditions would multiply as time went by, as shall be seen in later chapters.

growth in 2012?[13] The answer, again, was the wondrous impact of the structural reforms. But could the Greek private sector really generate all the dynamism needed to replace the drain on the economy from the huge contraction in the public sector — especially when the country's banks were frantically curbing credit in response to swelling bankruptcies? Some of the specific projections about the performance of the private sector strained credulity. Exports of Greek goods and services were assumed to increase by 65 percent over six years, for example — a rate of growth even surpassing that of the German export juggernaut during its most competitive years.[14]

The dubiousness of the program's assumptions was the subject of a memo authored by Blanchard, who in addition to his position as the IMF's chief economist headed its Research Department. The degree of budgetary belt-tightening required for Greece to meet its fiscal targets "has never been achieved" by any other country, warned the memo, which was dated May 4 and was based partly on contributions from two high-ranking Research Department economists, Jonathan Ostry and Giovanni Dell'Ariccia. Furthermore, "even with full policy compliance…there is nothing that can support growth against the negative contribution of the public sector…the recovery would likely be L-shaped, with a recession deeper and longer than projected," Blanchard wrote. "The projected V-shaped growth pattern is overly optimistic…it is unlikely that strong productivity gains can play a meaningful role."

13 In retrospect, one of the mistakes made at this time was the size of the "fiscal multiplier" — that is, the economic impact of cuts in government spending or increases in taxes. The IMF staff paper on the program did not specify what multiplier was assumed, but according to Fund documents published later, Fund economists evidently used a multiplier of 0.5, meaning that every €1 of spending cuts or tax hikes would reduce GDP by €0.50. Research led by IMF chief economist Blanchard indicated that a much higher multiplier would have been appropriate — in other words, the May 2010 assumptions about the program's impact on the Greek economy were insufficiently pessimistic. But this research surfaced only later, in the fall of 2012, so the issue will be covered in chapter 15.

14 For the assumptions and projections underlying the program, see IMF, 2010, "Greece: Staff Report on Request for Stand-By Arrangement" (see footnote 11 in this chapter). The projection regarding growth in exports is on page 43.

Taken together, these concerns led to disquiet about the most critical assumptions of all — the debt figures. The plan anticipated that the debt-to-GDP ratio would top out at 149 percent in 2013 and gradually decline in years thereafter. As harrowingly high a debt-to-GDP ratio as 149 percent was, keeping it from soaring even further depended on two stupendous gambles paying off: not only would the Greeks have to implement the measures as promised, those measures would have to engender the anticipated benefits on confidence and growth. In other words, prospects for stable debt dynamics were shaky at best.

A graphical depiction helps make this crucial point more comprehensible. The dark solid line in the graph (below) shows the projected path for Greece's debt — first peaking, then sloping back down to relatively sustainable levels — if all the assumptions in the program proved valid. The gray dotted line shows what would happen, according to figures published in the IMF's May 2010 staff report on the program, if just one of the major assumptions proved too optimistic — that is, if economic growth turned out to be one percentage point a year worse than projected. Under that less rosy scenario, the debt-to-GDP ratio wouldn't decline; it would stay very high, almost certainly above sustainable levels. An even more explosive debt path (reaching

Greece: Debt-to-GDP Projections, May 2010

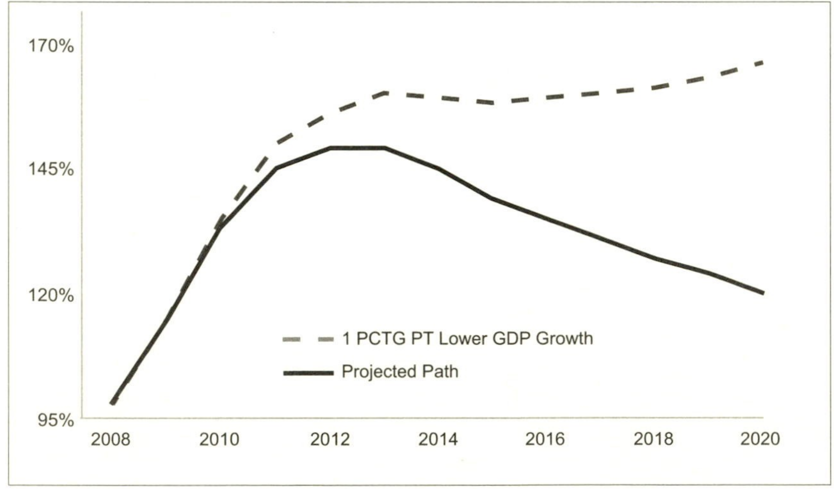

Source: IMF.

230 percent of GDP) would result if several of the assumptions went unmet, the IMF's figures revealed.

Based on the likelihood that something like the less rosy scenario would unfold, Blanchard and his colleagues urged in their memo that a secret deal be struck in advance envisioning the adoption of more radical steps if necessary — presumably including the restructuring of Greece's debt. "Even with perfect policy implementation" — that is, even if Athens did everything it was supposed to — the program may well go "off track," the memo stated. Thus "it is critical to reach a clear and confidential understanding with the [Greek] authorities and the EU on how to proceed forward should such circumstances materialize (this may possibly involve a side letter)." This recommendation went unheeded, however.

Small wonder that, as analysts scrutinized the plan in detail, markets began to swoon anew in the days after the package was unveiled. By May 7, the day after the Greek Parliament approved the deal (following deadly rioting in Athens the day before), yields on Greek government bonds were above 12 percent, and the extra yields that investors demanded to hold Portuguese and Spanish bonds rather than safer German bonds reached euro-era highs.

Small wonder, too, that a number of independent economists and analysts expressed dismay at the program's lack of a debt-restructuring plan. "It beggars belief that Greek government debt can top out at 150 percent of GDP, as the IMF envisages," wrote Barry Eichengreen, a Berkeley economics professor, in a commentary published five days after the accord's announcement. "Sooner or later, the creditors will have to exchange their existing bonds for new ones worth at most 50 cents on the euro. This will leave Greece with more public money for basic social services. That in turn will make it a tiny bit easier to achieve social consensus on the needed measures. It will show the Greek in the street that he is not simply making sacrifices to pay the banks. All these are reasons for proceeding sooner rather than later."[15]

15 Barry Eichengreen, 2010, "It Is Not Too Late for Europe," Vox.EU, May 7, www.voxeu.org/article/greek-crisis-it-not-too-late-europe.

Small wonder, too, that within the IMF staff, the question was being raised: how, in good faith, can we claim that this program complies with the No More Argentinas rule?

The €30 billion loan that the IMF planned to give Greece wasn't just bigger than any the Fund had given any other country; it was also more than 30 times (3,212 percent) of Greece's IMF quota — another record. It was therefore indisputably subject to the standards the IMF had established in 2003, after the Argentine default, restricting the use of giant loans to cases where they are clearly justified.

These standards, as will be recalled from the explanation of the No More Argentinas rule in chapter 2, required that a country receiving an extraordinarily large loan must have a "high probability" of debt sustainability. Unsurprisingly, the SPR department did not believe Greece met this standard — and SPR had unique leverage over this matter because its signature is required on any document of this kind going to the executive board.[16]

Strauss-Kahn was learning of the No More Argentinas rule for the first time, and during the first week of May 2010 he found himself in the middle of a bitter dispute that threatened to derail the Greek rescue, with potentially cataclysmic effects on markets. The board was scheduled to meet within days to formally approve the program — but what should the board be told? How could the board bestow its blessing, and allow the disbursal of IMF resources, if it was going to blatantly break the rule? What sort of message might the Fund send by doing so, regarding both Greece and future programs?

Moghadam and his SPR colleagues, backed by Hagan and a few others, were firmly dug in: the probability of debt sustainability was not "high." Even though the rule didn't specify a numerical meaning for "high

16 Technically, IMF management could have brought the document to the board without the SPR department's signature, but that would have been extremely awkward and embarrassing.

probability," it surely meant something in the 75 to 80 percent range, and based on graphs (called "fan charts") showing the range of possible outcomes for Greece's debt-to-GDP ratio using various assumptions, the probability of debt sustainability was, if anything, "low." Thus the SPR department could not certify that the program fulfilled the criteria for an exceptionally large loan. Simply pretending otherwise would make a mockery of a rule that, for good reasons, was supposed to prevent the Fund from making bad mistakes, SPR argued. At the board meeting, senior staff members would be queried closely; how could they say, with straight faces, that they had reached comforting conclusions about Greece's debt based on "rigorous" and "systematic" analyses, as the rule required?

Their position elicited a torrent of denunciations from other members of the staff as well as some of the deputy managing directors, who accused Moghadam and his allies of risking a global crisis over a bureaucratic obstacle. Some rules are made to be broken, they contended, and this one surely merited bending under the circumstances. Determining debt sustainability is not like measuring temperature, or atomic weight; it is a subjective judgment. The European Department believed in good faith that the program stood a chance of working, which ought to suffice. "It seemed to a lot of us that [Moghadam and Hagan] were thinking about how their reputations might be affected," said one participant in the debate. "Your ultimate objective is protecting the global financial system, not your good name."

To the irritation of Moghadam's foes, Strauss-Kahn declared that he wouldn't force anybody to sign something they were uncomfortable with. But the managing director was also determined for the program to go forward, with the big dollop of IMF cash that Greece had been promised. A compromise emerged: instead of certifying that Greece had a high probability of debt sustainability, the staff would tell the board that "on balance," the country's debt appeared sustainable. At the same time, the Fund would create a new exception to its rule, dropping the high-probability requirement for crises that risked general contagion (defined as "systemic spillovers"). This new exception could be applied in all future cases, not just Greece.

Among those supporting this approach as the least of all evils was Blanchard. "The program fails to pass [the test for debt sustainability]," the Fund's chief economist wrote in his memo. "Fudging with the numbers will likely undermine the credibility of the program... It would be better to recognize openly (at least internally) that this criterion can be waived for cases with exceptional contagion risk. Then, a careful strategy would have to be devised to communicate with the public without undermining (further) the credibility of the program. Markets, so far, seem to be seeing through the rhetoric anyway."

The IMF's first serious test of its No More Argentinas rule was ending in a cop-out. "Nobody was really happy," Strauss-Kahn acknowledged. But uppermost in his mind at the end of the first week of May were other developments: the negative market reaction to the Troika deal with Greece was reaching a crescendo; a new plan was in the offing for dealing with future European crises; and the Fund was once again in danger of being sidelined.

It was when Bank of England Governor Mervyn King, a fan of the Aston Villa Football Club, began reading soccer scores to his fellow participants in an international conference call that the shambolic nature of global economic policy making during the weekend of May 7–9, 2010, became most apparent. Along with Fed Chairman Ben Bernanke, King was on the phone, impatiently awaiting the start of a discussion among the G7 finance ministers and central bank governors, but the conversation couldn't get under way until it included the euro zone's top economic policy makers, who were embroiled in a crucially important meeting in Brussels. Since those who had joined the call were already bored making small talk, King turned in desperation to the results of that day's football matches, figuring he may as well recite them aloud to convey his sentiment that he and his colleagues had other important things to do.

So it went during that weekend's marathon series of meetings, which immersed Europe's political and economic potentates in discussions spanning three different countries. It was "a weekend of destiny," and "the moment of truth," Sarkozy told his fellow leaders — just two examples of the grandiloquence gushed during many debates. As for Strauss-Kahn, he arrived on May 9 in Basel, Switzerland, for a conclave of central bankers, and spent much of the evening on the phone trying to make sure the IMF would remain involved in any future crises in the euro zone. "That was my fight for this night," Strauss-Kahn recalled. "It was a real fight."

Much is known, from articles and books written by others, about these meetings.[17] This is a book focusing on the IMF, so a detailed account of the machinations among European policy makers that weekend is not necessary, especially since the Fund played a minimal role in the most consequential discussions. The decisions taken had major import, however; a summary of events is therefore in order.

The fundamental challenge was to establish a "firewall" that would keep turmoil from spreading, by showing markets that Europe had both the financial resources and the institutional infrastructure to respond if any other euro-zone country came under speculative attack. A chart displayed by Trichet at a Friday evening summit dinner in Brussels on May 7, showing how Portuguese government bonds were tracking Greek ones, had the desired sobering effect on the leaders, as did the central bank chief's remarks citing similarities with the period of the Lehman collapse. Exhortations were also forthcoming from Washington, where President Barack Obama and Treasury Secretary Tim Geithner — keenly aware that their country's economy was also at risk, given US banks' $3.6 trillion exposure to European

17 For the most comprehensive and authoritative account of these meetings, on which a number of others appear to rest, see Peter Ludlow, 2010, "A View on Brussels: In the Last Resort: The European Council and the Euro Crisis, Spring 2010," EuroComment, briefing note vol. 7, No. 7/8, June. See also Marcus Walker, Charles Forelle and Brian Blackstone, 2010, "Currency Union Teetering, 'Mr. Euro' Is Forced to Act," *The Wall Street Journal,* September 27; Ben Hall, Quentin Peel and Ralph Atkins, 2010, "The Day That Tested Limits of the Union," *Financial Times,* May 10; Tony Barber, 2010, "Danger Zone," *Financial Times,* May 16; and Barber, 201, "Dinner on the edge of the abyss," *Financial Times,* October 10. For books, see Irwin, *The Alchemists,* chapter 13 (see footnote 13 in chapter 3); and Bastasin, *Saving Europe,* chapter 14 (see footnote 15 in chapter 5).

banks[18] — spent hours working the phones to prod bold action from their counterparts across the Atlantic. Fearful that the currency union might not survive the following week if they failed, the European leaders resolved to unveil a plan by the time Asian markets opened on Monday.

Several of the leaders, led by Sarkozy, demanded at the May 7 summit that the ECB assume major firewall responsibilities by using its euro-creation powers to buy the bonds of the most imperiled governments. Predictably, Trichet retorted that such political pressure would never influence him and his central bank colleagues — on the contrary, it would backfire, "with disastrous consequences." He did not tell the leaders that the previous day, the ECB governing council had secretly agreed in Lisbon on a selective program to buy bonds of vulnerable countries. He kept that initiative under wraps for the time being because he wanted to make sure governments would also shoulder a hefty portion of the burden for the firewall; his reasoning was that they wouldn't deliver if they thought they could depend on the ECB as a backstop. His strategy, and well-orchestrated theatrics, began to pay off when the governments drew up plans on Sunday, May 9, at another Brussels meeting for a sizable "stabilization fund" that could lend hundreds of billions of euros to crisis-stricken countries.

But battling over the terms dragged well into the predawn hours in Brussels on Monday, May 10 — with one of the unsettled issues being the IMF's role, which was the focus of Strauss-Kahn's attention.

Joining the IMF managing director in Basel was Trichet, who was also attending a regularly scheduled meeting of central bankers at the Bank for International Settlements. The two men, huddling together with a handful of others, stayed in constant contact throughout Sunday evening with the finance ministers who were thrashing out the deal in Brussels. As Strauss-Kahn knew, the argument that Europe should handle its own affairs, with no outside interference, was gaining fresh momentum. A proposal tabled in the afternoon by the European Commission, with

18 Nelson D. Schwartz and Eric Dash, 2010, "Greek Debt Woes Ripple Outward, from Asia to U.S.," *The New York Times*, May 8.

strong backing from Sarkozy, envisioned no IMF role in the new rescue mechanism. Once again, the anti-IMF forces were up against Merkel, who was sticking to her view that Fund involvement was essential. But the dispute over the IMF was just one among many, and events took an unexpectedly chaotic turn when German Finance Minister Wolfgang Schäuble, whom Merkel dispatched to Brussels to insist on terms Berlin wanted, was rushed to the hospital because of an allergic reaction to medication, obliging Germany to send another minister in the evening, with only a few hours to go before the opening of Asian markets.

This time, Strauss-Kahn had Trichet's support for IMF involvement. The ECB chief no longer wanted to keep the IMF out; he had swung around to Merkel's position on the value of the Fund's expertise and credibility. Moreover, Strauss-Kahn could offer something else that European leaders wanted — money for the firewall, or at least the theoretical prospect thereof. He had no legal authority to commit IMF resources; only the board could do that. But he was willing to put his name and prestige in support of a statement that the IMF would presumably match a portion of the European commitment, at a ratio of €1 from the Fund for every €2 from Europe. The 1-for-2 ratio appealed to him because, although the IMF would have to continue as junior partner in the Troika, contributing less than one-third of the total would risk putting the Fund in too junior a position. Since Europe was by then contemplating a firewall totalling €500 billion, the amount from the IMF could be up to €250 billion.

Just as Asian markets were opening, the deal was announced creating the European Financial Stability Facility (EFSF), which was in effect a bailout fund for a region that ostensibly had a no-bailout rule. As iniquitous as this might appear on the surface, the EFSF's purpose — lending money to euro-zone countries in financial distress — did not violate the rule, which prohibited member countries from "assuming the commitments" of others. The EFSF would be based in Luxembourg and could raise up to €440 billion in financial markets, backed by guarantees from European governments. Combining that €440 billion with the European Commission's rescue fund, which then stood at €60 billion, the total European firewall would be €500 billion. Furthermore, the agreement envisioned replacing these facilities after three years with a more permanent arrangement for providing assistance, called the European Stability Mechanism (ESM), which would be based on a treaty and would have paid-in capital from member states. The sentence Strauss-Kahn wanted was included in the announcement: "The IMF will participate in financing arrangements and is expected to provide at least half as much as the EU contribution."[19]

Trichet also got most of what he was seeking, so at 3:15 a.m. on May 10 he announced the plan that the ECB governing council had endorsed the previous Thursday, called the Securities Market Programme (SMP). Its centrepiece was the purchase of bonds that had been issued by financially stressed governments, a move that was depicted variously as a courageous crossing of the Rubicon or (especially among German monetary purists) a betrayal of the ECB's founding principles. The ECB carefully circumscribed its commitment, saying that the scope of operations would be "determined by the Governing Council." Seeking to preempt any complaints about violating the rules against deficit monetization or bailouts, the ECB said it was acting because of "severe tensions in certain market segments which are hampering the monetary policy transmission mechanism." This wasn't a "whatever-it-takes" move, in other words; it was limited and temporary.[20] But it was significant, enough so that it drew public repudiation from Bundesbank President Axel Weber, who had voted against it in his capacity as a governing council member.

The IMF's junior partnership in the Troika was intact. Meanwhile, as the frantic goings-on in Brussels and Basel were taking place on May 9, another important meeting was taking place at IMF headquarters. It was Mother's Day in Washington; the unfortunate timing was attributable to the urgency of the agenda.

19 Council of the European Union, 2010, "Press Release: Extraordinary Council Meeting, Brussels," May 9/10, available at: http://europa.eu/rapid/press-release_PRES-10-108_en.htm?locale=en.

20 One reason this initiative's effectiveness was limited was that the ECB insisted on retaining seniority over private bondholders in the event of a Greek default. This created a double-edged sword: on one hand, the ECB's purchases of Greek bonds added to demand for them, lowering their yield; on the other hand, it scared away private bondholders by subordinating them to the ECB. In later years, under Mario Draghi, the ECB would change this policy.

7

"THERE IS NO PLAN B"

An oval chamber 60-feet long and two stories high with plush blue carpeting and suede-and-wood panelling, the IMF boardroom is designed to convey the majesty of the international community passing judgment. There, the Fund's executive directors gathered at 10 a.m. on Sunday, May 9, settling into their grey swivel chairs around a horseshoe-shaped table with microphones in each place, while staff members took seats a few feet away from the table. Lipsky was presiding, since Strauss-Kahn was in Basel. The board's task was to consider the IMF program for Greece, the historical importance and unprecedented size of which was lost on nobody. Each member had received copies in advance of the staff report, a 144-page document loaded with analysis, data, charts and projections explaining how the Troika-backed loans and Greek policy changes were supposed to work.[1]

As they entered, the directors and other IMF personnel attending the meeting knew how it would end. Given the combustible market environment, the board was certain to approve the program, based on the usual consensus or something very close to it. But the attendees also knew that incisive criticism and awkward questions were going to be raised. Preliminary statements by directors from outside the

1 IMF, 2010, "Greece: Staff Report on Request for Stand-By Arrangement" (see footnote 11 in chapter 6).

euro zone, circulated internally in advance of the meeting, reflected profound skepticism about the wisdom of imposing austerity on Greece without requiring the country's creditors to accept any losses. This meeting would thus afford a striking illustration of the IMF's capacity for maintaining a unified facade in public even when it is splintered internally.

The complete minutes of the meeting, which were released in mid-2015, show the depth of the IMF's reservations in proceeding with the approach being taken in the Greek rescue. The minutes also reveal something that the directors didn't know at the meeting's outset — that the Fund's rules were being changed in a manner that can fairly be described as fast and loose. The board members were about to discover, although only near the end of the meeting, that an unwelcome surprise regarding the No More Argentinas rule lay buried within the staff report.[2]

Powerful backing for the program predictably came from directors representing euro-zone countries. Six of them joined in a statement to their colleagues on the board saying: "Given the Greek authorities' extraordinary commitment to implement an exceptional adjustment program, we strongly support" the rescue, which "is appropriately comprehensive and addresses the relevant policy challenges." The Europeans said they were "fully aware that this is a very challenging program, which is not free of risks. However, the current situation makes hardship unavoidable and this program is the only alternative left to prevent a significantly worse scenario from happening."

Directors representing countries with far fewer votes took a much dimmer view. A number of their prepared statements and oral remarks are worth quoting for their prescience about what lay in store for Greece.

2 IMF, 2010, "Minutes of Executive Board Meeting 10/45-1," May 9 (published in the IMF Archives in July 2015), http://adlib.imf.org/digital_assets/wwwopac.ashx?command=getcontent&server=webdocs&value= EB/2010/EBM/353745.PDF.

Arvind Virmani, who represented India, fretted that the planned fiscal tightening would be a "mammoth burden [that] could trigger a deflationary spiral of falling prices, falling employment, and falling fiscal revenues that could eventually undermine the program itself," so a default or restructuring might be "inevitable." Poignantly, the Argentine director, Pablo Andrés Pereira, harkened back to "harsh lessons from our own past crises" in urging consideration of a debt restructuring for Greece sooner rather than later. "In 2001, somewhat similar policies [as those in the Greek program] were proposed by the Fund in Argentina," Pereira said. "[The] catastrophic consequences are well known....Beyond economic theories, there is an indisputable reality that cannot be contested: a debt that cannot be paid will not be paid without a strong process of sustainable growth."

The assumptions in the staff report about Greek growth "seem to be overly benign," said René Weber, a director from Switzerland who represented his own country and seven others. "Even a small negative deviation...would make the debt level unsustainable over the longer term." Weber exhorted management and staff "to prepare contingency scenarios....Among these contingency measures, serious consideration should be given to debt restructuring as a means to achieve fiscal sustainability and make private creditors shoulder some of the adjustment burden." Indeed, he asked, "Why has debt restructuring and the involvement of the private sector in the rescue package not been considered so far?" Along with a couple of others, Weber also voiced concern about the Troika arrangement: "While close coordination with the EU and the ECB will be key, we wonder whether such joint review [of Greece's progress] could hinder the independence of Fund staff assessment," he said.

Echoing similar sentiments about the need for contingency planning, Christopher Legg, an alternate executive director from Australia who represented a constituency of 13 countries, said: "I understand why there is a huge reluctance to countenance any kind of debt restructuring.... But it is clear that the markets are not convinced that the program will be sufficient. While we must not speak the unspeakable, certainly not outside this room, we need to be thinking the unthinkable."

Unsurprisingly to his colleagues, the most caustic comments came from Paulo Nogueira Batista, a Brazilian with swept-back salt-and-pepper hair who was the board's most outspoken detractor of the Fund's governance. As the representative from a BRIC country that was taking the lead in seeking a reordering of control over institutions like the IMF, Nogueira Batista took discernible pleasure in goading the Atlantic powers for what he saw as their arrogance and hypocrisy. ("Why do they need a European Monetary Fund?" he chortled at one board meeting when the idea was proposed by the German Finance Ministry. "They already have one here.") Characteristically, his attack on the Greek program dispensed with the diplomatic niceties favoured by his board allies; he used the term "Panglossian" to describe the staff report's projection of a V-shaped recovery. The program, he declared, "may be seen not as a rescue of Greece, which will have to undergo a wrenching adjustment, but as a bailout of Greece's private debt holders, mainly European financial institutions."

With so many aspects of the program to criticize, none of these directors bothered to mention one of its most preposterous assumptions — figures projecting that from 2014 to 2020, Greece would run primary budget surpluses of about six percent of GDP. By assuming that the government would extract such a surfeit in tax revenue over a number of years, the staff report could conclude that Greece would pay off enough of its debt to make its burden sustainable by the end of the decade. Few countries have mustered the discipline necessary to generate large primary budget surpluses over prolonged periods, and the IMF itself — in public comments by Christine Lagarde during her fifth year as managing director[3] — would later decry the absurdity of pretending that Athens could manage such a feat. But at this board meeting the issue wasn't discussed.

As expected, US director Meg Lundsager threw her country's 16.8 percent vote behind the program, but she interjected a couple of caveats aimed at protecting the IMF's financial interests in case the rescue failed. "We take note of and welcome the extensive support

3 IMF, 2016, "Press Briefing of the Managing Director," April 14, www.imf.org/external/np/tr/2016/tr041416.htm.

of Greece's European partners," she said, but added: "We simply and strongly reiterate the Fund's seniority and preferred creditor status." This was a pointed reminder that if Greece was unable to repay all of the loans it was receiving, the Fund's claims would get priority over any amounts owed by Athens to other lenders, including European governments. Then Lundsager suggested that Europe's financial responsibilities might go even further than preferred-creditor status required. "In the event that there are setbacks or additional financing requirements, we will look to continued European leadership in meeting those challenges in Greece and other countries in the region," she said.

Ludsager's words were diplomatic — intentionally so, because she was raising a delicate question: if Greece proved unable to repay its loans to the IMF, who should bear the loss? A persuasive argument could be made that the member countries of the euro zone should assume responsibility for covering any losses incurred by the Fund; in other words, the IMF should not only be paid before any other creditors, it should be indemnified against loss by countries that were benefiting most from the Fund's loan. After all, the Fund was lending an extraordinarily large amount of money, on extraordinarily risky terms, with one of its important motivations being the euro's salvation. And for the IMF to suffer a significant loss on such a large loan would be disastrous for its ability to serve as lender of last resort.

In her cautiously phrased statement, Lundsager stopped well short of demanding that Europe indemnify the IMF. She could be construed as merely asserting that Europe might have to lend Greece more money at some future time. Her European colleagues did not respond directly to her point, and the official records of the meeting do not indicate that anyone else did either. As we shall see, the issue of preferred creditor status and Europe's potential obligations to the Fund would arise often at future board meetings. Members of the Fund staff would grow increasingly concerned about the Fund's exposure to Greece, and some would internally advance the case for an ironclad European guarantee to cover the Fund against loss. But the Europeans would get away without making, or even being asked for, such a guarantee.

Once all the directors had spoken, it was Thomsen's turn as mission chief to respond to their questions and concerns, starting with the point about the Troika. "To be clear, as an independent institution, the Fund will make its own judgment on program performance," the Dane said. "[I]f the Fund assesses that conditions have not been met, we will not disburse, irrespective of the judgment reached by the Commission and the European Central Bank. In this regard, let me stress that we are off to a very good start…in terms of our cooperation."

Thomsen was a true believer in the program — or at least in the plausibility of its chances for success — and having negotiated it for the IMF, he delivered a spirited defence, focusing on the element he had always considered the linchpin of the whole undertaking. "The key issue...is really the government's ability to overcome what undoubtedly will be fierce resistance from vested interests to structural reforms," Thomsen said. "This will be challenging....Even if Greece were to mobilize the political resolve to implement the fiscal program, if the structural reforms do not happen, the strategy will not be sustainable, and I think that the government is very mindful of that." Nonetheless, he argued, "our assumption is that we can put Greece over the hill in a couple of years and set it on a credible fiscal path that promises a gradual reduction in debt."

As for debt restructuring, Thomsen — who had opposed the idea in internal staff debate — told the board: "From the outset of the discussion, the [Greek] authorities were firmly of the view that debt restructuring is not on the table. In this regard, one of the reasons was clearly that Greece was at a point where it needs to move away from a model very much dependent on the public sector and give much better conditions for the private sector. It would be a mistake not to honor contracts."

Nobody voiced outright opposition to the program, despite the disdainful comments. Even Nogueira Batista said he was in favour; he could do no more than thunder, "Our decision to go along with this problematic and risk-laden program should not be taken to mean that we will support it in the future."

But fresh controversy arose when the realization spread that, along with the Greek program, the board was taking another important step that day — modifying the No More Argentinas rule. The manner in which this emerged aroused suspicion that approval for a significant policy change was being sought without directors being alerted, which would constitute a breach of proper international governance.

The issue came to the fore when Weber, the Swiss director, cited a passage on pages 19 and 20 of the staff report, which he had noticed while poring over the document on a long plane flight to Washington. He said he "had some difficulties finding that spot and realizing that this is a proposed policy change." The passage read as follows:

> On balance, staff considers [Greece's] debt to be sustainable over the medium term, but the significant uncertainties around this make it difficult to state categorically that this is the case with a high probability. Even so, Fund support at the proposed level is justified given the high risk of international systemic spillover effects. Going forward, such an approach to this aspect of the exceptional access policy would also be available in similar cases where systemic spillover risks are pronounced.[4]

In plain English, this language effectuated the compromise reached at the staff level on the No More Argentinas rule: henceforth, in cases where contagion was feared, the IMF could give exceptionally large loans to countries even if their debt sustainability couldn't be certified as highly probable. Normally, a policy change of this sort would be subject to careful deliberation, as it had been in 2003, perhaps over the course of several board meetings. Instead it had been inserted into a jargon-filled passage of the staff report, apparently without providing directors with an advance briefing.

Confusion reigned among many if not all of the board members about the implications of this passage. "I admit I did not pick this up either

4 IMF, 2010, "Greece: Staff Report on Request for Stand-By Arrangement" (see footnote 11 in chapter 6).

in my quick read of the documents," Lundsager told her colleagues. Several others, including Canadian director Thomas Hockin, declared themselves prepared to exempt Greece from the No More Argentinas rule as long as no precedent was necessarily being set for future crises. But that underscored his lack of understanding about what was being proposed; staffers at the meeting said that such a case-by-case approach wasn't permissible.

Hagan, the general counsel, explained that "uniformity of treatment" among member countries — a fundamental IMF principle — required consistent applicability. "When a general policy is established, it must be applied in all cases to all countries," he said. "If in fact a situation arises where a country does not meet that policy, the board has no authority to make an ad hoc exception." In the case of the Greek program, he added, the board could either make a determination that Greece met the "high probability" standard for debt sustainability, "or alternatively, [the board] must change the policy and, as a result...those changes would be applicable to future cases."

An indignant Nogueira Batista suggested that the policy change was being snuck past the board. Noting that directors would have misunderstood what they were doing had Weber not pressed the issue, he demanded: "Should we not have a separate decision...instead of just a sentence on page 19 of the staff report, which would then be used as a precedent?" Weber chimed in too, complaining that the rule change was "kind of hidden."

Was this episode as deplorable as such rebukes would imply? The best gloss that can be applied is that it was a lamentably hasty way to do what had to be done. The Greek rescue had to go forward, without further ado. IMF rules could not be grossly flouted, but they could be fudged, and there was no time for the kind of debate that would normally precede an important change in policy. The board went along with shredding the No More Argentinas rule, once members understood this step to be inseparable from approval of the Greek program.

Seeking to bring the meeting to a close, Lipsky played down the fuss about the change in the No More Argentinas rule. "Ideally, it would have been better to have held a discussion separately. That point should be self-evident," said the IMF's no. 2 official. "We are meeting on Sunday, because of the need for urgent action. So, we have dealt with it as best we can."

Then Lipsky pronounced himself "a little disturbed by the suggestion that the Fund program should obviously have involved debt restructuring or even default." There were good reasons for eschewing such an approach, according to Lipsky, who had been one of the most powerful opponents of debt restructuring during the IMF's internal debates that spring. "Greece has a very large — very large — primary [budget] deficit that would have remained even if all debt payments were suspended," he said. "Such an action would have had immediate and devastating implications for the Greek banking system, not to mention broader spillover effects."

That prompted a rejoinder from Nogueira Batista, who said Lipsky's comments "reveal what we suspected — that management had been looking carefully at the issue of debt restructuring....perhaps an eventual Plan B."

"There is no Plan B," Lipsky shot back. "There is Plan A and a determination to make Plan A succeed; and this is it."

Lee Buchheit, a partner at the New York law firm Cleary Gottlieb Steen & Hamilton, was not bound by anybody's strictures to make Plan A succeed. In many of the financial crises that have occurred since the 1980s, Buchheit was the attorney whom over-indebted countries sought for legal counsel. His first big client was Mexico; later came Russia, the Philippines, Iraq and Iceland, among others. Erudite and whimsical, he was a frequent writer and speaker on sovereign debt issues, and although some of his adversaries in the creditor community hated to admit it, he was an intellectual giant in the field.

Buchheit would eventually represent Greece, and play a key role in its crisis, as shall be seen in chapter 14. In May 2010, he was merely a bystander; he had not been retained by Athens, but he was fascinated by the debate over the country's travails. On economic grounds, he was sympathetic to the view that the country *should* restructure its debt, although as a lawyer, he wasn't sure at first how it *could*. One of the arguments advanced against a restructuring was that Greece would end up submerged in a legal morass, just like the country that held the previous record for a restructuring — Argentina.

"Everyone at that point had 10 years of looking at Argentina, and nobody wanted to bring those problems into the belly of Europe," Buchheit told me. "So people were saying, 'All this talk of restructuring Greek debt is fatuous. It simply couldn't be done.'"

Ever since its default, the Argentine government had been the target of creditor lawsuits, led by billionaire Paul Singer, a New York hedge fund executive. Although Buenos Aires had induced the vast majority of its bondholders to accept a restructuring in 2005, offering new bonds worth roughly 33 cents on the dollar, Singer and other bondholders were holding out against the deal and continuing to pursue litigation demanding full payment of principal plus accumulated interest. Since Argentina had sold many of its bonds to big financial institutions in the United States based on promises that any disputes would be subject to New York law, the holdouts could take advantage of the American legal system to press their claims. Sure enough, federal courts issued judgments in favour of Singer and his fellow holdouts, whose bonds contained covenants (legal provisions) clearly entitling them to full payment. Not that the holdouts could force Argentina to hand over money; a sovereign government is pretty well protected against foreign legal judgments that it deems invalid, and most of its assets abroad (embassies, for example) are immune from seizure. But Singer's lawyers skillfully used the courts to harass Buenos Aires — filing claims against overseas accounts belonging to the Argentine central bank, for example, and even seizing money from a Science Ministry account at a US bank that was intended to pay for telescopes. In addition to making it risky for Argentine government-related entities to operate internationally, this litigation made it impossible for the Argentine government to raise new funds in international debt markets.

The complexity of Greece's government debt, which totalled about €320 billion, made Argentina's woes seem almost puny by comparison. Not only did Athens owe several times the amount that Buenos Aires ever did, its outstanding bonds had been issued in 130 different series, each with its own maturities, interest rates and other terms. "The expectation was that in any restructuring, holdouts would eat the transaction alive," Buchheit recalled.

But an ingenious solution occurred to Buchheit and one of his former law associates, Duke University Professor Mitu Gulati, as they deliberated by phone and email. Greece had one advantage that put it in a far better position than any of the emerging-market debtors in modern history: most of its debt, about 90 percent, was governed by its own national law. This meant that Greece could conceivably facilitate a restructuring by changing the bonds' terms in an act of Parliament, which would be immune from challenge in foreign courts. Not that Athens should blithely renounce its obligation to pay; that would be a gross abuse of power for which the country would suffer long-lasting reputational damage. But other "balanced and proportional" options were available, making it possible for Greece to deal with the holdout problem, as Buchheit and Gulati wrote in a paper they posted online on May 7, 2010.[5]

In the paper, titled "How to Restructure Greek Debt," Buchheit and Gulati suggested that Greece could enact legislation effectively inserting collective action clauses (CACs) into its Greek-law bonds. It will be recalled from chapter 2 that these clauses help limit the power of holdouts. The way they work is by binding all bondholders to the terms of a restructuring provided that a supermajority (say, 75 percent) accepts the deal. Suppose, for example, that a financially strapped country offers its bondholders new bonds worth 50 cents on the dollar. If more than three-quarters of the bondholders take the offer, then CACs prevent the ones who refuse from holding out for a better deal; the terms on their bonds are automatically revised

5 Lee C. Buchheit and G. Mitu Gulati, 2010, "How to Restructure Greek Debt," Social Science Research Network, May 7, http://papers.ssrn.com/sol3/papers.cfm?abstract_id=1603304.

to match the principal and interest payments due on the new bonds. (Argentine bonds did not include such clauses, making it possible for holdouts to demand full payment.)

"The question of the hour was, could the Greek debt stock be restructured without a massive holdout creditor problem? Mitu and I thought there was a way, and we decided to put out ideas on a public website to encourage debate," Buchheit said. "We deliberately limited our focus to *how* it might be done and did not volunteer a public view on *whether* it should be done (which would have involved issues such as contagion, effect on the banking sector and so forth). The paper got tens of thousands of hits and downloads."

There, in cyberspace, it sat unused, for much longer than it should have been.

On May 13, four days after the board meeting on Greece, Strauss-Kahn called Panagiotis Roumeliotis, who represented Greece at the IMF as an alternate executive director, to his office. The two men had known each other since the 1970s, when both were studying at the University of Paris. According to Roumeliotis, the managing director urged him, in confidence, to convey to Athens the need for an early debt restructuring, perhaps by September, as well as a reduction in the interest rates that European governments were charging on their loans to Greece. On May 24, Roumeliotis met again with Strauss-Kahn, and the managing director reiterated his belief in the need for a restructuring. Strauss-Kahn confirmed Roumeliotis's account of their conversations.

This episode reflects well on Strauss-Kahn's perspicacity. It also raises one of the most troubling questions about the Greek rescue, because the fact is that in the months immediately after May 2010, no strenuous efforts were forthcoming to launch a process for reducing Greece's debt burden. Why not?

The IMF had good reasons to avoid risking a restructuring during the spring of that year. Substantial time would have been required, and failure by Athens to make the payments due to its creditors on May 19 might well have led to a "Lehman moment," given the lack of a firewall and other groundwork that would have been necessary for bondholders to accept losses. But suppose Strauss-Kahn had quietly told the IMF's Troika partners that very soon thereafter, the Fund would insist on a restructuring. He might have said that the Fund could simply not lend its good name and credibility to a plan with insufficiently high likelihood of leading to debt sustainability. He might have said that while Europe was free to do as it pleased with its own money, the IMF's loan would be contingent on a restructuring taking place later in 2010, so that Greece would get the relief it needed in a timely fashion and taxpayers would not end up assuming losses that banks ought to incur.

Such an approach would have required confronting Europe's high and mighty. It presumably would have also required overcoming resistance from the US government, which was still suffering from post-Lehman trauma. Although American officials were playing a much less dominant role in this crisis than they had in previous ones, the United States was still the IMF's single most powerful shareholder, and its officials were opposed to any debt restructuring in the absence of a strong firewall.

Most daunting of all would have been the face down with Trichet. As noted in the previous chapter, the ECB president was prone to umbrage when the subject of restructuring a euro-zone country was broached and he had declared himself loath to take the kinds of monetary policy steps that would have been needed to limit contagion. Without his cooperation, a Greek debt restructuring would put the global financial system in danger of reverting to the horrors of September 2008.

The poker play would have been one of the greatest in the history of the global economy: If the IMF had forged ahead with a Greek debt restructuring, how would Trichet have reacted? Would he have stood his ground, even at the cost of allowing his beloved currency union to break up? Or would he have grudgingly used every conceivable monetary policy instrument to pacify market alarm about the creditworthiness of other euro-zone countries? At this sort of poker, Trichet's mastery was unsurpassed. The stakes were much higher than a poker game, though, and he wasn't bluffing. Or was he? Wouldn't he have folded?

The IMF did not attempt this audacious step because — to carry the poker metaphor further — its managing director believed the Fund would only have gotten itself expelled from the card table. "We were just recovering, trying to re-establish our role in the global system," Strauss-Kahn said in response to my question about this imaginary showdown. "I couldn't accept the idea, which would have been lethal to the IMF, that the Europeans would handle the crisis by themselves. I could play this game a little. But I couldn't go too far."

Strauss-Kahn's grasp of *realpolitik* is hard to refute, no matter how lamentable that *realpolitik* might be. It might seem right and proper that an institution representing the international community, and providing a global public good, could insist on preserving its credibility in circumstances such as the ones above. It might seem right and proper that the IMF could demand fair and sensible burden-sharing for an individual member country seeking its assistance. It might seem right and proper that the IMF, having overridden the objections of proud Asian mandarins and strongmen to its policy prescriptions, could do the same with powerful European policy makers who needed international help in saving their dysfunctional currency union. But the world in which Strauss-Kahn was operating did not work that way.

A comfortable alternative to confrontation was available. The IMF could allow the program in Greece to start running its course, banking on the hope that the Greeks would deliver on their promises to the Troika, confidence would return and growth would surprise on the upside. Debt restructuring could be put off for at least a while, and when the inevitability of some sort of restructuring became evident, perhaps the cost of delay would be manageable.

For a while after May 2010, this approach showed some promise. But other events soon intervened. For reasons completely different from those at work in Greece, the crisis was about to claim another victim.

8

CHASTITY AND CONTINENCE, BUT NOT YET

If only Greece would get its political act together, and swallow the necessary economic medicine, it could regain the favour of financial markets and recover from crisis. This was the message from Europe's most austerity-minded leaders in the spring of 2010. After all, the Greeks could just follow the splendid example of another country — Ireland — that had embarked on a tough-minded budget-cutting program, and was enjoying relatively low interest rates compared with the yields on Greek bonds. Impressed by Ireland's exemplification of fiscal virtue, and seeing it as an admirable counterpoint to Greece's profligacy, the European establishment showered Dublin with hosannas.

"Greece has a role model, and that role model is Ireland," Jean-Claude Trichet declared in late March. "Ireland had extremely difficult problems and took them very seriously — and that's now been recognized by all."[1]

At the time the ECB president uttered those words, Ireland was less than seven months from becoming the second euro-zone country to undergo a Troika rescue. Although Ireland's economy would not contract nearly as sharply as Greece's did, the events of late 2010 would be an ugly comedown for a country that only a few years earlier was basking in its "Celtic Tiger" era, when GDP per capita rose to almost the highest in Western Europe.

---

1 Liam Halligan, 2010, "Rebounding Celtic tiger offers UK harsh lessons in demolishing debt," *The Telegraph*, April 3.

No matter how disciplined its fiscal policy, Dublin was bedevilled by a problem — a banking system full of rotten loans — that did not lend itself to the same sort of cure that had been administered to Athens. Starting in the early years of the twenty-first century, Irish banks had gone on a property-lending binge, making heavy use of funds from abroad, and by 2010, a collapse in real estate was well under way, leaving large tracts of land all over the country covered by half-finished developments with nobody to pay for them. To top it all off, the Irish government had guaranteed the banking system's obligations during the depths of the global financial crisis — and an enormous bill was coming due.

In the process, many financiers were amassing billions of euros in profits, backed by the Irish state, that they deserved to lose. As we shall see in this chapter and the one that follows, the IMF would make commendable efforts in late 2010, when the country's crisis erupted, to effectuate a fairer outcome for the Irish people, only to find itself thwarted — an embittering manifestation of its standing in the Troika.

The Fund also deserves credit for doing a better job than European institutions of recognizing Ireland's weaknesses in the spring of 2010. A few days after the Greek bailout in May, Patrick Honohan, the governor of the Central Bank of Ireland, was at London's Heathrow Airport when he received a call on his mobile phone from the IMF in Washington. According to Honohan, the caller — Ashoka Mody, the Fund's mission chief for Ireland — had an unexpected proposition: would the Irish authorities consider fortifying their country against a severe crisis by seeking one of the IMF's new "precautionary" loans?

Mody's proposal went nowhere; the Irish Finance Ministry rejected it. Still, as Honohan wrote later in an essay, the episode shows that "Only the IMF clearly appreciated the risks at this stage."[2]

The IMF had not always been so farsighted regarding Ireland as it was in the spring of 2010. During the Celtic Tiger's heyday, the Fund was

2 Patrick Honahan, 2014, "Brian Lenihan and the Nation's Finances," in *Brian Lenihan: In Calm and Crisis,* edited by Brian Murphy, Mary O'Rourke and Noel Whelan, Sallins, Ireland: Merrion Press.

overly enthralled with the Irish economy's dynamism. Some of the wording in the Fund's pre-crisis surveillance of the country deserves a special place in the vast archive of laughably complacent official appraisals that have come to light since 2008.

To understand the fate that befell the Irish economy, a brief history of one bank in particular neatly encapsulates the country's rise and fall. This bank's seamy saga also helps account for the sense of injustice that arose in many quarters over what happened when Ireland found itself in the not-so-tender clutches of the Troika. The name of this bank, Anglo Irish, is today cursed throughout the Emerald Isle.

When 32-year-old Sean FitzPatrick was named general manager of Anglo Irish Bank in 1980, the bank had just four employees, and Ireland was one of Europe's poorest countries, suffering from high unemployment and emigration. For most of the first decade and a half thereafter, the bank specialized in modest loans to pubs, restaurants, hotels and warehouses. But FitzPatrick was a master at networking and inspiring his troops, and in the mid-1990s, when Ireland's property market began to flourish, Anglo Irish surged ahead of its much bigger rivals in furnishing credit. From 1994 to 1999 its loans swelled nearly sixfold, to €5.7 billion, as FitzPatrick's lending officers aggressively sought business with developers who were racing to keep pace with demand for new homes and apartment buildings.[3]

3 Much of the information about Anglo Irish in this section is derived from Simon Carswell, 2011, *Anglo Republic: Inside the Bank That Broke Ireland,* Dublin: Penguin Ireland. Much of the other information about the Irish crisis and its background comes from Matt Cooper, 2011, *How Ireland Really Went Bust,* London: Penguin Books; also Irwin, *The Alchemists* (see footnote 13 in chapter 3); Bastasin, *Saving Europe* (see footnote 15 in chapter 5); Barry Eichengreen, 2015, *Hall of Mirrors,* Oxford University Press; John Peet and Anton La Guardia, 2014, *Unhappy Union: How the euro crisis — and Europe — can be fixed,* London: Profile Books Ltd.; Martin Sandbu, 2015, *Europe's Orphan: The Future of the Euro and the Politics of Debt,* Princeton, NJ: Princeton University Press; and Michael Lewis, 2011, "When Irish Eyes Are Crying," *Vanity Fair,* March.

The run-up in real estate stemmed at that time from fundamental economic factors. Ireland was transforming itself from Europe's sick man to an export-based powerhouse where multinationals such as Dell, Intel and Merck were drawn by low corporate tax rates and a skilled labour force of English speakers willing to work at competitive wages. Falling unemployment and rising incomes helped spur purchases of homes, and an even bigger factor was a sharp decline in interest rates that accompanied Ireland's entry into the newly created euro zone in January 1999. Just as in Greece, Irish borrowers — including homebuyers — enjoyed the interest rate advantages that came from being able to tap vast pools of European capital without risk of currency movements. In stark contrast to Greece, though, the Celtic Tiger boasted a high degree of competitiveness.

As tales of bidding wars and property-flipping fortunes spread, bubble psychology began to play an increasingly important role in driving real-estate prices upward starting around 2002, and under FitzPatrick's continued incitement, Anglo Irish maintained its status as the nation's most opportunistic bank, opening its credit spigots ever wider. Although Dublin's banking giants such as Allied Irish Bank and Bank of Ireland were exploiting the boom too, they couldn't match Anglo Irish for the speed with which it disbursed loans to cash-hungry developers. These borrowers — many of whom were former bricklayers, plasterers or tilers — knew they might approach Anglo Irish on a Monday for a property-development loan of several million euros, and receive approval the following Friday, according to *Anglo Republic: Inside the Bank that Broke Ireland*, by Simon Carswell of *The Irish Times*. One former bank manager told Carswell that the Friday meetings of the bank's credit committee were "a cross between a Nuremberg rally and the half-time talk to an American football team....No one was going to dissent in that atmosphere." Even when the bank's top officers began to worry in 2005 that their exposure to land and development should be cut back, they found it impossible to stop lending more amid the fevered ascension in property prices, which in 2006 reached more than 3.5 times the 1997 level. Part of the problem was the lack of checks and balances; during a two-year period when the bank's lending more than doubled, nobody on the board was given responsibility for overseeing risk. By 2007, the loan book of this once-tiny bank stood at

€68.7 billion. That year, the total GDP of Ireland, a land of 4.6 million people, was €190 billion — it too had grown impressively, by an average 5.6 percent per year since 2002 — but it was now dwarfed by the amount of credit extended by the country's banks. The biggest bank, Allied Irish, had launched a determined effort in 2004 to fight back against Anglo Irish by going on a property-lending spree of its own.

To fund all of its lending, Anglo Irish could not rely solely on deposits from Irish savers, companies and pension funds. Instead, it borrowed significant sums elsewhere in Europe, mainly by selling bonds to European financial institutions that were eager for extra yield and saw Ireland's leading property lender as a lucrative bet. Again, raising money in this manner was all the easier because both creditor and debtor were using the same currency. By 2007, Anglo Irish had sold €23 billion of such bonds in Europe; its rivals had also raised extensive amounts from abroad.

All the while, the IMF was essentially cheering Ireland on. Article IV reports were especially enthusiastic about the budget surpluses that the government recorded every year from 2003 to 2008, and the low level of total government debt, which fell to 25 percent of GDP in 2007. This fiscal rectitude turned out to be a chimera of sorts — not because of any Greek-style accounting trickery, but because roughly one-third of government tax revenue depended on the thriving property and construction sectors. The Fund was not oblivious to the implications of developments in the housing market; as early as 2003, the Article IV report included substantial analysis on the question of whether a bubble was in the making. The conclusion, after much "on the one hand, on the other hand" examination of the evidence: "[T]here is a substantial risk that house prices could be overvalued."[4]

Most dismally wide of the mark was a report produced by a mission that went to Dublin in the summer of 2006. This mission was an FSAP, which stands for Financial Sector Assessment Program. Started in 1999 in the wake of the Asian crisis, FSAP missions are separate from

4 IMF, 2003, "Ireland: 2003 Article IV Consultation—Staff Report," Country Report No. 03/242, August, www.imf.org/external/pubs/ft/scr/2003/cr03242.pdf.

the annual Article IV checkups; they take place every five years or so, and in the words of the IMF's website, they provide "a comprehensive and in-depth analysis of a country's financial sector," with the Fund's focus being "to gauge the [financial system's] stability." The program was aimed chiefly at emerging markets, because of widespread concern that countries in the developing world would remain susceptible to more crises if they did not strengthen banking regulation and clean up their systems for allocating capital. But most advanced countries dutifully agreed to receive FSAP missions — Ireland was one of the first, in 2000 — the hope being that doing so would set a good example for emerging markets, where all the serious problems were assumed to be festering.

Ireland's banking sector was in fine fettle, according to the report of the 2006 FSAP mission. "There are concerns that house prices are now becoming overvalued," the report acknowledged, citing the average 10 percent annual appreciation in Irish real-estate prices since 2000, which substantially outstripped growth in household income. Even so, "the financial system seems well placed to absorb the impact of a downturn in either house prices or growth more generally," the report said. "The results of stress tests confirm that the major domestic lending institutions have adequate capital buffers to cover a range of large but plausible hypothetical shocks." Although the report offered a few suggestions for improving Ireland's regulatory and supervisory framework, the mission gave the regulators high marks, and added: "financial institutions have improved their own risk management practices, so that the financial system as a whole is better placed to identify and manage risks."[5]

Other IMF reports included finger wagging about the need to keep fiscal policy as tight as possible in case a housing downturn deprived Dublin's coffers of revenue, and they also contained cautionary passages about the banking sector's exposure to property. But taking comfort from the 2006 FSAP, the IMF's bottom-line conclusion in its

5 IMF, 2003, "Ireland: Financial System Stability Assessment Update," Country Report No. 06/292, August, www.imf.org/external/pubs/ft/scr/2003/cr03242.pdf.

2007 Article IV, published in September of that year, was the following: "Economic performance remains very strong, supported by sound policies."[6]

Within months of that report, the economy was headed into a deep, three-year-long recession, as a cooling of the housing market in 2007 became a vertiginous slide in 2008 — and Anglo Irish was again on the cutting-edge of the trend. Recognizing the bank as an Irish version of America's go-go subprime-mortgage lenders, investors began taking a cynical view toward the quality of the bank's balance sheet as well as its ability to raise funds. In the spring of 2008, when major tremors on Wall Street caused global credit markets to seize up, Anglo Irish suffered severe outflows of deposits because of fears that losses on its property loans would bleed the bank dry. That was just a warm-up, though, for the Lehman shock of September 15, which put Anglo and other Irish banks in their most precarious situation yet. Having suddenly lost access to the foreign funds on which they had grown heavily dependent, Irish banks underwent a twenty-first-century bank run, as depositors — instead of thronging in person at the bank's front doors — used computer keystrokes and mouse clicks to move their money to safety. Large companies and financial institutions that had placed deposits in the €50 million to €200 million range into Anglo began withdrawing them en masse in the second half of September. Within two weeks, so much cash had been drained from Anglo that the bank was within hours of following Lehman into bankruptcy.

Late into the night of September 29, one of the most chaotic days of the post-Lehman period, Brian Cowen, the Taoiseach (Irish prime minister), met with top members of his cabinet and took a fateful step that had not been adopted by any other country during the great crisis. Terrified of the implications for the rest of the country's banking system if Anglo Irish went under, the Irish government issued a blanket guarantee, valid for two years, of nearly all the liabilities in six major financial institutions, including Anglo Irish — some €440 billion worth, all told. This approach, modelled on a successful bank

6 IMF, 2007, "Ireland: 2007 Article IV Consultation—Staff Report," Country Report No. 07/325, September, www.imf.org/external/pubs/ft/scr/2007/cr07325.pdf.

rescue launched by Sweden in the early 1990s, meant that if these banks couldn't pay the amounts that they owed at any time in the subsequent two years, the state would pick up the tab. For a country with a GDP less than half the amount of the sum guaranteed, Ireland was taking a monumental roll of the dice, and the guarantee went much further than was customary in a bank failure, by covering not only deposits but also other liabilities as well. Depositors, especially small ones, reasonably expect to be protected against loss, because they can pull their money out of the bank on demand and their confidence is essential to the functioning of the system. But Dublin's guarantee, although designed to halt an outflow of funds, also covered claimants who could not withdraw their money right away — namely the bondholders, many of them large European institutions, which Anglo Irish and its rivals had tapped to fatten their balance sheets. These kinds of creditors are presumed capable of understanding the risk they have taken, so in a failure they normally lose their investments or undergo conversion of their holdings into stock.[7]

Brian Lenihan, the finance minister, defended this decision as necessary under Irish law, and his confidence in the righteousness of the blanket guarantee grew as the panic withdrawals from the nation's banks subsided, as if by magic. He declared that Ireland was getting off cheaply compared with other countries, where governments were pouring vast emergency investments of taxpayers' money into banks to boost the capital levels necessary for prudent operation and, in some cases, taking full state control. Lenihan's boast might have been valid so long as the losses on Irish bank loans were modest enough to avoid triggering the guarantee, but that calculation would eventually prove to be colossally incorrect. In fairness to Lenihan and his colleagues, they might have drawn a different conclusion if they had been aware of laughter-and-joke-filled phone conversations among Anglo Irish executives indicating that the bank was lying about the extent of its troubles in the days before the issuance of the guarantee. In one of these conversations, tapes of which came to light five years later, one

7 Some of those present at the meetings that night had qualms and preferred less sweeping solutions, according to testimony later given in an Irish parliamentary inquiry, but they were overruled.

senior executive explained how he calculated the figure of €7 billion the bank was telling government officials it needed: "Picked it out of my arse."[8]

The truth began to unfold within months: Irish banks were not merely illiquid, they were insolvent, and Anglo Irish was the most insolvent of all. Deepening losses on Anglo Irish's books — and a series of scandals involving loans the bank had made to FitzPatrick and other top executives — forced the Cowen government to nationalize the bank. In April 2009, Dublin also established a state-owned "bad bank," called the National Asset Management Agency, to acquire toxic assets from the banks in the hope that, free of doubt about their balance sheets, they could restore their health. But property prices continued to spiral downward, compelling the government to keep raising its estimate of the cost taxpayers would have to bear. Meanwhile the Irish state budget went deeper and deeper into the red, as tax revenues — no longer bloated by real estate and construction activity — shrank from €47.25 billion in 2007 to €33.1 billion in 2009.[9] The budget deficit swelled in 2009 to 14 percent of GDP, and although Dublin resolutely responded with spending cuts, fiscal probity would not suffice to spare the country from its fate. On May 22, 2010, a couple of weeks after the Greek rescue, Morgan Kelly, a professor at University College Dublin, shocked the Irish public (and infuriated the government) by prophesying in a newspaper column: "It is no longer a question of whether Ireland will go bust, but when."[10]

Incredibly, not a single Irish bank — not even Anglo Irish — "failed" when European banking regulators conducted a stress test in the summer of 2010 that, like the US authorities' 2009 test, was supposed to determine whether the region's banks had enough capital to cushion losses in a variety of different scenarios. The ostensibly heartening results in Ireland were matched elsewhere; of the 91 European banks

8 Paul Williams, 2014, "Inside Anglo: the secret recordings," *The Irish Independent*, June 24.

9 Cooper, *How Ireland Really Went Bust*, chapter 32 (see footnote 3 in this chapter).

10 Morgan Kelly, 2010, "Burden of Irish debt could yet eclipse that of Greece," *The Irish Times*, May 22.

tested, only seven were deemed to need additional capital, in an amount totalling €3.5 billion. The guffawing that greeted this outcome when it was announced on July 23 reflected the low esteem that private analysts held for Europe's financial regulatory system, with its profusion of national regulators bent on cosseting their banking champions. As was widely observed, the test was not very stressful, having ignored the possibility of losses on the vast bulk of sovereign bonds that European banks held. Events soon to materialize in Ireland would expose the ludicrousness of this exercise as a fair appraisal of European banks' capital adequacy.

By late summer, Irish banks were once again bleeding deposits, especially after a stunning estimate by Standard and Poor's (S&P) on August 25 that the banks' losses would lift the cost of the bailout to upward of €45 billion, with €35 billion of that attributable to Anglo Irish. The 2008 bank guarantee was nearing its two-year expiration, hastening the withdrawal of funds by investors who in any case were harbouring grave doubts about the soundness of the government behind the guarantee. Frozen out of private credit markets, Irish banks had no choice but to obtain cash from the ECB, which as lender of last resort for the euro area would provide unlimited loans of up to three months to banks, provided the banks posted eligible collateral. A blog post on September 2, 2010,by Simon Johnson, a former IMF chief economist, and his colleague, Peter Boone, declared Ireland "insolvent" based on its current trajectory. "The ultimate result of Ireland's bank bailout exercise is obvious," they wrote. "One way or another, the government will have converted the liabilities of private banks into debts of the sovereign (that is, Irish taxpayers), yet the nation probably cannot afford those debts."[11]

11 Simon Johnson and Peter Boone, 2010, "In Ireland, Dangers Still Loom," *Economix* (blog), September 2, http://economix.blogs.nytimes.com/2010/09/02/in-ireland-dangers-still-loom/?_r=0.

On September 30, dubbed "Black Thursday" by the Irish commentariat, Lenihan appeared before the media for yet another confession that the numbers were worse than previously acknowledged. The Irish finance minister had ample grounds for feeling depressed. He had been diagnosed in late 2009 with inoperable pancreatic cancer; he was continuing at his job despite knowing that he stood a scant chance of living for very long. Now he had to admit that the cost to the government of Anglo's losses would indeed be on the order of magnitude specified by S&P — it would be somewhere between €29 billion and €34 billion. And he announced additional news that, to use the Irish vernacular, was even more gobsmacking: mainly because of the rising bank-bailout cost, Ireland's budget deficit for 2010 would be 32 percent of GDP. This would be just a temporary spike in the gap between outlays and revenue, the finance minister hastened to add. But it underscored the reasoning behind the parallels between Ireland and Greece: Ireland's debt-to-GDP ratio, which as noted above had been just 25 percent in 2007, was now officially projected at 98.6 percent at the end of 2010, both because of the bank bailout and plummeting government tax revenue.

The IMF was gearing up for another Troika operation. At the 2010 annual meeting of the Fund and the World Bank in Washington in early October, Lenihan and some of his aides met with Mody and other IMF staffers responsible for Ireland to discuss what a rescue program might entail, although the finance minister was loath to request outside help at that point. According to an in-depth inquiry conducted years later by the Irish Parliament into the country's crisis,[12] Fund staffers raised a key question at these October meetings that would soon become one of Ireland's most explosive controversies: What should be done about the billions of euros worth of bonds that had been issued by Anglo Irish and other banks? Should the government continue making full payment on those bonds? Or should it haircut them — that is, reduce the amount paid to well below 100 cents on the euro?

12 This inquiry provided a wealth of testimony about what key figures were doing and saying during the crisis, and its contents, used extensively in the next chapter, are available at: https://inquiries.oireachtas.ie/banking/.

If ever a moral argument could be made for administering a haircut, these bonds were a canonical case. The investors, which included a number of French and German banks, had provided much of the financing that inflated Ireland's property bubble; the justification for their repayment under the 2008 guarantee had always been questionable, and the justification seemed downright flimsy now that the two-year guarantee had expired and Ireland was economically prostrate. Instead of continuing to use Irish taxpayers' money to ensure that these bondholders were paid in full, a haircut would help ease the nation's fiscal burden. Exactly how much that burden could be reduced depended on the level of seniority of the bonds included in the haircut, the health of the bank that had issued the bonds and how deep a haircut would be applied. Unfortunately, many of the bonds had already been paid off by October 2010, which reduced the amount of savings to be reaped. Investors in junior (subordinated) bonds, which had relatively weak legal claims to repayment, were definitely obliged to suffer losses, but nearly €20 billion in senior bonds were still outstanding and being fully serviced, including about €3.7 billion of Anglo Irish bonds. (Since Anglo Irish was no longer even trying to raise money in financial markets, its bonds were considered particularly vulnerable to being haircut.) Estimates of the potential savings ran between €3 billion to well over €10 billion — not a trivial percentage of Ireland's GDP, and enough to spare Irish citizens from a substantial portion of the inevitable increase in their tax bills and loss of public services.[13]

In testimony before the parliamentary inquiry in 2015, Alan Ahearne, an Irish academic economist who served as an adviser to Lenihan, recalled his October 2008 discussions in Washington as follows: "I met with a couple of IMF officials…they said, 'Is the minister aware that there's about €4 billion of Anglo bonds that are now unguaranteed, senior non-guaranteed?' I said he is aware of that….They said, 'It's a lot of money,' and I said, 'He's aware of that.'"[14]

13 Landon Thomas Jr., 2010, "In European Debt Crisis, Some Call Default Better Option," *The New York Times*, November 22.

14 Ahearne's testimony is available at https://inquiries.oireachtas.ie/banking/hearings/alan-ahearne-early-warnings-divergent-contrarian-views/.

Indeed, Lenihan and his colleagues in the government were facing a mounting outcry to "burn the bondholders," based on the increasingly clear perception of how poor a deal the 2008 guarantee had been. Although the finance minister was giving the idea considerable thought, according to Ahearne, he was reluctant to act, mainly because of the possible impact on the willingness of investors to buy Irish government bonds. The Irish government was still raising money in financial markets, at increasingly high interest rates, and Lenihan did not want the interest cost to rise further, lest the expense outweigh whatever savings might be obtained by bondholder burning.

Meanwhile, even as the IMF was actively pondering the contours of an Irish program, it was blindsided by developments at the highest levels in Europe.

Whenever the IMF provides a rescue loan, the country being bailed out formally promises to inform the Fund, and seek its advice, before taking any major economic policy initiatives. Logic dictates as much. Having put the resources of the international community at the disposal of a country's authorities, the Fund legitimately expects to receive prior notice of actions that may materially affect the country's economic fortunes. The programs for Greece, for example, as well as Hungary and other Eastern European countries, included boilerplate language in which the governments pledged to "consult with the Fund before...adopting new measures that would deviate from the goals of the program."

A similar arrangement with the euro area would have made considerable sense. The IMF was playing a key role in saving the euro, so European policy makers might have felt obliged to ask the Fund's opinion in advance of any big steps that could affect confidence in the common currency. But no such understanding existed, either formally or informally. The euro zone wasn't party to an IMF program, and the continent's leaders weren't in the habit of submitting their decisions to international institutions for approval or even informational purposes.

Just how far key European leaders were willing to go without bothering to notify the IMF became jarringly clear on October 18, 2010, when Fund officials learned to their stupefaction of a "Franco-German Declaration" agreed by Sarkozy and Merkel at the seaside resort of Deauville, France.[15] Under the accord, which the French president and German chancellor had drafted after a walk on the beach, future rescues of euro-zone countries would include "adequate participation of private creditors" — that is, some sort of restructuring of debt. But this new requirement would not take effect immediately; it would apply only to rescues starting in 2013. Although the declaration had no legal force, it appeared certain to be implemented in some form, given its sponsorship.

The impetus behind the initiative was mounting discontent in Germany over the sweet deal that banks and investors were getting under the program for Greece. The moral hazard inherent in giving Greece's lenders a full bailout, with no haircut, offended German sensibilities to the point of righteous anger, and members of Merkel's shaky ruling coalition were agitating for rules that would prevent the same from happening again. This instinct was understandable, even praiseworthy. But to win French support, Merkel offered Sarkozy concessions on fiscal issues that he cared about — and somehow, in the process of Franco-German haggling, a proposed rule had emerged in Deauville that was nonsensical both in its rigidity and delayed implementation. IMF economists were hardly alone in their disbelief and dismay; other European governments had also been taken by surprise, and Trichet was beside himself, berating high-ranking French and German finance ministry officials attending a meeting in Luxembourg that day. Investors unloaded bonds of countries — Greece, Ireland and Portugal in particular — to which the rule might apply.

One big problem with the Deauville declaration, which drove markets into their tizzy, was that it evidently envisioned debt restructurings in all rescues, which made no more sense than ruling restructurings out. As for waiting until 2013, that was a worst-of-both-worlds compromise.

15 "Franco-German Declaration," www.eu.dk/~/media/files/eu/franco_german_declaration.ashx.

It scared investors into concluding that haircuts were in store for their bond holdings eventually, while seemingly increasing the possibility that any rescues in the near future would be guaranteed haircut-free. This was akin to fashioning financial policy around St. Augustine's prayer, "Grant me chastity and continence, but not yet."

Merkel staunchly defended the deal's underlying rationale: "We cannot keep constantly explaining to our voters and our citizens why the taxpayer should bear the cost of certain risks and not those people who have earned a lot of money from taking those risks."[16] But the uproar in the markets, as well as pressure from Trichet and other policy makers, obliged her to backpedal in subsequent declarations issued by European leaders. The new approach would not apply to bonds issued for the next three years; it would come into effect only with the inauguration in mid-2013 of the permanent firewall institution, the ESM, which was to replace the temporary EFSF. Moreover, haircuts would be in order only for the bonds of countries that were clearly insolvent.

Deauville was a watershed event, which made the crisis more difficult to manage. Exactly what kind of watershed, however, remains a subject of debate. By some reckonings, the official endorsement of haircuts, regardless of how carefully it was hedged, poisoned market sentiment permanently by signalling that Europe was more tolerant of default than had been previously assumed. According to this perspective on events, the chances for a gradual return to normalcy in Europe had been increasing over the summer, with spreads narrowing between yields on the vulnerable countries' bonds and those on German bonds. The ECB's bond buying had produced a salutary effect, as had the agreement in May to establish a substantial government-backed firewall; the Luxembourg-based EFSF was prepared to mobilize hundreds of billions of euros in emergency aid for any euro area country that might need it. Moreover, the Greeks were showing early signs of compliance with their program. In early August, a Troika mission to Athens had given a solid "thumbs-up" to a quarterly disbursement

16 Peter Spiegel and David Oakley, 2010, "Irish contagion hits wider eurozone," *Financial Times*, November 11.

of funds, saying Greece was off to a "strong start."[17] Talk of haircuts was therefore gratuitous and incendiary — and a terrible disservice to Greece and Ireland, which lost whatever chance they had to regain the confidence of investors.

This school of thought about Deauville took intellectual succor from an IMF "staff position paper" that had been released six weeks before Merkel and Sarkozy's walk on the beach.[18] Co-authored by Carlo Cottarelli, the head of the Fund's Fiscal Affairs Department, the paper was titled "Default in Today's Advanced Economies: Unnecessary, Undesirable, and Unlikely." It presented rebuttals to arguments made by analysts who were inclined toward haircuts for Greece and other euro-zone debtors, noting for instance that a number of countries in the past three decades had undergone painful deficit-cutting exercises of magnitudes not that dissimilar to what the Greek rescue required. In a briefing with reporters about that paper and two others, Cottarelli carefully pointed out that "these views...do not reflect the view of the institution. These are the views of the staff who wrote the papers."[19] That was true; Strauss-Kahn neither solicited nor encouraged the paper's publication, and many Fund staffers vehemently disagreed with the analysis. Still, the paper drew considerable public attention.

There is another way of viewing Deauville, not as an event that made haircuts more likely, but as one that made them harder to achieve even when advisable. The declaration's impact on markets was undeniable, but only temporary, and it should hardly be considered a game-changer for Greece or Ireland, whose bond yields were already well above pre-

17 IMF, 2010, "Statement by the EC, ECB, and IMF on the First Review Mission to Greece," Press Release No. 10/308, August 5, www.imf.org/external/np/sec/pr/2010/pr10308.htm.

18 Carlo Cottarelli, Lorenzo Forni, Jan Gottschalk and Paolo Mauro, 2010, "Default in Today's Advanced Economies: Unnecessary, Undesirable, and Unlikely," IMF Staff Position Note 10/12, September 1, www.imf.org/external/pubs/ft/spn/2010/spn1012.pdf.

19 IMF, 2010, "Transcript of a Conference Call on Release of IMF Staff Position Notes on Fiscal Matters," September 1, www.imf.org/external/np/tr/2010/tr090110.htm.

crisis levels.[20] In Ireland's case, the writing on the wall had appeared weeks before Deauville, when Anglo Irish was recognized as an even bigger drain on the government than anyone had imagined, and the cost of the overall bank bailout began to swell far beyond the country's means. Indeed, Deauville's most important upshot was arguably to dampen prospects for haircuts in 2010 or 2011, because policy makers like Merkel had to stress the "not until 2013" aspect of her declaration with Sarkozy.

How the crisis might have unfolded in the absence of Deauville will never be known. Whatever impact it had, the Franco-German declaration would not be the last time that European policy makers would catch the IMF unawares. And one other point can be made with certainty: regardless of what Merkel and Sarkozy said in Deauville, their doughty rhetoric about "adequate participation of private creditors" would ring hollow in the rescue of Ireland. Those European financiers who had bought senior bonds of Anglo Irish and its ilk were going to get off scot-free.

20 Ashoka Mody, 2014, "The ghost of Deauville," VOX, January 7, www.voxeu.org/article/ghost-deauville.

9

OFFERS THAT IRELAND COULDN'T REFUSE

When the G20 met for its annual summit on November 11-12, 2010, Irish ears were burning. No Irish officials attended the summit, which took place in the South Korean capital of Seoul, on the other side of the world from Ireland. But policy makers in Dublin were aware, in part because of questions they were getting from reporters, that their country's crisis was one of several major topics of discussion in Seoul. Speculation was mounting that Ireland must soon seek an international rescue, an opinion heartily shared by one of the most influential attendees at the summit — Dominique Strauss-Kahn.

With Irish housing prices down about 36 percent from their peak, the losses of the nation's banks were continuing to mushroom, leading depositors to withdraw their money at an ever-faster clip, and financial markets were driving the yield on Irish government 10-year bonds close to nine percent, not far behind the 11 percent yield on comparable Greek bonds. Members of the Cowen cabinet, who perceived submission to the Troika as a national humiliation that would destroy the political fortunes of their governing coalition, were continuing to deny that Ireland needed outside help. The government held enough cash to cover all state obligations coming due until the middle of the following year, Irish officials repeatedly noted.

In deference to Dublin's sensitivities, Strauss-Kahn took a hands-off stance in public, telling reporters during a stop in Japan: "So far I haven't received any kind of request. I think they can manage well. If at one point in time, tomorrow, in two months or two years, the Irish want support from the IMF, we will be ready."[1] But in a private meeting with top G20 policy makers in Seoul, the IMF managing director struck a different note, reflecting Fund dogma that countries are better off obtaining financial assistance before desperation forces their hand. According to an attendee, Strauss-Kahn told the group he had seen a survey of bank economists showing that 60 percent believed Ireland needed a rescue program — a result, he said, implying that "40 percent of bank economists ought to be fired."

Pressure on the Irish from European policy makers was unrelenting in the days thereafter, in the form of phone calls, emails and face-to-face meetings. On November 16, when Lenihan arrived at a finance ministers' meeting in Brussels, he was appalled by the bluntness of Germany's Schäuble, who essentially demanded that Lenihan announce to the media after the meeting that Dublin was requesting a Troika program. Explaining Schäuble's position, his deputy, Jörg Asmussen, later recalled: "It was made very clear to the Irish finance minister that it is not just about Ireland — it was made very clear that... the functioning of the currency union was at stake."[2]

The urgency was valid. Whereas Greece required financial assistance because its government might otherwise default on a debt payment, Ireland's need stemmed from the risk of cascading bank runs. Between September and November 2010, roughly €60 billion had left the country, both in the form of withdrawals of cash by bank depositors and refusals by foreign financial institutions to continue lending to Irish banks. In their scramble to assure they had enough cash to fulfill demands, the banks were borrowing massive amounts in emergency loans from the ECB, which had legitimate grounds to wonder whether it was providing

1 Kathleen Chu, 2010, "Strauss-Kahn Says IMF Can Help Ireland's 'Difficult' Situation," Bloomberg News, November 13.

2 Dan O'Brien, 2011, "The Bailout Boys Go to Dublin," BBC Radio 4, April 27, www.bbc.co.uk/programmes/b010mryv.

lender-of-last-resort assistance to banks that would prove incapable of repaying the money. A failure by one or more major Irish banks to meet their obligations could generate incalculable knock-on effects elsewhere, as depositors keeping money in other European countries with financially strapped governments might well conclude that their euros ought to be shifted immediately to safer locales. Foreign banks' exposure to Ireland heightened the potential for contagion; German and UK banks held €113 billion and €107 billion worth of Irish assets respectively, followed by US banks with €47 billion, French banks with €36 billion and Belgian banks with €24 billion.[3]

At the Brussels meeting, Lenihan indignantly rejected Schäuble's demand to announce a rescue request, noting that he lacked the authority to act without cabinet approval. But he agreed to a compromise: experts from the Troika institutions would be publicly invited to come to Dublin later that week to analyze the nation's banking system. Clinging to hopes of preserving sovereignty over budget and tax policy, the Irish government insisted that fiscal matters were not on the agenda; the banking analysis was the only purpose for the visits. The IMF promptly issued a statement: "At the request of the Irish authorities, an IMF team will participate in a short and focused consultation, together with the European Commission, and the ECB, in order to determine the best way to provide any necessary support to address market risks."[4]

Thus it was that Ajai Chopra, a deputy director in the IMF's European Department, found himself besieged by media crews on the morning of November 18 as he walked from his Dublin hotel to Ireland's central bank, passing three homeless panhandlers on the way — scenes that were instantly flashed around the world. At that point, top Irish leaders had nearly resigned themselves to the inevitable; the editorial in that day's *The Irish Times* captured the national mood: "Was it for this?" the

3 IMF, 2010, "Ireland: Request for an Extended Arrangement—Staff Report," Country Report No. 10/366, December 17, www.imf.org/external/pubs/cat/longres.aspx?sk=24510.0.

4 IMF, 2010, "IMF Statement on Ireland," Press Release No. 10/441, November 16, www.imf.org/external/np/sec/pr/2010/pr10441.htm.

paper asked, borrowing from a Yeats elegy to the martyrs of a failed Irish uprising. "Having obtained our political independence from Britain to be masters of our own affairs, we have now surrendered our sovereignty to the European Commission, the European Central Bank, and the International Monetary Fund."[5]

But with no formal request yet forthcoming from the government, Trichet took matters into his own hands, sending a confidential letter to Lenihan dated November 19. The ECB president's message: Dublin must apply to the Troika for a program, lest Irish banks lose access to emergency funding. This was the proverbial offer that Ireland could not refuse. Without the euros that banks needed to continue functioning, people would be unable to withdraw money or pay bills until a new currency was introduced — by which time the entire national economy would have imploded.

At Trichet's insistence, the content of his letter remained secret for years; even the IMF economists who worked on Ireland never saw it until the ECB finally released it under pressure in late 2014.[6] The letter began with the observation that the emergency cash infusions the ECB was giving to Irish banks had "risen significantly over the past few months to levels that we consider with great concern. Recent developments can only add to these concerns." (The letter didn't mention a figure, but according to Trichet's later estimate, the combined total that Irish banks had borrowed from the ECB and their other lender of last resort, Ireland's own central bank, was about €140 billion, representing 85 percent of the nation's GDP.) Lenders of last resort are supposed to lend without limit to cash-strapped banks when the loan is sure to be repaid, but not when repayment is questionable. Accordingly, Trichet continued, "[I]t is only if we receive in writing a commitment from the Irish Government...on the four following points that we can authorize further provisions of [emergency liquidity assistance] to Irish financial institutions." The first point was: "The Irish government shall send a

5 *The Irish Times,* 2010, "Was it for this?" November 18.

6 ECB, 2014, "Irish letters," November 6, www.ecb.europa.eu/press/html/irish-letters.en.html.

request for financial support to [euro-zone finance ministers]," and the second point was: "The request shall include the commitment to undertake decisive actions...in agreement with the European Commission, the International Monetary Fund and the ECB."

Trichet's letter "was not well received by us," as Cowen delicately put it later, because he and his cabinet were already on the verge of taking the required action by that point and didn't appreciate the additional bullying.[7] But the threat was taken seriously, and it would have a subsequent impact on the outcome of the program. Two days later, the government finally requested a full-fledged rescue, at which time official negotiations began — although in a somewhat disorganized fashion at first, as some negotiators had to sit with their laptops on the floor because of the lack of desks in government buildings.

It did not take long for the Irish media to catch wind of important differences within the Troika — in particular, the inclination of the IMF representatives to take positions that were less austerity-oriented, and more closely aligned with Irish interests, than those taken by the other two Troika partners. Chopra, who grew up in India and holds a Ph.D. from the University of Virginia, displayed a flair for speaking empathetically about Ireland's plight, which soon made him something of a celebrity in Dublin. "I'm not used to a situation where I've been so recognizable," he told the state broadcaster RTÉ. "People have come up to me — and called me by my first name as well — but they've done so in a very polite and very gracious way and they've always wished me the best." Anguished as the Irish were by scenes of Troika officials marching into government ministries, their resentment was tempered by the recognition that the original sinners were their own bankers, developers and politicians. Chopra later recalled with amusement seeing a tabloid newspaper headline — "Indians Take Over From Cowboys" — which was accompanied by a photo showing him walking down the street with Ashoka Mody, who shares Chopra's nationality.

7 The remark was one that Cowen made in his testimony to the Irish parliamentary inquiry, available at: https://inquiries.oireachtas.ie/banking/hearings/brian-cowen-regarding-his-role-as-former-taoiseach/.

(Mody, the mission's no. 2 official at that point, had ceded the title of mission chief because of his lack of program experience.) "No prizes for guessing who the cowboys were!" Chopra said.[8]

As in Greece, the Fund favoured a gradual tightening of budget and tax policy, based on the belief that curbing spending power too quickly would only make it harder for Ireland's already depressed economy to recover and generate the revenue the government needed to restore its fiscal health. This view was not shared by the discipline-minded ECB, which wanted the budget deficit cut by €8 billion in the program's first year — nearly twice as much as Chopra and his colleagues deemed advisable. The Irish Department of Finance itself, though, had prepared an austere budget in advance; its officials were willing to accept a €6 billion cut for 2011, and the Fund team acquiesced, aware that it could offer no precise estimates about the economic impact of such measures.

A second issue on which the IMF was correctly perceived as being on Ireland's side was that of the interest rates on rescue loans — although here, in another reprise of Greece, there was no argument within the Troika, but rather two separate approaches on two technically separate loans. In accord with its established formula for loans of this type to member countries, the IMF would charge about 3.34 percent, whereas European rescuers would charge about 5.8 percent. The theory behind the much higher European interest rate, as in Greece, was that "you didn't want to reward a country that ended up in a program," as Marco Buti, the top economic official at the European Commission, later explained.[9] This reasoning was absurd; no rational government tries to "reward" itself by getting into a situation like Ireland's in the hope of borrowing at low interest rates, and European policy makers would later recognize the mistake of extracting high interest payments from

8 Chopra's recollection came in an interview that was published on the IMF's intranet (internal website) when he was leaving the IMF ("Ajai Chopra Reflects on Lessons Learned and Life after the Fund," November 5, 2013.)

9 Buti's explanation, which did not indicate that he agreed with the reasoning involved, came in his testimony to the Irish parliamentary inquiry, available at: https://inquiries.oireachtas.ie/banking/hearings/marco-buti-european-commission/.

a country that was under tremendous financial strain. But northern European governments, keenly cognizant of the no-bailout rule, were anxious to avoid any hint of providing subsidized aid.

One issue above all set the IMF Indians apart from the others in the Troika — and the whole manner in which it arose indicated to Irish officials that among their rescuers it was an extremely sensitive, almost taboo, subject.

During a dinner break at around 8:00 p.m. on November 18, the first day of meetings between Irish and Troika policy makers in Dublin, the IMF's Mody presented a new idea as everyone was lining up for sandwiches. The fact that he was speaking at that point was a tacit acknowledgement that his comments were technically separate from the official discussions that had taken place earlier. To the evident discomfort of some of the Troika representatives in the room, Mody asked about the possibility of haircutting the senior bonds that had been issued by Anglo Irish and other banks.

Up until then, Lenihan was continuing to reject political pressure to "burn" the bondholders. Standing by his public defence of the government's initial guarantee, the finance minister had been vigorously contending that honouring the senior bondholders' claims was a legal obligation of the state, and that breaching it would come at dear cost to Dublin's credit standing. But Ireland had abandoned efforts to raise money in financial markets — that was the rationale for calling in the Troika — and if the Troika were to encourage the Irish authorities to impose a haircut, that would be a different matter entirely. "We were very excited by this," Honohan, the central bank governor, recalled in his 2015 testimony at the parliamentary inquiry. "There was a unanimous view on the Irish side that this was a great opportunity.…the reputation risk of burning bondholders would be greatly diminished if it was at the behest of the IMF."[10]

10 Honahan's testimony to the inquiry, available at: https://inquiries.oireachtas.ie/banking/hearings/patrick-honohan-governor-central-bank-of-ireland/.

But there was a fly in the ointment. "The team from the [European] Commission and the team from the ECB were saying, 'This is off the agenda, we're not talking about it,'" Honohan said.

Predictably, Trichet's opposition was no less adamant than it was to a haircut for Greek debt. The ECB president's reasoning was similar to the stance he had taken in the Greek case: he feared a market panic. A haircut on the senior bonds of an Irish bank, he believed, would lead investors to question the security of similar bonds issued by other banks in Europe, threatening the survival of some of the region's biggest banks that had large exposures to such risk. Chopra and Mody disagreed, with backing from colleagues in Washington. They believed the contagion could be contained, especially if the only bonds affected were those of banks like Anglo Irish, which was due for closure as soon as it could be wound down and could thus be seen as an exceptional case, with no implications for healthy banks elsewhere. The IMF staffers quietly encouraged Irish officials to take the necessary legal steps for senior bondholders to "share the burden" with taxpayers (to use the euphemism favoured by Fund economists in situations such as this.)

"The IMF was not just saying…that they were in favour of [imposing a haircut on these bondholders]…in some ways they were saying, 'We might even make it a requirement [for a rescue],'" recalled Kevin Cardiff, who was the senior civil servant responsible for banking issues in the Finance Ministry. "They said, 'Look, we've talked to Dominique Strauss-Kahn. He thinks that he can get the other parties, the big European and American governments over the line. He thinks he can persuade them that this is a good thing to do.'"[11]

Looking back on this debate at an Oxford seminar in March 2015, about a year after he retired from the IMF, Chopra explained his position as follows:

11 Cardiff's testimony to the parliamentary inquiry, available at: https://inquiries.oireachtas.ie/banking/hearings/kevin-cardiff-former-secretary-general-department-of-finance-resumed/.

> The reason we were in favor [of imposing haircuts]—most fundamentally it just reduces the cost the public sector has to bear. It reduces moral hazard. It's more equitable.
>
> The European partners were dead against, especially the ECB. The Commission was initially on the fence, but they quickly joined the ECB....We thought the reasons given by the Europeans were exaggerated. Yes, there would have been spillovers. But if you looked at spreads on the senior debt at the time—they already suggested that the market was expecting...haircuts on this. It would not have been so much of a disaster. [And] the ECB could have stepped in, and said, "Look...we'll give liquidity support." That's what a central bank is for, to deal with these sorts of spillovers....And why should the Irish taxpayer cover the cost of bearing these spillover concerns in the rest of the euro area?[12]

The ECB, for its part, posted an explanation of its stance on its website, which said:

> One has to bear in mind the situation at the time, as well as the counterfactual scenario....[haircuts on senior bondholders] would first and foremost have had negative spillover effects on the financial stability of Ireland, as well as on other European countries.
>
> [Moreover], one fact that is often overlooked in commentaries is that there was a substantial bail-in of subordinated debt issued by the Irish banks. Over the period 2009–2011, the total cash gained from the burden-sharing of subordinated debt was just under €14 billion.[13]

12 Ajai Chopra, 2015, "Lessons from Ireland's financial crisis," presentation at Oxford University, March 10, www.youtube.com/watch?v=6XDomfai7DY&feature=youtube.

13 ECB, "Irish letters" (see footnote 6 in this chapter).

Who was right? Would a major reduction in the amounts the Irish government paid to the senior bondholders have sparked a fresh market conflagration? The answer is unknowable because it was not tried. In a meeting at the Department of Finance with Lenihan and the three Troika heads that went late into the evening of November 26, 2010, Klaus Masuch, the ECB representative, conveyed his boss's position that if the government failed to pay the bonds in full, there could be no Troika program — and given what Trichet had written in his letter the previous week, the implication was that the ECB would halt emergency lending to the banking system. Trichet's opinion, therefore, was not just one influential voice in the debate; his institution was providing Irish banks with life-sustaining transfusions of cash, without which Ireland's economy would be in an even greater fix than it already was. Although Chopra continued to take the position that the program could include a haircut, a crestfallen Lenihan concluded that he had no choice but to go along with the ECB.

In any event, on the day after the late-night meeting on November 26, word came from Washington that the IMF, as an institution, was unwilling to go to the mat on this issue either. This was because in a conference call of G7 finance ministers and central bank governors, Strauss-Kahn had encountered overwhelming opposition to imposing any haircuts on the senior bondholders, not only from Trichet and other European participants but from Tim Geithner. The US Treasury secretary shared Trichet's concerns about contagion, and like other Obama administration policy makers he remained deeply concerned about the danger that Europe's crisis posed to the still-fragile American recovery. He sympathized with the argument that the bondholders deserved a haircut, but contended that no such action should be taken before Europe had a much sturdier firewall than the one it had thus far erected.

"I was on the Cape [Cod] for Thanksgiving, and I remember doing a G7 call…in my little hotel room," Geithner told an interviewer for his book, *Stress Test*. "I said, 'If you guys do that [haircuts], all you will do is accelerate the run from Europe....until you have the ability to in effect protect or guarantee the rest of Europe from the ensuing contagion, this is just [a] metaphor for our fall of '08."[14]

Strauss-Kahn likewise recalled that Thanksgiving-weekend call: "We had a house in the forest for a couple of days with my kids, and I had a very bad phone connection," he told me. "Everybody was against me [on the haircut issue]. With Tim plus Trichet, at the end of the day, I was too weak. It was a real pity."

Irish officials heard from the Fund team in Dublin "that the programme would not go ahead if senior bondholder burden sharing was contemplated," according to Cardiff's recollection. "[T]he IMF negotiators despondently confirmed that this was now also the official position of the IMF."[15]

A hail of scorn thus greeted the Irish government when its agreement with the Troika was finalized on Sunday, November 28. Recalling that day in a radio interview shortly before his death the following year, Lenihan said: "I believed I had fought the good fight and taken every measure possible to delay such an eventuality. And now hell was at the gates."[16]

The package totalled €85 billion in loans, of which €22.5 billion would come from the IMF — about 2,300 percent of Ireland's quota — and €40 billion from the EFSF and European Commission. (The rest was from sources such as the UK government and Ireland's own national pension reserve.) The Irish banking system would undergo a drastic downsizing and thoroughgoing examination of its assets followed by

14 Peter Spiegel, 2014, "Draghi's ECB management: the leaked Geithner files," *Brussels Blog* (*Financial Times* blog), November 11, http://blogs.ft.com/brusselsblog/2014/11/11/draghis-ecb-management-the-leaked-geithner-files/.

15 Cardiff's (prepared) witness statement to the parliamentary inquiry, available at: https://inquiries.oireachtas.ie/banking/wp-content/uploads/2015/06/Opening-Statement-Kevin-Cardiff.pdf.

16 O'Brien, "The Bailout Boys Come to Dublin" (see footnote 2 in this chapter).

large-scale government injections of capital aimed at regaining the confidence of depositors once and for all, in the hope that the surviving banks would no longer require drip-feeds from the ECB.[17]

Opposition politicians howled at the average 5.8 percent interest rate the European creditors were charging, but the chief focus of their derision was on what was missing from the package — a haircut for the senior bank bondholders. By assuring continued full payments from government coffers to the bondholders, the deal "makes Irish taxpayers the sacrificial lambs for European financial stability," fumed Joan Burton, the Labour Party deputy leader. "Developers and bankers here were crazy borrowers. But so were German and French banks which backed them with finance."[18] Similar sentiments were voiced by respected economic analysts both in Ireland and abroad. Barry Eichengreen of the University of California at Berkeley was again one of the most passionate critics, pointing out that instead of giving the bondholders a free pass at Irish expense, there was a much fairer way of dealing with contagion worries.

"[P]olicy makers in Germany—and in France and Britain—are scared to death over what Ireland restructuring its bank debt would do to their own banking systems," Eichengreen wrote. "If so, the appropriate response is not to lend to Ireland—to pile yet more debt on the country's existing debt—but to properly capitalize their own banking systems so that the latter can withstand the inevitable Irish restructuring." And why wasn't this option even being considered? Because, he continued, "European officials are scared to death not just by their banks but by their publics, who don't want to hear that public money is required for bank recapitalization."[19]

17 IMF, 2010, "Ireland: Request for an Extended Arrangement—Staff Report" (see footnote 3 in this chapter).

18 Cooper, *How Ireland Really Went Bust,* chapter 11 (see footnote 3 in chapter 8).

19 Eichengreen's article was published in German in *Handelsblatt,* but an English version was posted on *The Irish Economy* (blog), under the heading "Barry Eichengreen on the Irish bailout," on December 1, 2010, www.irisheconomy.ie/index.php/2010/12/01/barry-eichengreen-on-the-irish-bailout/.

In other words, the Irish program was, in substantial part, a bailout of European banks. If such a bailout was needed, fine; but why put so much of the burden on the Irish government budget instead of, say, those of France and Germany? As Martin Wolf put it in his weekly *Financial Times* column: "If the eurozone is not a 'transfer union,' that has to work both ways; taxpayers of one state should not rescue those of others from having to save their banks from their follies."[20]

The possibility remained that bank bondholders might be burned in the future — and the IMF staff report on the program, dated December 4, included a paragraph suggesting that this ought to happen. "The [government's] obligations will…be lower if the debt owed by banks is restructured," the report said, indicating that haircuts ought to apply at least in the case of banks like Anglo Irish that were being wound down after government takeovers. "[W]here a bank has lost substantial value—and [is] indeed, insolvent—the debt holders should share in the losses. Further such action is contemplated for banks that have received substantial state assistance."[21]

A fresh chance arose a few months later to save Irish taxpayers some money at the expense of bondholders, with the IMF again supportive of doing so. But Trichet intervened again — this time, according to testimony by Irish officials, with even more colourful and menacing language.

Michael Noonan had been Ireland's finance minister for only three weeks when, on March 31, 2011, he attempted to initiate a process aimed at leading to a haircut on the €3.7 billion worth of remaining Anglo Irish senior bonds. Noonan's party, the centre-right Fine Gael, had won power in an election the month before by riding a wave of popular disgust at Cowen and Lenihan over the way the economy had been run. Among the major election issues was the treatment of bank

20 Martin Wolf, 2010, "Why the Irish crisis is such a huge test for the eurozone," *Financial Times,* November 30.

21 IMF, 2010, "Ireland: Request for an Extended Arrangement—Staff Report" (see footnote 3 in this chapter).

bondholders; during the campaign Fine Gael leaders had issued frequent and brassy promises to get a better deal for Ireland on that score.

March 31 was the deadline for the new government to submit a plan for implementing the Troika's conditions regarding the financial sector, thereby coming to grips with Ireland's banking problem once and for all. The plan, which Noonan was scheduled to deliver to Parliament that evening, included measures to shrink the size of the financial system by off-loading a large amount of the banks' loans, completing a review of bank assets, reducing the number of large institutions to two "pillar" banks, and lowering the system's dependence on both outside funding and ECB support. This package, for once, would not be overtaken later by events.

The IMF, which was watching this development closely from Washington, received a proposed draft statement from Dublin in which Noonan would say that, at least for the senior bonds of Anglo Irish and one other small bank that was also slated for closure, the government would introduce legislation empowering it to impose haircuts. Even though the savings might only be a couple of billion euros, that was a sum well worth seeking for Irish taxpayers, and it would restore a measure of fairness to the program. Chopra and other top Fund officials reviewed the draft and sent word back: It was OK as far as they were concerned.

When word reached the ECB, however, Noonan got a call from Trichet asking what Dublin was doing. "I told him that as part of the programme, we were burning bondholders....I had the authority of the government to do so," Noonan said in his testimony to the parliamentary inquiry. In response, Trichet "asked me was I aware this would be treated by the markets as a default," Noonan continued, adding that although the ECB president didn't explicitly say that this would lead to a cut-off of emergency loans — on which the Irish banking system remained heavily dependent — "the implications of that to me were clear. [Emergency loans] could be suspended."[22]

22 Noonan's testimony to the inquiry, available at: https://inquiries.oireachtas.ie/banking/hearings/michael-noonantd-minister-for-finance/.

Confronted by such formidable opposition, Noonan said he would have to consult with the new Taoiseach, Enda Kenny, and he later called Trichet back. "I said we were still disposed to burn the bondholders," Noonan recalled. "[Trichet] sounded irate…he said 'If you do that, a bomb will go off and it won't be here, it'll be in Dublin.'"

At that point, Noonan proved no more willing to defy Trichet than his predecessor was. "I had some conversations with my key staff," Noonan said, "and I decided to advise the Taoiseach that the risk was too high for the amount of gain that was involved and I changed my script and did not promise burden-sharing."

Trichet has denied using the word "bomb" or resorting to threats, telling the parliamentary inquiry that it "would have been totally not in line with the relationship I had with the government." The more accurate way of describing what happened, he said, was as follows: "[T]he Governing Council of the ECB considered it was not appropriate for Ireland…to go along with this burning and that you would have had probably a lot of very adverse consequences." Ultimately, he added, Ireland was not coerced into dropping the proposal; rather, its officials saw the light: "It was finally what was decided by the [Irish] Government….The decision was not taken by the ECB."[23] (Asked about Trichet's denial, Noonan testified: "I can assure this committee he said it….He said a bomb will go off.")

Whatever precise words were uttered, Noonan's capitulation meant that the bondholders would continue to receive their money, and Irish citizens would get no relief from this particular quarter.

The next day was April Fool's Day. "I wanted to send an email to the [IMF's Ireland] team saying U2 was going to hold a "Burn the Bondholders" concert in Dublin, and we'd all been invited," Chopra recalled. "But I was told it would be a bad idea to send that email, so I didn't."[24]

23 Trichet's presentation to the inquiry, available at https://inquiries.oireachtas.ie/banking/hearings/jean-claude-trichet-iiea-event-not-an-official-inquiry-hearing/.

24 Chopra, "Lessons from Ireland's financial crisis" (see footnote 12 in this chapter).

Hark back to an episode recounted in chapter 4, when the IMF's Reza Moghadam sent an email to colleagues regarding the proposed rescue of Latvia. As director of SPR, Moghadam evidently felt duty-bound to try rallying the Fund into saying "no" to Europe — that is, to refuse participation in the Latvian rescue if the Fund strongly disagreed with the terms. "We need to explain to the Europeans that we cannot delegate responsibility for use of Fund resources....The Fund needs to be able to have...underlying policies that enable us to support the program," Moghadam wrote.

By many accounts, the view that the IMF ought to be saying "no" more often to Europe was taking hold at Fund headquarters after the Irish rescue. Many on the staff agreed with commentaries such as Eichengreen's and Wolf's, and were sickened that their institution was supporting such an unfair use of taxpayer money to continue bailing out the bondholders in Irish banks. Some found it mystifying that the ECB had gotten its way so easily. What would Trichet have done, they wondered, if the Irish government had insisted on a haircut for the bondholders that could have saved taxpayers billions of euros? Again, the poker analogy applies: Would the ECB have folded? Or would it have stood its ground and pulled its cash from Irish banks, knowing that the likely result would be the destruction of the euro?

At this point, the pitfalls of the Troika arrangement, and the IMF's junior partner status, were becoming more manifest. To be sure, Ireland was not a clear-cut case of Europe imposing its will on the Fund, because the United States — the Fund's biggest shareholder — had also opposed burning the bondholders, which made it near-impossible for Strauss-Kahn to disagree in the end. But as the above retrospective shows, the Irish had already surrendered by that point, the reason almost entirely being ECB intimidation.

Ireland's plight showed that the ills of the euro zone were much more pervasive and systemic than the fiscal irresponsibility of one member state in the Balkans. A number of region-wide steps were needed to contain the turmoil and ensure the euro's survival — large-scale recapitalization of big European banks being one example that Ireland's crisis had brought to light. A reasonable case could be made that the Fund had a legitimate right to demand the adoption of such measures, especially since its imprimatur as the agent of the international community (and its money) were being used to help preserve the monetary union. Instead of seeking to impose its will on the entire euro area, however, the Fund was going along with individual country programs that were in important respects inimical to its own principles.

Many of the current and former IMF staffers whom I interviewed for this book recalled sharing the frustration that the Fund was unable to prescribe the actions taken by European policy makers outside of the hardest-hit countries. In particular, Fund economists were increasingly upset over their inability to influence the ECB and contended that the central bank belonged on the other side of the negotiating table from them. Did the IMF have the authority to impose conditionality that extended beyond the country being rescued? Although this was a legally murky area — the euro zone is not itself an IMF member — there were precedents indicating that the Fund did have such powers. Indeed, in May 2010 (the same month as the Greek bailout was being finalized), the IMF approved a program for Antigua and Barbuda, a member of the Eastern Caribbean Currency Union, that included promises of certain actions by the regional central bank.[25] And even if such conditionality wasn't formally agreed, it was perfectly conceivable that the Fund might insist on striking clear agreements with European leaders on pan-European policies as a prerequisite for Fund involvement in the effort to save the euro. Ideas of this nature were the topic of considerable discussion between IMF staff and their European counterparts starting in 2011, according to people in both camps.

But these concepts, bandied about over dinners and in informal meetings, stayed in the realm of brainstorming rather than practical policy making. The dominant European reaction, as one senior Brussels-based official put it, was, "There may be some intellectual merit to your argument, but let's shut up and get on with the job." Fund

25 IMF, 2010, "Antigua and Barbuda: Letter of Intent," May 21, www.imf.org/external/np/loi/2010/atg/052110.pdf.

staffers saw little upside in pushing their case too far, given their boss's perspective; Strauss-Kahn had made the political calculation that the IMF would only get booted out of Europe if he dared assert the right to dictate to the likes of Trichet, Merkel and Sarkozy.

So the IMF had to be content with conveying its views on pan-European policies to the people who mattered, without invoking conditionality or even insisting on informal agreements. This was by no means a worthless endeavour; the Fund prides itself on acting as a "trusted adviser" to policy makers in cases where it lacks leverage. Time-wise, however, it was not the most expeditious approach. The IMF's recommendations were, in general, well-reasoned and in many cases ended up being adopted — albeit with a long lag before their merit was recognized in European capitals, according to a number of the European officials I interviewed. This finding dovetails with the conclusions of the study by the think tank Bruegel on IMF surveillance (first mentioned in chapter 3). "In general, the Fund pushed for more comprehensive and bolder solutions than the Europeans were willing to accept," the Bruegel authors wrote approvingly, based on their own interviews with participants.[26]

The word "comprehensive" is especially important in this regard. In the final weeks of 2010, after the agreement on the Irish program, the Fund began strongly pushing the case for what internally was called a "comprehensive approach." As noted in chapter 1, this set of policies — which would include action by the ECB and measures to strengthen the region's banking system, among other things — was supposed to have been high on Strauss-Kahn's agenda during his aborted trip to Berlin and Brussels in May 2011. In his first public call for the adoption of such a strategy, on December 7, 2010, the IMF chief exhorted Europe to embrace a "comprehensive, integrated" plan. "The piecemeal approach, [rescuing] one country after another, is not a good one," he stated.[27]

26 Pisani-Ferry, Sapir, and Wolff, "An evaluation of IMF surveillance of the euro area" (see footnote 18 in chapter 3).

27 Peter Spiegel, 2010, "IMF calls for 'comprehensive' euro solution," *Financial Times*, December 7.

The day before, behind closed doors in Brussels, the managing director had delivered a more impassioned and detailed version to finance ministers at a meeting of the Eurogroup. "Time is running out," he warned, citing worries that Spain and Portugal might be next to need rescues, according to notes taken at the meeting. He urged the Europeans to embrace a broad strategy that would "ring-fence" countries in financial distress — that is, prevent their troubles from spreading to other countries perceived as vulnerable. The most crucial step would be a substantial increase in the size and strength of Europe's temporary bailout fund, the EFSF. If the Europeans raised their financial commitment to the EFSF, the IMF would follow suit with a bigger commitment of its own cash, Strauss-Kahn told the group.

The EFSF was fully operational, with its own headquarters building in Luxembourg, its own staff of 12 people,[28] and a director, Klaus Regling (previously introduced in chapters 3 and 4), who was one of the most highly regarded economic policy makers in Europe. Its ability to borrow money was underwritten by guarantees from European governments. But no longer were markets impressed by the firewall that had been established in May, which was initially advertised as including €440 billion from the EFSF, €60 billion from the European Commission and €250 billion from the IMF. The EFSF's true capacity for lending to stricken countries turned out to be only a bit more than half of the claimed €440 billion, thanks to restrictions needed for it to maintain a high credit rating. Moreover, the cost of rescuing countries such as Spain — whose GDP was more than six times as big as Ireland's — would entail orders of magnitude more in funding. If investors perceived that there was no means of giving even solvent euro area countries sufficient emergency financing, future bouts of panic would be more likely to spread and intensify. And in addition to its size problem, the EFSF had a mobility problem. It was limited to buying the bonds of countries that were seeking rescues; it had no authority to help quell contagion by buying bonds of other affected countries. For these reasons, the IMF was a vigorous and early advocate not only of much greater funding for the EFSF (and the institution envisioned

28 In addition to those 12 staffers, the EFSF relied on employees from the German Debt Management Office for its funding activities.

to permanently replace it in 2013, the ESM), but also the granting of additional powers enabling them to purchase the bonds of countries under attack and help recapitalize their banks.

Besides pressing to beef up the EFSF, the Fund also advanced schemes to make greater use of the ECB's unlimited euro-creation powers, to ensure that both plenty of liquidity would be available for banks and plenty of financing for governments in the event of renewed turbulence. In supporting such proposals the Fund was hardly alone; a variety of think-tank and private-sector economists, as well as some European and American policy makers, were also promoting similar ideas, many of which went by names with the word "comprehensive" included. But most of these suggestions, including the Fund's, ran afoul of two problems at this stage of the crisis. One was the set of rules, enshrined in treaty, that differentiate the ECB from other central banks like the Fed — especially the prohibition against "monetary financing" of government borrowing. The other was the reluctance of Germany and its northern European allies to commit their taxpayers' hard-earned money to ever-bigger firewalls, whether via the EFSF or other avenues. Aside from political and legal considerations, German leaders had substantive reasons for their stance. Rightly or wrongly, they believed that if market pressures abated too readily, the euro zone's weakest economies would relax their efforts to reform, and would possibly abandon such endeavours completely. That would leave unaddressed fundamental problems including fiscal profligacy, lack of competitiveness and a host of other sins that were undermining monetary union. There could be no substitute for the euro area's countries "doing their homework," as the Germans never tired of reminding their European partners.

Stepping back from the intricacies of this debate, it is important to acknowledge the merits of all the major lines of argument. Those who favoured imposing haircuts on private creditors were justified in wishing to apportion burdens fairly, reduce moral hazard and minimize the risk of a catastrophic default by ensuring that countries' debts were sustainable. Those who shrank from this approach for fear of sparking contagion were justified in their conviction about the need to first create some sort of mechanism — whether it be a government-financed firewall or an all-out ECB bond-buying program — capable of preventing a "second Lehman." Those who resisted creating such mechanisms were justified in worrying that the removal of market pressure would eliminate incentives for lasting reforms, both in individual countries and in Europe writ large. Unless all three of these legitimate problems were addressed, the crisis would fester and intensify. The only way to break the Gordian knot in a speedy fashion was for some single authority to impel all parties — the prosperous "core" countries, the endangered periphery countries and the ECB — to do the right things. Was the Troika's junior partner up to this task? Perhaps, but in any event, it would not be allowed to try.

One obvious step toward compromise was for Germany to agree to bankroll a bigger and stronger bailout fund in exchange for pledges by other European countries to embrace more Germanic discipline, such as higher retirement ages and better-balanced budgets. Amid fanfare and a flurry of deal brokering by Brussels-based leaders at the European Commission and European Council, a "Grand Bargain," which went by various other names including "comprehensive package" and "Euro plus pact," emerged from summit meetings in March 2011. Hopes soared and markets rallied as the summits neared, but in the end the bargain lacked grandness, and the package lacked anything resembling comprehensiveness. German proposals for attaining more centralized coordination over member states' fiscal policies, labour rules and retirement ages were watered down, with no provisions for imposing sanctions on violators. Most disappointing was that one of the main goals touted by European policy makers, increasing the firepower of the EFSF, went unmet. Although the facility got some additional authority regarding how it might aid countries that were being rescued, it wasn't allowed at that point to buy bonds of troubled countries on the open market.[29]

That meant responsibility for buying such bonds remained with the ECB — much to the irritation of Trichet, who wanted governments to relieve the central bank of this duty. Shortly after the March 2011 Grand

29 Peter Spiegel, 2011, "Eurozone leaders reach deal on key reforms," *Financial Times*, March 13.

Bargain, the ECB's governing board decided to suspend purchases of Greek, Irish and Portuguese bonds.

The "piecemeal approach, one country after another" that Strauss-Kahn had decried was still very much in effect, and at that point there was no doubt which country was next.

On March 23, Portuguese Prime Minister José Sócrates announced his intention to resign amid record-high borrowing costs and intense opposition to his budget-cutting program that he had initiated in a vain effort to halt months of market pressure. A few days later, Portugal formally requested a rescue from the Troika. This was one country whose problems the IMF had been reasonably successful in identifying in advance, perhaps because although they were less egregious than Greece's fiscal misbehaviour or Ireland's banking excesses, they were more readily apparent on the surface — low productivity, poor competitiveness, sluggish growth, and large budget and current account deficits. Portugal's rescue would total €78 billion, including an IMF loan of €26 billion (2,300 percent of the country's quota). As with Greece and Ireland, the No More Argentinas rule would be waived; that is, the report submitted to the board would acknowledge that it was "difficult to state categorically there is a high probability that debt is sustainable over the medium term," but Fund support was justified "given the high risk of international systemic spillover effects."[30]

The rescue of Portugal does not require a detailed examination in this book because it raised no major issues regarding the IMF's integrity or governance. But one revealing episode merits mention — an attempt by Strauss-Kahn to say "no" to Europe. Fed up with the failure to adopt a viable comprehensive plan, the managing director told European finance ministers that he would refuse to allow the Fund to join the Troika for the Portuguese rescue.

30 IMF, 2011, "Portugal: Request for a Three-Year Arrangement Under the Extended Fund Facility," Country Report No. 11/127, June 7, www.imf.org/external/pubs/cat/longres.aspx?sk=24908.0.

"It was a meeting of the G7 [finance ministers] in April 2011, at the French embassy in Washington," Strauss-Kahn recalled. "I said, 'We're not going to be your companion in Portugal; the Fund is not going to put money in. You need to go for a comprehensive approach. If you want to go case-by-case, I'm not in.' Of course I had no power to do such a thing, and I remember [Germany's] Schäuble said, 'You can't do that!'"

"He was right. It was a total bluff."

10

HYPOCRISY AND TORTURED LOGIC

On April 6, 2011, George Papaconstantinou met in his Athens office with the three men whom many Greeks regarded as their country's de facto colonial administrators — Poul Thomsen of the IMF, Servaas Deroose of the European Commission and Klaus Masuch of the ECB. The Greek finance minister delivered a message that, he knew, would go down poorly with one Troika member in particular. His foreboding was correct, although the intensity of the response was jarring. Upon hearing what Papaconstantinou had to say, the ECB's Masuch excused himself from the meeting to make an urgent call to Frankfurt. The next day, a letter addressed to Prime Minister George Papandreou arrived from Jean-Claude Trichet. The ECB president's letter, the existence of which remained secret until a Greek newspaper disclosed it three years later,[1] echoed the one he had sent to Ireland. It threatened to terminate support for the nation's banks — action that would be certain to result in Greece's departure from the euro zone, with all the havoc that would ensue.

What did Papaconstantinou say in that meeting that might have evoked such a harsh response? Was Greece planning to start printing drachmas again, or renounce its obligation to repay any or all of its debt, or violate the EU treaty by imposing tariffs on imported European goods?

1 Yannis Palaiologos, 2014, "How Trichet threatened to cut Greece off," *Kathimerini*, November 3, www.ekathimerini.com/158504/article/ekathimerini/business/how-trichet-threatened-to-cut-greece-off.

No, the Greek finance minister was considering nothing so wild-eyed. Papaconstantinou's message was that Greece wanted to reschedule its debt — that is, negotiate the deferral of some payments.

Nearly a year had passed since the May 2010 rescue, and Greece was no closer to restoring market confidence than it had been before its deal with the Troika. Although Greek securities had staged a modest rally in the rescue's aftermath during the summer of 2010, the yields that investors demanded for holding risky Greek bonds had headed steadily upward since the fall, reaching 13 percent on 10-year bonds by early April 2011. The reasons for this were varied, starting with the Deauville episode, which had stirred anxiety among market participants about the fealty of European officialdom to principles of debt repayment. But developments in Greece itself were playing the biggest part in fomenting pessimism.

Despite the government's success at passing legislation to cut spending and raise taxes, its attempts to implement many aspects of the Troika program were encountering fierce resistance and practical obstacles at every turn. Ownership, to use the IMF's anodyne term, was starting to erode. One salient example was the "Can't Pay, Won't Pay" movement, in which increasing numbers of ordinary citizens simply refused to comply with measures such as a hike of up to 40 percent in ticket prices for buses and inner-city trains in Athens, the levying of special property taxes and the assessment of fees for patients in public hospitals. Although this phenomenon was partly attributable to resentment against impositions by foreigners, it also had domestic origins. As Yannis Palailogos explains in *The 13th Labour of Hercules*, "most Greeks, especially since the bailout and the pain of austerity that came with it, feel…put upon. Rightly or wrongly, they feel they are being asked to shoulder the burden of adjustment so that those who are truly responsible for the catastrophe can get away unscathed."[2] And the further the government went to meet Troika targets, the more aggrieved large segments of the populace became, owing in part to the perception of such injustices. A landmark pension reform approved

2 Palaiologos, *The 13th Labour of Hercules*, chapter 1 (see footnote 3 in chapter 5).

by Parliament in July 2010, for instance, significantly reduced benefits and raised retirement ages, but it retained separate arrangements for certain privileged professionals (lawyers, doctors and journalists among them), who would enjoy much more comfortable retirements. Public fury over the genuine impoverishment of many elderly Greeks was all the more intense as a result.

Even more important in throwing the program off track was a worse-than-projected deepening of Greece's recession, as fiscal stringency proved a bigger damper on the economy than the Troika had anticipated. Unemployment was heading into the high teens — it had been as low as 7.7 percent in 2008 — resulting in an erosion of tax revenues, which were falling short of target levels. (Continued evasion was also partly at fault; the lower people's incomes fell, the more determined they became to keep as much as they could for themselves.) A credit crunch was materializing amid an accelerating pace of deposit withdrawals from banks. Moreover, budget figures had to be revised yet again because of the previous government's accounting irregularities. As a result, the budget deficit for 2010 was 10.5 percent of GDP, rather than the goal of 8.1 percent of GDP, with the outlook for 2011 likewise shaping up poorly.

Any chance that the Troika program would lead to an economic transformation in Greece and enable the government to repay all of its debt in full and on time appeared dimmer than ever. Based on the levels at which Greek government bonds were trading, financial markets were showing a complete loss of faith that the government's obligations would be honoured. The longer this went on, the less stable Greece's debt dynamics would be, and the more absurd it was to maintain the program's assumption that Greece could return to raising funds on private markets in 2012.

A debt rescheduling (also sometimes called a "reprofiling") was an idea that Greek policy makers had been mulling for some months — as far back as the summer of 2010 — with quiet encouragement from a number of IMF officials. That was because even if the program worked more or less as planned during its three-year scope, an enormous amount of debt payments would come due after the program's end in

2013 and in years thereafter. At the very least, the government would have to ask its creditors to permit the postponement of some of those payments — that was clear to the government's own financial experts as well as many in the markets. The lack of a resolution for this problem was exacerbating investor concern about Greece's creditworthiness; as Papaconstantinou recalled: "We were convinced there was no way the program could be successful as long as markets believed Greece couldn't repay money coming due three years down the road. So there was a need to push those payments back in time."

The meeting in Papaconstantinou's office was the start of a process that would end in the biggest debt reduction for any nation in history, with the main element being haircuts of between 59 to 75 percent (depending on the calculation method) on bonds with a face value of about €200 billion. It was high time for this process to get under way; as noted in chapter 7, an earlier opportunity had been foregone. But in this initial phase, during the spring and summer of 2011, the discussion among policy makers was focused on just the first tentative steps — "a light dusting" of Greece's debt rather than "the Full Monty," as legal experts Lee Buchheit and Mitu Gulati put it in an article published at the time.[3] Although rescheduling debt entails an alteration in repayment terms, and is thus no trivial matter, it involves a postponement or stretching out of payments to creditors rather than a cut in the amount owed to them. Debate was in full swing among think tank and private market analysts during this period about whether Greece's debt needed a much heavier dusting than a mere rescheduling. But within top policy-making circles, the only options under serious consideration were of the light-dusting variety. This was another missed opportunity, in the view of many retrospective analyses, to relieve Greece's debt burden in a much bolder and more timely fashion.

The IMF staffers who encouraged Greece to consider debt rescheduling included some of the same ones who had expressed the greatest

3 Lee C. Buchheit and G. Mitu Gulati, 2011, "Greek Debt—The Endgame Scenarios," April 8, www.gramercy.com/portals/0/pdfs/Greek%20Debt%20Endgame%20Scenarios%204-08-11%20CGSH.pdf.

concern about the country's debt sustainability in the spring of 2010. Lorenzo Giorgianni, the deputy director of SPR who had conducted the secret talks about Greece's debt with French and German officials, met with Greek policy makers during the October 2010 IMF-World Bank annual meetings. "We looked at various scenarios with Lorenzo, from moderate reprofiling to those of a heavier nature, like a haircut," recalled one of the Greek participants. "He was always trying to solicit support for more drastic action." Later in 2010, other IMF economists travelled to Athens, without the knowledge of the other Troika members, to discuss possible debt-rescheduling options.

If anything, the case for "drastic action" on Greece's debt was even stronger in the spring of 2011 than it had been a year earlier. An analysis published in February by the think tank Bruegel, for example, concluded that even under the most optimistic scenarios for economic growth and interest rates, lowering Greece's debt-to-GDP ratio to safe levels would require budget surpluses over many years that would exceed those achieved by Norway, for example, a country blessed with bountiful oil revenue. "Greece has become insolvent," the study's authors argued, and the country needed a substantial haircut on its debt.[4] But those at the IMF who hankered for such an approach found themselves impeded anew, with more of the opposition coming from within the Fund than before.

The European Department was now under the command of a new director, Antonio Borges, a Portuguese economist and banker. Recruited by Strauss-Kahn in late 2010 in the hope that he would instill the department with some market savvy — he had held a high position at Goldman Sachs — Borges received shattering personal news soon after joining the Fund when he was diagnosed with pancreatic cancer, a disease from which (as in Lenihan's case) survival prospects are slim.

4 Zsolt Darvas, Jean Pisani-Ferry and André Sapir, 2011,"A Comprehensive Approach to the Euro-Area Debt Crisis," Bruegel Policy Brief, February, http://bruegel.org/wp-content/uploads/imported/publications/110207_A_comprehensive_approach_to_the_Euro-area_debt_crisis.pdf.

He confidentially informed his superiors, assuring them that while he would undergo treatment he wanted to continue in his job and would be able to fulfill his duties. But for many of his new colleagues and subordinates, who were unaware of his medical condition, his assumption of this key post was a source of consternation for other reasons. He promptly made it clear that he believed the Fund had been insufficiently imaginative in finding ways to overcome the Greek crisis. A fan of financial engineering schemes, he argued that the Troika had overlooked some innovative ideas, one of which in particular, he contended, offered enormous untapped potential: the privatization of state assets and property.

Finding private investors to buy or lease real estate and enterprises held by the Greek government made perfect sense in theory. By some estimates, the value of the assets under Athens' ownership was in the hundreds of billions of euros, enough to pay off much, if not all, of the government's debt. Among the government's holdings were a majority share in Athens international airport, a ritzy marina south of the capital, a casino, the state lottery and horse-racing concessions, the national railway, electricity and water utilities, venues from the 2004 Olympics, several ship ports, a golf resort on the island of Rhodes and countless beachfront lots. Some of these operations — the state railway being a notorious example — were rife with featherbedding and government patronage, so transferring them to private hands would serve the purpose of not only helping the government raise revenue, but also enhancing economic efficiency and competitiveness. Having seen privatization work well in Portugal, Borges was convinced that Greece could reap much more than the €5 billion over five years that had been targeted in the May 2010 program. He had some support in Athens; Papaconstantinou himself had been urging his fellow ministers since mid-2010 to privatize more assets. But largely at Borges' instigation, the Troika pressed in early 2011 for a much higher goal than Greek officials were contemplating — €50 billion in receipts from asset sales and leases by 2015, with €15 billion of that to come in the next two years. Following completion of a quarterly inspection visit to gauge compliance with program conditions, the Troika announced the €50 billion figure at a press conference in Athens on February 11, 2011. The

IMF's Thomsen assured reporters that ancient monuments such as the Acropolis were not on the block, but he argued, "The mismanagement of public property is a major source of waste" in Greece.[5]

Skepticism, even outright derision, greeted claims that privatization could generate so much quick cash. As a number of experts pointed out, the Greek government had been trying for years to squeeze revenue from its assets, with meager success. Hellenic Tourist Properties, a special agency set up more than a decade earlier, had flopped for lack of buyers for its collection of aging government-owned hotels, resorts and spas. As for scenic property, one big problem was *afthereta* — unauthorized construction of homes, the result being that ownership was often under great uncertainty, with property records in disarray and many thousands of families having taken up residence on land based on laws that used to allow for squatters' rights. According to a study by an Athens think tank that drew considerable attention in early 2011, "The Greek state literally does not know what it owns....There is no central control, and hundreds of hectares fall victim to encroachment," so less than one-fifth of the land supposedly belonging to one government-controlled real-estate enterprise might be possible to exploit, the study estimated.[6] Yet another major obstacle to sale of government assets was the difficulty of obtaining approval from a myriad of government agencies that had jurisdiction over environment, forestry, labour and other issues. And even if those problems could be overcome — the government was promising a "fast-track" procedure for speeding asset sales through the bureaucracy — there was the problem of investor willingness to pay anything more than rock-bottom prices in a country with such a dismal economic outlook. The lower the prices paid, the further away the government would be from its €50 billion target.

5 Petros Giannakouris, 2011, "Debt inspectors tell Greece to privatize €50 billion," Associated Press, February 11.

6 EUbusiness, 2011, "Greece targets tourism in 50-billion-euro state asset push," February 22, www.eubusiness.com/news-eu/greece-imf-finance.8px. Other articles recounting difficulties that afflicted privatization in Greece include: Charles Forelle, 2011, "Ailing Greece Tries National Tag Sale," *The Wall Street Journal*, June 28; and Liz Alderman, 2012, "Privatizing Greece, Slowly but Not Surely," *The New York Times*, November 17.

Borges is no longer around to defend his enthusiasm for privatization in Greece, having succumbed to his cancer in 2013.[7] By then, the effort to reap substantial proceeds from the sale and lease of government-owned assets had long been abandoned, recognized as an exercise in futility.[8] This was one glaring exception to the general rule that the IMF showed greater prescience than European policy makers in discerning how best to deal with the euro-zone crisis. One plausible excuse for Borges and his fellow privatization boosters is that in early 2011, the degree of the Greek state's dysfunctionality was not yet readily apparent. As for Strauss-Kahn, he was not inclined to rein in his new European Department head on this issue.

Whoever deserves blame, the expectation of a €50 billion privatization bonanza was officially inserted into Greece's program in the spring of 2011, together with commensurately higher forecasts of future Greek government revenue. That helped to make the country's debt look more sustainable on paper, much to the delight of European officials who hoped it would squelch pressure for a haircut. The privatization gambit did not impress markets, however; investors attached little credence to the undertaking, especially after a political furor erupted in Athens against this latest concession to the Troika. In the financial world, the Greek program continued to receive a vote of no confidence, with yields on the country's bonds rising steadily in February and March.

---

7 At an April 2011 press briefing, Borges explained his reasoning as follows: "We did a study of privatizations across Europe over the last 20 years or so. Plenty of countries privatized more than that, a lot more than that, up to 30 percent of GDP, including countries from Eastern Europe where there was a lot more uncertainty about ownership and about title and the legal status, all of that. So, this can be done. Of course, it has not been done in Greece until now because the Greeks didn't feel the need to do it. But now, the important new element is that the Greek Government accepts the priority that should be attached to this and, you know, privatizations can happen very quickly. In particular, if you decide to get the experts in and if you outsource it and find the right people to make it happen, it can happen very, very quickly, I can assure you." See IMF, 2011, "Transcript of a Press Briefing with IMF European Department Director Antonio Borges," April 15, www.imf.org/external/np/tr/2011/tr041511.htm.

8 It would resurface again in 2015 as part of Greece's third rescue program, due to pressure from European officials, as shall be seen in chapter 19.

At his April 6 meeting with the Troika, therefore, Papaconstantinou saw little alternative to stating officially — in confidence, of course — that Athens intended to pursue a debt rescheduling. "The aim was to push the debate forward and force decisions; everyone was talking about [a rescheduling] anyway," Papaconstantinou told me. Notwithstanding the lightness of the dusting that the Greek minister envisioned, the letter from Trichet that arrived the next day showed what the plan would be up against. The ECB president was as immovable as ever in his conviction that failure by a euro area government to pay its obligations punctually, in accordance with the original contracted terms, would both discredit the monetary union and destabilize the market for bonds of the zone's at-risk countries. Deauville had hardened his position; a debt rescheduling, he feared, would show investors that Europe was determined to take pounds of flesh from bankers without regard for the consequences.

"I am writing to inform you about the grave risks that the Greek government would take if it were to pursue at this juncture a rescheduling of its debt, even on a voluntary basis," Trichet wrote. ("Voluntary basis" means with the willing consent of creditors, as opposed to a unilateral failure to pay.) The ECB would respond to such action, the Frenchman warned, by denying Greek banks the billions of euros in short-term loans that it was providing as lender of last resort — the total that month was a whopping €87 billion. The central bank's governing council, he noted, had agreed to take Greek government bonds as collateral for those loans, even though the bonds' ratings had been downgraded below the level the ECB normally accepted. That agreement was "based on the current programme, and the current programme being on track. No debt rescheduling is compatible with the current programme. Therefore [the agreement to accept Greek bonds as collateral] would no longer apply."[9]

Translated into more straightforward terms, the ECB would pull the plug on Greek banks, terminating their supply of euros, which would force Athens to abandon the monetary union and print its

9 Yannis Palaiologos, 2014, "How Trichet threatened to cut Greece off" (see footnote 1 in this chapter).

own currency to keep the economy functioning at any semblance of normality. To underscore the point, Trichet closed by admonishing that it was "absolutely key" for Greece to fully abide by the program's terms, which would "put the Greek economy on a path that can ensure a smooth participation in EMU [European Monetary Union]."

Once again, Trichet was standing resolutely on principle — or using intimidation to defend a rigidly ideological position, depending on one's perspective. But Strauss-Kahn was about to counter with an ultimatum of his own.

The IMF managing director laid down the law on April 14, 2011, during a meeting in Washington of G7 finance ministers and central bankers at the French ambassador's mansion.[10] The Greek program, he warned, was not "fully financed" — and unless it was, the Fund would be unable to provide its next quarterly installment of loans to Athens in the summer.

The requirement for "full financing" is one of the IMF's more obscure rules. The Fund can disburse a loan payment to a country only if the program is fully financed for at least one year, which means the country can reasonably anticipate to have all of the money it needs for 12 months, whether that money comes from official sources (including the IMF itself), or from foreign markets, or from its own domestic economy. By the spring of 2011, the Greek program was clearly headed toward falling out of compliance with this rule. The €110 billion in loans that the Troika pledged for Greece in May 2010 was designed to cover all of Athens' financial needs — its long-term debt repayments, its government deficits, its bank-restructuring costs — for the first two years, but not for 2012 and early 2013, when Greece was expected to start raising money again, to the tune of about €40 billion, on private markets. As noted above, investors were evincing no sign of willingness

10 This was the same G7 meeting referred to at the end of chapter 9, in which Strauss-Kahn tried to bluff European officials regarding the IMF's willingness to participate in the rescue of Portugal.

to lend Athens money on affordable terms. Barring some miraculous change in investor sentiment, the program lacked full financing.

One way or another, Strauss-Kahn said, the program must be fully financed by late June, because that was when the IMF board was scheduled to approve the Fund's portion of a €12 billion quarterly loan disbursement to Greece. Without that €12 billion, Athens would default in July. The Fund was indifferent about how full financing would be achieved, as long as a solution was forthcoming by summer. "We need a decision," Strauss-Kahn said.[11]

This was a mantra IMF officials were to repeat often in subsequent months and years about Greece: the Fund would not dictate the precise policies that Athens should adopt or the financial concessions that Europe should offer, but it would insist that the numbers added up — that is, the Greek program must be fully financed and the country's debt headed on a sustainable path. Assuming Greece was already committed to doing everything it possibly could, there were three possible options for achieving full financing, each of which struck varying degrees of horror among the continent's power elite. Europe would have to pick its poison.

First on the list was private sector involvement (PSI) — that is, a restructuring of the debt owed to Greece's private creditors, which could be either of the light-dusting or full monty variety. A second was OSI, an acronym newly coined by IMF economists to stand for "official sector involvement." Greece's debt, after all, was owed not just to private bondholders but to public bodies, notably the European governments that had participated in the May 2010 rescue, and the payments on that debt might also be reduced or stretched out. A third option was for European governments to cough up more loans.

For those at the IMF who favoured PSI, this presentation of unappealing alternatives was a clever way of trying to maneuver Europe into making

11 A good account of this meeting can be found in Charles Forelle and Marcus Walker, 2011, "Dithering at the Top Turned EU Crisis to Global Threat," *The Wall Street Journal,* December 29.

the right choice. The Germans clearly could not abide the idea that fresh dollops of taxpayer money would go toward ensuring that bondholders got paid in full; in the moral-hazard minded German capital, that would never pass political muster. As for OSI, it was hard to swallow for any government, like Germany's, that had put great stock in the no-bailout clause; forgiving parts of the loans provided to Greece the previous year implied that those loans had just been gifts all along. Sure enough, as expected, Schäuble, who was representing Germany in the G7 meeting, put his government's formidable weight behind PSI, saying, "We cannot just buy out the private investors" with public money.

But also present was Trichet, who for the reasons mentioned above declared his firm opposition to PSI in the monetary union. The G7 meeting thus ended without resolution, and in the days that followed, the battle lines were drawn, as German officials and others from northern Europe began publicly expressing their desire for some debt restructuring while other formidable forces lined up against. Also chary of PSI, mainly because of fears about contagion, was the European Commission; "We do not see debt restructuring as an option," declared Olli Rehn, commissioner of economic affairs.[12] The same went for the French government, whose officials were less troubled by moral hazard than their German counterparts and shared Trichet's worries about the broader impact of PSI on the financial system. Asked about a debt rescheduling on French television, Finance Minister Lagarde rebuffed the idea.[13]

Investors were understandably rattled as intra-European squabbling turned uglier. A low point came on May 6, when reporters learned of a secret meeting that evening in Luxembourg among top financial officials to discuss Greece. The media was soon abuzz with accounts of how Trichet had stormed out after Schäuble started talking about possible PSI approaches. People who attended the meeting told me they recalled hearing the ominous sound of Trichet's car door slamming.

12 Jan Strupczewski, 2011, "EU's Rehn—Greek debt restructuring not an option," Reuters, April 14.

13 Siva Sithraputhran and Mark Brown, 2011, "Debt Worries Weigh on Europe Bond Sales," *The Wall Street Journal*," April 19.

By that point, Greek 10-year bonds were trading at yields in the 15 to 16 percent range, the cost of insuring against a Greek default stood at record highs, and yields on the bonds of other peripheral countries, notably Spain, were climbing as well. Was this because investors were taking fright over policy makers' willingness to consider a debt restructuring? Or was it because policy makers were shying away from dealing squarely with Greece's lack of debt sustainability? Or was it because there was still no adequate safety net in place to minimize contagion in the event of a Greek restructuring, default or exit from the euro? Anyone with a strong opinion about what to do could find supportive evidence in the markets' behaviour.

With Europe openly fractured, the time was ripe for a major mobilization of international resolve to keep the crisis from deepening and spreading. Something of that nature was what Strauss-Kahn was hoping to achieve at the meetings he had scheduled with Merkel and the Eurogroup in mid-May. "He was going to push for a big firewall," recalled one senior US official. "We were putting a considerable amount of expectation on the outcome of those meetings."

Whether those expectations were well founded or not, they came to nought. The episode at the New York Sofitel intervened, along with the other events recounted in chapter 1.

Strauss-Kahn's resignation was in hand, and the institutional trauma caused by his arrest was starting to subside, when the IMF board met on May 20, 2011, to consider the procedure for selecting a new managing director. As was his wont, Alexei Mozhin, who represented Russia on the board, could not resist interjecting some sardonic wit into the debate. When directors discussed wording proclaiming that the selection process would "take place in an open, merit-based, and transparent manner," Mozhin suggested the insertion of an additional clause: "as long as the winner will be French."

The chorus had begun to emanate from European capitals even before Strauss-Kahn had gotten the chance to acquaint himself with the unpleasantries of Rikers Island. According to top policy makers in Brussels, Berlin and elsewhere on the continent, the financial crisis necessitated the continuation — at least for a while longer — of the tradition that the managing directorship should be in European hands. European Commission President Barroso, Belgian Finance Minister Didier Reynders and a host of others made clear that this was no time to hand over the Fund's reins to someone from another part of the world. "We are in a very difficult European situation, and it's quite natural that we would have a strong European influence in the IMF," Anders Borg, the Swedish finance minister, told reporters.[14] Merkel agreed: "Naturally the developing countries have a claim on the highest position of the IMF or World Bank," she said, "but the current situation speaks for a European candidate given the considerable problems of the euro."[15]

The original logic for US-European control over the top jobs at the IMF and World Bank — putting management in the hands of creditors rather than borrowers — was being cynically turned on its head. The crisis in the euro zone did not fortify the argument for keeping a European at the helm of the IMF; on the contrary, it made the opposing case more compelling than ever. Since Europe was the region most desperately in need of IMF loans and IMF-guided discipline, how could Europeans claim, with straight faces, the right to choose the person with the greatest influence over the terms? When Latin America was the IMF's dominant focus in 1986, had anybody seriously proposed replacing the then-departing managing director (Jacques de Larosière) with a Latin American? Of course nobody had, and the blatancy of Europe's conflict of interest ought to have pricked the conscience of even the most hard-boiled believer in *realpolitik*, especially since the handling of the crisis had aroused widespread concern that Europe's leading officials were using their sway over IMF policy to obtain deals corresponding to their political advantage and policy preferences. Arguably, Strauss-Kahn's standing had already been compromised

14 Sandrine Rastello, 2011, "Europe Aims to Keep IMF Job as Strauss-Kahn Faces Exit Call," Bloomberg News, May 19.

15 Alan Beattie and Barney Johnson, 2011, "Europe rushes to stake claim to IMF job," *Financial Times,* May 20.

by the common knowledge that he might challenge Sarkozy for the French presidency; he was guilty of at least the appearance of conflict of interest. But he had gotten the managing directorship before Europe plunged into crisis. The candidate anointed by Sarkozy and Merkel to succeed Strauss-Kahn would surely have to overcome even deeper suspicions about where his or her loyalties lay.

People in high European places conveniently forgot the pledges made in 2007, at the time of Strauss-Kahn's selection, that he would be the last IMF chief to get the job under the US-European stitch-up. Those pledges had long been one of the Europeans' favourite talking points at international meetings such as G20 summits. European officials had relished playing the part of "good guys" on the issue of IMF governance reform at these gatherings, when communiqué-drafting sessions turned to the wording that would be used about the selection process for future heads of the Fund and the World Bank. The phrase "without regard to nationality" had been routinely inserted into the drafts, and the Europeans had routinely voiced support for that phrase because of their 2007 pledge, which meant that US representatives — who wanted to protect American control over the World Bank presidency — would be put in the embarrassing position of insisting on the phrase's omission. Now that the Europeans were reneging on their pledge, their hypocrisy on this issue was plain for all to see.

Hypocrisy and tortured logic notwithstanding, the Europeans could not be faulted for the talent and appeal of their candidate.

"And the winner is...Christine Lagarde," the *Financial Times* trumpeted when its panel of judges declared her "European finance minister of the year" in 2009. "France's finance minister has become a star among world financial policy-makers."[16] The accolade was attributable in part to the French economy's performance, but also to Lagarde's audience-wowing capacity; whether on TV or in person, she displayed a disarming

16 Ralph Atkins, Andrew Whiffin, 2009, "Ranking of EU finance ministers," *Financial Times,* November 16.

combination of poise and self-effacing humour. In an October 2008 speech to a crowd of bankers anxious to hear that global authorities were working in concert to cope with the Lehman shock, for example, Lagarde quipped that as a one-time member of the French national synchronized swimming team, she had gained valuable experience in both coordination and holding her breath.[17]

The daughter of teachers, raised in the Normandy port city of Le Havre, Lagarde spent part of her high-school years as an exchange student in the Washington suburbs, where she honed her English to native-speaker level. After a couple of unsuccessful attempts at gaining admission to the Ecole Nationale d'Administration, the university that trained the likes of Trichet, she went to law school instead and joined the Paris office of a giant US law firm, Baker & McKenzie, moving later to its Chicago headquarters. There Lagarde, a mother of two sons (her first husband died; a second marriage ended in divorce), became the firm's first female executive committee member and later its first female chairman. Bigger firsts soon followed. Recruited by French leaders in 2005 to return to Paris as trade minister, she stood out for her enthusiastic comments about globalization, in contrast with the frequent rants of her cabinet colleagues against Anglo-Saxon capitalism. Partly for that reason, she was sometimes dubbed *L'Américaine*, a term that was not meant endearingly, but that did not stop Sarkozy from elevating her in 2007 to the finance and economy portfolio — making her the first woman to hold such a post in a G7 country. After the outbreak of the financial crisis, when many of her counterparts in other countries came under withering criticism, Lagarde's profile rose in mostly favourable ways as she subjected the financial industry to some of its most trenchant lambastings. In one widely admired interview with *The Independent*, a British newspaper, she linked market malefaction to the aggressive atmosphere of male-filled trading rooms. "Gender-dominated environments are not good... particularly in the financial sector where there are too few women," she said. "In gender-dominated environments, men have a tendency to...

17 Ralph Atkins et al., 2008, "Whatever it took," *Financial Times*, October 15.

show how hairy-chested they are, compared with the man who's sitting next to them. I honestly think that there should never be too much testosterone in one room."[18]

Needless to say, such commentary stood her in good stead for leading the Fund at a time when it had been sullied by a sex scandal. Depicting her as the perfect antidote to the testosterone-besotted Strauss-Kahn, Maureen Dowd, *The New York Times* columnist, raved about Lagarde's "short silver hair and blue green eyes...melodic low voice...nude patent Christian Louboutin high heels" and the zebra-pattern carpet she had installed in her Paris office. Dowd's question of whether Lagarde had ever felt sexually harassed elicited a classic answer from the 1.8 m (5 ft. 11 in.) Frenchwoman: "No, I'm too tall. I've been in sports too long. [Would-be sexual harassers] know that I could just punch them."[19]

Whereas Lagarde enjoyed full support from Europe as well as elsewhere in the world, the candidates from other regions could not even muster unified backing from their own blocs of countries.

The IMF board members representing BRICS countries, including Mozhin, joined to issue a statement on May 24 demanding a "truly transparent, merit-based and competitive process" and condemning the "obsolete unwritten convention" of reserving the managing directorship for Europeans.[20] But their unity stopped there; they banded behind no candidate strong enough to garner more than a small percentage of the voting power. The media speculated about

18 John Lichfield, 2010, "Christine Lagarde: 'There should never be too much testosterone in one room,'" *The Independent*, October 23. Other information about Lagarde can be found in: Economist Intelligence Unit, 2005, "France Economy: Trade minister selling globalization's benefits," July 25; Carol Matlack, 2011, "Is Christine Lagarde Right for the IMF?" *Bloomberg Business Week*, June 9; Kambiz Foroohar, 2011, "Lagarde Uses IMF Role to Prod Europeans to End Debt Haggling," Bloomberg News, September 8; and Liz Alderman, 2011, "Mme. Lagarde Goes to Washington," *The New York Times*, September 24.

19 Maureen Dowd, 2011, "For Office Civility, Cherchez La Femme," *The New York Times*, May 28.

20 IMF, 2011, "Statement by the IMF Executive Directors Representing Brazil, Russia, India, China and South Africa on the Selection Process for Appointing an IMF Managing Director," Press Release No. 11/195, May 24.

many competent and attractive candidates hailing from countries as diverse as Turkey, Singapore, South Africa and India. Most demurred. Grigory Marchenko, who headed the central bank of Kazakhstan, threw his hat in the ring. A much more credible entrant in the race was the Mexican central bank chief Agustín Carstens, a former deputy managing director at the IMF who had also served as his country's finance minister. Despite being well-liked in international financial circles and highly regarded for his keen intellect and economic expertise, Carstens could not garner solid support in Latin America. His portly physique was one drawback, but his biggest problem was his nationality; Mexico is viewed in the region as too closely allied with Washington. Brazil declined, in the end, to back him. Canada and Australia were among the few countries with representatives on the board who voted for him.

Rivalries among the emerging powers were widely blamed for their failure to mount a strong challenge to the Europeans. Although that was clearly an important factor, there was a chicken-and-egg problem: "The difficulty the BRICS and other emerging markets had at that time was, although we did search for a non-European candidate, it was difficult to persuade strong names to run in an election that was seen as having a predetermined result," said Paulo Nogueira Batista, the Brazilian director. That was because, in the end, the decisive vote would be the United States; the combined US and European voting shares were almost impossible to beat. And the chances that the Obama administration would order its IMF director to vote against Lagarde seemed very slim.

"The US was in a very awkward position, because on the one hand, we were leading the charge for greater voice and representation of emerging market economies, and there were some credible emerging market candidates," said Charles Collyns, who at the time was assistant Treasury secretary for international affairs. "On the other hand, things were complicated by the fact that the U.S. very much felt it necessary to keep an American at the helm of the World Bank, and it would be hard to resist a European at the Fund while being able to keep the presidency of the Bank."

In this context, it is important to understand why the US government attaches such importance to its prerogative for selecting the World Bank president. In interview after interview, Collyns and other US officials, both current and past, said they did not believe that keeping the Bank's top job in US hands was necessary for maintaining American influence over the World Bank's policies. Rather, they were concerned about how Congress would react if a foreigner gained the post. Key lawmakers with major clout over legislation crucial to the Bank, such as appropriations for poor-country aid packages, evidently deem it essential to have an American as president if they are to pass the legislation the Bank needs. By taking patriotism to such ridiculous extremes, Congress makes it almost impossible for the Treasury to negotiate a termination of the "gentleman's agreement" regarding the Fund and the Bank's leadership. Deplorable as that is, at least the United States is not borrowing money from the institution whose head it chooses. The Europeans did not have that excuse regarding the IMF in 2011.

Even if she may have secretly felt confident that she could depend on US support in the end, Lagarde ran a near-flawless campaign, She launched her candidacy on May 25 with a masterfully nuanced statement about her nationality. "I am not basing my candidacy on the fact that I am European," she said, "My intimate knowledge of the European community, of the euro zone and its leaders, can help a bit but it should not be a plus on which my candidacy should be based."[21] To ensure that her support extended far beyond Europe, she travelled to Brazil, China, India, Egypt and other emerging markets, making promises to appoint as many people as possible from those types of countries to high posts.

21 Alan Beattie, 2011, "IMF succession: A contested quarry," *Financial Times,* May 25.

When she presented her candidacy to the board on June 23, she once again hit all the right notes. "I will not shrink from the necessary candor and toughness in my discussions with the European leaders," she said. "I am not here to represent the interest of any given region of the world, but rather the entire membership."[22]

That was a pledge Lagarde would get a lot of credit for keeping. The chapters ahead will provide evidence for whether she should be praised lavishly in this regard, or just modestly for failing to use the leverage she had to its full advantage.

22 IMF, 2011, "Statement of Christine Lagarde to the IMF Executive Board," Press Release No. 11/253, June 23.

11

THE LIGHT DUSTING

By pure coincidence, on May 12, 2011, two days before Strauss-Kahn's arrest, John Lipsky had announced plans to leave the IMF the following August, when his five-year term as first deputy managing director would end.[1] A Stanford Ph.D. with a bushy mustache and commanding height who had worked for 10 years on the Fund staff early in his career and later became chief economist at JP Morgan, Lipsky was facing an unexpected period of prominence following Strauss-Kahn's departure, heading the institution during an interregnum before Lagarde's arrival on July 5. In many ways his traits made him ideal for the task of caretaker. Although regarded by staffers as competent and congenial, Lipsky had been neither a major intellectual force at the Fund nor a close confidant of the managing director, and the fact that his days in office were definitely numbered meant he was in no position to assert himself aggressively.

Lipsky had been picked for the top deputy position in 2006 by the Bush administration (in keeping with the trans-Atlantic gentlemen's agreement), and the choice of his successor would now be up to the Obama administration, whose policy makers were planning to install someone else. In any event, he was not inclined toward significant new departures in policy, at least not regarding Greece, which was the big

1 IMF, 2011, "IMF First Deputy Managing Director John Lipsky Announces Departure," Press Release No. 11/173, May 12, www.imf.org/external/np/sec/pr/2011/pr11173.htm.

issue facing the Fund at that point. He had long placed primacy on the structural reforms that were central to the first Greek program; he believed that if only Athens would deliver on its promises to liberalize the nation's economy, it would restore economic health and make a debt restructuring unnecessary. While Lipsky was in charge, the staffers in SPR and elsewhere in the Fund who preferred the more radical approach of administering haircuts to Greek bondholders would have to lay low on that issue, in the hope that they could gain the support of the new management.

The interregnum was therefore to be a period of cautious inertia for the IMF, a mode that would continue for a few weeks even after Lagarde's arrival given the time required for her to settle into her new job. This suited European policy makers just fine. At this point they were looking to address the Greek crisis with quick fixes; the last thing they wanted from the IMF was a lot of a boat rocking. As this chapter will show, they would get the quick fix they sought — a deal on Greece's debt that would have the virtue of buying time, with the disadvantage of leaving the country buried as deep in its debt mountain as ever, while allowing more billions of euros in bailout money to go for payments to bondholders. By addressing Greece's debt problems only tentatively, and falling short on other crying needs facing the entire monetary union, the Europeans would ultimately incite more market tumult and expose the euro to even greater peril than before. But they were capable of little more that summer.

In the opinions of a number of insiders with whom I spoke, the IMF's rudderlessness led to a loss of valuable time and momentum in handling the crisis. Assuming that view is correct, questions arise: suppose Strauss-Kahn had never been arrested — would he have been able to persuade Europe to aim for a more ambitious outcome? If, as expected, he was going to resign fairly soon anyway to run for the French presidency, would he have avoided any risky new policy moves, or might he have ventured in the direction of measures that would establish himself as Europe's saviour? Unknowable as the answers may be, there is little reason to believe he would have pushed for a deep haircut on Greek debt at this point. He had already stated the position that the IMF's main requirement was full funding of the Greek program, and he had shown no stomach for confronting Trichet on this issue in the absence of powerful support elsewhere in Europe. On the other hand, there are grounds to conjecture that Strauss-Kahn could have made a compelling case for the "comprehensive approach" he favoured, including a bigger firewall and other elements — which, as this chapter will also show, Fund staffers were putting into their own public remarks and reports. Whether Strauss-Kahn would have succeeded is another matter. Perhaps he would have gotten nothing more than a respectful hearing.

For Lipsky, it was challenging enough, in any case, to ensure against the worst eventuality — that is, an outright Greek default, which loomed as a distinct possibility if the necessary steps were not in place for the Troika to disburse the €12 billion loan installment due in July. The Fund still needed assurances about the full funding of the Greek program before it could approve its portion of the aid. But Europe's internecine quarrels about how to proceed were becoming increasingly acrimonious.

In Berlin, a remarkable consensus prevailed across the political spectrum: PSI was a sine qua non; bondholders must start bearing at least some of the burden if Greece was to get a new aid program. From his perch at the finance ministry, Schäuble was the most prominent advocate of this view, and he was getting encouragement from the finance spokesmen for all parties in the Bundestag. Opposition to PSI at the Eurotower in Frankfurt, however, was so intense that Trichet's colleagues were going public with the threat to essentially disqualify Greek banks from emergency assistance if the country's debt was restructured. On June 1, in a meeting at the Hofburg Palace in Vienna, a spat continued into the wee hours after a meal in the banquet hall, with the chief antagonists being Germany's Deputy Finance Minister Jörg Asmussen and ECB Vice President Vítor Constâncio. When Constâncio — who had backing from France, Italy and Spain — warned that the application of PSI to Greece's debt would oblige the central bank to reject Greek bonds as collateral, Asmussen retorted coolly: "Without private-sector involvement, there will be no program."[2]

The Germans, it should be noted, were proposing nothing more radical than what Papaconstantinou had put forward at his April 6 meeting with the Troika — that is, a rescheduling of Greece's debt, with bondholders accepting repayment over a longer period of time. Any PSI would be voluntary and market based, meaning creditors would have the right to decide, as opposed to a deal being crammed down their throats by government fiat. By emphasizing voluntariness, the Germans hoped to minimize the danger of an adverse market reaction and, at the same time, appease the ECB, whose menacing position toward PSI could not be dismissed lightly. Of course, the more voluntary a deal is — that is, the more rights of approval that creditors retain — the greater the likelihood that the final agreement will be a light dusting rather a full monty.

Going further toward appeasement of the ECB, top European policy makers were nearly unanimous in their expressed desire to avoid one eventuality — "triggering" credit default swaps (CDS), that is, actuating payments on these contracts, which as previously noted in chapter 5 provide a kind of insurance against bond defaults. This meant that any Greek debt operation must not cause a "credit event" that might legally require payments to investors who had bought CDS. "No credit event," Trichet thundered at a press conference,[3] a view espoused by Lagarde herself, who by then was the clear front runner for the IMF managing directorship. "We are not debating that," she told reporters.[4]

That ruled out all but purely voluntary debt restructurings, since a credit event would include a deal that, even if accepted by most creditors, would force others to go along. And it was yet another obstacle for anyone in a position of power who dared to broach the possibility that

2 Forelle and Walker, 2011, "Dithering at the Top Turned EU Crisis to Global Threat" (see footnote 11 in chapter 10).

3 Reuters, 2011, "No credit event, no selective default: ECB's Trichet," June 9.

4 Stephen Fidler, 2011, "Debt Calculations Weigh on Restructuring Decisions," *The Wall Street Journal,* May 20.

Greece needed a much more thoroughgoing restructuring of its debt than the ideas on the table for official consideration.

As far as the private sector was concerned, this was the ideal environment in which to become "involved."

On the very day in late June 2011 that Lagarde was presenting her candidacy to the IMF board, Charles Dallara was in Athens, seeking to convince Greek government officials that they ought to deal with him and his organization if they wanted to get their country out of its fix. Dallara knew a thing or two about the IMF and financial crises; he had represented the United States on the board for five years. He also knew quite a bit about reducing and rescheduling countries' debts. As assistant Treasury secretary for international affairs in the late 1980s, he had been one of the architects of the Brady Plan, the initiative (introduced in chapter 2) that helped Latin American countries ease their debt burdens after the region's "lost decade." Now he was representing private lenders, as managing director of the Institute of International Finance (IIF), a group of more than 400 banks, investment houses, insurance companies and other financial firms from around the world.[5] With him was Jean Lemierre, who was also well versed in these issues given his former positions as director of the French Treasury and president of the European Bank for Reconstruction and Development. Like Dallara, Lemierre had moved to the private sector, having become a top adviser to the CEO of BNP Paribas, France's largest bank, which, as the holder of about €5 billion in Greek bonds, was the country's biggest private foreign creditor.

The main message from Dallara and Lemierre to the government in Athens was that if Greece wanted to restructure its debt in some form, the major private creditors were willing to negotiate terms. Put another way, PSI was not necessarily objectionable to the private sector. No lender wants a borrower to become completely unable to

5 Stephen Fidler, 2011, "Eyeing the Brady Plan as a Model for Greece," *The Wall Street Journal,* June 24.

pay its loans, after all; better to settle in an orderly fashion for new terms of repayment that reflect the reality of the debtor's circumstances than allow a disorderly default in which both sides lose. Provided the agreement would be voluntary and market based, the IIF was prepared to negotiate a deal by which the vast majority of bondholders would presumably accept repayment on less favourable terms than their bonds legally entitled them to. Since much of Greece's debt was held by members of the IIF, Dallara and Lemierre could credibly negotiate on behalf of the creditor community.

The talks promptly got under way as close to 50 people, many from the French and German banking and insurance industries, gathered in Rome on June 27 for the first round of negotiations. The debtor in question was, of course, Greece, and Greek officials were present. But the lead negotiator on the opposite side of the table from the banks wasn't Greek. He was Vittorio Grilli, an Italian deputy finance minister who headed a key group of euro-zone finance deputies. This was deeply emblematic of what was happening: Greece had little control over the outcome concerning its debt or even the negotiating stance that was being taken on its behalf. Grilli was the point man dealing with Athens' creditors, having been given the responsibility of making sure that Europe's requirements were fulfilled in whatever emerged.

Leading the creditor side was Dallara, who was hoping the talks would lead to some variant of the Brady Plan (although he took care to refrain from using the term often, lest the region's officials take offense at the analogy with Latin America). One of the Brady Plan's features was the big haircuts that creditors took on their holdings of Latin debt, but a big haircut was obviously not Dallara's goal when it came to Greece now that he was on the banks' side. The Brady Plan had another key element, namely "enhancements," which were essentially mechanisms to guarantee creditors that if they accepted reduced or deferred payments on the amounts they were owed, the new bonds they received would be gold-plated, triple-A rated securities, with no uncertainty about whether future payments would be forthcoming. The most straightforward kind of enhancement was an up-front cash payment of some fraction of the original amount owed. Other enhancements were more complex, typically involving the creation of escrow accounts, which would contain triple-A rated government bonds. Creditors could rest easy in the knowledge that, in the event of a future default, they could tap the escrow accounts to obtain repayment.

While the Grilli-Dallara negotiations continued, the generally agreed approach of buying time for Greece was progressing on other fronts. The Greek government, anxious to get its €12 billion quarterly disbursement from the Troika, came through with its part of the bargain at the end of June, narrowly winning parliamentary approval for billions of euros in spending cuts and tax increases that the Troika had required to get the program back on track. That victory had followed weeks of protests in Athens that often turned into rampages, and Papandreou's cabinet nearly collapsed, forcing him to replace Papaconstantinou at the finance ministry with a political rival, Evangelos Venizelos, thereby patching up a semblance of Socialist Party unity. A day after the Greeks delivered, Germany and other euro-zone countries announced approval of their portion of the loan disbursement. By that time, European finance ministers had already made pledges sufficient to satisfy Lipsky and the IMF board that the Greek program would be fully funded — with some new, as-yet-unspecified combination of fresh loans and PSI.[6]

Now it was time for action at the IMF, where the interregnum was coming to an end.

A burst of applause from IMF staffers greeted a beaming Christine Lagarde as she entered the Fund's main headquarters building on July 5, her first day as managing director, one week after her official selection by the board. Wearing a dark-blue suit adorned with a silver starfish pin, her every smile and wave captured by a horde of photographers, Lagarde strode up a set of marble stairs where Lipsky

6 James G. Neuter and Jonathan Stearns, 2011, "Greece Buys Time as Europeans Press to Conclude Bailout," Bloomberg News, July 4.

and Shakour Shaalan, the dean of the board, officially welcomed her with handshakes; the three of them then posed together amid a din of clicking camera shutters.[7]

A "town hall" meeting that day with the staff drew a huge and enthusiastic crowd, and to underscore that a new leaf was being turned over, the IMF website posted Lagarde's job contract, technically called "terms of appointment," which conspicuously included the following passage: "As Managing Director, you are expected to observe the highest standards of ethical conduct, consistent with the values of integrity, impartiality and discretion. You shall strive to avoid even the appearance of impropriety in your conduct." (Strauss-Kahn's terms of appointment had said only that he was expected to observe the same rules of conduct as the staff, including the avoidance of conflict of interest.)[8] At a press conference the following day, Lagarde adroitly fielded questions about issues such as her lack of formal training in economics: "Without being too poetic about it," she said, "not all conductors know how to play the piano, the harp, the violin, or the cello. So I'll try to be a good conductor."[9]

Her first major order of business was scheduled for just two days later — a July 8 board meeting to consider the IMF's portion of the disbursement for Greece. Accordingly, the managing director began receiving a crash course from top-level staffers on the key issues, by listening to lengthy debates in her office pitting those who strongly doubted Greece's debt was sustainable (notably SPR's Reza Moghadam and the Research Department's Olivier Blanchard) versus those who believed that a modified version of the first program still stood a chance of working (a decided minority by this point, including mission chief Poul Thomsen

7 Associated Press, 2011, "Raw Video: New IMF Chief Lagarde Arrives," July 5, www.youtube.com/watch?v=hmfRIjYajPg.

8 IMF, 2011, "Terms of Appointment of Christine Lagarde as Managing Director of the International Monetary Fund," Press Release No. 11/270, July 5, www.imf.org/external/np/sec/pr/2011/pr11270.htm. Strauss-Kahn's terms of appointment are available at: www.imf.org/external/np/sec/pr/2007/pr07245.htm.

9 IMF, 2011, "Transcript of a Press Conference by International Monetary Fund Managing Director Christine Lagarde," July 6, www.imf.org/external/np/tr/2011/tr070611.htm.

and his department director, Antonio Borges, as well as Carlo Cottarelli, the director of the Fiscal Affairs Department). Some of the participants in those debates were surprised at how much educating Lagarde needed on the subject of debt sustainability; her grasp of the economics was rudimentary at that early stage of her Fund tenure.

Not that there was any doubt concerning the outcome when she presided over the board for the first time at its July 8 meeting. Since the Greek and European governments had fulfilled their obligations, the IMF directors would unquestionably approve the new loan tranche, which would give the Fund's tacit blessing to the approach being taken in the debt negotiations with the private creditors. But plenty of doubt could be discerned in the report submitted for the meeting by the IMF staff about whether, on its present path, Greece could avoid exploding debt dynamics. The report, which was completed on July 4, evinced considerable skepticism among Fund economists that the light dusting the debt negotiators were discussing would be adequate.[10]

"The challenge posed by Greece's heavy debt burden has, from the time of program inception, been enormous," said the report, adding that a host of problems has "elevated the challenge further." Even if Greece did everything it was promising — cut its budget deficit from sky-high levels to below the EU treaty limit, reap fantastic sums from privatizing state assets, and overcome political resistance to structural reforms — and even if the result helped shift the economy from recession back to growth starting in 2012, government debt would still peak at 172 percent of GDP, according to the Fund's projections, and then decline to 130 percent of GDP by 2020. The graph on the next page illustrates what this debt path looked like — and although it appears to resemble the comparable graph in chapter 6, the figures are substantially worse; the initial program, it will be recalled, projected debt peaking at 149 percent of GDP, then declining to 120 percent of GDP.

10 IMF, 2011, "Greece: Fourth Review Under the Stand-By Arrangement and Request for Modification and Waiver of Applicability of Performance Criteria," Country Report No. 11/175, July 13, www.imf.org/external/pubs/cat/longres.aspx?sk=25038.0.

Greece: Debt-to-GDP Projections, July 2011

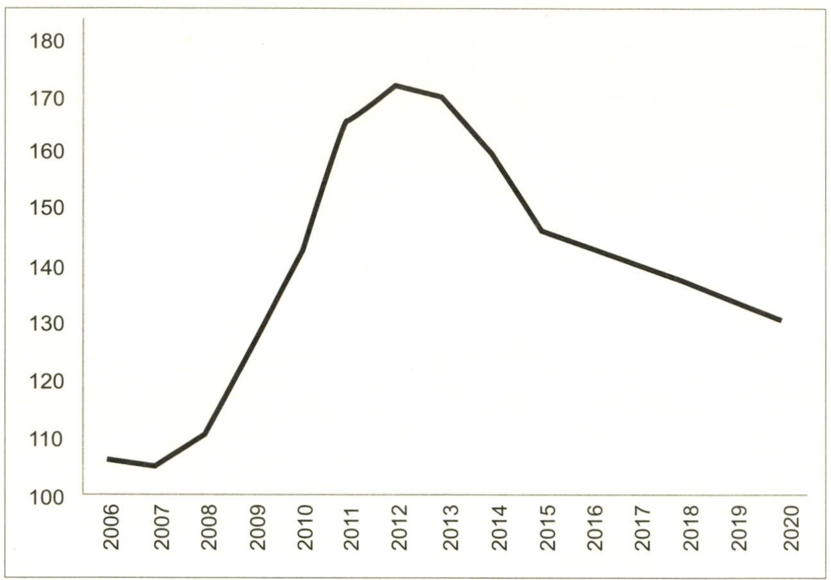

Source: IMF.

To give an idea of how heroic the assumptions underlying that projection were, the report spotlighted a few credulity-strainers, including the following about the primary budget surplus: "At the end point, Greece would be targeting a primary surplus of 6 1/2 percent of GDP" — in other words, Greek citizens would be paying vastly more in taxes than the government would be spending on benefits and services — "and would need to maintain this for the foreseeable future." The report noted that a surplus of that magnitude "is at the very high end of the range of international experience."

And suppose any single one of those developments didn't work out quite so beneficially as expected? "The debt dynamics show little scope for deviation," the report warned. If economic growth were just a percentage point lower than forecast, that "would render debt unsustainable," and the same went for privatization sales that fell short of the program's "very ambitious" targets, or for a primary surplus that was less spectacularly austere than the 6.5 percent of GDP goal. To graphically depict an outcome in which several of these assumptions

Greece: Debt-to-GDP Projections, July 2011

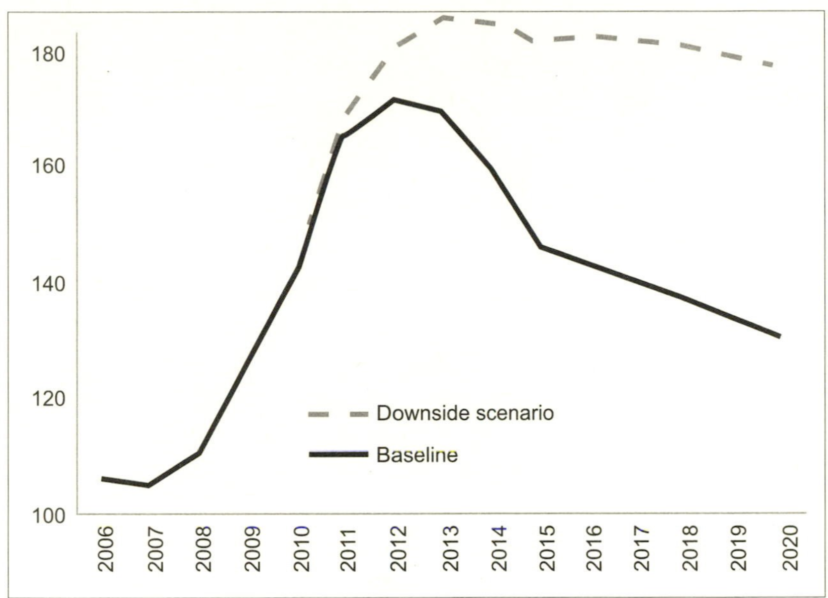

Source: IMF.

disappointed on the downside, the report showed the debt-to-GDP path following the dotted line (see above) instead of the solid one.

At the July 8 board meeting where this staff report was presented, plenty of reservations were expressed about continuing the Greek program as it stood at the time — with one director voicing a particularly negative stance. True to form, Brazil's Paulo Nogueira Batista took the highly unusual step of stating for the record (albeit confidentially) that he was abstaining from the decision to disburse the next tranche of the IMF's loan. "Our chair has repeatedly argued that solvency was the underlying issue," he said, according to the statement he submitted. "We recognize that the adjustment efforts made by the Greek government... have been immense. However, these efforts have been insufficient to render public debt sustainable. The road taken so far is not capable of leading Greece out of the crisis."

Nevertheless, the decision was approved as expected, ensuring that Greece would get its €12 billion from the Troika. The IMF's press release did not mention any dissent at the meeting (such details are customarily not disclosed). Included was a statement by Lagarde: "The program is delivering important results: the fiscal deficit is being reduced, the economy is rebalancing, and competitiveness is gradually improving," although she added that "Greece's debt sustainability hinges critically on timely and vigorous implementation of the adjustment program, with no margin for slippage."[11]

This step, by forestalling default that summer, was supposed to have helped maintain sufficient calm in Europe as to enable negotiators to return to the table in the fall and thrash out the details of a new, longer-term Greek rescue program. But hopes for such calm were evaporating even as Lagarde picked up the gavel in the boardroom that day.

In bold italic letters, on the eighth page of the report written in June 2011 by the IMF's Article IV mission for Italy, were the following words: "***No immunity from spillovers from the European sovereign debt crisis.***"[12] By an unfortunate coincidence, the accuracy of that warning became manifest during the end of Lagarde's first week as managing director. On July 8, the same day as the board meeting on Greece, yields on Italian 10-year bonds jumped to 5.27 percent, up nearly half a percentage point from the start of the week. Stock prices on the Milan bourse tanked, with shares of Italian banks taking a particularly steep dive.

Fears that the crisis might engulf one of the euro zone's larger economies had long plagued both European policy makers and the IMF. Speculation had focused mainly on Spain as the big country most likely to follow Greece, Ireland and Portugal into the euro zone's maelstrom. Instead, the country that was fuelling the most investor

11 IMF, 2011, "IMF Executive Board Completes Fourth Review Under Stand-By Arrangement for Greece and Approves €3.2 Billion Disbursement," Press Release No. 11/273, July 8, www.imf.org/external/np/sec/pr/2011/pr11273.htm.

12 IMF, 2011, "Italy—Staff Report for the 2011 Article IV Consultation," Country Report No. 11/173, July, www.imf.org/external/pubs/ft/scr/2011/cr11173.pdf.

jitters in early July 2011 was Italy, whose status as the currency club's third-largest economy significantly raised the stakes involved.

The cause of the market upheaval was the latest controversy involving Silvio Berlusconi, the roguish media mogul who had dominated Italian politics since the mid-1990s and was the country's longest-serving postwar prime minister. Perennially beset by charges of financial chicanery, conflict of interest and sexual shenanigans (he was facing trial for having paid an underage dancer for sex and using his position to cover it up), 74-year-old Berlusconi was fighting to revive his popularity after recent setbacks for his party in local elections. He pinned the blame for his deteriorating political fortunes on an austere emergency budget submitted by Giulio Tremonti, the finance minister, whom markets regarded as the guardian of Italy's fiscal virtue. The spending restraint in that budget was essential to safeguarding Italy from financial turmoil, Tremonti contended, but it interfered with Berlusconi's plans to spread around government largesse, and the prime minister launched an open verbal assault on his finance minister, declaring that Tremonti "thinks he is a genius and believes everyone else is a cretin." This ridicule reinforced a growing impression of disintegration in the top ranks of the Italian government; exacerbating the problem was an investigation of corruption charges against one of Tremonti's closest associates, which threatened the finance minister's job security.[13]

It was not news — but to skittish investors, it suddenly mattered a lot — that Italy's government debt stood at about 120 percent of GDP, second only (in the euro zone) to the Greek ratio and nearly twice the Spanish ratio. Nor was it news that the Italian economy was one of Europe's most sluggish performers; it had grown by less than two percent annually in all but two of the previous 10 years, thanks to a tangle of bureaucratic obstacles and legal inefficiencies. But that, too, was suddenly drawing a great deal of market attention.

13 Information about Italy's financial situation at this point, including Berlusconi's derisive quote about Tremonti, can be found in *The Economist*, 2011, "The Road to Rome," July 4; see also *The Economist*, 2011, "The man who screwed an entire country," and "For ever espresso," June 9; also Guy Dinmore, Giulia Segreti and Rachel Sanderson, 2011, "Finance minister denied moment of glory," *Financial Times*, July 13.

None of this meant that Italy was facing the kind of crisis that had struck its smaller euro-zone partners. The government's budget was in surplus, on a primary basis (that is, excluding interest payments). Its debt had been incurred using relatively long-term bonds, with an average maturity of about seven years, which meant that even if interest rates spiked upward for a period of time, the government could afford to borrow the limited amounts it needed without risking explosive debt dynamics. Italian banks had not gone on any property-lending sprees, and relied heavily on domestic deposits, so they were presumably insulated from sudden stops by foreign creditors.

But the sheer size of Italy's debt — about €1.85 trillion — justified plenty of anxiety in both market and policy-making circles. That debt accounted for about one-quarter of the euro-zone total; Italian bonds were held in vast quantities by the region's financial institutions, with French banks alone holding about €100 billion worth. A large-scale dumping of those bonds, whatever the reason, could seriously erode and possibly wipe out the capital cushion of many a big bank. Moreover, Italy was both "too big to fail" and "too big to bail" — that is, an almost unimaginably large package of rescue loans would be required if the country found itself cut off from market sources of cash needed to pay off its obligations coming due.

With the flames of contagion continuing to lick at Italy during the week of July 11 — Spanish markets were heavily affected as well — European officials realized that they dared not let the crisis fester until autumn. Plans were soon set for an emergency summit, with the chief items on the agenda being the terms of a new rescue for Greece and mechanisms for protecting the rest of the euro zone.

To the IMF's credit, its economists had become more vocal about the need for "comprehensiveness" and what that would involve. One of the first to go public with this argument was Ajai Chopra, in his statements about Ireland. At a May 20 press conference in Dublin, he exhorted the Irish government to continue implementing its reforms, but added: "The problems that Ireland faces are not just an Irish problem. They're a shared European problem that requires a shared solution."[14] That, he said, ought to include "an EFSF upgrade" — that is, a bigger firewall, with a better-endowed European bailout fund and more authority for it to buy government bonds — as well as Europe-wide bank recapitalizations where necessary. A similar set of recommendations was forthcoming in the IMF's Article IV report for the euro area, completed on July 1. Extricating Europe from crisis required more than just Greece, Ireland and Portugal faithfully adhering to their promises of austerity and structural reform; "a cohesive and cooperative approach by all euro area stakeholders will be essential," the report said. "[IMF] Staff emphasized the need to quickly scale up the capacity and flexibility of the EFSF...[which was] important to confirm that member countries 'will do whatever it takes to safeguard the stability of the euro area.'" Furthermore, "having in place adequate bank recapitalization plans is essential to mitigate contagion from sovereign tensions," and if banks couldn't raise enough capital from private sources, injections of public money "should be coordinated across the EU."[15]

But to the IMF's discredit, it was going along with European plans for a light dusting of Greece's debt. The defects of this approach were perfectly evident; the phrase "kicking the can down the road" cropped up repeatedly in media stories and independent analyses during this period. So did the phrase "worst of both worlds," which referred to the perplexing fact that a historic revision was occurring in the repayment terms of a euro-zone nation's debt, without going nearly far enough to assuage fears about a much more devastating default later on.[16] At least the IMF can claim, in its defence, that when the key details were worked out late at night by Merkel, Sarkozy and Trichet, nobody from the Fund was invited.

14 IMF, 2011, "Transcript of a Conference Call on the First and Second Reviews under Extended Fund Facility Arrangement for Ireland," May 20, www.imf.org/external/np/tr/2011/tr052011.htm.

15 IMF, 2011, "Euro Area Policies: 2011 Article IV Consultation—Staff Report," Country Report 11/184, July, www.imf.org/external/pubs/ft/scr/2011/cr11184.pdf.

16 See, for example, Alan Beattie, "Dithering Risks Creating the Argentina on the Aegean," *Financial Times,* July 1; Stephen Fidler, 2011, "Move Buys Time for Greece, But Growing Debt Looms," *The Wall Street Journal,* July 1; and *The Economist,* 2011, "The Euro's Real Trouble," July 14.

Duck breast and vegetables were on the dinner menu when the French president arrived at the German Chancellery at around 5:00 p.m. on July 20. It was the eve of an emergency European summit aimed at outlining a new program for Greece and other measures to address the crisis. Merkel and Sarkozy were at loggerheads over some of the major issues and, as was their custom, they wanted to reach a Franco-German accommodation in advance to maximize chances for success at the next day's summit, which would take place in Brussels.

The key issue was PSI. Up until that point, the French had vigorously opposed German demands for a rescheduling of Greek debt, but top aides to Merkel and Sarkozy had discussed a compromise, and over dinner the two leaders closed the deal: France would support Germany's ideas about how bondholders should be "involved." In return, Berlin would drop its resistance to giving the EFSF greater flexibility to buy bonds of countries under market attack.[17]

It was necessary, but hardly sufficient, for these two to concur. They still needed to bring Trichet on board; the ECB president was still unwavering in his opposition to PSI, having only recently given a newspaper interview in which he renewed threats to refuse emergency loans to the banks of a country in default. So at the invitation of the two leaders, the ECB president caught the last Lufthansa flight from Frankfurt to Berlin and joined them at around 10:00 p.m. He grudgingly agreed, although only with a host of conditions, to the PSI approach for Greece that Merkel and Sarkozy were proposing. In addition to being voluntary, Greece's deal would have to be deemed "exceptional and unique," and all other countries in the monetary union would pledge to "honour fully their own individual sovereign signature," which would effectively achieve one of Trichet's long-standing goals — gutting the Deauville accord. Furthermore, the ECB would not suffer losses on its own holdings of Greek bonds, and euro area governments would also indemnify the

17 For a thorough account of this episode and the summit that followed, see Peter Ludlow, 2011, "The meeting of the Euro Area Heads of State and Government of 21 July," EuroComment, Preliminary evaluation, July 29. Also see Forelle and Walker, "Dithering at the Top Turned EU Crisis to Global Threat" (see footnote 11 in chapter 10).

central bank against losses on collateral posted by Greek banks. Finally, euro area governments would be responsible for shoring up the capital of Greek banks, which themselves held billions of euros worth of their government's bonds.

There followed "a moment of low comedy after several hours of high drama," according to an account published shortly thereafter by Peter Ludlow, a Brussels-based analyst who specializes in chronicling key EU meetings. Merkel, Sarkozy and Trichet shared a single mobile phone to convey the terms of their agreement to Herman Van Rompuy, the president of the European Council, who despite the late hour was in his Brussels office preparing for the next day's summit. With the phone being passed from the German chancellor to the French president to the ECB president, depending on the points each wanted to emphasize, communication was difficult. Fortunately their top advisers sent an email shortly thereafter setting out the terms of their understanding, so that Van Rompuy's team in Brussels could start incorporating it into a draft communiqué.

The summit, which started in the early afternoon of July 21 and lasted about eight hours, was the first attended by Lagarde in her capacity as IMF managing director. By the time she left for Brussels, she had gotten up to speed on Greece. The argument she had absorbed — and was prepared to make at the summit — was that Athens needed debt relief one way or another, either by PSI or OSI. In other words, if private bondholders were not going to accept reduced or delayed payments on the money Greece owed them, then European governments would be obliged to do so.

Perhaps an even more important new presence at the summit was a group of bank executives from the IIF, led by its director, Dallara, and its chairman, Josef Ackerman, the chief executive of Deutsche Bank. Although barred from entering the summit meeting room, they were in constant touch with the leaders and allowed to socialize with them during coffee breaks. The bankers were there to finalize the negotiations on PSI that they had started in Rome — and they were doing very well at it.

Under the deal that was on the table as the summit began, holders of Greek bonds that matured anytime over the next decade would swap their old bonds for new ones with maturity dates 15 or 30 years in the future, thereby relieving Athens of much of its immediate worries about raising cash. As promised, this swap was purely voluntary, but Dallara's organization contended that the overwhelming majority of bondholders would accept. Creditors would get a "menu" to choose which flavour of new bonds they wanted; some new bonds would pay a reduced principal but earn more interest, while others would preserve the principal but offer lower interest. Most important, the deal envisioned Brady Plan-style "enhancements" for the new bonds aimed at assuring investors that they needn't fret henceforth about default. The bonds would be backed by €35 billion worth of collateral, in the form of triple-A securities and cash deposited in an escrow account, which investors could draw on if necessary to obtain what they were owed.[18]

To hear the bankers' group tell it, the deal would entail a loss of 20 percent in "net present value" on Greek bonds. This did not mean that Greece would get anything like a 20 percent cut in its debt burden. Rather, it meant that after Greece's debt obligations were rescheduled into the future, the value of the payments to be received by bondholders would be worth 20 percent less to them than the amounts due under their original claims. Net present value, which is the way of making this calculation, is based on a simple truth: money is worth more now than later on; after all, money can be invested to earn a return. But the math is highly subjective, even susceptible to manipulation, because assuming a higher rate of return will render a bigger loss, and vice versa. To take a simple example, suppose a bondholder who is due to receive a €1,000 payment tomorrow agrees to postpone receipt of the cash for five years. That would translate into a significant relinquishment of money based on the assumption that during those five years the

18 Less important, but also noteworthy, was a debt-buyback plan, under which Greece would borrow €20 billion from its European partners to purchase its own bonds at a discount, thereby retiring more debt than it had incurred. Based on the IIF's estimates, the end result of the bond swaps and the buybacks would be a reduction in Greece's debt burden of €26 billion, or about 12 percent of GDP.

investor could have earned a handsome return on that €1,000 of, say, 10 or 15 percent. The loss would be smaller if the assumed return were changed to a more paltry, single-digit number.

The leaders at the July 21 summit presumably didn't understand the math involved, but as their talks dragged on they sent word that they wanted the bankers to offer a bigger sacrifice. Their instincts were sound, because as subsequent calculations showed, the banks weren't about to take nearly as big a hit as the 20 percent net-present-value loss would imply.[19] Dutch Prime Minister Mark Rutte was up in arms over one back-of-the-envelope calculation indicating that the bond swap would shrink Greece's €350 billion-plus debt by a mere €19 billion. The demands by Rutte and other leaders for bigger bondholder losses irritated Deutsche Bank's Ackerman and his fellow bankers, who fumed that these last-minute changes violated an understanding they thought they had with Merkel. But in a show of magnanimity, the bankers agreed to raise the net-present-value loss they would absorb on the new bonds — by one percentage point, to 21 percent.

Was everyone satisfied? That was the question put forward at a side meeting among some of the highest-powered names in international banking and European economic policy making — Ackerman, Dallara and Lemierre for the banks; plus the top financial deputies for Germany, France, the Eurogroup, the European Commission and Greece. Most of the attendees assented, with the notable exception of the IMF's representative. Sitting at the end of the table, Lorenzo Giorgianni, the deputy director of SPR who had long been urging "drastic action" on Greek debt, expressed doubt that the country's sustainability would be restored by the steps being taken that day, so he would have to seek the views of higher-ups before giving the Fund's approval. His injection of this sour note elicited a furious denunciation from Dallara, according to the recollections of several attendees.

19 Jeromin Zettelmeyer, Christoph Trebesch and Mitu Gulati, 2013, "The Greek Debt Restructuring: An Autopsy," Peterson Institute for International Economics, Working Paper 13-8, August, http://iie.com/publications/wp/wp13-8.pdf.

Resistance was futile; Lagarde had only just assumed her new position, and if the IMF wanted to raise objections to the approach being taken, the time had long since passed. The Fund's formal endorsement was soon in coming, as Lagarde issued a statement declaring that the summit's outcome would "provide significant support to growth and financial stability in Greece and in the euro zone."[20]

European leaders were also bursting with self-congratulatory rhetoric. "Today, with all these decisions, we have shown that we will not waver in the defence of our monetary union and our common currency," Van Rompuy said.[21] And to be fair, this emergency summit had achieved a good bit more than just the Greek PSI deal. Under the accord reached that day, Greece was promised €109 billion in new Troika loans over the next three years, with the European portion of the money henceforth coming from the EFSF, so there would no longer be any doubt about Athens' access to cash as long as it complied with the Troika's conditions. Furthermore, Greece would be allowed to repay its European partners over a significantly longer period, and at significantly lower interest rates (about 3.5 percent) compared with the terms imposed in May 2010 — and Ireland and Portugal got similar reductions in their interest charges.[22] Finally, the EFSF would get additional flexibility that had been under consideration for months,

20 IMF, 2011, "Statement of IMF Managing Director Christine Lagarde on the Eurozone Leaders' Summit," Press Release No. 11/289, July 21.

21 European Council, 2011, "Remarks by President Van Rompuy at the press conference following the Eurozone Summit," July 21

22 By reducing interest charges on loans to Ireland, European policy makers believed they were taking compensatory action of sorts for having insisted that Dublin bear the cost of bailing out senior bondholders of Anglo Irish Bank. The Irish view was that the interest rates on the loans were too high to begin with, as noted in a retrospective by Arthur Beesley, economics editor of *The Irish Times*. In Beesley's December 13, 2013, article, titled "Dealings with troika developed a give-and-take quality," he wrote: "The view within the troika was that the interest rate cut represented a 'fair deal' for Ireland after the imposition of losses on senior Anglo Irish Bank bondholders was ruled out by the ECB. István Székely, mission chief to Ireland for the commission, told a forum in Brussels that the rate cut might be worth €12 billion while the most to be gained from 'burning' bondholders was €3 billion. 'There was no such deal really involved, but to me that seems pretty substantial burden-sharing.' Ireland would have preferred to take the €3 billion on top of the €12 billion."

eliminating the restriction that it must buy only the bonds of countries receiving Troika programs. Now it would be allowed, under certain conditions, to buy bonds of other countries.[23]

This was not a shabby showing considering the cumbersome decision-making apparatus of the euro zone. It would be hard to expect a lot more from an agglomeration of democracies that had pooled some of their sovereignty while retaining many of the features of nation-states. Some of the key players had not only shifted far from their initial positions, they had starkly reversed themselves. Merkel, for example, had insisted in the spring of 2010 that aid should be given to countries only on an *ultima ratio* basis, and only on punitive terms that honoured the spirit of the no-bailout clause. Now she was conceding that the EFSF, of which her country was the biggest backer, might buy bonds of governments that were merely seeking to fend off contagion. Moreover, she was allowing rescue loans to be given at much more generous cost to borrowing nations, and at much easier terms. This was a step — albeit implicit rather than explicit — toward a transfer union; a loan extended at heavily subsidized interest rates is akin to a grant. For yielding on those two points, the German chancellor had won on others, notably PSI, where Trichet and Sarkozy had ceded ground.

But the firewall was not being enlarged, because of reluctance among leaders of big European countries to pour more of their taxpayers' money into the EFSF. A metaphor by Willem Buiter, the chief economist of Citigroup, vividly identified the problem: "The EFSF has gone from being a single-barreled gun to a Gatling gun, but with the same amount of ammo" — that is, an insufficient sum to deal with Italy and Spain — and Buiter, along with many other analysts, argued that it was "urgent" to provide more.[24]

23 The EFSF would never exercise this power; the conditions specified in the summit decision were quite rigorous. The decision gave the EFSF the power to purchase bonds of euro-zone countries "on the basis of an ECB analysis recognizing the existence of exceptional financial market circumstances and risks to financial stability and on the basis of a decision by mutual agreement of the [euro zone] member states to avoid contagion."

24 Simon Kennedy and Jonathan Stearns, 2011, "EU May Accept Greek Default as Crisis Fight Intensifies," Bloomberg News, July 22.

As for Greece, the danger of a disorderly default had certainly not been eliminated. Perhaps the most telling evidence of the country's continuing plight was the sense of relief that bankers confidentially shared with each other about how lightly they had gotten off in the negotiations over PSI.

"At the end of the day, I think we were surprised that we were able to get a deal with the [terms] that we did," Dallara said, and Lemierre told me: "I remember well taking the train back to Paris, and saying to Dallara, 'Let's plan on meeting in September. This will not fly long.'"

The IMF had largely been a bystander through all of this. Next it would see its traditional role usurped.

"We trust that the [Italian] Government will take all the appropriate actions."

"We are confident that the [Spanish] government is aware of its highest responsibility in the good functioning of the eurozone in the current conjunction, and that it will adopt in a decisive manner the necessary measures to regain the confidence of the markets."

So ended two letters sent by Trichet on August 5, 2011, ostensibly in confidence. The first went to Berlusconi; it was co-signed by Mario Draghi in his capacity as governor of the Banca d'Italia.[25] The second went to Spanish Prime Minister José Luis Zapatero; it was co-signed by Miguel Angel Ordóñez, governor of the Banco de España.[26] The letters landed in Rome and Madrid at a time when investors were relentlessly pummelling these two countries' securities. Yields on 10-year Italian

25 *Corriere della Sera*, 2011, "Trichet e Draghi: un'azione pressante per ristabilire la fiducia degli investitori," September 29, showing the original English version of the letter, available at: www.corriere.it/economia/11_settembre_29/trichet_draghi_inglese_304a5f1e-ea59-11e0-ae06-4da866778017.shtml.

26 *Open Europe* blog, 2013, "Where to publish an ECB letter setting your country's economic policy?" November 28, http://openeurope.org.uk/blog/ecb-letter-set-spain-economic-policy/.

government bonds rose above 6.2 percent on August 4, compared to 4.8 percent a month earlier, and the Milan stock market fell more than five percent. Borrowing costs for Spanish bonds were likewise reaching euro-era record levels. Persistent evidence of disarray in Rome, combined with disappointment over the results of the July 21 summit, were major factors in this market rout, and the ECB's actions were also having a dampening effect on market sentiment. At its regular monthly meeting, on August 4, the central bank's board had decided to resume the government bond-buying program first launched in May 2010 — but as market professionals could plainly see, the only countries whose bonds were receiving support were Ireland and Portugal, while Italian and Spanish bonds were being left to the mercy of supply and demand.

The letters to Berlusconi and Zapatero were different from the ones that had been sent to the leaders of Greece and Ireland. These letters contained neither explicit threats nor explicit promises of ECB action. But the quid pro quo was unmistakable: the central bank would intervene to prop up the bonds of Italy and Spain only if their governments complied with a number of demands, ranging from labour market reform to energy prices to product markets to fiscal policy. The requirements were far more precise and detailed than in Trichet's previous letters. In Italy's case, for example, the central bankers stated that it was "crucial" to achieve a budget deficit of one percent of GDP and a balanced budget by 2013; they further specified that they expected implementation by decree laws, "followed by Parliamentary ratification by end September 2011." Spain was ordered to "announce, by the end of this month," measures to shrink its 2011 budget deficit by at least 0.5 percent of GDP. By Sunday, August 7, both governments had issued public pledges to take the requisite actions, and in a conference call that afternoon, the ECB board voted to start buying Italian and Spanish bonds, which touched off a rally the following week as the Frankfurt-based central bank went on a purchasing spree in the tens of billions of euros.

"The letters were of an extraordinary nature," Trichet wrote several years later in a series of articles reflecting on his life and career.[27] That was quite an understatement. The types of policy changes being demanded, and the level of specificity, went far beyond the normal remit of a central bank. Although the ECB publicly claimed that its actions were designed "to ensure price stability in the euro area," and were thus a necessary part of monetary policy, the central bank was, in effect, acting like a European version of the IMF, setting forth lists of fiscal and structural conditions for aid. Indeed, the move so rankled one board member, Jürgen Stark, that he felt he had no choice but to announce his resignation the following month — the second German to do so since the crisis began. The ECB was blatantly violating its mandate, in Stark's view, by financing government borrowing and, worse yet, making that financing conditional on policy changes by individual countries.[28]

The Italian daily *Corriere della Sera* learned of the existence of the letters very soon after they were sent, and reported some of the details of the one to Berlusconi, although the full content of that letter was not leaked until September 29. The content of the letter to Zapatero did not become public until Zapatero himself, by then long out of office, disclosed it in a memoir published in 2013.

It might be assumed that Trichet consulted with IMF officials, or at least informed its top management, about these letters. That assumption would be misplaced. "The letters were totally confidential. They were the property of the addressees, the prime minister of Italy and the prime minister of Spain, so it was for them to decide whether to disclose them," Trichet told me. "This was something we considered our own ECB responsibility in a dramatic situation which called for extremely swift decisions taking into account the state of the European and global financial markets....I considered it was neither timely, nor appropriate to inform in detail other European governments, the

27 Jean-Claude Trichet, 2014, "Letters to two prime ministers," *Nikkei Asian Review*, September 25.

28 Peter Müller, Christoph Pauly and Christian Reiermann, 2011, "ECB Chief Economist Quits," Spiegel Online International, September 12.

Commission and the international community, via the IMF, of what was an extraordinarily acute and brief episode of the relationship between the Governing Council of the ECB and two countries in major difficulties." He also noted that at that point, the IMF "had with Spain and Italy the normal relationship it had with all member countries" — in other words, it was not providing any loans or other unusual support.

The policies demanded in the letters were reasonably appropriate. The letter to Berlusconi, for instance, drew heavily on Draghi's expertise about the chronic ills that were sapping the Italian economy's vitality and raising concern about its capacity to sustain a large debt. Draghi, who was designated heir to Trichet as ECB president, had delivered a farewell speech at the Banca d'Italia highlighting his country's lamentably poor productivity (output per worker), which had fallen by five percent during the first decade of the twenty-first century. The underlying cause, he contended, was government policies that "fail to encourage, and often hamper, [Italy's] development."[29] These included a civil justice system clogged with cases that typically took years to resolve, and laws and regulations engendering a two-tier labour market in which fortunate insiders enjoyed protection from competition, as if they were exclusive brotherhoods, at outsiders' expense. Accordingly, the Trichet/Draghi letter put top priority — even ahead of deficit cuts — on growth-enhancing structural reforms. It called for a wide range of politically sensitive measures including "full liberalization of local public services and of professional services" and an overhaul of the rules regulating hiring and firing of employees.

Perhaps the ECB's letters and bond-buying interventions in August 2011 saved the euro. It is impossible to say what might have happened had Trichet not seized the initiative. But was there an alternative? Suppose Italy and Spain had been bullied into accepting Troika programs, in a similar manner to the Irish case. To be sure, there was not enough money in IMF coffers, nor in the EFSF, to fully back these

29 Mario Draghi, 2011, "The Governor's Concluding Remarks," Banca d'Italia, May 31, www.bancaditalia.it/pubblicazioni/interventi-governatore/integov2011/en_cf_2010.pdf?language_id=1.

two countries' potential financing needs. But the ECB could have promised to buy unlimited quantities of Italian and Spanish bonds, with the proviso that Rome and Madrid would abide by conditions set by the IMF. This, again, is akin to the approach the ECB would later take (after Draghi had become president) in 2012.

Instead, the ECB went ahead by itself in August 2011. At first, Italian and Spanish markets rallied. But the results would prove far from ideal. Within weeks, the Berlusconi government would be backtracking on its "commitments" to the central bank, predictably sowing renewed panic among investors.

Reactions at the IMF to this episode were mixed. Some people whom I interviewed expressed bitterness, describing the ECB's move — and lack of pre-communication with the Fund — as indicative of what a difficult partner it could be. Others shrugged it off, noting that at the time, the Fund was simply in surveillance mode with Italy and Spain, and therefore had no reasonable expectation of being foisted on them as rescuer.

In any case, it would soon be Europe's turn to be surprised, and upset, with the IMF, which was about to emerge from its era of inertia.

12

A DEAL IS NOT A DEAL

For economic policy makers who have spent too much time cooped up in sterile meeting rooms such as the ones in the headquarters of the European Union in Brussels, there are few better refreshments for mind and soul than viewing the snow-capped peaks of the Grand Teton mountain range looming through the panoramic window of the Jackson Lake Lodge in Jackson Hole, Wyoming. Every year in late August, the lodge is the site of a conference, sponsored by the Federal Reserve Bank of Kansas City, at which top central bankers gather, along with a few dozen other policy makers, analysts and journalists. Attendees typically indulge in hiking, river rafting and tennis playing in the afternoons, but mornings are devoted to sessions on big-think economic topics, where speakers — sensitive to the sophistication of their audience — usually feel obliged to say something exceptionally pithy, noteworthy or headline-generating. Among the most eagerly awaited speakers at the August 2011 conference was Christine Lagarde, who was delivering her first major public address as IMF managing director. She did not disappoint.

The attention-grabber in her speech was a passage on European banks. They "need urgent recapitalization," Lagarde said. "This is key to cutting the chains of contagion. If it is not addressed, we could easily see the further spread of economic weakness in core countries, or even a debilitating liquidity crisis."[1] The solution, she added, should be "mandatory" — that is, requiring banks to boost their capital, and injecting public funds into them if they couldn't raise the money from private sources. Since European governments were already under financial strain, it would probably be advisable to tap the EFSF, or other European-wide funding, "which would avoid placing even greater burdens on vulnerable sovereigns," Lagarde said.

The reaction from Europe was a mixture of indignation and disdain. "Confused" and "misguided" were some of the accusations hurled at her by European officials, speaking anonymously in the *Financial Times*,[2] and Christian Noyer, governor of the Banque de France, told French radio: "Perhaps she was very badly informed by her staff."[3] One of the complaints against Lagarde was that she seemed unaware that European banks had already started raising tens of billions of euro in capital over the previous year. Also widely quoted, since he delivered his own remarks at the conference, was Trichet, who disputed the suggestion that the problems Lagarde was worried about might cause European banks to run short of cash. "The idea that we could have a liquidity problem in Europe," Trichet said, "is plain wrong."[4]

This episode was the first indication that Lagarde's arrival at the IMF might portend a kind of regime change toward greater independence from Europe — and that was how it was portrayed in the media. "[J]ust as important as what Ms Lagarde said was the fact that she said it," *The Economist* editorialized. "Her stern words for Europe assuaged worries that a former French finance minister would be too cosy with her erstwhile colleagues."[5]

1 IMF, 2011, "Global Risks Are Rising, But There Is a Path to Recovery: Remarks at Jackson Hole," Speech by Christine Lagarde, August 27, www.imf.org/external/np/speeches/2011/082711.htm.

2 *Financial Times*, 2011, "European officials round on Lagarde," August 28.

3 Quoted in David Enrich and David Gauthier-Villars, 2011, "Struggling French Banks Fought to Avoid Oversight," *The Wall Street Journal*, October 21.

4 *Financial Times*, 2011, "European officials round on Lagarde," August 28.

5 *The Economist*, 2011, "A Call to Arms," August 28.

In fact, Lagarde was not spoiling for a fight in this instance. The criticism surprised and upset her, according to several of her new IMF colleagues. She even wondered at first whether the top advisers chiefly responsible for the speech — Olivier Blanchard, the Fund's chief economic counsellor, and José Viñals, director of the Monetary and Capital Markets Department — had overstated their case. She thought she was highlighting an important but relatively indisputable point about the European banking system, which was consistent with what the IMF had been saying for months. On the other hand, once she was reassured that she was standing on solid ground, Lagarde was delighted that the attacks were redounding to her political benefit.

Even more gratifying was the vindication that would come in following weeks, when European officialdom began to acknowledge the truth of Lagarde's admonition. The region's leaders were coming around to the realization that bank recapitalization was indeed a pressing necessity, for the sake of bolstering the banks against a default or plunge in government bond prices, and also for the sake of increasing banks' willingness to lend. (Undercapitalized banks tend to reduce lending, for fear of being unable to meet regulatory requirements.) The only questions were how much new capital was needed, how fast it should be obtained and where the money would come from.

As noted in chapter 8, European banks had undergone stress tests in mid-2010 that were jeered for being insufficiently rigorous. And a few weeks before Lagarde's 2011 speech, the European Banking Authority, a newly created agency, released results of a second test, which showed that nine banks in the region needed to raise a combined total of €2.5 billion in capital to ensure they could survive the worst. Once again, serious doubt was expressed about the test's stressfulness (though the criticism was tempered by appreciation for the greater amount of detail that was disclosed), and once again mockery ensued when one of the giant banks that "passed," Franco-Belgian Dexia, had to be broken up three months later.[6]

6 David Enrich and Sara Schaefer Muñoz, 2011, "Few Banks Fail EU Exams," *The Wall Street Journal,* July 16.

All along, the IMF had been urging European authorities to stop trivializing the financial system's woes, much to the irritation of the Europeans. How non-trivial did the Fund believe the situation was? One answer could be found in a provocative analysis that Fund officials were confidentially circulating around the time of Lagarde's speech — a draft of the semi-annual "Global Financial Stability Report." In this report, the Fund estimated that if European bank holdings of Greek, Irish, Portuguese, Italian, Spanish and Belgian bonds were valued at market rates, the banks' capital base would take a hit totalling about €200 billion, with the loss reaching €300 billion once other assets from the most affected euro-zone countries were included. European officials angrily declared the methodology behind the calculations badly flawed for the purpose of calculating bank capital needs — in fact, tensions over the draft report were one of the reasons for the criticism levelled at Lagarde, even though she didn't mention the figures in her speech. Fund officials, while accepting that their data was not necessarily an ideal indication of how much capital the banks needed, contended that it showed the general dimensions of the problem were much greater than the figures in the European stress tests.[7]

Ultimately, it was the verdict of markets that helped shift the attitudes of European policy makers toward the IMF view. US money-market funds, which were major sources of credit for European banks, were pulling vast amounts of money out of the region in the second half of 2011 — $100 billion from French banks alone[8] — and European pension funds and insurers were also balking at buying the banks' debt. The reason was simple: they feared the banks' condition was much worse than the publicly available data showed. The harder it got for banks to attract funds from such investors, the more they had to curtail lending and even dump assets, with deleterious effects on the whole European economy.

7 Alan Beattie and Chris Giles, 2011, "IMF and eurozone clash over estimates," *Financial Times,* August 31.

8 IMF, 2012, "Euro Area Policies: 2012 Article IV Consultation—Selected Issues Paper," Country Report No. 12/182, July 3, www.imf.org/external/pubs/ft/scr/2012/cr12182.pdf.

Most ominous of all was a vicious circle reflecting the waning financial strength of both banks and their governments — a "doom loop," as pundits and analysts were increasingly calling it. As confidence in banks sank, along with their holdings of government bonds, investors were waking up to the fact that the European governments standing behind those banks might have difficulty mustering the necessary resources if major banks required bailouts. That in turn was eroding faith in government bonds even further, deepening anxiety about the banks and the potential cost of government bailouts — and so on. Ireland had already presented a canonical case of this syndrome, but now even France was falling victim to a certain extent, as ratings agencies were starting to suggest that the nation's triple-A rating was imperiled.

On October 4, a ray of sunshine broke through when EU finance ministers, meeting in Luxembourg, admitted they needed to do more to persuade markets of banks' ability to withstand a worsening in the crisis. "Capital positions of European banks must be reinforced to provide additional safety margins and thus reduce uncertainty," the European Commission's Rehn told the *Financial Times*.[9] A couple of days later, the European Banking Authority disclosed that it would take a significantly harder look at the soundness of banks.[10]

Inadvertent though it may have been, Lagarde's clash with the Europeans over the banking issue gave her a welcome boost in stature in the opening weeks of her IMF tenure. And other important changes were afoot in the Fund's executive suites.

Given Lagarde's lack of economic expertise, whoever came in as the new first deputy managing director could be in a position to exert a much more substantial influence over IMF policy than Lipsky had.

9 Peter Spiegel and Alex Barker, 2011, "EU examines bank rescue plan," *Financial Times*, October 5.

10 Patrick Jenkins, Alex Barker, Peter Spiegel, Gerrit Wiesmann and Hugh Carnegy, 2011, "Banks face new European stress tests," *Financial Times*, October 5.

Whereas Strauss-Kahn tended to form his own views and often implemented them by giving strong direction to individual staffers, Lagarde was more inclined to run the Fund as a sort of chairman of the board, soliciting a variety of opinions before reaching decisions. She also tended to be hierarchical, limiting those from whom she sought advice to members of top management, department heads and a few others.

Shortly before Strauss-Kahn's arrest, the Obama administration had submitted David Lipton, senior director for international economic affairs at the White House National Economic Council, as its candidate for the IMF's no. 2 position. Lipton had gone for an interview with the Frenchman — a formality of sorts, since the decision is technically up to the managing director — but before the news could be announced, the events at the Sofitel put the appointment on hold. Now that Lagarde was in charge, Lipton's appointment, announced on July 12[11] (after she, too, interviewed him), was all the more laden with potential significance.

Lipton had been a key player, along with Larry Summers and Tim Geithner, on the Treasury team that handled the emerging markets crises of the late 1990s. By contrast with his peppery, sometimes pugnacious Treasury colleagues, Lipton was soft-spoken and diplomatic, but he was an out-of-the-box thinker who had no trouble holding his own in high-intensity policy debate.

His friendship with Summers dated back to the early 1980s when they were both Ph.D. students in economics at Harvard; the two were frequent study-group colleagues and tennis partners. After getting his doctorate, Lipton spent eight years on the IMF staff, then served as an adviser to the governments of Russia, Poland and Slovenia during their transitions from communism. He joined the Treasury in 1993, becoming undersecretary for international affairs at the time Summers

11 IMF, 2011, "IMF Managing Director Christine Lagarde Proposes Appointment of Mr. David Lipton as First Managing Director and Mr. Min Zhu as Deputy Managing Director," Press Release No. 11/275, July 12, www.imf.org/external/np/sec/pr/2011/pr11275.htm.

was deputy secretary; Geithner was then his immediate underling. Starting in 1998, he moved to the private sector — first at Moore Capital, a hedge fund, followed by a stint at Citigroup, where his title was head of global country risk management. When Obama won the presidency and Summers returned to Washington as chairman of the National Economic Council, Lipton also joined the White House unit, where he again was often teaming up with Geithner.

One episode during Lipton's Treasury days, epitomizing the domination that the United States was then exerting over the IMF, tinged his Fund appointment with controversy. Dispatched undercover to Seoul in November 1997 at the height of a crisis in South Korea, he checked into the Seoul Hilton, where a Fund mission was scrambling to cobble together a rescue, and without publicly disclosing his presence he forcefully conveyed the US view about what the program ought to contain to both the Fund team and the Korean negotiators — an extraordinarily intrusive act of oversight. Only when word of his involvement in the talks reached Korean journalists was he "outed," with his photo splashed in the media and his visage featured in anti-IMF and anti-US cartoons. The episode rankled some Fund staffers, who felt it made their institution look too much like America's puppet.[12]

In view of that episode — and Lipton's long association with Geithner and Summers — a big worry in 2011 among many on the IMF staff was whether the new first deputy managing director would take his cues from his former US administration colleagues, especially regarding debt restructuring. American policy makers — Geithner in particular — had opposed imposing losses on bondholders, both in Greece and Ireland, based on the fear that the firewall was inadequate in strength and size.

But haircut proponents on the Fund staff soon found that in Lipton they had a powerful patron. Despite sharing the first three letters of their last names, Lipton and Lipsky differed on a number of substantive issues. Lipton did not share his predecessor's faith in the efficacy of structural reforms in Greece (at least not to the same extent), and

12 Blustein, *The Chastening*, chapter 5 (see footnote 1 in chapter 2).

he was much more open to a debt restructuring. Importantly, one of his first major efforts at the Fund was to push for more realistic debt sustainability analyses, which would have a huge impact on the debate over Greece, as subsequent events will show.

Yet another major personnel switch in the fall of 2011 involved the European Department. Antonio Borges, the champion of Greece's privatization initiative, resigned from the IMF in November, a year after becoming the department's director. Borges cited "personal reasons" (and he had them, given his aforementioned battle with cancer), but he had also committed an embarrassing gaffe that appalled many at the IMF's headquarters. At an October 5 briefing on Europe, Borges suggested that the IMF might join the EFSF in buying bonds of countries such as Italy and Spain — an idea that red-faced Fund officials had to quickly disavow because the Fund only lends to governments.[13]

Since Borges, like Lipsky, wasn't keen on debt restructuring, his departure was seen internally as potentially heralding a significant shift in policy — all the more so because the new director of the European Department was Reza Moghadam, the director of SPR. Moghadam's appointment, although a lateral move, was a sign that he would remain just as powerful under Lagarde as he had been during the Strauss-Kahn regime. And given the role he played in the early stages of the Greek rescue, as chronicled in chapter 6, his replacement of Borges marked an important gain for the forces favouring a debt restructuring.

The new team at the top of the IMF hierarchy might look as if it would be gutsier than the old one, and therefore better able to insist on policies that would be adopted in the fall of 2011, notably a full monty restructuring of Greece's debt. But attributing forthcoming events to the change in IMF personnel would be wrong, or at least exaggerated. Many other forces were at work altering the state of affairs in which the Fund was operating. Trichet's term at the ECB was ending. The

---

13 IMF, 2011, "Transcript of a Press Briefing by David Hawley, Deputy Director, External Relations Department," October 6, www.imf.org/external/np/tr/2011/tr100611.htm.

Greek economy was weakening further, and that was leading German leaders to recognize the need to push for much deeper PSI than the July 21 agreement. Finally, the IMF no longer had to be concerned about being excluded from the efforts to save the euro. By the latter months of 2011, it was reasonable to wonder what had ever possessed the Europeans to think they could manage their crisis without the Fund's help.

Glittery social gatherings abound during the annual meetings of the IMF and World Bank, affording opportunities for financiers and top economic policy makers from all over the world to rub shoulders, and the conclave held in Washington the last weekend of September 2011 was no exception. At a soiree hosted by UBS, the Swiss banking giant, dance music serenaded guests as they sipped champagne; other banks hosting cocktail parties included Citigroup and JP Morgan. The biggest get-together, as always, was the dinner at the annual meeting of the IIF, the group of major financial institutions whose director, Charles Dallara, had negotiated the July 21 agreement to reschedule Greece's debt. About 1,000 people feasted on truffled potato crepes and beef tenderloin stuffed with red chard, dates and pine nuts at the September 24 dinner, which was held at the National Building Museum, a nineteenth-century edifice with 23-meter-high Corinthian columns that has been the site of many inaugural balls.

Yet as the liquor flowed and the tuxedo-clad waiters hovered, the mood among partygoers was bleak, thanks to the dismal state of global economic affairs. Markets were in such a funk, chiefly over the deepening crisis in the euro zone, that numerous participants, including Summers, were pronouncing themselves more alarmed than they had been even at the 2008 annual meeting in the aftermath of the Lehman bankruptcy. And for the bankers belonging to the IIF, fresh grounds for hand-wringing materialized in the form of comments from Schäuble. The German finance minister dropped an unmistakable hint that Berlin was inclined to revise the terms of the July 21 debt deal — by making creditors take a substantially bigger hit on Greek debt. "One has to see whether what has been envisaged in June, July, is still sustainable in light of more recent developments," Schäuble said. In private, IMF officials were likewise pushing strongly during this meeting for a larger haircut, regardless of the July pact. These views drew a swift rebuttal from Josef Ackermann, the Deutsche Bank CEO, who was speaking in his capacity as chairman of the bankers' group. "It is not feasible to reopen the agreement," Ackermann told reporters. "It was not a contract, but it was a clear agreement in Brussels with the official sector."[14]

The light dusting of Greece's debt agreed on July 21 was indeed endorsed by all parties — the banks, the euro-zone leaders, the ECB and the IMF — on that score, Ackermann was of course correct. But the transaction had not yet taken place. Although Dallara and other banking-industry leaders had already started the process of holding meetings around the world with Athens' private creditors, with the aim of persuading them to accept it, a voluntary bond swap involving so many different securities takes considerable time to organize and legally effectuate. And in the two months that had passed since the Brussels summit, the Greek economy was starting to emit its most abysmal indicators since the crisis began, providing striking evidence of how far off track the rescue effort had gone. That in turn was fuelling second thoughts among some policy makers about the July debt deal — and greater conviction that the time had come for a full monty.

Greece's economic outlook for 2011 had already been downgraded by the Troika in July — to a 3.8 percent contraction in GDP, compared with an original forecast of a 2.6 percent downturn at the time of the first program in May 2010. A mere two months later, in September 2011, even the July projection was looking insufficiently pessimistic. Consumer spending, which accounted for two-thirds of the Greek

14 Information about developments at this meeting, including the gloom and jockeying over Greece between bankers and officials, can be found in Christine Harper, Dawn Kopecki and Simon Kennedy, 2011, "Banks Splinter on Europe Crisis as Tension Pervades Meetings," Bloomberg News, September 26; Alan Beattie and Tom Braithwaite, 2011, "Debt talks fail to agree solution," *Financial Times,* September 25; and Christopher Spink, 2012, "Greek Tragedy Averted," *International Financing Review,* www.ifre.com/greek-tragedy-averted/21052459.fullarticle.

economy, had plummeted by seven percent over the previous year. In the 30- to 44-year-old age group, the unemployment rate was nearly 15 percent, while fully one-third of those aged 15 to 29 were jobless. One in four retailers in central Athens had closed since the onset of the crisis, and some 80,000 businesses around the country had gone bankrupt. Hospitals were reporting shortages of medical supplies; public health-care facilities were especially overwhelmed with patients because private care had become unaffordable for so many people. Suicides were rising, to roughly double the pre-crisis rate — six per 100,000 population, a low level compared with many other countries but an indication of the toll the crisis was taking on mental health.[15]

This misery could be dismissed as the price Greece had to pay for having lived higher off the hog for a longer period of time than it had any right to do. Moreover, any sympathy that Europeans felt for the Greek people was tempered by a continuing stream of reports about waste and abuse by the nation's bureaucracy, many of whose members had obtained their jobs through political connections. Some ministries still employed people whose sole task it was to record the arrival of documents on a paper ledger, as if email had never been invented.

Most aggravating of all were the mounting signs of failure by the Greek authorities to do what they had promised. Since his appointment to replace Papaconstantinou in mid-June, Venizelos had shown himself to be considerably more defiant than his predecessor; the burly finance minister was essentially halting implementation of structural reforms, which were supposedly the key to reigniting growth. In apparent violation of pledges to the Troika that only one new civil servant would be hired for every 10 who retired, figures reported in the Greek media showed that nearly 7,000 new public employees were on the job in the first seven months of 2011, while less than 20,000 retired. The highly touted €50 billion privatization initiative was going nowhere; only one sale had been completed by the third quarter of

15 Information about the societal effects of the crisis at that time can be found in Costas Paris and Alkman Granites, 2011, "Greek Cuts Erode Livelihoods," *The Wall Street Journal,* August 23; and Marcus Walker, 2011, "Greek Crisis Exacts the Cruelest Toll," *The Wall Street Journal,* September 20.

2011 — a 10 percent stake in Hellenic Telecom, purchased by Deutsche Telekom for €390 million. When Venizelos rejected the Troika's new demands in early September, its three representatives demonstrated their displeasure by leaving Athens and suspending talks concerning an €8 billion tranche of rescue funds that was due for disbursement later in the autumn — money that the government needed to continue normal operations. Upon their return, Troika representatives found themselves locked out of late-September meetings by protesting civil servants who were barricading the finance ministry, transport ministry and other agencies.[16]

But the main reason for the woes afflicting the Greek program was the counter-productive effect that fiscal austerity was having on an economy that had no real means of stimulating growth in the short term. The government had largely delivered on vows for steep cuts in public-sector salaries, bonuses and allowances, and it had significantly raised the value-added tax, fuel tax and other levies. Even so, the budget deficit was running well above the 7.6 percent of GDP goal for the year, and the Troika estimated the gap would probably end up at around 8.8 percent of GDP. The above-target budget deficit was a natural consequence of the deeper-than-expected economic slump and its predictably negative impact on tax revenue. Privatization, too, was heavily affected by the viciousness of the economy's downward cycle, as potential investors — anticipating a possible Greek default, or perhaps exit from the euro zone — were figuring that they ought to wait until they could pick up assets at much lower prices.[17]

These harsh realities were driving the IMF, along with the Germans and their northern European allies, toward the conclusion that

16 Information about problems afflicting the Greek program during this period, including the government's failures to deliver on its promises, can be found in Peter Spiegel and Kerin Hope, 2011, "Greek bail-out: A pillar in peril," *Financial Times*, September 12; Harry Papachristou and Lefteris Papadimas, 2011, "Greek state workers disrupt audit talks, again," Reuters, September 30; and Kerin Hope, 2011, "Uphill struggle to patch Greek budget holes," *Financial Times*, September 15.

17 Spiegel and Hope, "Greek bailout: A pillar in peril" (see footnote 16 in this chapter).

the July 21 accord was untenable. Schäuble deemed the situation sufficiently grim that in September he secretly told Venizelos that Greece should consider exiting the euro zone. Explaining his proposal to his shocked Greek counterpart, Schäuble said that assistance from Europe would help ease the economic trauma, which he likened to his own bullet wound. "I said to him: the adjustments you will have to make are extremely difficult if you are unable to use the tool of external devaluation," Schäuble recalled telling Venizelos. Leaving the currency union "would be a terrible step, and the population would suffer. However, things would start heading uphill on the very next day. I've experienced that myself. Someone shoots you, and you find yourself lying on the ground. At some point, your situation begins to improve, and then it gets a little better every day."[18] Greek leaders rejected that idea, but the conversation threw enough of a scare into them that it helped boost momentum for the enactment of additional measures demanded by the Troika.

At the very least, Greece had to receive more debt relief than the July 21 pact implied if the country was to stand any chance of avoiding a hard default. The evidence that banks ought to take a bigger haircut was utterly obvious in one key respect: Greek bonds were by that point trading at such low levels — less than 40 cents on the euro, down from about 75 cents on the euro in mid-July — that any bank accepting the "net present value loss" of 21 percent would still earn well above market prices.[19]

The case for revising the July 21 agreement continued to draw resistance from predictable sources — the ECB and the French government, which worried about triggering renewed contagion — and the banks. "A deal is a deal," Dallara protested in media interviews.[20]

18 Gabor Steinhart, 2016, "Those Who Engage in Politics Are Not Without Fault," *Handeslblatt* Global Edition, May 13 (interview with Schäuble).

19 Landon Thomas Jr., 2011, "European Banks Face Huge Losses From Greek Bonds," *The New York Times,* October 4.

20 Peter Spiegel, 2011, "Investor threat to second Greek bail-out," *Financial Times,* October 14.

Not this deal. The clinching argument came in the form of a Troika document dated October 21 and labelled "strictly confidential." Drafted mainly by IMF staffers, it blew away any modicum of credibility that the July 21 accord might have retained. It was distributed to euro-zone governments just as a top-level meeting of finance ministers in Brussels was getting under way, and a leaked copy was soon posted on the *Financial Times* website.[21]

The document was a new debt sustainability analysis that took account of the deterioration in the Greek economy and evidence that the original conditions of the program were far beyond Athens' capacity to implement. It started with another ratcheting down of the nation's economic forecast. Instead of the 3.8 percent contraction in 2011 and resumption of growth in 2012 that had been projected in July, the new analysis was based on the prediction that GDP would shrink by 5.5 percent in 2011 and another three percent in 2012. (Even this would later prove too rosy, by quite a large margin.) Privatization receipts were also assumed to be lower than earlier projected, and further adjustments were made in expectations about Athens' capacity for running large budget surpluses for many years in the future.

Under those assumptions, "debt...would peak at 186 percent of GDP in 2013 and decline only to 152 percent of GDP by end-2020 and to 130 percent of GDP by end-2030," according to the analysis — all much higher figures than in comparable previous exercises. Wouldn't the July 21 agreement make a big difference in this regard? Sadly, no, the document's authors explained: "The financing package...does help the debt trajectory, but its impact is more than offset by the revised macro and policy framework." And if conditions continued to worsen, even the very high debt-to-GDP projections would prove optimistic. Assuming that growth was permanently lower by one percent each year "would render debt clearly unsustainable," the document said, "while higher growth (+1 percentage point each year) would lead debt to fall to just under 130 percent of GDP by 2020." As for policy slippage, "Significant shortfalls relative to the revised fiscal and privatization targets would

21 Available at: http://blogs.ft.com/brusselsblog/files/2011/10/Greece-DSA-Oct-2011.pdf.

deteriorate debt dynamics even further." Graphs, similar to the ones shown in chapters 6 and 11 (although with grimmer data) depicted these outcomes.

Nowhere did this document explicitly say that any euro-zone country with such a debt burden would be highly likely to default; that was supposed to be understood by readers, and the drafters were aware of the potential for leaks. Rather, the authors of the analysis pointed directly at the main solution. "Deeper PSI...has a vital role in establishing the sustainability of Greece's debt," they wrote — and by "deeper PSI," the document was referring to haircuts in the 50 to 60 percent range, which would dwarf the amounts agreed on July 21. Only by applying a haircut in which private creditors would accept half the face value of their bonds could Greece's debt have a chance of falling to 120 percent of GDP by 2020, according to the analysis. A footnote hinted at continued disharmony among the Troika on the whole issue of haircuts: "The ECB does not agree with the inclusion of these illustrative scenarios concerning a deeper PSI in this report."

The implications were not lost on the markets: Greece's creditors were in for a much worse drubbing. Fortunately, plenty of discussion was also going on in high places about what could be done to minimize the fallout to other countries in the euro zone, by strengthening firewalls and shoring up bank capital. Unfortunately, those efforts were plodding.

In addition to cocktail-sipping and shoulder-rubbing, the annual meetings of the IMF and World Bank involve a number of lengthy official gatherings, some of which are notorious for their soporific effect on participants. Among these is the meeting of the International Monetary and Financial Committee (IMFC), a group of finance ministers from member countries that is often referred to as the IMF's "steering committee." More than 200 people usually attend IMFC meetings, which take place around a massive table and at one time consisted almost entirely of prepared speeches (although the time set aside in recent years for informal interactive discussion has alleviated the tedium). These meetings are where many major changes in Fund policy are officially put on the body's agenda and acted upon by the membership. At the September 2011 IMFC meeting, Lagarde launched a major initiative when she presented a three-page "Managing Director's Action Plan," containing a key paragraph that proposed a significant expansion in the amount of money the IMF would have at its disposal. "The Fund's credibility, and hence effectiveness, rests on its perceived capacity to cope with worst-case scenarios," stated the action plan, adding that the Fund's current lending capacity, which then totalled $384 billion (€285 billion), "looks comfortable today but pales in comparison with the potential financing needs of vulnerable countries and crisis bystanders."[22]

Only two and a half years earlier, it will be recalled, the IMF had tripled its war chest at the April 2009 London summit of G20 nations, when the world's economic elites were responding to fears that the Lehman shock would overwhelm emerging-market economies. In fact, the Fund was potentially in even better shape financially thanks to another step taken in 2010, aimed at improving on the ad-hoc approach taken in London. At the November 2010 G20 summit in Seoul, member countries had agreed to double IMF quotas, which would expand the Fund's pool of hard currency on a more permanent basis than the London deal. Accompanying this quota-doubling agreement was an agreement to reapportion voting shares, mitigating a little of Europe's over-representation and the corresponding under-representation of fast-growing emerging economies. The 2010 agreement was not yet implemented; it required legislative approval in many countries, and was languishing politically — most importantly in the United States, where Congress, especially the Republican-controlled House of Representatives, was hostile toward funding an institution involved in European bailouts. But in the meantime, the London boost in the IMF's borrowing arrangements was still operative.

Lagarde's "Action Plan" was based on much bigger worries than those that had prompted the earlier agreements. The "worst-case scenarios" to which she referred meant that the crisis in Europe might reach mammoth proportions, requiring an even better-endowed global

22 IMF, 2011, "Managing Director's Action Plan, IMFC, September, www.imf.org/external/np/pp/eng/2011/092411.pdf.

financial firefighter. Beyond that, her proposal reflected a tectonic shift that was taking place in the relationship between the IMF and Europe. Keeping the IMF out of euro-zone rescues had once been a key objective of many top European policy makers. In the fall of 2011, nobody in Europe's elite policy circles was thinking anymore about ridding the continent of the IMF's involvement. Quite the contrary: throughout the region's capitals, the Fund was now seen as potentially crucial to salvation. As one European official confided to the *Financial Times* that fall, "We're increasingly coming to the view that the eurozone crisis is too big a problem for Europe to solve on its own. If you want to sort it out properly you need American and Chinese money, which means the IMF."[23]

Especially now that a deep debt restructuring loomed for Greece, Europe needed a bigger and more formidable firewall, to show convincingly that resources were available for bailouts of all vulnerable euro-zone countries, lest markets fear that the Greek solution would become the model to be followed elsewhere. And ideas for mobilizing more European money — another big topic of conversation at the Washington meetings in September — were encountering resistance at every turn, despite exhortations by both US Treasury and Fund officials for Europe to consider creative approaches.

The EFSF, which had helped bankroll the rescues of Ireland and Portugal, had only about €250 billion left, a relatively puny-looking sum now that Spain and Italy were in investors' gunsights. The most obvious solution, pumping more money from European governments into the EFSF, was less attractive than ever, not only because taxpayers in Europe's healthy economies would object, but because of the potential impact on big European countries that were under financial strain — Italy and Spain being prime examples, along with France, given its endangered triple-A credit rating. The EFSF's ability to raise money for rescues depended on guarantees provided by euro-zone member states, based on their shares of the region's output. How could Italy and Spain risk guaranteeing some portion of a loan to a troubled country? How could France, if it lost

23 Alan Beattie, Alex Barker and Joe Leahy, 2011, "Emerging countries in talks on IMF boost," *Financial Times*, October 14.

its triple-A rating — which would then harm the EFSF's credit rating, causing the whole rescue mechanism to come unstuck? In its inimitable style, *The Economist* likened France and the EFSF to "tottering drunks holding each other up."[24]

Instead of filling its coffers directly, the EFSF could use "leverage" to give itself added financial heft, under a variety of ideas cooked up by Managing Director Klaus Regling and his staff at the EFSF's Luxembourg headquarters. One proposal that received intense consideration at the IMF-World Bank meetings envisioned the EFSF guaranteeing bondholders of certain euro-zone countries that it would cover losses of up to 20 percent of their bonds' value, rather than the full amount; the EFSF could then use its €250 billion to back more than €1 trillion worth of bonds. Other proposals focused on giving the EFSF access to the unlimited euro-creation powers of the ECB. If the EFSF got a banking licence, for example, it could borrow vast amounts at very low cost from the central bank. But these financial engineering schemes also ran afoul of various fundamental factors. With fewer and fewer European governments endowed with sterling credit, using the EFSF — whose credit depended on that of its member countries — became increasingly problematic, regardless of the mechanism involved. And both the ECB and German government rejected any approach that appeared to infringe on the ban against monetary financing of deficits.

Another obvious solution, taking full advantage of the ECB to reassure bondholders that they could sell to a buyer with an unlimited supply of euros, also continued to face strenuous opposition from the central bank and the German government. The ECB's purchases of Italian bonds was already turning into a fiasco, because Berlusconi was failing — for reasons of both political will and political muscle — to fulfill his government's promises that had been made in response to the Trichet/ Draghi letter of August 5. In German eyes, this was proof, if any were needed, that using the ECB to ease pressure on member states would only increase the temptation for politicians to pursue reckless policies.

24 *The Economist,* 2011, "No big bazooka," October 29.

Pumping up the IMF, therefore, offered appealing options, at least by comparison with many of the alternative ideas for strengthening financial safety nets. And Lagarde had grounds for hope that the Fund could again tap the BRICS, the world's biggest accumulators of hard-currency reserves. China, Russia and Brazil were heavily dependent on European markets for their exports, so they were understandably nervous about the potential impact on their own economies of a severe recession in the euro zone. The BRICS issued a statement during the IMF meetings declaring themselves "open" to the idea of contributing more money to the Fund for the sake of fostering global financial stability.[25]

Proposals to increase IMF resources initially encountered strong push-back from the United States and other Anglospheric countries, including Britain, Canada and Australia. (Japan was also in this camp.) Leading the opposition was the US Treasury, whose officials contended that the Fund was too heavily exposed in Europe already, and that non-European nations should not assume the burden of bankrolling the effort to contain the region's crisis. As the Treasury saw it, the problem wasn't lack of money at the Fund; it was lack of will among European policy makers to overcome their bureaucratic strictures against taking decisive crisis-fighting action.

"The IMF has very, very substantial uncommitted resources because of the actions we took in '09 and 2010 in the crisis to substantially expand the IMF's financial capacity," Geithner said in a televised interview during a mid-October G20 finance ministers meeting. "The financial problems they face in Europe, they're complicated to solve, but they're well within the resources that [are] available to Europe and the stronger countries in Europe."[26]

25 "BRICS Finance Ministers' Joint Communiqué Issued at the end of Meeting in Washington," September 23, 2011, http://pib.nic.in/newsite/PrintRelease.aspx?relid=76189.

26 CNBC, 2011, "CNBC Transcript: CNBC's Steve Liesman speaks with Treasury Secretary Timothy Geithner," October 14, www.cnbc.com/id/44875650.

One interpretation of Geithner's stance — echoed by many who favoured boosting IMF resources — was that it stemmed from domestic US politics, namely the difficulty in securing congressional approval for such a measure. But there was ample merit to the case that the Fund was taking too much risk in Europe, and the Europeans should be obliged to put up more money for the firewall first. In a sense, the Treasury was commendably trying to safeguard the Fund's financial integrity.

Whatever the opponents' motives, Lagarde's initiative at the 2011 annual meetings would bear fruit. She would eventually secure a major injection of money from a number of IMF member countries — another illustration of how America's once-invincible grip over the Fund has loosened. But all that would come months later. In the fall of 2011, more pressing tasks were at hand.

13

SUMMIT FOLLIES

IMF managing directors are expected to maintain personal decorum in international negotiations, even when it is necessary to issue threats. So as the clock ticked past midnight in Brussels on the evening of October 26, 2011, Lagarde stayed mostly silent during a confrontation in the EU's Justus Lipsius Building between a handful of Europe's top leaders and two representatives of the banking industry. Although she may have been tempted to act in a menacing fashion, she didn't have to, because her former boss was doing a perfectly fine job of it.

Denouncing the banks as *voleurs et menteurs* (thieves and liars), Sarkozy blustered that they would be "destroyed" if they did not accept the losses on their Greek bonds that Europe was demanding. The men at whom the French president's tirade was directed — Charles Dallara of the IIF and Jean Lemierre of BNP Paribas — could only grit their teeth and wait until he had finished venting.[1]

This was a turning point. The full monty was at hand. Up until then, Sarkozy's government — including Lagarde, when she was in it — had been a resolute advocate for caution regarding the treatment of

1 Although much of the material in this section is based on interviews, I also rely heavily for details (including Sarkozy's insults to the banks) on Peter Ludlow, 2011, "A Tale of Five Summits: October & November 2011," EuroComment, Preliminary Evaluation, November 30.

European banks, for fear of the contagion that might result from a restructuring of Greece's debt. Now the French president was comporting himself as the banks' worst nightmare. The IMF's debt sustainability analysis (cited in the previous chapter) had left little choice: only a massive haircut of Greek bonds would credibly render the country solvent, so the banks would have to forgo enormous amounts of their legal claims for Greece to stand any reasonable chance of fulfilling its payment obligations.

At the time of Sarkozy's outburst, the heads of state and government of euro area countries were holding their second meeting within four days — an extraordinarily frenetic period of summitry even by the standards of the previous two years. The leaders were desperately seeking to reach an accord that would finally get them out in front of the crisis besetting their currency union. Whereas previous "comprehensive" deals had flopped, this one would prove worthy of the term, the summiteers hoped, by conclusively addressing Greece's debt problem and taking measures guaranteed to safeguard the rest of Europe. One reason for the leaders' urgency was the continued hammering that European securities were taking in financial markets. And there was another, political imperative for success at the Brussels conclave that was especially important to Sarkozy, rendering him even more mercurial than usual: the French president was scheduled to host the annual G20 summit in Cannes in early November. If Europe's crisis response was still floundering by then, the diplomatic mortification — for all of Europe, but for the host government in particular — would be excruciating.

As shall be seen in this chapter, the flurry of summits in the fall of 2011 would plumb fresh depths of disappointment. The aftermath of the Cannes G20 parley would be one of the most harrowing phases of the euro-zone crisis. This is not to say that advances were entirely absent during this period; the agreement in principle for a Greek debt restructuring of full-monty proportions was a major step, heartily welcomed by the IMF, which had played a significant part in providing the analytical case for such a move. Yet even this development must be kept in perspective. At the same time as Sarkozy was shaking his fists at the banking-industry leaders, he was clinging to the principle that the deal must be voluntary. For all his bravado, he remained worried that if the banks were pushed too far, an imposed default would ensue, with unfathomable consequences. How could these seemingly irreconcilable positions be squared? Therein lies a little-understood story about that night's events.

A three-fold package of measures was on the agenda for the Brussels summiteers. First, they wanted to show that Greece's debt would be shrunk to manageable dimensions, which meant striking a deal with the banks involving a much bigger haircut than the July 21 agreement. As in the case of the earlier pact, Dallara and Lemierre were speaking for the creditors, with Greek officials present, but leaving the chief negotiating role to Italy's Grilli, who represented the Eurogroup. Dallara had abandoned efforts to preserve the July 21 terms; indeed, he knew that many of the financial institutions he represented had practically given up hopes of recovering anything on their Greek bonds. But he was repeatedly warning, both publicly and privately, that there were limits to the losses those institutions could accept on a voluntary basis. For its part, Greece would have to deepen its commitments to austerity to get this debt relief together with new loans that would be part of a new program with the Troika.

The purpose of the summiteers' two other objectives was to limit any possible contagion from the Greek restructuring or other similar shock. The political and economic situation in Italy was deteriorating particularly fast (more about that in the next section), and European leaders wanted to enhance the EFSF's capacity for handling rescues of big countries. They agreed to leverage the EFSF in two ways: the first was based on the hope that extra-large sums might be forthcoming from China, Japan and other major investors outside of Europe, such as Middle Eastern sovereign wealth funds. Under this approach, the EFSF would create "special purpose vehicles" to attract the overseas investors, with the funds available for tapping if necessary. The second method involved the use of what was called "risk insurance," which was essentially the same as the bondholder-guarantee proposal discussed at the IMF-World Bank meetings. Under this scheme, the EFSF would guarantee investors against loss on some portion of the bonds issued by member states, so instead of being able to buy just €250 billion worth of bonds, the EFSF would use its resources to back the purchase of several times that amount.

The EFSF plans were the summit's second objective; the third was to assure markets that European banks could readily absorb losses on their European government bonds, by mandating an increase in their capital to substantially safer levels than before. The leaders endorsed new findings by European regulators that the region's banks needed approximately €106 billion in capital — considerably more than had been conceded earlier — and they also backed more stringent standards for capital levels than had been previously required. As Lagarde had suggested in her Jackson Hole speech, banks needing additional capital to fulfill the standard would be expected to try raising it first in private markets, then from their own governments, and then — if their governments were strapped — from the EFSF. Whether these measures went far enough was questionable; at least they went in the right direction.

As talks on these issues dragged on into the evening of October 26, Sarkozy was champing at the bit to assail the bankers on the Greek debt issue. Reports of painfully slow progress were coming from negotiations under way several floors below in the Justus Lipsius Building, where Dallara and Lemierre were meeting with Grilli and a handful of other officials. The French president knew he could count on Merkel to join him in intervening, but she refused to do so before midnight. For one thing, the summiteers had plenty to discuss as they went through their lengthy communiqué paragraph by paragraph. The fine print was especially important for some items regarding new disciplines that euro-zone countries were agreeing to apply to their fiscal policies — a German initiative, predictably. These new rules included pledges for member countries to put balanced-budget requirements in their constitutions, and new powers for the European Commission to blow the whistle on national spending plans that skirted the bounds of profligacy. Another reason the German chancellor wanted to wait before muscling into the talks with the bankers was to allow a decent amount of time for the negotiators to narrow their differences over several complex points.

The size of the haircut that would be applied to Greek bonds was naturally the main focus of attention. It must be at least 50 percent instead of the 21 percent agreed in July, and it must be a reduction in the nominal amount of the bonds (that is, their face value) rather than the more slippery figure of net present value — on that, Merkel and Sarkozy were agreed, and they couldn't afford to yield without looking feckless; the media had reported it. Whatever the exact figure, it would have to be sizable, because an appallingly large amount of Greece's private debt had been paid off already — much of it with money the Troika had lent to Athens — leaving less that could be subjected to a haircut. Of the €320 billion in private debt that Greece owed at the time of the first Troika program in May 2010, only about €206 billion remained outstanding, which meant that the percentage reduction on that amount would have to be all the larger.

For Dallara and Lemierre, the number that mattered almost more than anything was the sweetener — the enticement for banks to exchange their old bonds for new ones of lower face value. They initially wanted something similar to the deal they had negotiated in July, under which the new bonds would be backed by collateral consisting of Triple-A securities.[2] But to the bankers' amazement and delight, they realized they were going to get something much better.

European negotiators insisted at the October 26 meeting that the sweetener should be in the form of cash instead. In other words, Greece's bondholders would receive an up-front payment of euros in partial satisfaction of their claims. An up-front cash payment is obviously preferable, from an investor's standpoint, to the same amount of collateral held for years to guarantee repayment. And serendipitously, it suited the European governments too, because of complex budget accounting rules that made cash a better alternative for them politically. The money for making these payments would be lent by European governments to Greece, which would then hand the cash over to its bondholders.

2 According to the terms of the July agreement, Greece would be obliged to buy the securities, which would be set aside to assure bondholders of repayment, in a complex scheme involving the EFSF.

The only question was how big the cash sweetener would be. Dallara and Lemierre maintained that €30 billion was necessary if the deal was to win the voluntary assent of creditors; Grilli said he had no mandate to approve anything.

When midnight approached, Sarkozy tapped his watch. It was time to browbeat the bankers. Dallara and Lemierre were summoned to the office of European Council President Van Rompuy, who joined Sarkozy along with Merkel, Lagarde, Grilli and the heads of two other European bodies; no staffers were allowed except for Sarkozy's interpreter. Incredibly, no Greek officials were present for this meeting either, even though it was their debt that was on the line.

Sarkozy's rant about "thieves and liars" set the initial tone, and Dallara was sorely tempted to issue a rebuttal, but before an argument could get started, Merkel piped up. "She said in a very calm voice, 'Mr. Dallara, we would like to find some solution here. Tell me your thoughts,'" Dallara recalled. "And then we began a dialogue. I emphasized the importance of the 30 billion [euro sweetener]. She emphasized the importance of a haircut that was in the range of 50 percent."

A discussion on debt sustainability followed, in which Lagarde offered a few remarks. The hardest bargaining, though, was over the sweetener. European officials' initial negotiating position was to give nothing; the bankers held out for more, and kept getting it — €10 billion, €20 billion and finally €30 billion, provided the banks agreed to the 50 percent haircut. The details would be worked out in ensuing weeks and months, because these broad parameters left open many fine points, such as the maturities and yields of new bonds that would be exchanged for old ones.

Merkel "finally reached out — we were sitting in these big chairs — and handed me a draft press release," Dallara continued. "She said, 'Why don't you take this, mark it up, and get it back to me, if possible, within an hour?' The numbers were missing, but the terminology was already there. I said, 'We'll get back to you to confirm, but I think we have an understanding.'"

It was then after 2:00 a.m. Dallara and Lemierre left with the draft press release, hardly believing their luck in having negotiated such a substantial sweetener. As tough as the 50 percent haircut would be for some investors, it had been widely anticipated, and the pain would be easier for bondholders to take since they would be getting immediate cash payments equal to 15 percent of the amount they were owed, in addition to new Greek bonds. Together with one of Dallara's top aides, Dallara and Lemierre made modest wording changes — regarding the goal set for Greece's debt sustainability, for example, they made sure the banks would not be held accountable for failure to reach any particular target, since that would depend on many other factors outside the banks' control. Then a logistical problem arose: they couldn't find a computer and printer on which to print out an amended draft, "so we found a Belgian security guard who opened up an office, presumably against all EU procedures," Dallara recalled, "and he used somebody's computer terminal to type it up and print it out for us." Their handiwork was incorporated into the twelfth paragraph of the communiqué issued in the early dawn hours that morning.

Media coverage gave the impression that Dallara and Lemierre had simply capitulated in the face of intimidation from heads of state. *The New York Times* account was typical: "In the end, it was Chancellor Angela Merkel of Germany and President Nicolas Sarkozy of France against the European banking establishment — and the bankers blinked," the paper reported.[3] Other news articles described the French and German leaders as having delivered an "ultimatum" to attain the banks' assent.[4] In fact, many of the officials who scrutinized the details of the accord with Dallara and Lemierre were concluding that the banks had once again gotten more favourable terms than they had any right to expect, especially given the €30 billion cash sweetener. As a German policy maker (who wished to remain anonymous) told me: "It was great spin [to characterize the banks as surrendering], but the PSI was not as deep as was portrayed."

3 Steven Erlanger and Stephen Castle, 2011, "Calling Bankers' Bluff, Merkel Won Europe a Debt Plan," *The New York Times*, October 27.

4 Tony Czuczka and Helene Fouquet, 2011, "Sarkozy Temper Boils, Banks Yield in Six-Day War Saving the Euro," Bloomberg News, October 28.

Still, this was hardly a light dusting. And the bankers would not be the only ones subjected to reprobation at this summit.

As a multilateral institution, the IMF is supposed to distance itself completely from domestic politics in member countries. While promoting policies they deem wise, top management and staff scrupulously avoid, as best they can, the slightest appearance of aiding or damaging the fortunes of any political party or individual politician. Nevertheless, in the fall of 2011, the Fund was seen in some quarters as the means by which a monumental political shift might take place in Italy.

The chief source for this information is no less an authority than Tim Geithner. In the former Treasury secretary's words: "At one point that fall, a few European officials approached us with a scheme to try to force Italian Prime Minister Silvio Berlusconi out of power; they wanted us to refuse to support IMF loans to Italy until he was gone. We told the President [Obama] about this surprising invitation, but as helpful as it would have been to have better leadership in Europe, we couldn't get involved in a scheme like that. 'We can't have his blood on our hands,' I said."[5]

That passage comes from Geithner's book, *Stress Test*, which was published two and a half years after Berlusconi's November 2011 ouster. The publication of that single paragraph in a 592-page book caused a sensation in Rome. Ever since Berlusconi was forced from office and replaced by Mario Monti, an economist and former EU competition commissioner, suspicion had swirled among Italians about who was pulling the strings, with international plots high on the list of likely sounding theories. The removal by subversive means of a democratically elected head of government, no matter how offensive his character, is obviously a legitimate topic of inquiry — all the more so if foreigners and multilateral organizations are playing a part.

5 Timothy F. Geithner, 2014, *Stress Test: Reflections on Financial Crises,* New York, NY: Crown Publishers, chapter 11.

It is fair to say that those seeking regime change in Italy during the late summer and early fall of 2011 were sorely provoked. A multiplicity of erratic moves by Berlusconi and others in his government in the late summer and early fall sparked incredulity abroad, both in official quarters and in financial markets. One week the prime minister would unveil a budget-tightening package with a dramatic flourish, only to be followed a few days later by an about-face or at least partial withdrawal of some of the most controversial pieces. Tax surcharges on high-earning Italians were announced in mid-August ("Our hearts are streaming with blood. We find ourselves before the biggest planetary struggle," Berlusconi lamented when he made the proposal),[6] but they were dropped in favour of a plan to delay government pension payments, which in turn fell prey to furious opposition from unions and business leaders. Headlines quoting Berlusconi denouncing Italy as "this shitty country" in a phone conversation further eroded his crumbling authority, as did continued lurid revelations in the judicial inquiries against him involving alleged corruption, tax fraud and sexual misconduct.[7] Hostility between Berlusconi and his finance minister, Tremonti, continued to flare, and Tremonti's own behaviour sometimes deepened the dismay of European officialdom even further. At a meeting of G7 finance ministers and central bankers in late September, jaws dropped when Tremonti warned that if an Italian crisis caused the disintegration of the euro zone, Germany would suffer as much as Italy, or perhaps even more. "Schäuble was shocked. Everybody was shocked," recalled one participant. "There really was a problem of trust in the Italian government."

Who, then, were the "European officials" who sought US help in using the IMF to topple Berlusconi from power? Italian journalists have besieged Geithner with questions on that subject. To the best of my knowledge, neither the former Treasury secretary nor people who served with him in Washington have furnished any answers, although some of his own words hint strongly that Merkel and Sarkozy were

6 Christopher Emsden and Stacy Meichtry, 2011, "Italy Unveils Measures to Balance Budget, *The Wall Street Journal,* August 13.

7 Guy Dinmore, 2011, "Berlusconi hangs on amid cuts and sex sagas," *Financial Times,* September 2.

supportive of the effort.[8] I can say, based on what I have been told, that the schemes for getting rid of Berlusconi bandied around in the fall of 2011 included a variety of approaches, some of which seemed to contradict each other. For example, one idea was to force the prime minister into the arms of the IMF, in the expectation that his failure to abide by Fund conditions would prove his undoing; other ideas involved withholding international aid in the hope of obliging him to quit lest the Italian economy collapse. Although none of these ploys seem very likely to have succeeded, or even very sensible to pursue, the fact that they were discussed at high official levels is noteworthy.

It is no secret that Merkel and Sarkozy had completely lost confidence in their Italian counterpart by the fall of 2011, and fervently hoped he would be replaced by a competent leader in Rome. At one point, Merkel even called Giorgio Napolitano, the president of Italy who, as head of state, held the power to select a new prime minister if parliamentary backing for the incumbent evaporated. In that conversation, which took place on October 20, Merkel expressed concern about whether Berlusconi was strong enough to deliver the necessary reforms, and when Napolitano noted that Berlusconi had barely survived a recent vote of confidence in Parliament, Merkel said she would be grateful for the president doing whatever was "within [his] powers" to promote reform. That phone call, details of which were disclosed by *The Wall Street Journal*,[9] provides strong evidence of the German chancellor's eagerness to see Berlusconi go. But whether she or Sarkozy, or anyone acting at their behest, approached Geithner or other US officials to propose specific anti-Berlusconi plans cannot be confirmed. As for the

8 A transcript of a conversation Geithner had with assistants preparing his book quotes him as saying, "I thought what Sarkozy and Merkel was doing was basically right which is this isn't going to work. The German public [was] not going to support a bigger firewall, more money for Europe if Berlusconi was presiding over that country. He was at that point in the midst of one of his trials for, you know, sex with minors and things like that." He was then asked: "So did they essentially do that?" Geithner's reply: "They ultimately did it, but they did it pretty deftly actually. He stepped down." This transcript is not public; I was given access to a copy.

9 Marcus Walker, Charles Forelle and Stacy Meichtry, 2011, "Deepening Crisis Over Euro Pits Leader Against Leader," *The Wall Street Journal*, December 30.

IMF, officials there stoutly deny being involved in any talks regarding such plans.

Powerful figures in Italy, notably Napolitano, were quietly paving the way for Berlusconi's exit — for that, ample evidence also exists, raising questions about whether the octogenarian president abused the constitutional powers of his office. Napolitano met in the summer of 2011 with Monti, the technocrat who would eventually be tapped for the prime ministership, and soon thereafter Monti was discussing with at least two leading Italians the possibility that the president might ask him to form a government, according to statements by the people involved.[10] Whether these machinations constituted the preliminary stages of a "coup" against a sitting prime minister, as some in Italy have charged, is beyond the scope of this book.

By the time of the two late-October summits in Brussels, dealing with Italy had risen to the top of European leaders' agenda, along with restructuring Greek debt, strengthening the firewall and recapitalizing banks. At the first summit, on October 23, Merkel and Sarkozy went public with their low esteem for Berlusconi, rolling their eyes and grimacing at a press conference when asked for comment on the Italian situation. That cosmetic humiliation was followed by a more meaningful one — a demand for Berlusconi to commit, in writing, to a specific and far-reaching set of economic measures. Van Rompuy sent a letter to Berlusconi spelling out what was required, evoking a bellicose response from the Italian prime minister, who declared on October 24, "No one in the EU can nominate themselves as special administrators and speak in the name of elected governments and the European people. No one is in the position of giving lessons to his partners."[11] But he was cornered, knowing how markets would react if he refused to comply. The following night, the eve of the October 26

10 Alan Friedman, 2014, "Italy: Monti's secret summer," *Financial Times*, February 10. This article also disclosed that Napolitano asked an influential banker, Corrado Passera, to draft a detailed, confidential plan for delivering economic "shock therapy" to Italy, and Passera shared it with Monti, whose cabinet Passera later joined.

11 Guy Dinmore, 2011, "Berlusconi faces the ultimate downgrade," *Financial Times*, October 24.

summit, he submitted a 14-page document (largely drafted by officials at the European Commission and European Council) containing a detailed plan including asset sales, an easing of labour laws and an increase in the retirement age of Italian workers to 67 by 2026 — a major concession that his allies in Parliament had bitterly resisted.[12] And at the summit itself, he even agreed to passages in the communiqué stating that the Commission would "provide a detailed assessment of the measures" and "monitor their implementation."[13]

Italian economic policy, previously subject to a detailed diktat from the ECB in August, was now effectively under supervision from Brussels. The IMF's turn to get involved in Italy was coming next, and at that point, whether by some calculated scheme or the accumulated effect of his own misdeeds, Berlusconi's days in office would be numbered in the single digits.

Swords raised in salute, a French honour guard in red-plumed gold helmets and white breeches stood at attention as Christine Lagarde disembarked from her car onto the red carpet of the Palais des Festivals in Cannes, the famed promenade of Hollywood stars, on November 2, 2011. The annual summit of the G20 was under way. It was getting off to a rocky start, and omens regarding the final outcome were not promising. Although she couldn't have known it as she entered the Palais that day, the IMF managing director would be virtually the only participant to leave Cannes with any legitimate claim to accomplishment.

Flanked by the honour guard, an animated Nicolas Sarkozy was waiting to greet Lagarde along with heads of state and government as they arrived. For the French president, the summit afforded a long-anticipated moment to shine on the world stage. He had once

12 Peter Spiegel, Hugh Carney and Quentin Peel, 2011, "Leaders struggle for eurozone deal," *Financial Times*, October 26.

13 "Euro Summit Statement," October 26, 2011, www.consilium.europa.eu/uedocs/cms_data/docs/pressdata/en/ec/125644.pdf.

envisioned France's turn to host the G20 as an opportunity to orchestrate fundamental reform of the international monetary system, and he was still professing grand ambitions for this Riviera gathering, as witnessed by banners decking the streets proclaiming, "History is being written in Cannes." But plans for the summiteers to dwell on such long-range issues were going up in smoke, as short-term emergencies regarding the euro zone were, perforce, topping the agenda. The measures taken at the European summits of late October were exerting none of the desired effects. Indeed, the crisis was taking turns for the worse on multiple fronts, with financial markets sinking accordingly.

Greece's woes, which were supposed to be in at least temporary abeyance following the debt deal with the banks, were again stoking doubt about the monetary union's durability. On October 31, Papandreou jolted the world by calling for a national referendum on Greece's latest agreement with the Troika, throwing into question whether the country would adopt the policies required for continued membership in the euro zone. Papandreou's motives for taking this dramatic step stemmed from the unnerving reality he encountered upon returning to Athens after the October 26 summit, including some exceptionally frenzied anti-austerity riots and a rebellion in Parliament by both the main opposition party and members of the prime minister's own Socialists. He was taking a gamble — one he felt confident he would win — that the electorate, confronted with the alternative of national bankruptcy and possible exit from the euro, would vote in favour of the bailout package, thereby disarming the parliamentary opponents. But understandable from a purely Greek perspective as it might be to seek a mandate from the people, the referendum raised the prospect that uncertainty about Greece's future would persist for months to come, with markets remaining in turmoil pending the voters' judgment. Moreover, the announcement had come as a shock to other European governments, many of whose officials were apoplectic over Papandreou's unilateral move. With the G20 summit just 48 hours from opening, Sarkozy and Merkel agreed in a phone call that the Greek leader should be summoned to Cannes to be informed that the referendum must be an up-or-down vote on the straightforward question of whether Greece wanted to stay in the euro zone or not.[14]

Italy, meanwhile, was continuing to fare poorly in the markets despite the 14-page list of reforms Berlusconi had submitted to his fellow leaders at the October 26 summit and his acceptance of European Commission oversight. Yields on Italian government bonds climbed to euro-era highs, with the nation's Treasury forced to pay 6.06 percent on 10-year debt in an October 28 auction. Skepticism about Berlusconi's intentions deepened when, shortly before his departure for Cannes, his cabinet approved a plan that clearly fell short of his European partners' expectations. Although it included measures to sell state property and cut red tape, the plan lacked provisions aimed at curbing costly pensions and heavy labour regulation that economists widely blamed for the country's stagnation; moreover, parliamentary approval of even the stripped-down package was uncertain. A number of lawmakers from his coalition signed a letter asking him to step down, and rumblings about his imminent resignation grew deafening as the G20 summit opened amid reports that Tremonti himself had told him: "I am saying that...there will be a disaster in the markets if you, Silvio, stay at your post and do not go. Because the problem for Europe and the markets, correct or not as it may be, is in fact you."[15] But Berlusconi was vowing to stay in office and fighting hard to win parliamentary confidence votes.

As for the plans agreed on October 26 to magnify the firewall fund, they were showing scant sign of producing results either, and they were drawing a cacophony of criticism. The EFSF's Regling embarked in the closing days of October on a much-ballyhooed trip to China and Japan,

14 Detailed accounts of the Cannes summit can be found in Ludlow, "A Tale of Five Summits" (see footnote 1 in this chapter), and in Peter Spiegel, 2014, *How the Euro was Saved,* London: The Financial Times Ltd. I have supplemented that information with my own interviewing.

15 Peter Spiegel and Guy Dinmore, 2011, "Berlusconi under pressure at G20 and in Rome," *Financial Times,* November 3.

where he made a pitch for Asian money that his institution could tap to expand its financial firepower. Asian buyers accounted for 40 percent of the bonds the EFSF had previously issued, after all, and both Beijing and Tokyo pledged to continue buying them. But the Asian response to the new approach was wary.[16] Investing in EFSF bonds guaranteed by European governments was one thing; it was far from clear how safe money invested in special purpose vehicles would be. Explaining Beijing's concerns, Yu Yongding, a prominent Chinese economist, wrote in a *Financial Times* op-ed: "The Chinese people will ask: If Germans do not want to contribute more money, why should China bother?"[17] Moreover, the uncomfortable prospect loomed that Chinese officials might expect a quid pro quo from the desperate Europeans for any money that might be forthcoming. A number of commentators and editorialists fretted that Beijing might insist upon, and obtain, concessions such as a toning-down of official European complaints about human rights, or changes in the way Chinese products were treated in trade disputes.[18]

The upshot was one of the oddest G20 summits ever. The elephant in the room — the crisis in Europe — was barely discussed in the leaders' main meetings, since everyone knew intensive negotiations were taking place at side meetings that included Lagarde, Merkel, Sarkozy and the heads of major European bodies, together with a handful of other top euro area policy makers. The hope and expectation among the non-European G20 participants was that, under the glare of worldwide attention, the side meetings would produce some kind of breakthrough, which the summit would endorse. Nothing resembling a breakthrough ever came.

At 5:30 p.m. on November 2, Sarkozy convened the first of the side meetings, concerning the proposed Greek referendum, to prepare

16 Charles Forelle, 2011, "Europe Tries to Rescue Its Rescue," *The Wall Street Journal*, November 8.

17 Yu Yongding, 2011, "Beijing will not ride to the eurozone's rescue," *Financial Times*, October 31.

18 See, for example, "Do not rush to pawn the euro," *Financial Times*, October 31, 2011.

for a confrontation with Papandreou, who was flying in from Athens accompanied by his finance minister, Venizelos. (No honour guard was on hand to welcome the Greek leaders.) Later that evening the Greek leaders joined this elite group for dinner, where Papandreou would undergo the EU equivalent of being mugged by a gang. He knew his hold on the prime ministership was tenuous; he did not realize how this episode would finish him.

A single sheet of paper containing six points spelled out the terms Papandreou would have to accept if he was to proceed with the referendum. The vote would have to take place by the first week of December; the choice would be staying in the euro zone or leaving it; and Athens would receive no new disbursements until the Greek Parliament approved the terms of the plan agreed on October 26. As was his wont, Sarkozy again played the role of browbeater-in-chief, virtually accusing Papandreou of betraying Europe after having been promised such huge debt relief. Others present, although uncomfortable at the harshness with which one European leader was dictating to another, did not back away from the demands. Papandreou's explanation of his decision made some sense; he argued that a referendum was his only way of overcoming opposition from politicians who were claiming they could have negotiated a better deal. He also agreed to hold the vote within a month, and bowed — after putting up some feeble resistance — to making the poll an up-or-down vote on euro-zone membership. But some of the European leaders still wanted to kill the referendum entirely, and they had their agent in Venizelos, who had never liked the referendum and was known to covet Papandreou's job. Upon returning to Athens early the next morning with Papandreou, Venizelos issued a statement, effectively undercutting the prime minister, declaring that Greece's membership in the euro zone "cannot be put in doubt... [and] cannot depend on a referendum." With that, the hue and cry for Papandreou's resignation became deafening.

The day after Papandreou's Cannes ordeal, it was Berlusconi's turn.

Once again, Sarkozy was using histrionics to make his point, at a Cannes meeting on Italy that started shortly before 11:00 a.m. on November 3. He "almost shouted out at Berlusconi….he was very emotional," according to the recollections of Barroso, who was attending in his capacity as European Commission president.[19]

The French president wanted the Italian prime minister to accept an idea advanced by Lagarde at this meeting. Depending on who is asked, the proposal was either sensible, imperative, unnecessary or fraught with risk to the point of being crazy. Nobody, including the IMF managing director herself, claimed that it was ideal.

The idea was for Italy to ask the IMF for a precautionary credit line (PCL), which is designed for countries that fear becoming vulnerable to balance-of-payments crises even if they are not yet suffering from a full-fledged one. Sarkozy was the most ardent champion of this approach, and he was joined at the meeting by Schäuble in clamouring for Berlusconi to recognize the necessity of Fund help in quelling market turmoil. The yield on Italian 10-year bonds was rising that day to yet another euro-era high of 6.4 percent, which aggravated the urgency of the French president's desire for a major step that could serve as a summit accomplishment. "Silvio, the G20 starts in two hours," he said, according to participants' records of the meeting. "Will you please ask for a PCL from the IMF."

It is worth pausing to reflect that this was the same Sarkozy who, the previous year, had fought vehemently to keep the IMF out of the euro-zone crisis. Now he was beseeching the prime minister of the zone's third-largest country to seek the Fund's aid. If ever there was a moment revealing how the tables had turned in the IMF's favour relative to Europe by the fall of 2011, this was it.

Lagarde offered several points in support of Sarkozy's argument. First, she said, the Italian government had lost credibility — with markets, with the public both domestically and abroad, and with European

19 Alan Friedman, 2015, *Berlusconi: The Epic Story of the Billionaire Who Took Over Italy*, New York, NY: Hachette Books, chapter 12.

partner governments. An IMF program could restore that credibility, by showing that Rome's commitments to adopt reforms would be subject to international oversight. In deference to Italy's political sensitivity about being lumped with Greece, Ireland and Portugal, Lagarde said she recognized that a regular IMF rescue wasn't in order, which was one of the great advantages of a PCL, since it was different from the rescues those countries had received. Although the program would involve risk, it was the best solution, Lagarde contended.

Berlusconi scoffed at the idea that his country needed IMF assistance. He noted the list of actions he had already promised at the late-October Brussels summit, which the European Commission was supposed to monitor. Then, echoing a refrain he had often expressed in public, he argued that the Italian economy was in much better condition than was widely perceived. The country's restaurants were full, he observed, and even if market pessimism persisted for a while the government could afford to borrow at relatively high interest rates, since so much of its debt was long-term.

European Commission and European Council officials were also dubious about the value-added of an IMF program, considering the pledges the Italian government had already made and the Commission's plan to monitor them. When Van Rompuy asked Lagarde how much money would be available to Italy under a PCL, the reply — about €80 billion — met with more scorn, from both EU and Italian policy makers present. Looking at what their government would need in cash if it couldn't borrow on the open market for two or three years, Italian finance ministry officials estimated that a rescue program would have to be €600 billion, if not more. Announcing an IMF program would highlight Italy's vulnerability, and if the funding was inadequate, investors would take no comfort — on the contrary, they would fear being trampled in a stampede. "I can think of better ways of committing suicide than going to the IMF," Tremonti quipped, according to people who were present. Italian officials proposed an alternative, in which Italy would submit to joint European Commission and IMF monitoring, but without an actual Fund program of any kind — a suggestion that EU officials endorsed, since no dollar or euro figures would be included.

"Frankly, I said that €80 billion was peanuts compared to what we were doing with the other countries," Barroso recalled. "It was less than we had given to Greece. If news got out that Italy was getting an €80 billion rescue loan from the IMF, then that would be a disaster."[20]

Some Italian officials held the PCL proposal in such low esteem that they wondered later whether it was part of the alleged secret plot by Merkel and Sarkozy to topple Berlusconi from power. This degree of cynicism appears completely misplaced. For one thing, a similar rescue for Spain was proposed at Cannes, according to a book by Spanish Prime Minister José Luis Zapatero[21] — and there was certainly no scheme against Zapatero, who had already announced plans to step down.

The proposed PCL for Italy may have been hastily conceived, but it was no Machiavellian ruse to unseat the Italian prime minister. A number of officials who were involved in the discussions contend that the proposal was sincerely intended as offering the best hope for Italy to minimize its chances of severe crisis. Rather than providing the Italian government with all the money needed for two or three years in the absence of market financing, the theory was that the program would help Italy continue to raise money in the markets at a time when the government needed to borrow tens of billions of euro per month. The credibility conferred by IMF oversight, plus the availability of the €80 billion should the Italians need to draw it, could be reasonably beneficial in this regard, Fund staffers believed. As one explained:

> The idea was never to take them out of the market. The idea was to support them being in the market, by having a backstop. They were coming to a period where they had massive financing needs, something like €30 billion a month. The Italians themselves were obsessed with the idea that they would need so much money. But the idea was, with a precautionary program, they could maintain

20 Ibid.

21 Paul Taylor, 2013, "Merkel tried to bounce Spain into IMF bailout: ex-PM," Reuters, November 25.

> market access, and have some money in their pocket if they needed it. That was all we could do. We always knew that taking them out of the market was impossible.

The IMF position had an important subtext: a rescue for Italy would entail a new, more senior status for the Fund, meaning the right to negotiate conditionality for the entire euro zone. IMF staffers, backed by officials in the US and UK Treasuries, were making it clear that a program for Italy could not be run in the way previous programs had been, with the Fund sitting on the same side of the table as the ECB and going along with the central bank's policy demands. This time, changes would have to occur in the relative status of Troika members; although Lagarde didn't raise this point during the discussions with Berlusconi and the others, her subordinates were delivering the message to European officials.

"The ECB's argument was that they make monetary policy not for Greece or for Ireland or for any individual country, but for the euro zone," said Jörg Asmussen, who was Merkel's Sherpa at Cannes. "But when there were debates about a program for Italy, then the Fund said, 'For the small states, you might be correct [about limiting conditionality to the country in question]. But if Italy moves into a program, then there has to be [pan-European] conditionality for monetary policy.'"

It was a moot point. Berlusconi's rejection of an IMF program for Italy meant that the Troika arrangement would remain intact as it was. The most the Italian premier's interlocutors could persuade him to accept that morning was Fund involvement in monitoring implementation of his previous pledges. This was a letdown for Merkel, and especially for Sarkozy, who wanted a much meatier summit outcome. The frustrated French president called for a second meeting to take place that evening, after the G20 had adjourned for the day.

Imagine people so frantic for cash that they resort to searching their sofas, pulling off the cushions and sticking their hands into the crevices in the hope of plucking out some loose coins. That is an apt metaphor for what was transpiring in Cannes when the group of top Troika and euro-zone policy makers who had met on the morning of November 3 to discuss Italy reconvened at around 9:40 p.m. Joining them, and chairing the session, was US President Barack Obama, who was assuming this role at Sarkozy's behest in the hope that he would use his powers of persuasion to mobilize a consensus for action.

Obama's main goal, long shared by both his government and Sarkozy's, was to augment Europe's firewall, the ultimate aim being to keep the crisis from raging out of control. The most obvious approaches — obtaining more contributions from European governments to the EFSF, or using the unlimited euro-creation powers of the ECB — were moribund at that point, for the economic and political reasons cited above. The same went for the various ideas to leverage the EFSF's financial resources. So with French backing, Obama was promoting a new stratagem, which involved the IMF using its power to create SDRs at the touch of an "enter" button and allocate them to all of its member countries. In a scene bordering on the surreal, this esoteric quasi-currency became the topic of an extended and emotional discussion among the heads of state and other political leaders meeting that night in the Palais des Festivals.

Initially invented with the worthy aim of reducing the world's dependence on the US dollar, SDRs were comprised of a basket of four major currencies,[22] as will be recalled from chapter 4. Although not used as money in ordinary transactions (and unsuccessful in displacing the dollar), they can be converted into usable cash, once changed into their constituent currencies. As will also be recalled from chapter 4, the 2009 G20 summit in London had directed the IMF to allocate $250 billion worth of SDRs to all of its member countries, the idea being to help combat the global crisis by increasing the reserves held by the world's central banks. Under Obama's 2011 proposal, the IMF would make another such allocation, with euro-zone countries using their share of the two allocations — worth about €140 billion — to contribute to the EFSF. In this way, Europe would bear the primary burden for firewall-building, rather than putting the IMF at greater risk, although European government budgets would not be unduly strained either.

22 The Chinese yuan is slated to be added as a fifth currency in October 2016.

Gimmicky as this plan was, it appeared to avoid the problems that had plagued other proposals. But to Obama and Sarkozy's dismay, Merkel said that her government could not go along. The Bundesbank was objecting, she explained, and under German law, the Bundesbank is technically the IMF's shareholder, with legal responsibility for assets and obligations arising from Germany's membership, including SDRs (although the finance ministry decides the position the country takes on IMF policy matters).

Bundesbank officials were not in Cannes, but shortly before the opening of the summit they had learned about the SDR scheme, and they saw right through it. The SDRs allocated by the IMF to euro-zone countries would eventually be converted into euros, since that was the currency needed by crisis-stricken countries. And who would create those euros? The ECB would — and that, according to the Bundesbank, would violate the ECB's mandate. It was one thing to use SDRs to boost central bank reserves around the world, as had been agreed in 2009; it was quite another to use SDRs for bailouts.

Merkel made a counter-offer, to increase the firewall in a more straightforward way: she would try to get her Parliament to approve more German funds for the EFSF, provided Italy agreed to request the €80 billion IMF PCL. But Berlusconi was immovable on that subject, and Obama was sympathetic with the Italian view that an underfunded rescue program might only spawn market panic. "I think Silvio is right," he said.

Having been cornered into being the sole opponent of the SDR proposal, a plan that most others in the room favoured, Merkel uncharacteristically became teary-eyed, depicting herself as being asked (like Tremonti) to "commit suicide." Going against the Bundesbank, or seeking more money for the firewall without a commensurate concession from Italy, would be tantamount to signing her own political death warrant, she contended. Taken aback by her breakdown, Obama and Sarkozy dropped the subject of SDRs.

The evening meeting thus ended without any progress, other than final agreement that the IMF would support the Commission in monitoring Italy. Even this minor triumph degenerated into a turf battle when Barroso made clear that his institution would be taking the lead. "If the IMF wants to join us, I have no problem," he said, according to notes of the meeting. "But we will never accept the IMF replacing the Commission. European rules must be respected."

One saving grace of the otherwise ill-starred Cannes summit was a strong signal that a massive injection of new money might be in store for the IMF. The leaders of the BRICS, who held a separate meeting of their own at Cannes, generally expressed preference for helping to resolve the euro-zone crisis by channelling their resources through the Fund, rather than the EFSF or other direct forms of aid to Europe. Money that went to the Fund, after all, could theoretically be used to rescue any country in need, not just a wealthy European one. The presidents of Brazil and Russia, Dilma Rousseff and Dmitry Medvedev, were particularly emphatic that the only way in which they could provide financial support would be via the Fund — carefully adding that they expected governance reforms to be implemented as well.[23]

Delighted by this turn of events, Lagarde used her closing press conference to quote verbatim from the G20 communiqué, which said: "We will ensure the IMF continues to have resources to play its systemic role to the benefit of its whole membership….We stand ready to ensure additional resources could be mobilized in a timely manner."[24]

But how much? The communiqué didn't say, because contrary to speculative reports during the summit, the G20 wasn't ready to decide on even an approximate augmentation for the IMF. To a number of prominent economists, it seemed increasingly clear that the sum should, and could, be very large, in the many hundreds of billions

23 BRICS Information Centre (University of Toronto), 2011, "The BRICS at the G20 Cannes Summit," November 3, www.brics.utoronto.ca/reports/111130-leaders-as.html.

24 IMF, 2011, "Transcript of a Press Briefing with Christine Lagarde," November 4, www.imf.org/external/np/tr/2011/tr110411.htm.

if not trillions of dollars.[25] European countries that had once been leading creditors of the Fund were now big borrowers, or potentially in the queue. And countries that had recently ranked among the biggest borrowers — Brazil and Russia, for example — were now creditors, with the capacity to lend a lot more.

The vague promise of a strengthened IMF could not prevent an investor run to the exits in the days and weeks after Cannes. Having perceived the G20 as flailing for solutions, markets continued to deliver a thumbs down even when technocratic governments came to power in Europe's most troubled economies. In Greece, Lucas Papademos, a former ECB vice president and Columbia University economics professor, became prime minister on November 11; in Italy, the aforementioned Mario Monti succeeded Berlusconi on November 12. Bond yields in Italy and Greece continued to rise nonetheless, reaching 7.5 percent on Italy's long-term government bonds, and similar distress was besetting the governments of Spain, Austria, Belgium and even France, which had to pay record differentials above German bond yields to borrow money. The victory in Spain on November 20 of a new centre-right government led by the ostensibly reform-minded Mariano Rajoy also failed to halt the market slide more than temporarily. By the end of the month the news media was full of speculation that European monetary union could soon be torn apart.

25 See, for example, Barry Eichengreen, 2011, "The IMF must be empowered now," *Emerging Markets,* November 3; and Arvind Subramanian, 2011, "Mme. Lagarde: Where Are You When the World Needs You?" RealTime Economic Issues Watch, Peterson Institute for International Economics, November 11.

14

THE BARBER'S SHEARS

On rare occasions, members of the IMF board receive numbered documents, to inhibit them from giving copies to outsiders. One example was the document circulated to executive directors on January 5, 2012, two months after the washout at the Cannes G20 summit. Underscoring the need for avoiding disclosure, the document stated on its cover: "It is not intended that this paper will be published on the Fund's external website owing to extreme market sensitivity considerations."

The document was nicknamed "the doomsday paper" by some on the staff. "On current policies, the outlook for the world economy is bleak," it said on its summary page. "No economy — whether advanced, emerging or low income — is immune to an escalation of the crisis." According to the paper, a "new paradigm" was at work: "Whereas country shocks in the 50 years prior could largely be considered *idiosyncratic* in that they did not destabilize the entire system, shocks in the advanced economy core...are now effectively *systemic.*"

The aim of the document was to explain the need for increasing the IMF's war chest. On the inside pages was a colour-coded map of the world labelled "a simulation of intensification of the euro area debt crisis," with countries shaded in blue, yellow or red to show how badly their economies could be hit. The scenario was based on the assumption that "confidence and asset price shocks are offset by policy tightening in the absence of external assistance." In more straightforward terms, this meant that if vulnerable euro-zone countries suddenly found themselves cut off from borrowing in private markets and also unable to obtain sufficient amounts of emergency funding from international institutions such as the IMF, they would have no alternative but fiscal austerity. And as more countries cut government spending or raised taxes, the result would be a self-reinforcing contraction that would affect countries elsewhere depending on their economic and financial linkages with Europe. Output losses in blue-shaded countries, which included China and India, would likely be less than one percent; economies of those shaded in yellow, which included the United States, Japan, Brazil and South Korea, would probably contract between one and three percent; the red-shaded countries — predictably including Italy, Spain, Portugal, Belgium and Greece — would slump the most. Such were the risks, the paper's authors warned, of "an escalating crisis…[in which] spreads on government borrowing in some large advanced economies have risen to historical peaks…[and] confidence in banks has eroded, prompting a contraction of credit." In this kind of situation, "no economy…is immune to the unfolding tensions."

The paper estimated that $2 trillion in official financing could conceivably be needed over the following two years, both for rescues of countries in crisis and for precautionary programs. This implied a "global gap" of almost $1 trillion in the amounts available for such purposes, of which "half…could be filled by the Fund," the paper said — meaning that the IMF ought to obtain an extra $500 billion in lendable resources.

The board met on January 17 to discuss the paper. Most of those present endorsed the general approach, while emphasizing that the Europeans must increase their own firewall institutions, according to notes of the meeting taken by a participant. "Staff has made a compelling case," said Alex Gibbs, who represented the United Kingdom, and Christopher Legg, the Australian director, agreed that the paper was "persuasive," adding: "As the region at the epicenter, the euro zone has the chief role to play. Equally, the international community has to build on the recent G20 commitment to ensure…a firewall sufficiently large that it will never need to be used."

The most negative note was sounded by Meg Lundsager, the US director, reflecting the Obama administration's argument that Europe was rich enough to take care of itself. Lundsager contended that the IMF should wait to see what the Europeans do first. "We'll be ready to support a review of [IMF] resources after a European review," she said. (Unmentioned in her comments was the fact that the administration stood no chance of obtaining the necessary legislation from Congress for an increase in US support for the Fund, which some of her colleagues viewed as the most important determinant of the US stance.)

Ironically, the gloomy paper came after a spate of developments in Europe in December 2011 that were helping financial markets to rebound somewhat from Cannes. At a European summit ending in the early morning hours of December 9, leaders agreed on new rules envisioning much tighter regional oversight over government spending and deficits. (Britain refused to go along, but since it isn't in the euro zone that didn't matter much.) Countries in breach of the currency union's deficit ceilings would be subject to "automatic" sanctions — or at least sanctions that would be much more difficult than before to block — and budget-balancing rules would be obligatory under constitutional amendments. Lending credence to this move was Monti's program, dubbed "Salva Italia" (Save Italy) when it was unveiled December 4, aimed at slashing the cost of government while raising the retirement age and hiking tax rates, which appeared likely to transform Berlusconi's empty promises into reality.

Also at the December 8-9 summit came a pledge to "make available additional resources of up to €200 billion to the IMF."[1] European governments, in other words, were going to mobilize money for the Fund in the hope that other countries would follow suit — thereby creating a bigger pool of financing for handling any major emergencies that might arise in the euro zone. This was yet another paradoxical twist for the Europeans given their initial resistance in 2010 to IMF

1 European Council, 2011, "Statement by the Euro Area Heads of State or Government," December 9.

involvement in the crisis. Chinese authorities reacted favourably, as did other BRICS governments, to the evidence that Europe was finally taking substantive action to save itself.

Most important of all was a nearly simultaneous decision by the ECB to erect a "wall of money" that could help protect Europe's most fragile economies. This was the first big move by Mario Draghi since taking over as ECB president, and in keeping with the obfuscatory traditions of central banking, the new approach had its own jargonistic name and acronym — Long-term Refinancing Operations (LTRO). Draghi had initially disappointed investors by reiterating Trichet's dicta against major increases in the central bank's purchases of government bonds; he was not about to arouse the fury of Europe's monetary purists by acting as a lender of last resort to governments. But now that the governments had embraced fiscal reforms at the December 9 summit, Draghi was prepared to help them by using a roundabout approach that took advantage of the ECB's powers to lend to banks — the assumption being that the banks would invest a hefty portion of their new cash in government bonds. Even under the Trichet regime, the ECB had been funnelling cash to banks under relatively relaxed terms, and Draghi persuaded his fellow governing council members to go much further, by providing banks with whatever liquidity they needed for only one percent annual interest and for a period of up to three years, while accepting lower quality collateral than before.[2] The LTRO scheme was akin to measures that IMF staffers had been urging, although it is unclear whether they had any influence in persuading the ECB to adopt it. Altogether, the ECB extended a little more than €1 trillion in cheap funding to banks in two separate operations in December 2011 and February 2012.

Rays of hope, albeit faint, were even emanating from Athens at the end of 2011. Papademos, the academic economist and former central banker who had assumed the premiership, headed a national unity government that included leading figures from both major parties, the

2 ECB, 2011, "ECB announces measures to support bank lending and money market activity," December 8, www.ecb.europa.eu/press/pr/date/2011/html/pr111208_1.en.html.

Socialist PASOK and the centre-right New Democracy. The coalition parties jointly endorsed the objectives of the Troika program, signifying a possible end to the partisan warfare that had hobbled Greek policy making.

Nobody was under the illusion that all was well in Greece, however. The worries expressed in the "doomsday paper" were not entirely misplaced. Athens was in the process of negotiating a second bailout to replace the first one, launched in May 2010. The need for such a new program had been clear once hope was abandoned in mid-2011 that the Greek government would be able to fund its operations by returning to financial markets in the foreseeable future. European leaders had pledged at the October 26 summit that Greece would get a total of €130 billion in loans under this new program, with the IMF expected to furnish some portion of that amount. The Fund was entering into this new bailout with misgivings equal to if not greater than the first one, as this chapter will show.

Moreover, it wasn't clear how one of the chief elements of the new program would work out — that is, the 50 percent haircut on Greek bonds, another goal set at the October 26 summit. A bitterly fought issue was about to be put to its first real test in the euro-zone crisis — whether private lenders should, and could, be induced to give up a significant portion of their claims on countries in financial distress, and how roughly those lenders might be treated. In the process, financial history, of both the good and bad sort, would be made during the early months of 2012.

At long last, the time was approaching to implement the plan, titled "How to Restructure Greek Debt," that had first been proposed in May 2010 by the veteran sovereign debt attorney Lee Buchheit and his academic collaborator, Mitu Gulati, as noted in chapter 7. Since July 2011, Buchheit's firm had been retained by the Greek government, and by the end of that year circumstances were dictating that he try putting his idea into action — fast. "The fuse was lit," he recalled, meaning there would be a race against time to get the job done before a financial explosion.

The fuse lighting had occurred when Merkel and Sarkozy staged their post-midnight confrontation in late October with Dallara and Lemierre. The 50 percent figure agreed for the haircut on holders of Greek bonds set the broad parameters for the debt restructuring, and meant as a matter of mathematical certainty that the amount of debt restructuring would be the most massive ever; Greece owed a little more than €200 billion to private bondholders, so if nearly all of them participated, a 50 percent haircut would shrink their claims by about €100 billion.

But countless details remained unresolved. What sort of new securities would bondholders be offered? What yield would these new securities bear, and which country's laws would govern them? How much inducement was necessary for bondholders to accept these new securities, beyond the cash "sweetener" that had been agreed? Would the deal be entirely voluntary, or might some element of coercion be involved for investors who were unwilling to accept the terms? Would Greek bonds held by official creditors such as the ECB also be subject to haircuts?

Moreover, even before the terms of its debt restructuring could be finalized, Greece had to reach agreement with the Troika on the terms of its new program. Nobody in a position of authority was going to allow Athens to lighten its debt burden without first accepting the need for a long-term plan aimed at restoring competitiveness and fiscal rectitude. Here too, an immense amount of negotiating lay ahead.

All of this had to be hammered out well before March 20, 2012, because on that date Greece was obliged to make a €14.5 billion payment to bondholders. Failure to pay the full amount on time would put Greece in default, which in turn would heighten the likelihood of exit from the euro zone, as the ECB would presumably withdraw support from the Greek banking system, depriving the economy of euros and forcing the government to issue drachma or some other new currency. A shuttering of Greek banks and the imposition of capital controls — regulations preventing the movement of money across Greece's borders — would likely ensue. The potential consequences of this chaos for the rest of Europe were hard to predict with precision, but appeared bound to be negative given that the expansion of the firewall was still a work in progress.

Obtaining the full cooperation of Greece's bondholders loomed as a major difficulty. They were well aware of the anxiety in policy-making circles to avoid a default, which naturally emboldened them against pressure to accept the 50 percent haircut on their investments. To be sure, a substantial portion of the Greek bonds in private hands — an estimated €120 billion worth of the €206 billion total — was held by banks and insurance companies, many of them located in Europe, which rendered them susceptible to arm-twisting by regulators; their willingness to participate in the restructuring was fairly well assured. But the same did not apply to the remaining bondholders. Each one of them, individually at least, potentially stood to gain by holding out — that is, declining to surrender bonds with a face value of twice the amount to be received in return. This was a classic example of what social scientists call a collective action problem, the most common allegorical metaphor being the mice who want to bell a cat. Collectively, the mice would all benefit if the cat were belled, but the decision by each individual mouse to refuse approaching the cat is entirely rational.

Thus went the logic behind Buchheit and Gulati's proposal. Collective action clauses (CACs) — which, as their name implies, are designed to deal with a collective action problem — would be inserted into as many Greek bonds as legally possible. As previously noted, a CAC discourages bondholders from holding out against a restructuring because the clause mandates that if the terms are accepted by a high proportion (say, 75 percent) of the holders, the same terms will be imposed on all. Although few of Greece's bonds had been issued with CACs, most of them were governed by Greek law, and under the Buchheit-Gulati plan the nation's Parliament would exercise its legal power to insert the clauses retroactively.

Fiendishly clever as it was, the plan had a big hitch. The bondholders' participation in Greece's debt restructuring was supposed to be "voluntary" — so said the communiqué issued at the October 26 summit, because of fears that the use of legal coercion would be tantamount to default. And if a minority of bondholders, even just a small minority, voted against the restructuring and suffered losses under terms imposed by CACs, wouldn't that vitiate the claim of voluntarism? In particular, it might lead to the legal declaration of a credit event, in which payments would be required to investors who had insured themselves against a Greek default by buying CDS. As noted in chapter 11, such an outcome was anathema to some in the European establishment; it conjured up memories of the post-Lehman period, when problems for firms active in CDS trading and issuance had exacerbated the breakdown in financial markets. ECB officials were especially adamant on this point: nothing about the restructuring could be involuntary.

As Buchheit put it: "There's very much an Old Testament flavour to how the ECB communicates its views. Someone comes down from the mountain, bearing tablets with commandments on them. And one of the commandments was, 'Thou shalt not trigger the CDS.'"

In the IMF, by contrast, Buchheit had an ally. There is "a real risk under a purely voluntary approach...[of] a significant amount of holdouts," the Fund said in a document published on December 13. "It will be critical... to deliver the near-universal participation necessary to bring Greek debt down by the targeted €100 billion." The document noted approvingly that "a key step now under consideration" was "possible legislation of CACs in domestic law bonds."[3]

Looking back at the complexity of the Greek debt restructuring, its completion on time could be considered almost miraculous. But it should have come much earlier than it did, and as shall be seen in due course, some unfortunate precedents would be set for other countries that may find themselves similarly in need of debt relief.[4]

3 IMF, 2011, "Greece: Fifth Review Under the Stand-By Arrangement," Country Report No. 11/351, December, www.imf.org/external/pubs/ft/scr/2011/cr11351.pdf.

4 Detailed information about the restructuring can be found in Jeromin Zettelemeyer, Christoph Trebesch and Mitu Gulati, 2013, "The Greek Debt Restructuring: An Autopsy," Peterson Institute for International Economics, Working Paper WP 13-8, August; Miranda Xafa, 2014, *Sovereign Debt Crisis Management: Lessons from the 2012 Greek Debt Restructuring*, Centre for International Governance Innovation, CIGI Papers No. 33, June; and Christopher Spink, "Greek Tragedy Averted" (see footnote 14 in chapter 12).

Unswervingly pressing the case for reducing Greece's debt, although he was a latecomer to the cause, was Poul Thomsen, who was above all a dedicated international civil servant. Thomsen remained a steadfast believer in the rescue program for Greece that he had negotiated in the spring of 2010. In conversations with Fund colleagues, he stuck by his conviction that the program could have worked at saving the Greek economy, without giving the country any debt relief, if only Athens had faithfully implemented the structural reforms it had promised, and if a few other untoward developments had not occurred — most notably the Deauville declaration.

But events had conspired against any chance the program had of succeeding, and Thomsen could hardly argue with the consensus view, as reflected in the decision of the October 26, 2011, European summit, that Greece's debt needed a full monty-type restructuring. In keeping with his sense of professional duty, he proved disciplined — and effective — at executing his superiors' wishes. His counterparts were often taken aback by the fervency with which he hounded them to agree on terms aimed at giving Greece a decent shot at debt sustainability. When he felt that Greek negotiators were yielding too readily to the demands of the country's lenders, for example, he was not shy about conveying his displeasure, according to those who recall being on the receiving end of verbal onslaughts such as the following: "Don't be afraid [of the creditors]! Give it to them!" or "Are you trying to cheat me? The IMF will never agree to this!" Indeed, as weeks passed after October 26, the tougher Thomsen became. Projections of Greece's debt sustainability were taking new turns for the worse. This implied that an even more stringent deal was in order.

Thomsen's lodestar was a numerical expression — 120 by 2020. Appropriately or absurdly, depending on one's point of view, these numbers had assumed totemic importance in Greece's debt drama. They referred to a target of 120 percent for Greece's debt-to-GDP ratio by the year 2020, which became the standard for determining whether Greece's debt was sustainable or not. It was widely acknowledged that this target was preposterously precise, considering how far in the future 2020 was and how many variables could affect both Greece's debt and its GDP by that time. Also widely acknowledged was the fact that the 120 percent figure was picked for a completely arbitrary reason, namely that it happened to be approximately the same debt-to-GDP ratio as Italy's, and aiming for anything lower than 120 percent for Greece would risk giving the impression that Italian debt was excessive. As regards who was responsible for devising this long-term goal, fingers point in every direction. Some people claim it started with the IMF; others attribute it to Schäuble; still others recall Grilli (the Italian finance ministry official who chaired some of the Greek debt talks) as the originator.

Whoever deserves credit (or blame), 120 by 2020 was the agreed target in the October 26, 2011, summit accord. Once this target was set, the IMF became its relentless enforcer — not because Fund economists liked it (they would have preferred striving for a substantially lower debt ratio, if anything), but because they found it essential as a disciplinary tool for keeping debt sustainability as the top priority of negotiations. How much difference would it make if Greece's debt, which stood at 163 percent of GDP in early 2012, was projected to decline to, say, 125 percent of GDP in 2020, or if the ratio were projected to stay above 120 percent until a couple of years later? Probably none at all, in substantive terms, but allowing any flexibility in the target, the Fund feared, would lead to loosening it still more, the end result being yet another unsustainable program. If extra sacrifice was required by any of the various parties to the talks, so be it, as far as the Fund was concerned — 120 by 2020 was *sine qua non*.

The most obvious reason for extra sacrifice would be fresh evidence of more weakness than expected in the Greek economy, which in the final weeks of 2011 was exactly what IMF economists were detecting. "We have revised GDP growth down rather significantly, to minus 6 percent in 2011," Thomsen acknowledged in a December 13 conference call with reporters, citing a number of factors, including the contraction of lending by Greece's loss-plagued banks and the government's failure to enact reforms necessary for an improvement in the investment climate.[5] (As with previous forecast revisions, even this latest one did not capture the full extent of the decline the economy would actually post for the year.) And if GDP was going to be lower than anticipated, the most obvious place to seek commensurate reduction in debt was PSI — that is, demanding greater involvement by the private sector in the form of an even bigger haircut.

The IMF's admonitions on this score infuriated Dallara, who together with Lemierre was again leading the committee representing private creditors. "This is what I called 'chasing the rabbit down the hole,'" Dallara recalled about the IMF's adjustments to the forecast and the accompanying calls for more debt relief. "The more you chased, the further the rabbit ran down the hole. The metaphor 'moving the goal posts' was also used a lot." Before long, Dallara and Lemierre were effectively boycotting direct talks with IMF staffers such as Thomsen, turning instead to Papademos as their main interlocutor. Prior to his appointment as prime minister, Papademos had written an op-ed that, in keeping with his ECB background, argued against pushing the private creditors too far, lest doing so result in a "default and a credit event" which, he warned, would drive up interest rates in other euro-zone countries and generate "large — possibly huge — aggregate losses for financial institutions."[6] Echoing other opponents of debt restructuring, Papademos had also pointed out that almost 30 percent of Greece's debt was held domestically, mostly by Greek banks, pension funds and insurance companies. Not that Papademos exerted much control over the size of the haircut Greece's bondholders would ultimately get; even though he was the debtor country's prime minister, the PSI terms were going to have to pass muster with Greece's overseers in the Troika and the Eurogroup.

Dallara and the bondholders he represented were not the only creditors of Greece upset with the IMF's hectoring. The same went for official sector lenders, because the Fund was taking the view that OSI would

5 IMF, 2011, "Transcript of a Conference Call on Greece," December 13, www.imf.org/external/np/tr/2011/tr121311.htm.

6 Lucas Papademos, 2011, "Forcing Greek Restructuring is not the answer," *Financial Times*, October 21.

be just as acceptable as PSI in cutting Greece's debt down to sustainable proportions. Of the Greek government's €356 billion in total debt, €116 billion was owed to the official sector, including European governments, the ECB and the IMF itself. The only official loans to Greece which must be treated as sacrosanct and repaid in full, in the Fund's view, were its own, in accord with its preferred-creditor status, which if violated would make the Fund's shareholders loath to approve rescues in the future.

"The Fund was totally alone on this," recalled Jörg Asmussen, the German deputy finance minister, who in late 2011 was in the process of joining the ECB as a member of the executive board. "There were harsh reactions, because the Fund has preferred creditor status. So people in the Eurogroup were saying, 'It's pretty easy to advocate OSI if you're not part of it.'"

It is worth stepping back to consider the big picture of the battle over OSI, which would continue to flare long after early 2012. The issue arose because the longer Greece kept paying off the principal amounts on bonds as they matured, the more its debt was owed to official creditors rather than private ones. That fact illuminates why bailouts of unsustainably indebted countries can be so injurious. One major drawback is the moral hazard that occurs when private lenders conclude they will be able to get their money back, courtesy of the public sector, no matter how foolish their loans may have been in the first place. Another problem, of more profound concern to citizens of the country being "rescued," is that debt to official bodies may be very hard to restructure, harder even than debt to private creditors. This is especially true for money owed to the IMF; failure to promptly repay the Fund stains a country's credit semi-permanently by putting it in notorious company along with the likes of Zimbabwe, Somalia and Sudan. The Greek case showed how tetchy other official lenders could also be about forgiving repayment.

The official creditors' hardline stance did not lack for supporting arguments. As in previous episodes where OSI had come up, Germany and other creditor governments were determined to stand by the treaty provision prohibiting the assumption of responsibility for the debts of other member states. The electorates of creditor countries had been promised that the monetary union would not become a transfer union

— a pledge that Europe's ruling elites felt bound (not least for the sake of their political survival) to honour. These tenets had been bent almost to the point of breaking when interest rates were reduced and other terms eased on loans to Greece, Ireland and Portugal in July 2011. But outright forgiveness of principal would constitute a blatant transformation of loans into gifts, an unacceptable step as far as Merkel and company were concerned.

For similar reasons, the ECB — the biggest single holder of Greek bonds, with about €42 billion worth in its portfolio — was digging in its heels against proposals that it should take the same 50 percent haircut as private creditors. The central bank had reluctantly started buying the bonds in May 2010, at prices ranging from 70 to 75 cents on the euro, the idea being that doing so would help keep Greece's borrowing costs tolerably low at a time when private investors were staying out of the market. Having acted on such noble intentions, ECB officials saw no reason why their institution should lose money. More important, they feared that a haircut on their bonds would be equivalent to providing retroactive monetary financing of a euro-zone government, in violation of their mandate. Although willing to consider schemes under which the ECB would forego any profit on its Greek bonds, central bank officials drew the line at taking a loss.[7]

But if not OSI, then what? Since private bondholders had already struck a deal for the approximate sacrifice they were going to make, how would the 120 by 2020 target be attained? The obvious alternative to OSI was Greece itself — that is, additional tightening of Greek belts so that the government would have more revenue to make debt payments. This was the option preferred by many European policy makers as negotiations ground forward in February 2012 on the terms of the new Greek program. In meetings of officials from finance ministries, representatives of countries such as Spain, Portugal and Estonia pointed out that their governments were making wrenching fiscal adjustments; why should they go soft on Greece?

7 Peter Spiegel and Ralph Atkins, 2012, "Lagarde presses ECB over Greek debt deal," *Financial Times*, January 24.

The problem, as IMF staffers repeatedly noted, was that another dose of austerity in Greece — where unemployment stood at 22 percent — might only deepen the country's recession and raise its debt-to-GDP ratio still higher. Both numerator (debt) and denominator (GDP) matter, after all, in the debt-to-GDP ratio. For that reason, the IMF was the Troika's "dove," in relative terms, concerning the imposition on Athens of requirements for more and faster cuts in government spending along with hikes in taxes. Reducing government borrowing as much as possible might help keep the absolute level of debt from rising, but if it depressed the economy further, a worse debt-to-GDP ratio would likely result. On fiscal matters, therefore, Fund economists "argued that demand effects...called for a longer adjustment period (thus allowing a more accommodative fiscal policy in the near term)," according to a Fund document published around that time.[8] The document lamented that this approach encountered "resistance from…European partners" and even from the Greek government officials, who feared that postponing tougher action "would be seen as a lack of commitment" to EU-mandated budget goals.

This is not to say that the IMF was dovish in all respects regarding the imposition of conditions on Greece. On the contrary, Fund economists agreed that debt relief was no panacea — it would affect only the numerator, not the denominator, of the debt-to-GDP ratio — and must be accompanied by structural reforms aimed at making the Greek economy more vibrant in the long run by ridding it of its inflexibilities. On this score, the Fund was much more hawkish, especially given all the pledges that Athens had failed to fulfill. Among the most salient examples of Greek heel-dragging were the slowness at which restricted professions were being opened up and union power curbed in collective bargaining. Moreover, the ostensibly technocratic Papademos government was showing signs of frailness, with a cabinet full of party leaders who were jockeying for political advantage in elections scheduled for later in the spring. Accordingly, the Troika concluded that it would have to make demands on Greece that were

8 IMF, 2012, "Greece: Request for Extended Arrangement Under the Extended Fund Facility—Staff Report," Country Report No. 12/57, March, available at: www.imf.org/external/pubs/ft/scr/2012/cr1257.pdf.

more exacting than ever in terms of the amount of detail and timing required for compliance, including long lists of "prior actions" to be taken before loans could be released and a new program approved.[9] And since the Greek government appeared unable to change its laws and rules regarding collective bargaining in meaningful ways, it would have to take more direct action to lower labour costs, most controversially by reducing the minimum wage, then set at €750 per month, by about one-fifth.

Mutual resentment between Athens and the Troika boiled over in an exceptionally hostile period of confrontation and recrimination.[10] On February 7, Greek unions called a 24-hour general strike that shut down government services, schools, docks and banks, in protest of Papademos's efforts to persuade the major parties in his governing coalition to accept new cuts in programs such as health care in addition to the lowering of the minimum wage. When the prime minister obtained party leaders' grudging assent to budget cuts on February 9, euro-zone finance ministers rejected the package as insufficient, delivering a public humiliation to Venizelos by sending him back to Athens amid widespread media accounts of how the Greek finance minister had been scolded like a wayward child. The unions announced another general strike, this one for 48 hours, and five ministers resigned from the cabinet, refusing to accept Papademos' insistence that the country would be even worse off without the Troika deal than with it. Although the remaining cabinet members endorsed the package and sent it to Parliament for approval, the streets outside were in chaos, as police battled with firebomb-throwing protesters. On Sunday the 12th, as Parliament voted approval, an estimated 80,000 people turned out in Athens to express their outrage, and rioters firebombed branches of two leading lenders, National Bank of Greece and Eurobank. Despite

9 Peter Spiegel and Kerin Hope, 2012, "Call for EU to control Greek budget," *Financial Times*, January 27.

10 Information about this series of events can be found in Maria Petrakis, Marcus Benasson and Natalie Weeks, 2012, "Papademos to Meet Greek Party Chiefs on Great Sacrifices," Bloomberg News, February 7; Stephen Fidler, 2012, "16 'Angry Parents' Lecture Greece," *The Wall Street Journal*, February 11; Kerin Hope and James Wilson, 2012,"Greece passes vote as violence erupts," *Financial Times*, February 13.

the parliamentary action, the Troika declared that funds still would not be released unless party leaders delivered written commitments to implement the plan fully, whatever the result of the pending election. Such a hard-nosed stance toward Greece was increasingly seen in European capitals — northern European capitals in particular — as relatively risk free, because financial markets in other countries were no longer moving in tandem with developments in Athens as they had the previous year. Bond prices in Italy, Spain and Ireland were on the rise; long-term Portuguese bonds were trading at even lower yields than before the events of October 2011 — all evidence that the ECB's new monetary approach was exerting the desired effect.

A document marked "strictly confidential" and dated February 15, 2012, conveyed the IMF's view of events at that point: the cliché about the impossibility of drawing blood from a stone was becoming apropos in Greece's case.[11]

The document was a nine-page debt sustainability analysis presented to euro-zone finance ministers. Although the IMF was publicly standing with its fellow Troika members in pressing the Greeks for concessions, this analysis tacitly acknowledged discomfort with the extent to which the burden of adjustment was being foisted on Athens. As beneficial as it might be to reduce Greek wages, the document's authors asserted, the corollary impact on Greek incomes and spending power was undeniable — as was the ultimate effect on the country's ability to climb out of debt. "There is a fundamental tension between the program objectives of reducing debt and improving competitiveness, in that the internal devaluation needed to restore...competitiveness will inevitably lead to a higher debt to GDP level in the near term," the document said.

Even if Greece did everything it was promising for its new program, and even if the 50 percent haircut to private creditors went through, and even if the Greek economy responded as positively as could be expected, the country's debt-to-GDP ratio would still be stuck

11 The document, which was first disclosed by Reuters, is available at: http://graphics.thomsonreuters.com/12/02/GreeceDSA.pdf.

at 129 percent in 2020, the analysis showed. This estimate reflected arithmetic updated to incorporate a long list of factors that had shifted in unfavourable directions during the period since the previous analysis in November. Both the economic outlook and government fiscal accounts had "deteriorated significantly," and the privatization program was generating even less revenue than previously adjusted forecasts. Moreover, the recapitalization of Greek banks — necessary because they were major holders of the government bonds that were going to undergo haircuts — was shaping up as more costly than initial estimates, to the tune of about €50 billion instead of €40 billion.

As with previous debt sustainability analyses, this one included a "tailored downside scenario" showing what would happen if greater pessimism proved justified regarding policy implementation and the health of the economy. "The Greek authorities may not be able to deliver structural reforms and policy adjustments at the pace envisioned," the document's authors noted, and since that would delay economic recovery for many years, the result would be "a much higher debt trajectory, leaving debt as high as 160 percent of GDP in 2020." Such towering debt would be perilously close to explosive levels, the document warned; relatively minor set backs "would produce unsustainable dynamics, leaving the program highly accident-prone."

The results of this analysis, the document concluded, "point to a need for additional debt relief from the official or private sectors to bring the debt trajectory down, consistent with the objective of reaching a 120 percent of GDP ratio by 2020." That might sound like clear evidence of rabbit chasing and goalpost moving; in a sense it was. But if anything, the rabbit ought to have been chased, and the goalpost moved, even further. As bad as the tailored downside scenario was, it would turn out to be more tailored to the upside than it ought to have been. The Greek economy would perform even more poorly in 2012, 2013 and 2014 than the downside scenario projected.

That wasn't all. Greece might well become dependent for a very long time on loans from its European partners, according to the document, because the way the haircut was going to work was likely to increase the country's difficulties in restoring its ability to borrow from financial markets. The terms of the deal for private creditors implied that Greece was promising them EFSF-type seniority on the new securities they were getting — in other words, failure by Athens to pay interest and principal on the new securities would be legally equivalent to defaulting to the EFSF. The problem with this arrangement was that, in the future, investors could become chary of buying new Greek bonds, which would have junior status. "Given the high prospective level and share of senior debt, the prospects for Greece to be able to return to the market in the years following the end of the new program are uncertain," the document said. "Prolonged financial support...by the official sector may be necessary."

Put another way, more blood drawing was in order, and it would have to come from stones other than Greece.

A long night of negotiations, with Greece's future hanging in the balance, lay ahead as members of the Eurogroup, together with Lagarde, began gathering in Brussels at 3:30 p.m. on February 20, 2012, to hammer out the final terms of the new rescue package for Athens. In an unexpected last-minute addition to the meeting, Papademos flew in from the Greek capital, where the odour of tear gas was lingering in the city centre. As a prime minister, Papademos would not normally attend a gathering of finance ministers and other economic policy makers. But it was crucial for him to convey directly to the group how feverishly he had been mobilizing support for the actions required of Greece to secure its new bailout, and how committed the Greek body politic was to abiding by the conditions.

Only one month remained before the €14.5 billion payment owed to bondholders was due. To avert default, a number of procedures would have to be completed by that time, including ratification of the new program by the 17 euro-zone member states; moreover, the debt restructuring would have to be effectuated, which would require another series of time-consuming legal steps. On his way into the EU's Justus Lipsius Building, the man responsible for chairing the meeting, Eurogroup President Jean-Claude Juncker, told reporters:

"We have to conclude today. There's no more time to waste." Others, by contrast, were making clear their unwillingness to simply go along with whatever deal was on the table. "We can afford to say 'no' until Greece has met all the demands," media reports quoted Jan Kees de Jager, the Dutch finance minister, as saying. "It's probably necessary that there is some kind of permanent presence of the Troika in Athens, not every three months but on a permanent basis....We will see to a rigid and very strict implementation of those demands and only then will we make the next step."[12]

Casting a pall over the proceedings was the aforementioned IMF debt sustainability analysis. All of the parties to the talks felt as if their ability to contribute had already been taxed to the limit. Dallara and Lemierre, who were in the building with several members of the IIF staff, had agreed on bondholders' behalf to the 50 percent haircut; the Greek authorities had acceded to many of the Troika's demands; European governments had pledged a new package of loans totalling €130 billion plus OSI in the form of lower interest rates; and the IMF had agreed to replace its old stand-by loan with a new "Extended Fund Facility," providing credit over a longer term than before. But more would be needed from somewhere, since the IMF's analysis showed that Greece's debt would be 129 percent of GDP in 2020 — nine percentage points higher than the level deemed sustainable — even under fairly optimistic assumptions about Greek implementation, bondholder acceptance of the haircut and the economy's response.

The evening wore on without any sign that a deal was near. Newswires quoted anonymous sources indicating that progress was being made — but slowly; by 10:30 p.m. ministers had reportedly found ways to cut Greece's debt to around 124 percent of GDP by 2020. The European Commission's website promised for hours that a press conference

12 Information about this meeting comes in part from interviews with participants and also from three live blogs of the event, one in the *Financial Times*, available at: http://blogs.ft.com/the-world/2012/02/eurozone-crisis-live-blog-24/; one in *The Guardian*, available at: www.theguardian.com/business/2012/feb/20/debt-crisis-euro; and one in *The Telegraph*, available at: www.telegraph.co.uk/finance/debt-crisis-live/9094900/Debt-crisis-and-Greek-bailout-deal-as-it-happened-February-21-2012.html.

featuring Juncker and others would materialize — "timing unknown." After midnight, reporters began tweeting photos of an empty press room and posting blog items about the tedium involved in the wait.

One of the most hotly contested issues involved PSI, on which Dallara and Lemierre were conducting negotiations in a separate room from the main Eurogroup meeting. Up to that point, the 50 percent haircut was supposed to work like this: bondholders would get 15 percent of the face value of their old Greek bonds in cash — this was the sweetener that Dallara and Lemierre had jubilantly obtained in their deal with Merkel and Sarkozy the previous October — and the rest in new long-term Greek bonds with a face value equal to 35 percent of the old ones. Suddenly, much to the bankers' distress, the sweetener was in peril. For the sake of helping to reach the 120-by-2020 debt target, European officials proposed to reduce by one-third the €30 billion that was to be used for the sweeteners. Dallara and Lemierre were aghast; keeping the amount at the original level was a major goal for them, because a big cash sweetener afforded the one real consolation to bondholders for taking such a substantial write-down on their investments. As noted in chapter 13, most private investors vastly prefer cash in hand to long-term securities of uncertain value.

To keep the cash for the sweetener at €30 billion, Dallara and Lemierre offered a counter-proposal — a haircut of 53.5 percent instead of just 50 percent. In other words, bondholders would still get 15 percent of the face value of their old bonds in cash, but the new bonds would have a face value of only 31.5 percent of the old bonds. Whether this was better for Greece was beside the point; the officials with whom the bankers were negotiating were overjoyed at the prospect of a deeper haircut, which would play well politically in European capitals.

Now the lateness of the hour presented an unforeseen logistical problem, to the consternation of Juncker and his aides. It was important to determine whether the 120-by-2020 target was at last achieved, based on the new haircut and other deals worked out during the night.

The trouble was that the IMF, whose sophisticated model had become the accepted method for calculating debt sustainability, was shut down until morning; producing an authoritative analysis required input and review from several Fund departments. In a small but symbolic example of the incoherence that all too often plagues policy making at such times, the job was handed over to IIF economists, among them some former Fund staffers, who were both awake and ready to do the calculations on their laptops.

"We were turning numbers around with a snap of the fingers," Dallara recalled. "It was 3 or 4 in the morning. Juncker finally said, 'We can't wait any longer. The heads of state are looking for a deal. We'll go with the IIF's numbers.' He seemed to know that the debate about a debt sustainability ratio of 122 versus 124 percent debt to GDP was like angels dancing on the head of a pin. We gave our version of the numbers, and Juncker said, 'Let's go with these.'"

The long wait to exhale ended just before 5:00 a.m., when newswires flashed the first headlines that a deal had been struck and drafting was starting on an official statement for release at a press conference, which would commence at 6:20 a.m. The weary negotiators could take satisfaction at putting to rest, at least for the time being, fears of default and Greek expulsion from the euro. Thanks to their handiwork, the new program for Greece was now projected to lower the government's debt to 120.5 percent of GDP by 2020. The Greeks were accepting tighter monitoring in exchange for receiving their €130 billion loan package; the PSI was acceptable to Dallara and Lemierre; and the OSI included a further reduction of interest rates (to very low levels, charged retroactively) on European governments' loans to Greece, while stopping short of an outright forgiveness of principal — thereby maintaining the appearance of abiding by the rules governing monetary union. An ingenious scheme would extinguish some of the debt that Athens owed to the ECB without technically running afoul of the central bank's mandate or going so far as to impose losses of the sort private bondholders were having to take.[13]

It fell to Lagarde to inject a note of sobriety, according to Gikas Hardouvelis, who was then an adviser to Papademos: "At the very end, when people started congratulating each other, I remember Christine Lagarde turned around and said, 'Don't celebrate, guys. In a couple of years you're going to have to dig into your pockets again for Greece.'"

If any doubt existed prior to the all-night meeting of February 20-21 about whether the Greek debt restructuring would be purely voluntary, such doubt vanished thereafter. As Martin Blessing, the CEO of Germany's Commerzbank, put it at a news conference on February 23, "The participation in the haircut is as voluntary as a confession during the Spanish Inquisition."[14] (His peevishness reflected the €2.2 billion loss that Commerzbank was taking on its investment in Greek bonds.) On that same day, the Greek Parliament approved legislation decreeing that, for all government bonds covered by Greek law, a CAC mechanism would apply, on a retroactive basis. Provided a sufficiently large majority of bondholders went along with the deal, any investor owning a Greek law bond would stand no chance of holding out against it, like it or not.

13 Eurogroup statement, February 21, www.consilium.europa.eu/uedocs/cms_data/docs/pressdata/en/ecofin/128075.pdf.

Under the agreement, the European Commission would have "an enhanced and permanent presence on the ground" in Greece. The Greek government would put money corresponding to the following quarter's debt-servicing bill into a special segregated account, and Athens would also introduce a change in the Greek constitution to ensure priority was granted to debt payments.

As for the ECB, it would distribute profits on its holdings of bonds to national central banks, which could pass on the profits to Greece.

OSI was achieved via a further reduction in the interest charges on the €53 billion in loans that had been made during the rescue agreed in May 2010.

14 Laura Stevens, Harriet Torry and Eyk Henning, 2012, "Greek Bond Deal Makes German Banker See Red," *The Wall Street Journal*, February 24.

This degree of coercion suited the IMF, which as noted above saw a need to overcome the collective action problem so that Greece's private debt would be reduced by a sufficient amount. The only major questions were whether the operation could be completed soon enough before the drop-dead date of March 20, and whether markets would react badly if, as seemed likely, a credit event was declared and CDS triggered. Such an event would depend on the judgment of a secretive 15-member body, the International Swaps and Derivatives Association (ISDA), which consists of representatives from large banks, investment houses and hedge funds. The ISDA holds oversight power on CDS contracts; its members could decide whether investors who had bought this type of default insurance on Greek bonds were entitled to collect.

With dispatch, the Greek government and its advisers initiated the necessary procedures, using a website, greekbonds.gr, to provide information bondholders would need to make their decision. As per the agreement reached on February 20-21, all bondholders were being offered pretty much the same terms, regardless of whether they held short-term Greek bonds that would mature in a few weeks or long-term Greek bonds that would mature in a couple of decades.[15] For every €1,000 in face value of old Greek bonds they held, investors would receive €150 in cash (or EFSF notes that could be easily converted into cash) and new bonds with a face value of €315, maturing in 30 years. These new bonds would pay a mere two percent interest through 2015, although the rate would rise in later years, at an average rate of 3.6 percent over the bond's duration, and they would be governed by English law, thus carrying more legal protection if Greece defaulted again. As an extra inducement, participants in the swap would get a "GDP-linked" bond that would provide a small stream of income if Greece's economy performed better than expected.

With the terms now legally specified, suspense mounted over the possible triggering of CDS — and the implications thereof — as the ISDA met on March 1 to begin weighing the legal and financial implications.

15 This was an important difference from the July 21, 2011 deal, which offered investors a "menu of options."

At first glance, it seemed obvious that triggering CDS might well prove catastrophic, because nobody knew exactly which firms would be exposed to severe losses in such a situation — and there was no shortage of hand-wringing commentary in the media. But a number of prominent observers were arguing that benefits might actually accrue from a ruling declaring CDS to have been triggered, because this would show that this sort of insurance offered practical protection against sovereign default. Otherwise, CDS would appear to have little purpose.[16]

Rarely in the history of international finance has such a long-dreaded event proved so anticlimactic.

On March 8, after expiration of an 8:00 p.m. deadline for bondholders to make their decisions, a small group of Greek finance ministry officials stayed up through the night to tally the results. Early the next morning, the ministry announced that investors holding almost 86 percent of Greece's private debt agreed to participate in the restructuring, more than enough to activate the CACs. Once the CACs forced other holders of Greek-law bonds to participate, the percentage would go up to 95.7 percent, the ministry said. Later that day, the ISDA declared that a credit event had occurred, requiring payments of about $3 billion on CDS contracts.

Markets barely moved; the news of a credit event elicited yawns from investors. The biggest debt restructuring in history was going forward, in a euro-zone country, with enough coercion involved to entail payment of default insurance — and the ensuing cataclysm predicted by ECB officials proved, in the words of Mark Twain, to have been greatly exaggerated.

Under the circumstances, it was only natural to wonder whether the Buchheit-Gulati proposal might have been put into action a lot sooner. By the same token, it was natural to worry whether the operation was being put into action too late. A related question dominated discussion when the IMF board met the following week: did the new rescue for Greece stand any better chance of working than the first one had?

16 Brian Milner, 2012, "No Greek credit default swaps," *The Globe and Mail,* March 2.

With 22 months having passed since their meeting in May 2010 to approve the first Greek program, members of the IMF board were commensurately better informed about all the things that could go wrong when they met to consider the second rescue on March 15, 2012. As is customary, they circulated statements in advance of the meeting — confidentially, of course, to avoid allowing any critical comments to undermine the goals the Fund was attempting to accomplish. Excerpts from those confidential statements show how tightly board members were holding their noses even while bestowing formal approval.

"The approach so far…has only helped to keep contagion to the rest of Europe at bay, but without any tangible benefits to the Greek economy," said a statement submitted by Arvind Virmani, the Indian director. "We are not convinced that a program based on adjustment through austerity and prolonged recession, and the continued recourse to more debt to deal with severe indebtedness…will work." His Argentine counterpart, Alfredo Mac Laughlin, lamented that "with each [quarterly] review, the staff's projections deteriorate together with the economic and social reality," and Andrei Lushin, the Russian alternate director, complained, "[T]he 120 percent debt-to-GDP ratio is not a proper target. Such debt level will not allow Greece to resume market borrowing under reasonable terms. The debt level targets should be substantially lower — maybe between 70 and 90 percent. Unfortunately, even achievement of the 120 percent debt-to-GDP ratio by 2020 looks unattainable."

Thomas Hockin, who represented Canada and 11 other countries, hit the nail on the head: debt should have been "brought down to well below the level targeted in the program, through a combination of more ambitious PSI/OSI." Nonetheless, Hockin agreed to join the consensus to approve an IMF loan for lack of any viable alternative. "Our support for the program is entirely driven by the continued high risk of international systemic spillovers that would result from a hard Greek default," he said. The same went for Switzerland's René Weber: "It takes us a very large portion of pragmatism to support this arrangement, for which the rules may well have been excessively stretched," Weber said.

Perhaps because he had already expressed such negative sentiments toward the Greek program at previous meetings, Paulo Nogueira Batista rose to unprecedented heights of dudgeon. Under the new program, the IMF's "exposure to Greece will last 16 years," the Brazilian observed. "If all goes well, the country will only fully repay the Fund in 2026. Most [directors] that are now meeting to take the decision to lend additional resources to Greece will be retired by then. However, colleagues should not take comfort from this. The decision to lend additional resources to Greece may come back to haunt those that supported it well before that."

The staff report on the program, which directors had received a few days before their meeting, provided ample information and analysis to support such caustic appraisals. Notwithstanding some new elements, the program was infused with a "same-old, same-old feel." Greece was required to achieve a primary budget surplus of 4.5 percent of GDP by 2014 — and the program still assumed that large primary surpluses would continue for many years in the future, with the target staying at 4.5 percent of GDP until 2017, then dropping only slightly to 4.3 percent for 2020 and 3.5 percent for 2030. Although not quite as huge as the surpluses assumed in the first program, surpluses of these magnitudes would later be deemed by the IMF to be far beyond the Greek government's reach, as we shall see.

The report's bottom line was that the only way the staff could back the program was because European officials were promising that their wealthy governments, rather than the Fund, would be on the hook if Athens needed more money to pay obligations.[17] "[A]t the February 21 Eurogroup meeting, European partners confirmed their commitment to provide adequate support to Greece…for as long as it takes for Greece to regain market access, provided that Greece fully complies with the requirements and objectives of the program," the report said. This wasn't the same as a guarantee by the Europeans to indemnify the IMF against loss; crucially, they would be under no obligation whatsoever if Greece violated the program's conditions and collapsed

17 IMF, 2012, "Greece: Request for Extended Arrangement Under the Extended Fund Facility—Staff Report" (see footnote 8 in this chapter).

into default on all its loans. But at least the Europeans were pledging to provide additional aid if Greece hewed to the conditions and still came up short of cash. "The euro area member states' commitment [is]...a key consideration for staff's recommendation to approve the proposed arrangement," the report said.

Even if the IMF was protecting itself financially to some degree, it was providing its imprimatur to the new rescue, and a close reading of the report showed that the Fund's own rules were once again being badly bent in the process. As in several previous instances, the Fund was getting around the No More Argentinas rule by employing the waiver it had hastily adopted in May 2010. Although it was "difficult to categorically affirm that debt is sustainable with high probability," Greece should get a large loan "given the continued high risk of international systemic spillover effects," the report said.

Adherence to other, related rules was clearly a stretch as well. Under the set of lending criteria established after the Argentine default, the IMF isn't supposed to give a country a large loan unless the country "has prospects" for regaining access to private financial markets "within the timeframe when Fund resources are outstanding." But as acknowledged in the staff report for the new Greek program, the chances of Athens borrowing from private lenders in the foreseeable future appeared dim: "The scale of Greece's challenges, including its emergence from the largest debt restructuring ever done and the perceived senior status of all debt relative to any new issuance, make it inherently difficult to project the volume and timing of Greece's return to the markets in the immediate post-program years." In all likelihood, the report said, Greece would be able to borrow only small amounts, for short-term periods, because the interest rates charged by lenders "could destabilize debt dynamics if borrowing took place in large volume."

The rule subject to perhaps the greatest torture was another of the lending criteria, which permits large loans only in cases where the program affords "reasonably strong prospect of success." To meet this standard, the IMF is supposed to satisfy itself not only that the borrowing country was adopting adequate policies but also that the country has the "institutional and political capacity to deliver that adjustment."

"Capacity to deliver" is a key phrase in this regard; did Greece have a realistic hope of fundamentally altering the workings of its economy? The staff report gamely contended that the program met the standard required by the rule. Under Papademos's leadership, Athens had "demonstrated ownership and policy resolve" by completing "prior actions" demanded of it by the Troika, according to the report's authors; "further confidence" could be derived from the letters sent by major political party leaders promising faithful delivery on program conditions. But lest this sound Pollyannish, the report continued: "Even with these assurances and undertakings of the authorities, it should be stressed that program implementation risks are likely to remain very high....even with political resolve, the breadth of the reform agenda may test the authorities' administrative capacity."

Indeed, in other parts of the 232-page report, the IMF staff raised serious concerns about the capacity issue. The authors gave Greece credit for achieving "a good deal" of progress in meeting the targets set under the first program for cutting government spending and shrinking the budget deficit. But as for improving competitiveness and reviving growth through structural reform, the report essentially conceded failure. "[T]he strategy required rapid, full and effective implementation of reforms to have a chance of success. Time has revealed that Greece does not have the capacity for this type of success."

The time had come, therefore, "to recalibrate the program strategy," the report said, heralding a shift from the approach taken in the first rescue. The new strategy would "directly prioritize internal devaluation... primarily through nominal wage reductions." The ultimate aim was for Greece to revive growth by closing a gap with competing countries whose unit labour costs were roughly 15 percent lower. This was the rationale behind the 22 percent cut in the minimum wage as well as measures designed to further weaken the bargaining power of unions. In addition, implementation of reforms would be subject to far more intense oversight than ever, with the "Memorandum of Understanding on Specific Economic Policy Conditionality" spelling out an extremely detailed list of actions that the Greek government was obliged to complete according to rigid timetables for each action.

At the board meeting, Nogueira Batista again registered his discontent by abstaining from the vote to approve the program. Others who reluctantly joined the consensus could feel some measure of relief that the IMF's share of the funds for the new program was being reduced to about 16 percent of the total, compared with 27 percent in the first program.[18] They could also take a little comfort from the words contained in a joint statement by their European colleagues on the board, providing assurances that the IMF would be paid back ahead of European official bodies and reiterating for the record the promises mentioned in the staff report. "The Fund's preferred creditor status has always been acknowledged by euro area partners," the Europeans' statement said. "The euro area leaders have consistently reiterated their commitment to provide adequate support to Greece during the life of the program and beyond until it has regained market access, provided that Greece fully complies with the requirements and objectives of the adjustment program."

The most satisfying aspect by far about the new program was the major haircut taken by private bondholders. But this should not be overstated. Although the haircut had extinguished €106 billion worth of Greece's debt, the impact on the country's overall indebtedness was less impressive. Greek banks were among the bondholders taking large losses — and to recapitalize them, the amount Athens needed to borrow was commensurately larger, to the tune of about €38 billion. The net reduction in debt was thus in the €68 billion range.[19]

18 This was not because the IMF was trying to reduce its exposure to some particular percentage of the total rescue package. Rather, the Fund contended that it should provide aid only for balance-of-payments support and the Greek budget, not for the recapitalization of Greek banks. For the bank-recapitalization cost, European creditors assumed full responsibility for providing loans, while the amount for the rest of the package was split between the Fund and Europe.

19 Xafa, 2014, "Sovereign Debt Crisis Management: Lessons from the 2012 Greek Debt Restructuring" (see footnote 4 in this chapter).

Moreover, some private bondholders — one fabulously rich one in particular — had evaded the barber's shears. Therein lay a dilemma, the resolution of which would have nettlesome and lasting ramifications.

When Philippos Sachinidis became Greece's finance minister on March 21, 2012, shortly after the completion of the debt restructuring, he knew he would hold the job only a brief period. National elections were scheduled for May 6, and Sachinidis, an economist belonging to the Socialist Party, planned to step down at that time along with the rest of the provisional government led by Papademos. But Sachinidis found himself stuck in office for a bit longer than he expected after the election when the vote produced no sufficiently large mandate for any of the major parties to form a new government. This was especially discomfiting because of a big decision that loomed in the days immediately following the election.

At issue was whether Greece should pay bondholders who had rejected the debt restructuring. Although nearly 97 percent of the government's outstanding bonds had undergone a haircut, owners of the remainder — about €6.4 billion in face value — were holding out; they could do so because the bonds they held were covered by foreign law rather than Greek law and were thus not subject to the legislation that had been enacted by the Greek Parliament. A payment of €436 million was due to be paid to some of those bondholders on May 15, and although Greek officials had previously blustered that holdouts shouldn't expect to be rewarded, failure to make the payment would constitute a blatant act of default and would surely trigger lawsuits by the investors in countries holding legal jurisdiction over the bonds.

The quandary was all the more vexing because the vast bulk of that €436 million — almost 90 percent of it — was owed to Dart Management, a Cayman Islands-based investment fund controlled by Kenneth Dart.[20] A member of a reclusive, strife-ridden Michigan family that had made billions of dollars from manufacturing Styrofoam cups, Dart

20 Landon Thomas Jr., 2012, "Bet on Greek Bonds Paid Off for 'Vulture Fund,'" *The New York Times*, May 15.

was a caricature of an avaricious coupon-clipper. According to one of his brothers, from whom he was estranged, he once considered making his home on his 220-foot yacht, which was armoured to withstand torpedo fire. He had escaped federal tax liability by renouncing his US citizenship and becoming a citizen of Belize; he gained notoriety in the 1990s when he sought to become a Belizean consul based in Sarasota, Florida, where his parents, wife and children lived.

Like Paul Singer, the New York hedge-fund executive introduced in chapter 7, Dart was one of the world's most successful "vulture investors," the pejorative for money managers who squeeze funds out of financially distressed countries by buying their bonds at deep discounts and using the threat of litigation to extract maximum payment. Dart and Singer honed their skills at this technique during various debt crises of the 1990s, reaping hundreds of millions of dollars in profits on bonds of countries such as Peru, Brazil and Nicaragua. Both men had also invested heavily in Argentine bonds, buying at bargain prices as the country slid toward default and then filing suits to recover the full face value of the bonds plus interest. Greece was a logical candidate for Dart's attention; he had bought most of his Greek bonds at prices that traders estimated at 60 to 70 cents on the dollar, carefully focusing his holdings on issues that were legally protected from the Buchheit-Gulati scheme.

Distasteful though it might be to yield to such extortionate tactics, Sachinidis was worried about the consequences of default. Greece was in political disarray and market turmoil had returned following the inconclusive election of May 2012; litigation by combative investors like Dart might complicate the situation further by raising doubt about whether Athens could smoothly obtain bailout funds under the new Troika program. Moreover, as a short-termer in high office, Sachinidis was concerned about the precedents he might be setting. Any action he took could presumably bind future Greek governments to follow suit. And the broader implications were perhaps most troublesome of all: if Greece paid holdout investors like Dart, how might that affect future efforts by other countries to restructure debt? The more creditors saw holdouts getting lucrative payments, the more difficult it would become to persuade creditors in general to accept a reasonable reduction in their claims.

"I was just an interim minister of finance at that point, as long as we were lacking a new government," Sachinidis told me. "I needed to make sure that the basis I should make the decision, whether to pay or not, was solid." With the aim of obtaining political backing for a decision one way or another, he continued, "I asked Prime Minister Papademos to raise the issue at a summit that took place with the President of the Greek Republic, where the heads of all the major parties were attending to see whether it would be possible to form a coalition government. The decision was that Greece should pay."

Asked whether the IMF intervened in the decision, Sachinidis said the Fund "didn't directly contact me on this particular issue. But I did inform the Eurogroup. I told them, 'Be careful, this is a unique situation, and this decision will affect the future, because to the extent that those who don't participate in an exchange will be paid, it may undermine future debt restructurings in Europe.' I don't remember anyone fighting for the argument that we shouldn't pay, and if anyone did take that position, it wasn't a strong position."

Thus did Dart, with an estimated net worth of $6.6 billion, get a big payday on May 15, courtesy of the Greek taxpayers (using money borrowed from the taxpayers of Europe and elsewhere in the world). On every occasion thereafter that a payment to holdouts came due, Athens continued to disburse the full amount owed. The clear message sent to investors around the world — that holding out pays off — is the main reason why the Greek debt restructuring, as much of a watershed event as it was, may be hard to duplicate should the need arise elsewhere. Another reason is the unlikelihood that an up-front cash payment as sweet as the one given to Greece's bondholders would be forthcoming in future cases.

But long-term issues such as future debt restructurings were getting little notice in mid-2012, because of developments that are the subject of the next chapter. Greece was going back into the cauldron, and it was not the only euro-zone country doing so.

15

BREAKING THE VICIOUS CYCLE

Even by the usual standards for IMF managing directors, Christine Lagarde's travel schedule during early 2012 was exceptionally gruelling. Not only was she making frequent transatlantic trips to participate in crisis-related meetings, she was also jetting off to world capitals seeking support from shareholder countries for the half-trillion-dollar increase in IMF resources that had been proposed in the January doomsday paper. Although her energy showed little signs of flagging, the globe-trotting binge took a toll, ending with her hobbling around on crutches and canes during much of the spring.

Lagarde made her pitch in late January to global leaders attending the World Economic Forum in Davos, Switzerland, where she evoked laughter in one session by brandishing her Louis Vuitton handbag and declaring, "I am here, with my little bag, to collect a bit of money."[1] The following month she journeyed to Saudi Arabia, and then to Mexico City for the meeting of G20 finance ministers, followed by trips to China and India in mid-March (she had already been to Brazil, Russia and Japan in late 2011 after the Cannes summit). Her main message concerned the necessity of fattening the IMF's coffers to underpin global financial stability, although she also emphasized that she was prodding European governments to endow their own rescue funds,

1 Philip Aldrich and Angela Monaghan, 2012, "IMF chief Christine Lagarde will struggle to bag more funds for a 'firewall,'" *The Telegraph*, April 14.

the EFSF and ESM, with bigger sums. (The ESM, the more permanent, treaty-based facility, was due to be inaugurated later in 2012, roughly a year earlier than the original schedule.)

It was on the last of her trips that Lagarde suffered a debilitating injury. As was her daily custom while on the road, she swam laps at the hotel pool in New Delhi on March 20, exerting herself with extra vigour because she was about to head to the airport for a long journey home. During a plane change in Paris, she began feeling twinges and snaps in her right knee, followed by such excruciating pain that she was rushed to George Washington University Hospital for surgery upon landing. To aid in her recovery, when she was confined to a wheelchair, her longtime partner Xavier Giocanti flew in from France, where he lives, as did her younger son Thomas, who was studying architecture in Chicago.[2]

At the same time as Lagarde was travelling these vast distances, the euro zone was enjoying a singularly long stretch of positive financial news. The terrifying market pressures of late 2011 were in abatement during the first quarter of 2012, thanks in part to the "wall of money" policy that the ECB had approved in December. Also contributing to the improved atmosphere was the performance of the Monti regime in Rome, which was exhibiting an impressive capacity to deliver on vows of fiscal reform. As bond yields of nearly all troubled euro-zone countries (with the exception of Greece) subsided to comfortable levels — Italian yields dipped to 4.2 percent on March 9 — elated European leaders issued a series of statements in March proclaiming the region to be emerging from danger. Sarkozy told a press conference in Brussels that "we're in the process of turning a page in this financial crisis,"[3] and Monti declared in Tokyo, "This crisis is now almost over."[4]

2 Ned Martel, 2012, "The economy of Christine Lagarde," *The Washington Post*, September 24.

3 Embassy of France in London, 2012, "President Sarkozy's press conference in Brussels," March 2, www.ambafrance-uk.org/President-Sarkozy-s-press,20678.

4 *The Guardian*, 2012, "Eurozone crisis live," March 28, www.theguardian.com/business/2012/mar/28/eurozone-debt-crisis-mario-monti-almost-over#block-4.

Even Draghi got a little carried away, telling an interviewer: "The worst is over."[5]

Despite all these cheery portents, the IMF did not abandon the effort to enhance its resources. That was fortunate, because the burst of optimism was to prove redolent of George W. Bush's "Mission Accomplished" message prematurely declaring success in the Iraq War.

Lagarde still needed a crutch, and kept her injured leg propped up while sitting, during the IMF-World Bank spring meetings in mid-April. But her rainmaking had paid off, and when she delivered a speech at the Brookings Institution on the eve of the meetings, she was in high spirits about the commitments she had secured from Fund shareholders. Harking back to the London G20 summit of 2009, when a tripling of IMF resources had helped to alleviate crisis conditions, she said, "some have called it the 'London moment.'...I believe that we may be at another such moment....Who knows, perhaps as we look forward to next week's Spring meetings of global financial leaders, this can be our 'Washington moment?'"[6]

Indeed, the spring meetings ended with the IMF securing most of the extra funding Lagarde had set out to raise — about $430 billion in pledges at that time.[7] It is important to note that this was money the member nations were promising to lend the Fund if necessary; it was not as permanent as quota contributions. The United States maintained its refusal to contribute, as did Canada, although they did not attempt

5 Matthew Brockett, 2012, "Draghi Says Worst of Debt Crisis 'Is Over,'" Bild Reports, Bloomberg News, March 22.

6 IMF, 2012, "Seizing the Moment—Thinking Beyond the Crisis," Address by Christine Lagarde, April 12, www.imf.org/external/np/speeches/2012/041212.htm.

7 This would rise to $456 billion when the amount was finalized at a G20 summit a couple of months later, with the $200 billion from the euro-zone countries supplemented by $60 billion from Japan, $43 billion from China, $15 billion each from the United Kingdom, Saudi Arabia and South Korea, and $10 billion each from Brazil, Russia, India, Mexico, Sweden and Switzerland, plus smaller amounts from a number of other members. See IMF, 2012, "IMF Managing Director Christine Lagarde Welcomes Additional Pledges to Increase IMF Resources," Press Release No. 12/231, June 19, www.imf.org/external/np/sec/pr/2012/pr12231.htm.

to block Lagarde's fundraising initiative. Meanwhile, Europe had upsized its own firewall (although not as generously as Lagarde and others had hoped) by raising the combined ceiling on lending by the EFSF and ESM, previously capped at €500 billion, to €700 billion.[8]

The increase in the IMF's war chest was timely, aimed in part as it was at easing market fears over the lack of official resources to deal with new financial tempests. As Lagarde told the news media on April 19: "We are seeing a light recovery blowing in the spring wind, but we are also seeing some very dark clouds on the horizon."[9]

The darkest cloud of all was the one hovering over a country with a €1 trillion GDP, the fourth largest in the euro zone, dwarfing the size of the economies that had been rescued before. The country was Spain — where, as in Ireland, a burst housing bubble was leading to angst about the banking system.

The selection of Rodrigo de Rato as IMF managing director in 2004 was a potent symbol of the acclaim Spain was drawing from all corners of the globe for its economic dynamism in the early years of the twenty-first century. The Spanish economy, which de Rato had steered as finance minister for the previous eight years, was in its eleventh consecutive year of growth. A number of widely admired multinationals were headquartered there, prominent examples including Telefónica, Repsol and Zara, which were giants in the global telecommunications, energy and fashion-retailing industries respectively, as well as Santander and BBVA in international banking. The nation's prosperity, combined with low interest rates, was generating one of the world's headiest housing booms, with residential developments springing up in the suburbs of major cities and coastal villages undergoing transformations to

8 Eurogroup, 2012, "Statement of the Eurogroup," March 30, www.consilium.europa.eu/uedocs/cms_data/docs/pressdata/en/ecofin/129381.pdf.

9 IMF, 2012, "Transcript of a Press Conference by International Monetary Fund Managing Director Christine Lagarde and First Deputy Managing Director David Lipton," April 19, www.imf.org/external/np/tr/2012/tr041912.htm.

accommodate demand for holiday villas from Spaniards and northern European retirees. Property prices peaked in 2007 at roughly triple the 1995 level.[10]

In 2006, the same year that an IMF FSAP mission went to Dublin to assess the Irish financial system, another FSAP mission landed in Madrid. With benefit of hindsight about subsequent developments in both countries, the report produced by the Spanish FSAP mission reflects a more appropriate degree of alarm than the Irish one. In addition to expressing concern about housing prices, which were estimated to be overvalued "on the order of 25 to 35 percent," the report warned that the double-digit expansion of credit in Spain over the previous five years was excessively rapid. "Staff attaches high priority to moderating housing credit expansion and mitigating credit risk," the report's authors said.

Still, the IMF's "overall message was fairly positive" regarding pre-crisis Spain, as a later report by the Fund's Independent Evaluation Office would acknowledge.[11] For example, the first sentence of the executive summary in the 2006 FSAP stated, in bold-faced lettering: "Overall Spain's financial sector is vibrant, resilient, highly competitive, and well-supervised and regulated." And the following year, in the Article IV report, the IMF staff forecast a "smooth landing" from the boom of the previous decade. Although the report fretted about "appreciable

10 Information about the strengths and weaknesses of the Spanish economy during the pre-crisis period can be found at: Raphael Minder, 2010, "Mix of Politics and Banking in Spain's Woes," *The New York Times*, June 3; Neil Irwin, 2010, "Despite E.U. rescue fund, Spain struggles with soured private loans," *The Washington Post*, May 12; *The Economist*, 2011, "Spain's Economy: Split Personality," July 7; Victor Mallet and Jonathan Ford, 2011, "Spain: Reluctant Retrencher," *Financial Times*, January 16; Landon Thomas Jr. and Raphael Minder, 2012, "Spain is Not Out of the Woods Yet," *The New York Times*, March 23; Eichengreen, *Hall of Mirrors* (see footnote 3 in chapter 8); and Amalia Cárdenas, 2013, "The Spanish Savings Bank Crisis: History, Causes and Responses," IN3 Working Paper Series, WP13-003, Universitat Oberta de Catalunya.

11 Nancy Wagner, 2010, "IMF Performance in the Run-Up to the Financial and Economic Crisis: Bilateral Surveillance in Selected IMF Member Countries," IMF Independent Evaluation Office, Background Paper BP/10/03, December 9, www.ieo-imf.org/ieo/files/completedevaluations/01102011Crisis_BP3_Bilateral_Surveillance_in_Selected_IMF_Member_Countries.pdf.

downside risks," the "main risk" was an economic slowdown, not anything remotely resembling the crisis that would eventually materialize.[12]

Plenty of sound reasoning underpinned the Fund's relatively sanguine view of Spain at that point. Fiscal policy was exemplary; the government had not run a budget deficit since 2002, and the government's debt-to-GDP ratio was below 40 percent — lower than that of Germany. Spanish bank regulators were regarded as not only prudent but almost zealously so, based on their adoption of a "counter-cyclical buffer" system that required banks to set aside more reserves during boom times, regardless of actual loan losses, so that they would be better fortified during bad times. (This approach would be incorporated into international banking rules in 2010.) Based partly on the high esteem accorded this system, de Rato in 2006 appointed Jaime Caruana, governor of the Bank of Spain, to head the IMF's Monetary and Capital Markets Department, a new department formed from the merger of two other departments. Faith in the resiliency of the Spanish financial system appeared justified in the immediate aftermath of the Lehman bankruptcy, when the nation's flagship banks weathered the storm without requiring rescues like many banks elsewhere in Europe and the United States.

But the stability on the surface masked troubles brewing in a less prominent segment of the system — the *cajas*, regional savings banks with cozy ties to local political elites. Quasi-public in function, with mandates to foster community development, the *cajas* were often run by retired politicians, whose lending preferences tended to be skewed toward projects benefiting the well-connected. These institutions had been by far the most enthusiastic bankrollers of Spain's housing-construction spree, so when the property market began its inevitable collapse, in 2008, a large and growing portion of the credit they had shovelled out to homebuyers and real-estate developers was turning out to be uncollectible. Worsening the condition of the *cajas* was a recession that, as in much of the rest of the world, started in late 2008

12 IMF, 2007, "Spain: 2007 Article IV Consultation," Country Report 07/175, May, www.imf.org/external/pubs/ft/scr/2007/cr07175.pdf.

and caused unemployment, a persistent problem in Spain, to shoot above 20 percent by early 2010, deflating incomes and demand for housing. From the standpoint of the overall Spanish economy, the woes of the *cajas* were hardly trivial; although they had accounted for 20 percent of the country's financial system in the 1980s, they had expanded at such a pace that their share of total financial assets was about 40 percent by the time Lehman collapsed. As the Greek crisis was unfolding in early 2010, Spain was awash in stories about ghost towns where thousands of unsold apartments were falling prey to vandalism and the few occupied units were inhabited by people who were behind in their mortgage payments. Despite furious efforts by Spanish officials to highlight the obvious disparities between their economy and that of Greece, speculation was rampant that the cost of bailing out the *cajas* might overwhelm Spain's fiscal wherewithal and that Madrid might even follow Athens into losing access to affordable market financing.

So concerned was Strauss-Kahn about the deterioration in Spain's fortunes that when he visited Madrid in mid-June 2010, about a month after the first Greek rescue, he privately proposed that the IMF might come to Madrid's assistance, according to José Luis Zapatero, who was the Spanish prime minister at the time. Zapatero had recently promised Parliament that the government's deficit, which swelled to 11 percent of GDP in 2009, would be slashed to the three percent euro-zone ceiling by 2013, so as he later recalled in a book he wrote, he was shocked to hear Strauss-Kahn's suggestion that Fund aid might still be necessary. Fearful of a financial panic if the IMF chief were to go public with a proposal that Spain needed an international rescue, Zapatero said his government wasn't interested, and he implored Strauss-Kahn to keep the idea under wraps. To the Spanish prime minister's immense relief, Strauss-Kahn did not mention anything about a rescue when he met the news media after their meeting; instead he effusively endorsed the policies Zapatero was adopting.[13]

Later that year, as the Irish crisis intensified, the Spanish government responded with still more initiatives to enhance investor confidence in

13 For a report about revelations in Zapatero's book, *El Dilema (The Dilemma)*, see *El País*, 2013, "Las tres amenazas de rescate contra el expresidente Zapatero," November 26.

the nation's economy. The most important of these was the merger in December 2010 of seven struggling *cajas* into one, dubbed Bankia, which was injected with €4.5 billion in government funds aimed at providing the solvency the enterprise needed to get off to a fresh start. Headquartered in one of Madrid's most innovative architectural structures, a sloping tower called the Gateway to Europe, this new financial institution was Spain's third-largest by assets, with more real-estate loans in its portfolio than any other — and its chairman was none other than de Rato, the former IMF chief.

The Bankia merger was part of a broader effort to address the *caja* problem that reduced their number from 45 to 11. But often, as in Bankia's case, this was achieved through mergers, and combining weak banks with other weak banks doesn't necessarily solve underlying problems. That concern weighed on financial markets in 2011 as contagion from the Greek crisis affected investor sentiment about Spain. The Spanish government managed to deflect some of the market pressure by responding positively to the secret letter sent by Trichet to Zapatero in early August 2011, drawing favourable comparisons to the inconsistent manner in which the Italian government responded to the letter received by Berlusconi. After the Cannes summit, however, Spanish securities underwent a renewed wave of selling, a particularly disturbing phenomenon because it persisted even after the centre-right Popular Party, led by Mariano Rajoy, won a landslide victory on November 20 that drove the Socialists from power — a development that markets were expected to welcome.

Only in December, when the ECB announced its LTRO program (the wall of money), and then followed up that month and again in February 2012 by lending hundreds of billions of euros to banks at rock-bottom interest rates, did Spain regain some semblance of financial normalcy. As envisioned, Spanish banks used much of their new cash to buy bonds that had been issued by their own government, and this surge of demand sharply reduced Madrid's borrowing costs, with the yield on 10-year Spanish bonds dipping to 4.9 percent at the beginning of March. This was the period during which "mission accomplished" rhetoric about the end of the crisis reached a crescendo.

The tranquility was deceptive, almost perversely so, especially in Spain's case. The LTRO was like a monetary drug, and as its effects began to wear off, realization set in that it was doing nothing to address systemic problems — indeed, it was aggravating them to some extent. Systemic problems required systemic solutions.

Here the IMF was ahead of the curve.

Media coverage of the euro-zone crisis was so intensive, with developments reported in minute detail not only in newspaper and magazine articles but also in blogs, tweets and various other forms of online communication, that important pronouncements by key policy makers rarely escaped notice. An unusual exception occurred on January 23, 2012, when Lagarde delivered a speech in Berlin. One passage in this speech went almost entirely unobserved in the numerous media accounts of the managing director's remarks, yet in retrospect, the new approach she advocated in this passage would prove crucial in alleviating the crisis. The pride the IMF takes in having pushed this argument is well earned.

"We must…break the vicious cycle of banks hurting sovereigns and sovereigns hurting banks," Lagarde said that day, and she continued: "To break the feedback loop between sovereigns and banks, we need more risk sharing across borders in the banking system. In the near term, a pan-euro area facility that has the capacity to take direct stakes in banks will help break this link. Looking further ahead, monetary union needs to be supported by financial integration in the form of unified supervision, a single bank resolution authority with a common backstop, and a single deposit insurance fund."[14]

The ideas put forward in that passage would come to be known as "banking union." As noted in chapter 4, the establishment of monetary union in Europe had never been matched by anything similar in the

14 IMF, 2012, "Global Challenges in 2012: Speech by Christine Lagarde, Berlin, January 23, www.imf.org/external/np/speeches/2012/012312.htm.

banking sector. On the contrary, bank regulatory and supervisory powers largely remained with individual member states, along with the responsibility for handling bank failures — a stark difference with the United States, where federal agencies in Washington hold such powers and responsibilities. Although this arrangement suited the propensity in many European capitals for nurturing national banking "champions," it posed a serious risk of generating the vicious cycle and feedback loop cited by Lagarde (the aforementioned phrase "doom loop" was also commonly used). As these terms suggest, a self-reinforcing, perpetual chain of causation was at play: banks were losing the confidence of depositors and creditors due to worries about whether their governments could support them; governments were suffering from fears that the cost of bailing out one or more banks would be too much for taxpayers to bear. The risk of such a doom loop materializing was all the greater in a common currency area where individual countries do not have separate central banks with the power to print their own money.

Even prior to the global financial crisis, the IMF had exhorted Europe to adopt a more integrated system for dealing with a meltdown in a large bank, as also noted in chapter 4. In a March 2010 speech, Strauss-Kahn advanced the argument further, calling for "a European Resolution Authority, armed with the mandate and the tools to deal cost-effectively with failing cross-border banks,"[15] and a working paper published at that time by several Fund economists made the case in greater detail.[16] These admonitions went unheeded, with European policy makers essentially clinging to their fragmented system even after the doom loop was drawing increasing attention in 2011. Behind the scenes, Fund economists often raised the issue, notably during a discussion among top policy makers at the September 2011 IMF-World Bank annual meetings.

15 IMF, 2010, "Crisis Management Arrangements for a European Banking System," Keynote speech by Dominique Strauss-Kahn at the European Commission conference, Brussels, March 19, www.imf.org/external/np/speeches/2010/031910.htm.

16 Wim Fonteyne et al., 2010, "Crisis Management and Resolution for a European Banking System," IMF Working Paper WP/10/70, March, www.imf.org/external/pubs/ft/wp/2010/wp1070.pdf.

In early 2012, the weaknesses embedded in Europe's banking arrangements were reaching the point of an existential threat to the euro. Nowhere would this be more evident than in Spain, whose banks were the biggest borrowers of ECB cash under the LTRO program. The €68 billion worth of government bonds that they bought, while causing yields to plunge in the first couple of months of the year, meant that the fates of the nation's banks and its government were intertwined much too closely for comfort. Spanish banks ended up holding a higher percentage of their government's debt — about two-thirds of the total — than the banks of any other country in the euro zone.[17]

Thus did the viciousness of the cycle cited by Lagarde in her Berlin speech intensify, and yields on Spanish bonds soared anew, with the 10-year bond yield reaching nearly six percent by April 20. Once the LTRO program ended, and the ECB stopped providing banks with cheap loans, market participants could see little reason why Spanish bond yields should stay low — and ample reason to see why the reverse ought to happen.

Not only had the linkages tightened between Spanish banks and the Spanish sovereign; both ends of the doom loop were emitting distress signals. The Popular Party, whose electoral victory in late 2011 had inflamed optimism in conservative European circles, was failing to live up to its advance billing for tough-mindedness and sure-footedness. Having inherited a 2011 budget deficit that was already well above the target set for that year, officials of the Rajoy government declared in early March 2012 that they intended to raise the target for the coming year to 5.8 percent of GDP instead of the 4.4 percent of GDP level previously agreed with the European Commission. The economy was sinking into its second recession since 2008, with unemployment climbing to almost 24 percent, so a looser fiscal policy made sense. But coming at a time when European leaders were embracing a new compact for region-wide budgetary restraint, Spain's seemingly cavalier approach drew a wrathful response from the guardians of fiscal probity in Brussels, who demanded — and got — a substantially narrower

17 Landon Thomas Jr., 2012, "Europe Fears Bailout of Spain Would Strain Its Resources," *The New York Times*, May 30.

deficit target. Regardless of whether this implied lack of discipline, as some analysts concluded, or acceptance of excessive austerity, as others believed, it shook investor confidence in Madrid.[18]

Meanwhile, the real potential budget-buster — a costly recapitalization of the *cajas* — loomed ever more menacingly in April and May, with Bankia the greatest source of anxiety. The growing number of unemployed homeowners and worsening housing bust fuelled pervasive suspicion in financial markets that Bankia's portfolio was far more laden with dud loans and its capital cushion much thinner than its officials were letting on. The Rajoy regime was clearly loath to crack down on an institution led by de Rato, a stalwart of the Popular Party; a number of other Bankia executives were also party figures with powerful allies, and they were vigorously defending the *caja* against allegations of capital deficiency. But deposits were flowing out of Bankia at an accelerating rate, and other large Spanish financial institutions were encountering difficulty attracting funds from abroad because of concern about how a Bankia implosion might affect them.

Help arrived from, of all places, another IMF FSAP mission.

Assessing a country's financial system, as IMF staffers do when they go on FSAP missions, is usually a dry and methodical chore, reflecting the long-term nature of an exercise that takes place once every five or six years. A different experience was in store for the FSAP team that, by coincidence, went to Madrid just as Spain's crisis was heating up in the spring of 2012. Fortunately, the head of the mission, Ceyla Pazarbasioglu, had plenty of practice in high-pressure situations. Her first assignment upon joining the IMF in 1992 was in Norway, during the Nordic banking crisis, which hit Sweden and Finland as well. Since that time she had worked on a number of similar cases, including one in her native Turkey in 2001, when she took a leave from the Fund to help Turkish bank supervisors cope with a hemorrhaging of cash from banks amid a crash in the currency and stock prices.

18 *The Economist*, 2012, "After the sugar rush," April 14.

Based on a quick stress test of the Spanish financial system using data furnished by the country's regulators, Pazarbasioglu's team reached the conclusion that with a handful of exceptions, most of Spain's major banks were fundamentally sound and could withstand a further weakening of the economy and house prices. The problem was that the whole system was at risk of being dragged down by the exceptions. In a statement issued on April 25 as it left Madrid, the FSAP mission urged that a thoroughgoing, independent examination of the system be conducted to help clarify which banks were imperiled and which ones were not. And the statement included one sentence that, without mentioning names, pointed the finger directly at where the danger lay: "To preserve financial stability, it is critical that [the most vulnerable] banks, especially the largest one, take swift and decisive measures to strengthen their balance sheets and improve management and governance practices."[19] Nobody had any doubt what "the largest one" meant; it was Bankia.

By many accounts, that single sentence provided unbiased, authoritative validation that enabled Spanish technocrats to overcome the powerful political forces that were shielding Bankia from regulatory intervention. On May 7, the Spanish government, which had insisted for weeks that it had a firm handle on the ills of the nation's financial system, announced plans to nationalize Bankia, which perforce meant a change in management. De Rato resigned, rocking the nation's political establishment.

Instead of taking comfort in Madrid's resolve, investors promptly went on a fresh rampage of Spanish bond selling, based on firmer conviction that the government must be hiding the truth regarding the amounts it would have to pony up for recapitalizations of Bankia and other institutions. The markets sank further upon the revelation on May 25 that €19 billion in new government capital would be required to prop up Bankia (on top of the €4.5 billion initially provided). Moreover, Bankia acknowledged that its performance in 2011 had been far worse

19 IMF, 2012, "Spain: Financial Sector Assessment, Preliminary Conclusions by the Staff of the International Monetary Fund," April 25, www.imf.org/external/np/ms/2012/042512.htm.

than previously stated, with losses totalling €4.3 billion rather than the €309 million profit posted before. This burst of candor served only to stoke more worries in the markets about the other nasty surprises that might be lurking in the balance sheets of Spanish banks.

Perhaps the market response to developments in Madrid would have been calmer had it not been for the rapid-fire series of thunderclaps that were resounding from other European capitals.

On May 6, one day before the Bankia nationalization, France held a presidential election runoff in which voters deposed Sarkozy from the Elysee Palace in favour of Socialist François Hollande. And in another sign of "austerity fatigue" among the European electorate, a populist party in Italy led by comedian Beppe Grillo scored some significant wins in local contests.

But by far the biggest jolt came from Greece, which was also holding national elections that day. Both the centre-right New Democracy Party and the Socialists, which had dominated Greek politics for decades, polled far below expectations, their support having been severely drained by parties once regarded as extremist fringe groups. Although New Democracy, led by Antonis Samaras, came in first with 18.9 percent, it lost so many parliamentary seats that it lacked any realistic hope of forming a stable coalition government, especially since popular fury over the country's fate had decimated the electoral strength of Papandreou's Socialists.

In second place, with 16.8 percent of the vote, was Syriza, an umbrella group of ex-communists, Trotskyists, socialists and greens led by a 38-year-old firebrand named Alexis Tsipras. These radical leftists had garnered less than five percent of the vote in 2009; now they were emerging as a political force to be reckoned with. Altogether two-thirds of Greek votes had gone to parties that took a rejectionist position toward the Troika program. On May 8, Tsipras refused to enter a coalition government with parties that had accepted the Troika's terms. "The popular verdict," he declared, "clearly renders the bailout deal null."[20] If so, the inviolability of membership in European Monetary Union was in doubt as never before.

When IMF officials say they analyze all plausible disaster scenarios during a financial crisis, they mean it, and the implications of a Greek exit from the euro zone was a subject the Fund had been considering from the early stages of the country's tribulations. Staffers who examined their files told me they found internal studies dating back as far as June 2010, and some recall the issue undergoing scrutiny even before that. More analyses followed as the crisis progressed, but the effort went into high gear in 2012, especially after Greece's May 6 election, with collaboration from officials in Brussels and Frankfurt. Although the European Commission and the ECB had shied from conducting in-depth work on the issue before 2012, for fear that leaks might spark panic in financial markets, they joined with the Fund in scenario-drafting and contingency-planning exercises in recognition that failure to prepare for such an eventuality would be irresponsible.

Extraordinary security surrounded this work, which was led by the IMF's Poul Thomsen, the ECB's Jörg Asmussen, the Commission's Marco Buti and an Austrian economist named Thomas Wieser, who headed the Euro Working Group, a committee of deputy finance ministers from euro area countries. Emails and other digital communications were all but forbidden. Written material was kept in hard copy form and, after distribution at meetings, collected for safekeeping. Greek officials were kept in the dark. A few hints were dropped, such as a May 16 statement by Lagarde on Dutch TV that the Fund had concluded Greek departure from the euro "would be extremely expensive and hard, and not just for Greece." The Fund, she explained, has to be "technically prepared for anything because it's our job."[21]

20 Kerin Hope, 2012, "Greece braced for repeat elections," *Financial Times,* May 8.

21 Sandrine Rastello, 2012, "IMF's Lagarde Says Greek Euro Exit Would Be Expensive," Bloomberg News, May 17.

A fuller picture of this mid-2012 activity came to light two years later, in a *Financial Times* article titled "Inside Europe's Plan Z," by the newspaper's Brussels bureau chief, Peter Spiegel.[22] One of the most sensational scoops of the crisis, the article reported that "a small group of EU and International Monetary Fund officials [were] working clandestinely for months....Their secret blueprint, known as 'Plan Z,' was a detailed script of how to reconstruct Greece's economic and financial infrastructure if it were to leave the euro." Although Spiegel said he was not given access to Plan Z documents, he learned many key details. I was no more successful than he was at obtaining the documents, but can offer a few elaborations on his reportage.

Perhaps most important, the term "Plan Z" was strictly that of the European Commission; the other institutions involved did not adopt it. This detail is not as trivial as it might appear, because the use of the letter "Z" was emblematic of the horror with which top Commission economists — Buti in particular — beheld the prospect of a Greek exit. Much more fervently than their counterparts at the IMF, Commission economists believed that every conceivable alternative ought to be tried before letting Athens go. That is not to say that Fund officials deemed a Greek exit to be desirable; quite the opposite, they believed Greece would suffer much more outside the euro zone than inside. But regarding the likely financial impact in the rest of the monetary union, the Fund — although by no means nonchalant — did not share the depth of the Commission's anguish, according to several participants in the exercise.

Nobody needed to know about these covert discussions to perceive how tenuous Greece's place in the euro zone was in the days following the May 2012 election. Economists at Citigroup, who had coined the term "Grexit" earlier in the year, raised their estimate of the odds to a range between 50 and 75 percent. Although new elections were called for mid-June, and polls indicated Samaras would probably succeed at forming a new government, the New Democracy leader was not guaranteed to maintain the Troika's financial lifeline. He

22 Peter Spiegel, 2014, "Inside Europe's Plan Z," *Financial Times*, May 14.

was held in ill odour in Berlin for his role during 2010 and 2011 in obstructing Papandreou's efforts to implement Troika demands; his frequent claims that he could secure a better deal for Athens disgusted Merkel despite their common bond as politicians in the federation of European centre-right parties. It was an increasingly open secret, too, that hardline policy makers in northern Europe, with Schäuble in the vanguard, had embraced the view that Grexit was an unfortunate necessity. As unimpeachable as Schäuble's European credentials were, he had concluded that Athens was probably incapable of the reform essential for its rescue to succeed, and therefore the country should be excised from the euro zone, like an infected limb, for the sake of the monetary union's long-term health.

The hardliners had no means of expelling Greece from monetary union, given the permanence and irreversibility of membership assumed in the treaty arrangement. But they had an indirect way of forcing Athens back on the drachma, simply by discontinuing the disbursement of rescue funds, which wealthier European countries had a perfectly legal right to do if the Greek authorities were failing to comply with the program. Once Greece was deprived of the euros needed to fulfill its obligations, it would default on its bonds, at which time the ECB would presumably cease providing the emergency loans needed to keep Greek banks operating. The nation's banks were in direr need than ever of those ECB loans after the May 6 election, because outflows of deposits increased significantly as worried Greeks sought to shelter their funds from the risks of political upheaval. Without the euros they needed to meet depositor demands, Greek banks would have to close their doors and the government would be compelled to replace the euro with a new currency.

It was within this context that the Troika institutions girded for Grexit. Part of their work was conceptual (that is, seeking to predict the consequences) and part was practical (that is, providing guidance for how to respond). According to people involved, the practical work culminated in an eight-page "cross institutional task list" consisting of 28 steps, each of which had a paper associated with it. The idea was to spell out instructions for what various government entities — in Athens, Frankfurt, Brussels and elsewhere — should do on the first morning after Grexit, and the first afternoon, and the second day, and so on, even down to the level of how to handle automatic teller machines. Each Troika agency took primary responsibility for drafting different aspects of these instructions, depending on its expertise. The IMF did most of the work on how to introduce a new currency; the Commission did most of the work on how to implement capital controls; the ECB did most of the work on how to establish a payments system — an especially daunting problem since Greece would be cut off from the ECB's giant computerized system, known as Target 2, by which cross-border transfers of funds are made within the European Union. If worse came to worst, the Greeks were to get a copy of this task list, with the accompanying papers, in time to prepare themselves. The IMF readied teams who would provide technical support.

Regarding the likely impact of Grexit, a summary version of the IMF's view was actually public, although it was buried so deeply in a long document published in the spring of 2012[23] that it went almost undetected. Most of the analysis focused on what would happen to Greece, and it wasn't a pretty picture, especially in the near term.

Greek GDP "could contract by more than 10 percent in the first year" after Grexit, the Fund warned. The reasons for the decline would include "disorganization effects" stemming from the fact that "the functioning of the payment system would be disrupted, and uncertainty would reign about contracts (with widespread litigation likely, aimed at testing any currency redenomination law). This could bring economic activity to a halt for some time." In other words, on the assumption that the drachma would become the country's new legal tender and would immediately depreciate in value against the euro, the Greek Parliament would have to approve legislation mandating changes in the terms of legal contracts so that money owed in euros could be repaid in drachmas, notwithstanding the lesser value of the drachma payment — and that would spark lawsuits, making it risky for people to consider entering into new contracts.

23 IMF, 2012, "Greece: Request for Extended Arrangement Under the Extended Fund Facility" (see footnote 8 in chapter 14), 46-47.

Another reason for the projected first-year plunge in GDP was "financing constraints" on business operations resulting from the damage to the banking system and the sharply higher risk of lending money in such an environment. "Liquidity and credit would dry up… leaving companies to rely on internally generated funds," the Fund analysis said.

After this intensely painful initial period, Greece could conceivably bounce back, the IMF said — but only if it maintained tight discipline over its newly autonomous ability to control its money supply. "Over time…depreciation would encourage a recovery" in certain segments of the economy where a cheaper currency would make a difference, "including manufacturing and tourism," the analysis said. "However, Greece would face many challenges to achieving a desirable steady state." Imports would become much more expensive, and if the government printed money to cover its budget deficits, that "could lead to a surge in inflation, followed by strong upward pressure on wages… quickly reducing any competitive advantage….[M]uch would depend on how well Greece conducted its policies post-exit."

What about the impact on the rest of the euro zone? With a much cheaper currency, fully paying back foreign loans denominated in euros would become impossible. "Post-exit, Greece's external debt burden would soar, making a default inevitable," the IMF said. That would be expensive for European governments and institutions, to whom Greece owed well over €300 billion by that point, including the roughly €130 billion in emergency loans extended by the ECB to Greek banks. More important, "Market perceptions of the Euro area's stability would suffer, and investors would attach increased probability to the possibility of additional Euro exits," the IMF analysis said. And if, as seemed likely, Greece were forced to take drastic measures such as deposit freezes and capital controls to keep money from flying out of the country, that "could spook depositors and investors in other weak Euro area countries, triggering preemptive deposit runs and capital flight."

European Commission economists perceived those risks in even more apocalyptic terms, according to people involved in the Grexit preparation exercise. To the Commission, one of the purposes of Plan Z was to show how nearly impossible it would be to contain the damage to Greece. The imposition of capital controls by the Greek government would very likely necessitate similar controls in Portugal, Cyprus and other members of the euro zone as panic took hold, in the view of the Commission — the result being a mockery of monetary union where capital is supposed to move freely. The Commission was also deeply concerned about the breakdown of social order in Greece, since the country would presumably remain in the European Union, which has rules permitting free movement of people.

Speculative though such anxieties may have been, it was only natural in mid-2012 to expect that a Grexit would reverberate far beyond Aegean shores.

When the time came at the end of May for the IMF to send a mission to European capitals for the 2012 Article IV assessment of the euro zone, there was little doubt that its findings would be downbeat, given the deteriorating state of affairs in both Greece and Spain. Still, this mission, led by Mahmood Pradhan, a deputy director of the European Department, arrived at conclusions that have rarely, if ever, been exceeded among Article IV's for their unsettling implications. The features of European Monetary Union that had appeared so benign and even beneficial to some at the Fund five years earlier were now going into reverse, straining the foundations of the common currency to the breaking point.

In a report published a few weeks after its May 29 arrival, the team recalled that during the period prior to the crisis, the euro zone "had achieved a very high degree of financial integration."[24] The report noted how differentials in borrowing costs across the zone had

24 IMF, 2012, "Euro Area Policies: 2012 Article IV Consultation," Country Report No. 12/181, July, www.imf.org/external/pubs/ft/scr/2012/cr12181.pdf.

almost vanished as large amounts of capital flowed from the surplus-generating core to the deficit-generating periphery, with the spread between the yields on German and Greek sovereign bonds oscillating between 8 and 37 basis points during the period from 2002 to 2007.

But the crisis had caused a torrent of capital to move in the opposite direction, the result being "financial fragmentation" of the monetary union, in the words of the report's authors. In both bond markets and interbank markets (lending by banks to other banks), hundreds of billions of euros had been withdrawn from cross-border transactions within the euro zone, data accumulated by the mission showed. Furthermore, the feedback loop between weak banks and weak sovereigns was subjecting member states to "starkly diverging perceptions of sovereign and banking risks," the result being increasing segmentation of the region's financial system along national lines. For example, whereas nearly one-half of Spanish sovereign bonds had been held by foreigners at the end of 2009, only one-third of them were held by foreigners at the end of 2011; the comparable figures for Italy had dropped from 44 percent to 34 percent. And European banks were charging interest to business borrowers based less on traditional credit considerations than on the country of operation.[25] Spanish firms had been able to borrow, on average, at just 6 basis points more than German firms in August 2008, but this spread had risen to 43 basis points in January 2011 and to 187 basis points in April 2012, "irrespective of [the companies'] profitability." Financing was therefore least available, and most expensive, in the countries where the crisis was most acute, which was leading to another mutually reinforcing impact — on the economy. Unemployment in the euro area stood at more than 11 percent in May, the highest level since the monetary union was launched.

The Article IV mission returned to Washington on June 11 — coincidentally, just as the crisis was about to worsen anew.

25 To some extent, this could be viewed as a rectification of the excessive convergence that had occurred previously.

Two days before, a Saturday, the announcement came that Spain would get up to €100 billion from one or both of the two European bailout funds, the EFSF and ESM. In this rescue, the IMF would not even get junior partner status. Although the FSAP report prepared by Pazarbasioglu's team was viewed in Madrid as helpful and influential, officials in the Rajoy government — who saw their country as belonging to an entirely different category than the likes of Greece — wanted no part of a traditional Troika program. To the extent aid was needed, they asserted, it should be focused solely on the banking system, with none of the austerity or intensive monitoring involved in the other three euro-zone rescues. Under its rules, the Fund cannot lend for such limited purposes; it could only provide technical assistance.

"This matter is now resolved," harrumphed Rajoy when the rescue was unveiled, and to underscore his belief that his country's troubles were over, he promptly flew that weekend to Poland, where he lent his prime ministerial support to the Spanish team at a soccer match.[26] He spoke way too soon; the announcement's impact could hardly have been more disappointing. By Tuesday the 12th, yields on Spanish 10-year bonds reached the highest level since the country's adoption of the euro, and two days later the yield topped seven percent, up from about 6.2 percent before the deal. Even after Madrid published stress tests conducted by two independent firms showing that Spanish banks' needs for new capital were somewhere in the range of €16 billion to €62 billion — well below many private analysts' estimates — markets remained rattled and yields stayed high.

Among the many factors explaining investors' negative verdict, one stood out as most crucial: the rescue would exacerbate, rather than fix, the doom loop linking the Spanish sovereign and Spanish banks. The European money being proffered, although accompanied by far fewer conditions than the loans for other countries, would come in the form of loans to the Spanish government rather than being injected directly into Spanish banks. That could add up to 10 percentage points of GDP

26 Raphael Minder, 2012, "Bailout in Spain Leaves Taxpayers Liable for the Cost," *The New York Times*, June 12.

to Spain's debt,[27] lifting the debt-to-GDP ratio to about 90 percent and raising new questions about Madrid's ability to shoulder the cost of the banking-system cleanup. The IMF — and a number of southern European governments, including Spain's — favoured an alternative approach, in which the money would go to Spanish banks in the form of new capital without going through Madrid. But Germany and other northern European countries nixed that approach, arguing that the euro zone must first adopt more rigorous rules for fiscal discipline over member states.

Amid a febrile atmosphere reflecting worry about the failure of the Spanish rescue to work, Lagarde appeared before the Eurogroup on June 21 in Luxembourg to present the findings and recommendations of the Article IV mission. At the end of the meeting, the IMF released the mission's preliminary statement, which warned: "Downward spirals between sovereigns, banks, and the real economy are stronger than ever....Contagion from further intensification of the crisis — including acute stress in funding markets and tensions involving systemically important banks — would be sizable globally."[28] Lagarde herself recited some of the main points at a news conference, where she solemnly declared: "At the moment, the viability of the European monetary system is questioned."[29]

There was no secret about the purpose for this public waving of red flags. The IMF wanted to intensify pressure on Germany into accepting several radical steps that Fund officials had long favoured, in some cases only privately. The opportunity for consideration of such steps was arising because the leaders of major European institutions — the Council, the Commission, the ECB and the Eurogroup — were working on their own report, to be submitted to leaders at an end-of-

27 This calculation assumes that the entire €100 billion that was made available to Spain would be used. In the end, Spain only had to draw down about €41 billion of the amount.

28 IMF, 2012, "2012 Article IV Consultation with the Euro Area: Concluding Statement of IMF Mission," June 21, www.imf.org/external/np/ms/2012/062112.htm.

29 James Kanter, 2012, "I.M.F. Urges Europe's Strongest to Shoulder Burden of Currency Bloc," *The New York Times*, June 21.

June summit, about long-term changes in the workings of monetary union. To a large extent, the Fund-backed measures already had support from key member states including France, Italy and Spain, but they faced resolute opposition or at least strong resistance in Berlin and other northern European capitals.

The "immediate priority" was concrete progress toward banking union, according to the IMF's Article IV statement. The principle of banking union had already gained support from Draghi, his influential ECB colleague Jörg Asmussen and the European Commission, as well as a lukewarm endorsement from Merkel. As obvious a solution as it might be for breaking the doom loop, however, achieving it was anything but simple. No sovereign government readily gives up decision-making power over whether a bank within its borders gets closed down or forced into a merger; such actions are often politically sensitive, and the prospect of ceding control to a central authority stirred up apprehension about creating a pan-European government with powers of micromanagement over local issues. Complicating matters further was the disparity between the banking systems in various euro-zone countries, especially France and Germany. Whereas French banks are mostly multinational giants and few in number, German banks include scores of small savings banks, and Berlin was particularly loath to yield much control over them to a supra-national authority — which in turn caused Paris to resist the idea of ceding supervision over French banks unless Berlin was going to do the same with German ones.

The biggest obstacle of all to banking union, though, was the suspicion it aroused in northern Europe that it was a backdoor way of getting wealthy, sober members of the euro zone to underwrite the recklessness of their less-prosperous neighbours. That is because one of the essential elements of a true banking union is a common deposit insurance scheme, with the deposits in one country covered against loss based on contributions from all over the union. On the face of it, creating such a Europe-wide deposit insurance scheme was crucial to short-circuiting the doom loop; worries about the potential costs to Madrid of covering Spanish depositors' losses lay at the root of Spain's crisis, and the same anxieties would apply to other countries in similar circumstances. But the very concept naturally triggered alarm among northern Europeans

— Germans in particular — that they would get stuck paying the bill for the follies of banks in poorly regulated countries.

Even more controversial was another IMF recommendation for the euro zone to embark on a path toward "more fiscal integration" — for example, enabling individual national governments to issue a certain amount of "eurobonds" that would be backed jointly and severally by all the zone's governments. Recognizing that this approach would run afoul of treaty bans against member states assuming the obligations of other countries, the Fund argued that new rules could be developed over time to prevent countries from running up excessive debts at their neighbours' expense. This idea had been bandied around almost since the start of the crisis, but it was a "non-starter" in northern Europe, as Merkel and her allies had repeatedly stated, unless member states were prepared to relinquish much greater sovereignty over their national budgets than could possibly be envisioned politically.

In addition, the IMF statement called upon the ECB to crank up its euro-creation machinery with a special focus on helping countries that were undergoing market pressure. In contrast to German officialdom's strict hands-off policy toward trying to influence ECB policy, the Fund said the central bank should "signal a commitment to a more accommodative stance for a prolonged period," and the statement continued: "If necessary, unconventional measures should be used," perhaps by reactivating past programs involving bond purchases (the SMP) and liquidity injections into banks (the LTRO).

Reporters attending Lagarde's news conference asked what she expected Germany to think about all these suggestions. The managing director smiled, and replied: "We hope wisdom will prevail."[30] And so it would, although not to the extent or in the manner that the IMF had prescribed.

30 Julia Kollewe, 2012, "IMF piles pressure on Germany to help struggling eurozone banks directly," *The Guardian,* June 22.

On June 29, 2012, after a flurry of meetings at lower levels, a summit of euro-zone leaders took what was arguably their biggest step toward solving the crisis — with a communiqué that in its first sentence borrowed almost verbatim words uttered by Lagarde in her January 23 speech. "We affirm that it is imperative to break the vicious circle between banks and sovereigns," stated the leaders, who went on to pledge that proposals for the first steps toward banking union would be considered "shortly."[31] By that point, to be sure, the "vicious circle" was a well-recognized phenomenon. Neither Lagarde nor other IMF officials were playing a major role in guiding this decision; the managing director and her deputies weren't even present for this summit, nor for the meetings that immediately preceded it. But the Fund could take some measure of satisfaction that, in its "trusted adviser" role, it had exerted influence and helped nudge policy in a favourable direction.

The European move toward banking union was still tentative at that point; numerous details remained to be specified. The summit endorsed only the establishment of a "single supervisory mechanism," with a target date of end-2012, without mentioning a centralized system for handling ailing banks or a euro-wide deposit insurance scheme, since German officials were particularly unready to go that far. But financial markets enthusiastically — and justifiably — welcomed the news as groundbreaking. Creating a common European supervisor would lead by almost ironclad logic to other elements of banking union, because it is essential to put the authority in charge of handling crises at the same level as the authority responsible for preventing them. In the absence of such consistency, a national government facing the necessity of closing down or merging a problem bank would point the finger at faulty supervision for having failed to detect the bank's weaknesses. In retrospect, the accord on a single supervisor can be viewed as the start of a giant shift toward deeper and fuller financial integration of the euro zone.

Another important agreement struck at the June 29 summit — also strongly favoured by the IMF, and also received joyously in markets —

31 Euro Area Summit Statement, June 29, 2012.

was that troubled euro-zone countries could tap Europe's bailout funds for the purpose of directly recapitalizing banks. For obvious reasons this new form of aid was a major goal of the Spanish government, since it held out the promise of enabling Madrid to repair its weak banks without the vexatious problem of adding to its sovereign debt load.

Almost no sooner had European policy makers made such progress, however, than they took back some of the most market-boosting parts. On July 6, the news media reported from Brussels that there had been some misunderstanding about the extent of the breakthrough reached at the June 29 summit. Although ESM funding could indeed go to recapitalize banks, the money would have to be channelled through the national government responsible for those banks — which meant that Spain would be on the hook after all for any amounts borrowed under this new scheme. The separation between ailing banks and sovereigns was not as definitive as initially thought; it would come only after full banking union, which required a long period of negotiation over details. Markets nosedived on the news, with yields on Spanish 10-year government bonds jumping back above seven percent, and yields on comparable Italian securities trailing at the six percent level.[32]

Never before, and never since, were the threats to financial stability in the euro zone so chilling as during the days that followed. Investors relentlessly drove yields on Spanish bonds higher and higher in July — the yield on the 10-year bond reached 7.5 percent on July 25, nearing impossibly expensive levels for borrowing on private markets considering that Madrid had to raise an estimated €385 billion over the next two and a half years to cover its obligations. The markets were effectively signalling that to keep its debt from swelling explosively Spain would before long need a full Troika rescue, which would require hundreds of billions of euros, straining the capacity of even Europe's newly fortified bailout funds and leaving little for other emergencies. Predictably, Spain's malady was infecting markets elsewhere in the euro zone, as Italian 10-year bond yields rose above 6.5 percent. Money, in the form of bank deposits and securities investment, was flooding in

32 Joshua Chaffin, 2012, "Euro doubts fuel leap in bond yields," *Financial Times*, July 6.

ever-greater quantities from the euro zone's peripheral countries to the safe-haven core, in particular Germany; as a result, businesses in the periphery were starved even more than before for capital while businesses in the core were flush with cash. Even the ostensibly sound northern tier got a nasty jolt when a Moody's report suggested that Germany, the Netherlands and Luxembourg might lose their triple-A ratings, in part because of the prospective cost of possible additional bailouts.

"We saw the risk of a complete collapse of all credit markets," Draghi recalled in a speech the following year. "Investors suddenly lost confidence that the euro area could survive in its current composition….In this environment, we once again had to act."[33]

The action taken by the ECB, dubbed "Outright Monetary Transactions" (OMT), can be seen in hindsight as the turning point after which the virulence of the crisis diminished, and in a much more sustained way than the "mission accomplished" episode earlier in the year. OMT was the decisive sort of move that the IMF and many others had long urged the central bank to take — although it was designed in an ingenious way that Fund officials admit they hadn't envisioned.[34]

The key was to make effective use of the ECB's unlimited euro-creation power while avoiding any blatant violation of the prohibition against monetary financing of deficits. Although a number of proposals were circulating for the central bank to simply buy as many bonds as necessary to cap borrowing costs for euro-zone governments, such as that of Spain, that were abiding by fiscal rules, Draghi and his colleagues rejected those ideas. Even if ECB officials had wanted to embark on such a course, they knew it would draw condemnation from Berlin, shatter German confidence in the central bank's stewardship of the

33 European Central Bank, 2013, "Stable Euro, Strong Europe," speech by Mario Draghi at the Wirtschaftstag 2013, Berlin, June 25, www.ecb.europa.eu/press/key/date/2013/html/sp130625_1.en.html.

34 Information about the development of OMT can be found in Irwin, *The Alchemists* (see footnote 13 in chapter 3); Spiegel, *How the Euro Was Saved* (see footnote 15 in chapter 13); and Brian Blackstone and Marcus Walker, 2012, "How ECB Chief Outflanked German Foe in Fight for Euro," *The Wall Street Journal*, October 2.

euro, and ultimately risk undermining support for monetary union in the euro zone's most important country. But they also recognized that previous ECB initiatives were inadequate; the SMP and LTRO had proven both limited in scope and temporary in impact. And they knew that only the ECB had the financial might to convince markets that a buyer stood ready to buy all bonds in a panic, even bonds of big countries such as Spain and Italy.

Starting in June 2012, Draghi began discussing a new mechanism with people in the ECB's inner circle. He had to gain support from one in particular — Jörg Asmussen, Germany's former deputy finance minister who was now the ECB's executive board member in charge of international and European relations. Two prominent Germans had already quit the ECB in protest during Trichet's reign over what they considered to be violations of the central bank's mandate; if Asmussen followed suit, it could be the death-knell for any new initiative. Fortunately for Draghi, Asmussen was less dogmatic — or at least more willing to accept that, as Asmussen put it later, there was a difference between what could be done in "wartime" versus "peacetime." Draghi also made sure he kept Merkel and Schäuble informed as the plan began to take shape. Opposition was almost certain to come from the Bundesbank, whose president, Jens Weidmann, sat on the ECB Governing Council, and Draghi was hoping to obtain political cover from other German leaders.

The first public hint that something dramatic was afoot came on July 26, when Draghi delivered a speech in London amid such deep gloom in financial markets that companies and banks were actively preparing for a bust-up of the euro. "The ECB is ready to do whatever it takes to preserve the euro. And believe me, it will be enough," Draghi vowed.[35] In fact, he hadn't fully vetted his plan at that point with all the people who mattered — he was essentially engaging in a central banker's version of bravado, in hope that it would at least keep the panic from worsening — but a few days later, he secured approval for OMT from the Governing Council at a dinner meeting in the Eurotower. The ECB

35 James Wilson, Robin Wigglesworth and Brian Groom, 2012, "ECB 'ready to do whatever it takes,'" *Financial Times*, July 26.

would stand ready to buy bonds in unlimited quantities of euro-zone countries subject to an important proviso: the countries would have to be entering into rescue programs with the EFSF or ESM — in other words, they would have to subject their policies to strict conditionality and monitoring, with heavy IMF input. The ECB would be able to claim that it was acting within its monetary policy mandate because it was acting to eliminate fears about the very survival of the euro, which were interfering with the ability of the central bank to influence monetary conditions throughout the euro area. Despite dissension and public criticism by Weidmann, the plan got sufficient endorsement from the other key Germans, who shared Draghi's conviction that it was needed to ensure the euro's continued existence. A full version of the plan was unveiled in early September, after which point yields on Spanish bonds dipped back below the six percent level.

The effect of OMT on market psychology was so potent that it has never had to be activated. As of this writing, the ECB has never created a single euro, or bought a single bond, in support of an OMT program, because markets are aware that the central bank stands ready to use its powers without limitation. Throughout the fall of 2012, the IMF was readying itself to join in an OMT-based program for Spain, providing expertise on conditionality and monitoring as specified in Draghi's plan. But the need did not arise. Yields on the bonds of the Spanish and Italian governments remained safely below the levels of summer 2012.

As with all of the major steps that European policy makers took during the crisis, this one had required a laborious process of consensus mobilization based on other measures being taken first. Intriguing evidence suggests that a key to success for Draghi's OMT gambit was the June 2012 agreement to embark on banking union[36] — so in that limited sense, the IMF, as a prime mover behind banking union, can claim to have played a helpful role in quelling the crisis. According to Van Rompuy, who chaired the June summit, "[Draghi] said to me, during that [summit], that [banking union] was exactly the game-

36 This insight comes from Nicolas Véron, 2015, "Europe's Radical Banking Union," Bruegel Essay and Lecture Series, Bruegel.

changer he needed."[37] Although Draghi himself has not linked the two decisions publicly — as a central banker, he would naturally feel constrained from acknowledging that monetary policy could be influenced by politicians — he has written that "the setting-up of European banking supervision has been the greatest step towards deeper economic integration since the creation of Economic and Monetary Union."[38]

Ending the virulent stage of the region's crisis did not mean that Greece's woes were sorted out, however. The threat of Grexit, still very much alive in midsummer 2012, would prove very tough to extinguish completely for a long time thereafter.

37 European Council, 2014, "Speech by President Herman Van Rompuy at the Brussels Economic Forum 2014—4th Annual Tommaso Padoa-Schioppa Lecture," June 10.

38 ECB, 2015, "Annual Report on supervisory activities 2014," March, foreword.

16

GETTING MOJO BACK

Bags were packed and briefing books ready for a visit to Athens in late June 2012 by the Troika "inspectors," including the IMF's Poul Thomsen. The purpose of the mission was to start discussions on how to resume the rescue program for Greece that had been finalized in March. A new government was coming to power, led by Antonis Samaras, whose centre-right New Democracy Party had won enough parliamentary seats in a second national election on June 17 to form a coalition with a couple of other parties, including PASOK. The Troika wanted to assess the damage inflicted on the economy by the political chaos that had prevailed in preceding weeks, and instill the proper sense of commitment in the new regime about the adjustment that would be necessary to secure its financial lifeline.

The mission would have to wait, however, because news arrived that authoritative interlocutors from the new government would be unavailable. Vassilis Rapanos, a 64-year-old economist and bank chairman who had just been designated as finance minister, was being rushed to the hospital after a fainting spell, and based on his doctors' advice, he decided to decline the ministerial post. As for Samaras, he too was in the hospital, to undergo emergency surgery for a damaged retina. Only hours before their scheduled departure on June 24, the Troika called off the trip.[1]

1 Kerin Hope, 2012, "Greek lenders postpone mission to Athens," *Financial Times*, June 24.

This episode was a harbinger of many frustrations the Troika was to have with the Samaras government. The new prime minister, who hailed from one of the most prominent families in Athens and held a Harvard MBA, had denounced previous bailouts during his years as opposition leader; he blamed the rescue terms for "suffocating" the economy. For that reason, among others, hardliners among Greece's official creditors regarded the new regime with jaundiced eyes. They suspected that these Greek leaders were, like their predecessors, beholden to special interests and too politically timorous to implement the kinds of reforms specified under the 2012 rescue program. The result was an increasingly unforgiving stance toward Greek failures to comply with program conditions.

The most hawkish in the Troika was the IMF, and particularly Poul Thomsen, whose skepticism about Samaras would deepen with the passage of time. His continuation as mission chief became a source of disquiet among some colleagues, partly because he was "invested" in the initial program, and partly because Greece's flaws — notably its clientelistic political system — seemed to be taxing his patience to the breaking point. Sometimes the Fund will assign a new mission chief to a country for the sake of a fresh start, especially when a new government takes power. On the other hand, keeping the same person in charge affords the benefit of expertise; even Greek officials were obliged to admit that Thomsen had a thorough grasp of their economy's inner workings. Thomsen also enjoyed the confidence of German officials, and Lagarde as well — as witnessed by his promotion in 2014 to the directorship of the European Department, where he would hold even greater sway over the Fund's Greek program.

Whether Thomsen and his IMF colleagues were overly exacting with Greece during this period is an important question, because as we shall see, the Fund's stance was a key factor in a Greek political impasse that would bring the radicals of Syriza to power in early 2015. To this day, an embittered Samaras and his allies accuse Thomsen of having caused their downfall by ignoring their genuine economic accomplishments and paying undue attention to deviations from program guidelines. The upshot, they argue, was surely much worse for Greece — the enormously costly showdown between Syriza and the nation's creditors, which is the subject of chapters 18 and 19. Some European policy makers, while acknowledging that the Samaras team gave Thomsen every reason to be fed up, also fault him for granting Athens no benefit of the doubt at critical junctures.

There is blame aplenty to be apportioned for the developments that led to the events of 2015. In defence of Thomsen (and the IMF more broadly), it should be noted that he didn't insist on the inclusion of austerity-oriented targets in Greece's programs. On the contrary, he often cautioned that ambitious goals for fiscal deficits and surpluses could exceed the government's capacity to achieve and might in any case prove counter-productive by stifling growth. But once Greek officials had committed to such targets (typically at the behest of European policy makers), Thomsen was remorseless at requiring delivery and standing fast against any loan disbursements until the necessary measures were taken. His endless renditions of the phrase "The numbers have to add up" not only suited his technocratic personality, he could ill afford to go before the executive board and seek approval for distribution of funds if he had overlooked substantial shortfalls in performance by Athens. Board members had amply demonstrated a readiness to pick on evidence that the Greek program was leading the country down an unsustainably indebted path. Thomsen therefore prided himself on resisting the temptation to go easy on Greek compliance, and if that meant he and the Fund would be perceived as "the bad guys," so be it.

The Fund's increasingly combative posture was not confined to Greece alone. It was also manifest in IMF relations with creditor Europe and with another country where a crisis was about to erupt — Cyprus. This was a period when, to use the vernacular, the Fund was trying to get its mojo back. Although IMF financial resources were not as essential to Europe once the ECB put its "whatever it takes" policy into effect, northern European policy makers — Merkel, in particular — continued to regard the Fund's participation in rescue programs as a political necessity. That gave the Fund a powerful hand to play when disputes arose.

At the time of the aborted Troika mission in June 2012, Greece was just emerging from two rounds of elections, during which government policy making was paralyzed and the economy was growing feebler. Fears that Grexit might be imminent were continuing to affect the behaviour of businesses and consumers — with good reason. Schäuble and his team in the finance ministry in Berlin still viewed Greece as an infected and ultimately incurable limb of the European Monetary Union that would be best to cut off. Only in late August was Greece's continued membership in the euro zone assured, when Samaras flew to Berlin for a meeting with Merkel. According to several accounts of that meeting, the Greek leader rehearsed his lines for hours in his hotel before going to see the German chancellor, and when the conversation turned to how stridently he used to criticize the Troika prior to his election, he assured his hosts that as prime minister he would take the measures necessary to keep his country in the European fold. As evidence of his new-found willingness to abandon political gamesmanship, he pointed to Yannis Stournaras, a respected, Oxford-trained economist with close ties to PASOK, whom he had selected as finance minister after Rapanos stepped aside. This effort paid off when Merkel ordered an end to Grexit speculation and delivered a visible show of support for Samaras by travelling to Athens in October for the first time since the onset of crisis.[2]

Even so, Greece's rescue program was veering far off track in the second half of 2012. Once again, growth figures were much lower than projected, and privatization — which was supposed to reap €12 billion in revenue for the government by 2014 — was completely stalled, as investors remained spooked by Grexit chatter. The Troika was withholding a €36 billion loan disbursement, originally scheduled for June, on the grounds that Athens had not yet come up with tens of billions of euros in budgetary savings and revenue-raising measures that were supposed to help generate the surpluses needed to pay down debt. With scarcely enough euros to pay pensions and government salaries, the Greek authorities were scrambling to raise cash by borrowing short-term from banks and squeezing suppliers.

2 Marcus Walker and Marianna Kakaounaki, 2015, "How Greece and Germany Brought Europe's Long-Simmering Crisis Back to a Boil," *The Wall Street Journal*, January 21; and Yannis Palaiologos, 2015, "The Greek-German breakthrough that didn't come," *Kathimerini*, May 17.

For the IMF, the qualms it had expressed earlier in the year about the program's viability were being confirmed. Management and staffers began girding themselves for intellectual battle.

Among the perennial routines of IMF-World Bank annual meetings is the release of the Fund's *World Economic Outlook* (WEO), a glossy publication loaded with charts, tables and analyses. The Fund's forecast of global growth tends to generate the most headlines, and in the days leading up to the meetings, wire-service reporters vie fiercely for scoops about that figure. But the WEO also includes several analytical chapters examining key issues in depth, which often contain some of the most noteworthy material. A classic example came during the October 2012 meetings in Tokyo, where controversy raged over a three-page box in the 250-page WEO, titled "Are We Underestimating Short-term Fiscal Multipliers?"[3]

The box was the latest, and most forceful, of the IMF's challenges to the high priests of economic austerity. The authors, Chief Economist Olivier Blanchard and one of his Research Department colleagues, Daniel Leigh, had already established themselves as trenchant critics of the most extreme claims for the benefits of budgetary discipline. As noted in chapter 6, this issue arose during the debate in spring 2010 over how to design the first Greek program, when some European policy makers embraced the view that cutting government spending and raising taxes in Greece would stimulate the economy's growth thanks to "confidence effects" that would lead to lower interest rates and increased investment. In the October 2010 WEO, a team of IMF economists led by Leigh presented research debunking this "expansionary fiscal contractions hypothesis" and defending the conventional Keynesian perspective on how fiscal policy affects economies. Based on an examination of episodes involving fiscal retrenchment over a 30-year period, this research found that when governments adopt programs of spending cuts and tax increases, economic output generally falls over

3 IMF, 2012, *World Economic Outlook*, October, 41–43, www.imf.org/external/pubs/ft/weo/2012/02/pdf/text.pdf.

the next two years by about half as much as the amount of the deficit reduction — in other words, for every $1 of deficit shrinkage, GDP falls by 50 cents. Although the authors were careful to note that "there is widespread agreement that reducing debt has important long-term benefits," they provided strong empirical grounds for rejecting the idea that benefits would be growth-stimulating in the short run as well.[4]

The box in the 2012 WEO went further, contending that fiscal austerity was having even more damaging short-term effects during the crisis than the previous research had indicated. Growth had been weaker, and recessions deeper, than initial forecasts had projected "in a number of countries" undertaking deficit-reduction programs, Blanchard and Leigh noted. One of the chief reasons for such an outcome, they asserted, was that "fiscal multipliers were underestimated....since the start of the Great Recession." In other words, instead of a 50-cent fall in GDP resulting from each $1 in deficit reduction (a multiplier of 0.5), the effect on GDP was turning out to be more like 90 cents to $1.70 (a multiplier of 0.9 to 1.7). The most plausible explanation for the bigger multipliers, the authors continued, could be found in analyses done by outside economists highlighting the importance of special circumstances arising during the crisis. Pretty much the whole global economy had softened — many countries were engaging in fiscal retrenchment simultaneously, and interest rates had fallen to zero or barely above zero, meaning that monetary policy had already been exhausted as a potential growth-booster. For all of those reasons, there was a lack of stimulatory factors to offset the negative effects of fiscal discipline, which were magnified accordingly.

Blanchard and Leigh's work came under immediate attack from European officials such as Rehn, who said the IMF was failing to appreciate the potential boost to confidence from rapid shrinkage in

4 IMF, 2010, *World Economic Outlook*, October, chapter 3, www.imf.org/external/pubs/ft/weo/2010/02/.

budget deficits.[5] Even within the Fund, staffers — Thomsen prominent among them — harboured doubts about the merit of the WEO box's findings. In Thomsen's view, Greece's slump was longer and deeper than initially anticipated for reasons that had little if anything to do with the multiplier used in the initial program. Rather, the unforeseen degree of contraction was attributable primarily to repeated political shocks causing investor flight, interest rate spikes, heavy deposit outflows from banks and failure to implement growth-oriented reforms.

Still, Lagarde stoutly backed her chief economist, telling reporters, "there is no difference between Olivier's views and my views."[6] And when asked whether these findings on budgetary austerity would exert any influence on IMF policy, she replied that she was trying to cut some slack for Greece, which had been begging its creditors for more time to deliver on promised spending cuts and tax increases. Instead of requiring the Greek government to generate a primary budget surplus of 4.5 percent in 2014, the new deadline should be 2016, the managing director contended; she also advanced the idea of another round of debt restructuring. European reaction to all this was predictably huffy. Although French officials indicated willingness to be flexible about the fiscal targets, Schäuble declared, "If you're doing a long run, you mustn't make it even longer by briefly running in the other direction."[7]

But even the northern Europeans could see that circumstances had changed so much in Greece since the March 2012 accord on the new program that revisions of some significance would be necessary. Another little bombshell in the IMF's WEO helped dispel any remaining doubts about the severity of the problem. One of the document's tables downgraded the forecast for the Greek economy to a six percent shrinkage in GDP for 2012 and another contraction of four

5 The European Commission produced its own analysis shortly thereafter, with different conclusions. European Commission, 2012, "European Economic Forecast," Autumn, Box 1.5, http://ec.europa.eu/economy_finance/eu/forecasts/2012_autumn/box_af12_-_multipliers_en.pdf.

6 IMF, 2012, "Transcript of a Press Briefing by Managing Director Christine Lagarde," October 11, www.imf.org/external/np/tr/2012/tr101112.htm.

7 Simon Kennedy, Jana Random and Patrick Donahue, 2012, "EU Girds for Summit as Nobel's Glow Fades on Crisis Response," Bloomberg News, October 15.

percent in 2013.[8] (In March, the projection had been for a 4.8 percent downturn in 2013, followed by flat growth the following year.)

This time, the new forecast would prove to be almost exactly right. That meant Greece's GDP, which had peaked at €242 billion in 2008, would shrink to €183 billion in 2013. Yet its government debt was continuing to climb, to a projected €346 billion, substantially higher than when the crisis began three years earlier. At nearly 190 percent, this ratio of debt to GDP was heading in the wrong direction.

If there was one senior European policy maker who sometimes elicited visible annoyance from Lagarde, it was Jean-Claude Juncker, the president of the Eurogroup, because of his penchant for lighting up cigarettes during meetings in EU buildings in defiance of no-smoking rules. On November 12, 2012, discord between the two of them flared openly at a post-meeting news conference in Brussels. Tobacco smoke, however, was not at issue. Greek debt was.

A reporter asked whether creditors were still using the previous benchmark for determining Greece's debt sustainability — that is, reducing the projected debt-to-GDP ratio to 120 percent by 2020. "There is a...probability that we move the target to 2022," Juncker replied, prompting a demurral from Lagarde, who said, "In our view, the appropriate timetable is 120 percent by 2020. We clearly have different views." When Juncker again maintained that the target year would be changed, saying, "I'm not joking," Lagarde's eyes rolled and she shook her head.[9]

IMF staffers were thrilled by media accounts describing the encounter as a "spat," "rare public breach" and "public manifestation of a fight

8 IMF, 2012, *World Economic Outlook*, October, 66.

9 Peter Spiegel and Joshua Chaffin, 2012, "EU-IMF feud erupts over Greek debt," *Financial Times*, November 12. A video of the press conference is available at: www.youtube.com/watch?v=D4vyqZuxpeA.

that has been simmering behind closed doors for months." Although the dispute over 2020 vs. 2022 looked trivial on the surface, many at the Fund saw their institution's credibility being challenged anew. Commentators were in full cry, recalling the Fund's apparent reluctance in acquiescing to the second bailout of March 2012, and noting that after just a few months the debt sustainability analysis underlying the bailout was woefully off base. Exhortations were mounting for the Fund to walk away if it was going to be dragged into yet another exercise in financial make-believe.[10]

The Europeans were doing just what IMF staffers had feared — chiselling away at the 120-by-2020 target. Although the target had no more analytical magic than when it was initially agreed, it had been accepted by all parties, and failure to honour it would risk eroding the primacy that ought to be accorded to debt sustainability. So what was going on? To the Fund, the answer was clear: the arithmetic of 120-by-2020 would require certain European governments to take steps they couldn't abide, so they were desperate to make the target more flexible.

To oversimplify the arithmetic somewhat, here's how it worked: a little more than €60 billion of Greece's debt — less than one-fifth of the total — remained in private hands, and that had already been haircut earlier in the year. The only big pot of debt that could be restructured was that owed to European governments and institutions. And the only plausible way to reduce the overall debt to 120 percent of GDP by 2020 was to haircut the European official debt as well — or at least that is what IMF debt sustainability analyses showed. Other options for reducing projected debt to the target level involved using accounting gimmicks, or assumptions about Greek growth or economic policies that the Fund deemed unrealistic — and the Fund was not about to accept such chicanery at this stage.

10 *Financial Times,* 2012, "IMF can end its agony over Greece," July 29; Alan Beattie, 2012, "Trouble in t'troika," *Financial Times, The World* blog, http://blogs.ft.com/the-world/2012/11/trouble-in-ttroika/.

Unsurprisingly, therefore, the countries most eager to tweak the target were the same ones that had long refused to countenance a haircut of principal on their loans to Greece — that is, Germany, the Netherlands and a few others. As previously noted, German officials from Merkel on down were insistent that European loans to Athens must be forever treated as loans rather than grants, to be repaid someday, even if not according to the initial timetable. They were grudgingly willing to consider other forms of OSI, such as granting Greece a further lowering of interest rates and longer periods to repay amounts coming due. But as far as Berlin was concerned, principal on its loans must not be alterable.

Not all European policy makers held this position. In the fall of 2012, officials in the French finance ministry secretly circulated a plan that envisioned eventual haircuts on official debt, according to several people involved in the discussion.[11] It was an ingenious scheme that would have combined debt relief with a mechanism to encourage the structural reforms, tax collection improvements and other measures essential to restoring Greece's economic health on a long-term basis. The model was a program launched in the 1990s, called the Heavily Indebted Poor Countries (HIPC) initiative, designed to cancel or reduce the debt of about three dozen countries, the majority of which were in Sub-Saharan Africa, including Ghana, Ethiopia, Senegal and Uganda. The IMF liked the suggestion to apply this approach to Greece because HIPC was not simply the unconditional forgiveness of debt; countries had to show over a six-year period that they were undertaking an economic policy program agreed with the Fund and the World Bank before they could get any of their obligations written off. Both numerator and denominator of the debt-to-GDP ratio were supposed to be altered, in other words, with the firm promise of debt relief held out as a sort of "carrot" to incentivize sensible policies.

11 This plan was the brainchild of Kemal Dervis, director of the Global Economy and Development Program at the Brookings Institution, where I was a nonresident fellow at the time. But Dervis was not the person who informed me about it; others involved were.

The French plan offered a new opportunity to pull the Greek economy out of its death spiral. If only that opportunity had been seized. But the German government quickly shot it down, which shows that an important role reversal had occurred between France and Germany. Whereas the Germans had ardently supported debt relief for Greece in the form of PSI, mainly because it was justified on moral-hazard grounds, the French had only reluctantly gone along because of fears about contagion. Once the debt relief in question involved OSI rather than PSI, and contagion was no longer a concern, the Germans became the chief obstacle.

While wrangling continued among Greece's creditors over the debt issue, the country's government was embroiled in the latest of many struggles to implement Troika-mandated measures. At the same time, finance ministry officials were hoarding every possible scrap of cash pending long-delayed disbursal of more bailout funding; the government's unpaid bills to suppliers totalled €8.3 billion at the end of September, and taxpayers were owed €738 million in late refunds. Despite more general strikes and protests on Syntagma Square pitting police against protesters hurling stones and Molotov cocktails, Parliament approved a package of austerity measures estimated at €13.5 billion on November 7, with 153 of the 300 deputies voting in favour. The savings included cuts ranging from five to 35 percent in pensions and public sector salaries, plus tax increases on fuel and cigarettes and higher charges for state health care.[12] Samaras promised that this would be the "last and final" round of such cuts, and his finance minister, Stournaras, helped rally support by persuading parliamentarians that this sacrifice was essential for Greece to obtain the €34.4 billion that was still due from the creditors — without which Athens would default.[13]

Now that the Greeks had fulfilled the Troika's requirements, and the time had come to approve the terms for disbursing their badly needed funds, which side would prevail in the battle over debt sustainability?

12 Kerin Hope, 2012, "Athens narrowly passes austerity bill," November 8.

13 *The Economist*, 2012, "Toil and Trouble," November 10.

Would the 120-by-2020 target remain intact, and a credible effort made to attain it, as the IMF wanted, or would the Europeans' chiselling campaign succeed?

Repeated meetings of the Eurogroup — including the one on November 12 featuring the tiff between Lagarde and Juncker — ended without agreement. Even after accounting for the impact of the measures Athens had just enacted, Greek debt was projected to fall no lower than 144 percent of GDP in 2020. Various ideas were circulating for how to shrink it a few percentage points more without running afoul of the German proscription against haircutting principal on official debt. Under one proposal, Greece would retire some of its €60 billion in privately held bonds — which were trading at around 28 cents on the euro — by offering to buy them from investors at a modestly higher price. Another idea was to slash the interest rate that Greece was paying on its loans from European governments to rock-bottom levels; over the years, those reduced interest payments would help lower the debt level.

On November 26, finance ministers assembled once again at the Justus Lipsius building, haggling for many hours into the early morning of the following day as Lagarde fought to keep the 120-by-2020 target. Late in the evening, one of the ministers proposed a compromise that might fairly be called chiselling with compensatory offsets: the target would be loosened, to 124 percent of GDP by 2020, in exchange for which Europe would commit to get debt levels "substantially below" 110 percent by 2022. A variety of measures such as the debt buyback and interest rate reduction would go part of the way toward reaching this new target.[14] And since even those steps didn't go quite far enough, Europe would pledge to take additional debt-reduction measures at some point in the future as long as Greece complied with program conditions and once it had fulfilled an important proviso — running a primary budget surplus.

14 An additional provision was an agreement by euro-zone governments to forego about €7 billion that they would otherwise receive from profits earned by the ECB on its purchases of Greek bonds. The profits were to go to Greece.

The deal was acceptable to Greece's representative, Stournaras, who was anxious to end his country's cash crunch. Although he knew many analysts doubted that Greece, with its long-standing deficit-spending habit, could possibly post a primary budget surplus anytime soon, he felt confident the recently enacted measures would suffice. Moreover, he saw no chance that joining Lagarde in holding out for the original target would lead to a haircut on Greece's official debt. As he put it later in an interview with the *Financial Times:* "Schäuble told me, 'Yannis, forget it.' So it cannot be done, so what can I do?"[15]

Facing unanimous pressure from the group, Lagarde also went along. If the deal had one great virtue, it would significantly lighten the annual burden to Greece of making principal and interest payments over the next decade or two. In addition to cutting the interest rates they were charging Athens, the European creditors were agreeing to delay the maturities of their loans by another 15 years, and defer some interest payments by 10 years. "I welcome the initiatives agreed today by the Eurogroup aimed at further supporting Greece's economic reform program and making a substantial contribution to the sustainability of its debt," Lagarde said in a statement after the meeting.[16] Also reasonably content was Reza Moghadam, the director of the European Department; he regarded the European pledge to provide the necessary amount of debt relief in the future as a breakthrough.

But other top IMF staffers were so dispirited about the latest twists in the Greek rescue that they concluded the Fund must take extraordinary action to protect its interests. Specifically, they argued that that the Fund was taking imprudent financial risks on its biggest-ever loan, and it should therefore demand a formal guarantee from euro-zone governments on its exposure to Greece. As preparations were under way for the board meeting to approve the Fund's €3.24 billion portion of the loan disbursement, these staffers — from departments including SPR, Legal and Finance — contended in discussions with Lagarde and

15 Peter Spiegel and Kerin Hope, 2014, "Yannis Stournaras urges 'troika' to ease demands on Greece," January 9.

16 IMF, 2012, "Statement on Greece by IMF Managing Director Christine Lagarde," November 26, www.imf.org/external/np/sec/pr/2012/pr12458.htm.

others that the financial assurances offered by the Europeans were insufficient under the circumstances. It was all well and good for Europe to declare its respect for the IMF's preferred-creditor status and to pledge adequate funding for the Greek rescue as long as Athens adhered to the program conditions. But that would not do the Fund much good if Greece went completely bust, re-adopted the drachma and could no longer fulfill its obligations. Although it went against the spirit of IMF lending to seek a guarantee — the Fund's protection is supposed to be the quality of the program — the political pressure driving the Fund's lending decision made this situation unique, according to this line of reasoning.

I was able to learn only the bare essentials of this sensitive internal debate — which the staffers lost. But the document published for the board meeting[17] contained passages that cogently set forth the extent of the gamble that the IMF was taking. The following paragraph summed up, in relatively jargon-free wording, how the Greek economy was faring at this stage:

> There should be no doubt on the part of Greece's European partners that it is enduring exceptionally painful adjustment in order to stay within the euro area. However, the manner of the adjustment leaves much to be desired. The fiscal adjustment has relied far too much on cuts in discretionary spending and increased taxation of wage earners, while the rich and self-employed have continued to evade taxes on an astonishing scale and bloated and unproductive state sectors have seen only limited cuts. Moreover, labor has shouldered too much of the burden as lower wages have not resulted in lower prices, because of failure to liberalize closed professions and dismantle barriers to competition….[T]he mounting sense of social unfairness is undermining support for the program.

17 IMF, 2013, "Greece: First and Second Reviews under the Extended Arrangement Under the Extended Fund Facility," Country Report No. 13/20, January, www.imf.org/external/pubs/ft/scr/2013/cr1320.pdf.

Alleviation from the pain did not appear to be anywhere in the foreseeable future. Greece was still expected to post a 4.5 percent of GDP primary budget surplus by 2016, and maintain a four percent of GDP surplus as far ahead as 2030. The country was thus "attempting to achieve an unprecedented amount of fiscal…adjustment under a fixed exchange rate, with a massive debt overhang, and weak confidence," the document said, noting that "a key risk for the program is diminishing support for reforms, particularly as Greece endures another year of deep recession. The latest opinion polls show dwindling support for the [governing] coalition parties and growing support for Syriza and other anti-program parties. This could…lead to a political crisis, triggering debt default and/or euro exit."

Even so, when the November 2012 agreement received its final blessing a couple of weeks later, unlocking the €34.4 billion, European and Greek leaders rejoiced at having triumphed over predictions that Greece would rend monetary union asunder. "Those Cassandras have been proved wrong," said Rehn, and Samaras declared: "Solidarity in our union is alive. Grexit is dead."[18]

For a while, anyway, worries about a return of the drachma were indeed put to rest. But in the meantime, collateral damage from Greece was buffeting a near neighbour. "Cyprexit" was to become the new Grexit.

Among the many pre-crisis words that IMF staffers must wish they could take back are the ones on page 30 of the Article IV report for Cyprus[19] published in September 2010.[20] On that page, the report gave the Cypriot economy high marks, based on "several indicators

18 Joshua Chaffin, Peter Spiegel and Kerin Hope, 2012, "'Grexit is dead' as €34bn loan agreed," *Financial Times*, December 13.

19 "Cyprus" refers here only to the southern (Greek) part of the island, formally known as the Republic of Cyprus. The island has been politically divided since 1974 into a Turkish north and Greek south.

20 IMF, 2010, "Cyprus: 2010 Article IV Consultation—Staff Report," Country Report No. 10/291, September, www.imf.org/external/pubs/ft/scr/2010/cr10291.pdf.

of vulnerability," compared with other euro-zone economies that were under pressure from financial markets. The Cypriot government budget deficit for 2009, for example, was "moderate" relative to the deficits posted elsewhere in the euro zone, and the debt-to-GDP ratio, at 56 percent, was "also well below" average for members of the monetary union. "All in all, Cyprus appears relatively robust compared to other peripheral [euro area] countries," the report said.

As the report noted, this Mediterranean island economy had enjoyed a long stretch of prosperity, with growth averaging 3.2 percent since the dawn of the twenty-first century, more than twice the euro-zone average, and low unemployment to boot. "Even during the global financial crisis, Cyprus outperformed its peers," the authors added, citing an unemployment rate that stood at just 5.4 percent in 2009 compared with a euro-zone average of 9.4 percent. More growth was in store, according to the report's forecast — 1.8 percent in 2011, 2.5 percent in 2012 and 2.9 percent in 2013.

It is now clear that the Cypriot boom afforded a classic illustration of how a country can go wrong when too much money flows in from abroad. With a GDP of just €18 billion, and a population of 800,000, Cyprus flourished thanks largely to the success of a banking sector that turned the capital, Nicosia, into a bustling international financial hub. The nation's banks, whose assets burgeoned to eight times the size of the economy, were especially popular among Russian elites looking for a secure and convenient place to deposit money with few questions asked. Entry into the euro zone came on January 1, 2008, and a couple of months thereafter, Cypriot voters deemed the economy solid enough to elect a president from the Communist Party, partly based on hopes that the new regime might succeed where others had failed at resolving the division of the island into separate Greek- and Turkish-dominated states.[21]

21 Information on how the crisis in Cyprus occurred can be found in Peter Coy, 2013, "Europe's Cyprus Crisis Has a Familiar Look," *Bloomberg Business Week*, March 21; and Athanasios Orphanides, 2014, "What Happened in Cyprus? The Economic Consequences of the Last Communist Government in Europe," LSE Financial Markets Group Special Paper Series, Special Paper 232, July.

At that time, the influx of funds was causing a property bubble to develop — house prices soared by about 50 percent during 2006 to 2008 — so regulators, sensibly fearing that the banks were drawing in more money than the economy could absorb, imposed curbs on domestic lending. The response from the biggest banks was to shift assets abroad, notably into the nearest economy that afforded both relatively attractive yields and a familiar culture — Greece.

The IMF mission that produced the 2010 Article IV report was by no means oblivious to the possibility that the banks' aggressiveness had put the Cypriot economy in danger. The number-one risk to the outlook was "spillovers from Greece due to the high exposure of the financial sector to Greek assets," according to the report. "[U]nder an adverse scenario cumulative losses on Greek exposure for local banks could be of the order of €2.0 billion (equivalent to about 12 percent of GDP)...by 2013-2014."

The adversity of that scenario soon proved far too mild. In fairness, the report's authors could not have foreseen some of the problems that would later develop, including the explosion of a major power plant in 2011 and the obstreperousness of the Communist government in failing to appreciate the need for prompt corrective action. In any event, Cyprus was shut out of financial markets by mid-2011; investors perceived that Nicosia could not muster the resources to save its banks from what was clearly impending, and the economy fell into recession. The death blow was the haircut imposed on Greek bondholders in March 2012, which cost the three big Cypriot banks €4 billion — for the second-largest bank, Laiki, the hit was €2.3 billion. On June 25, 2012, following a ratings downgrade on government bonds to junk status, Cyprus became the fourth euro-zone country to formally request aid from the Troika.

The rescue that ultimately emerged for Cyprus is often portrayed as a moral victory for the IMF, a sort of vengeance that the Fund exacted by forcing its will on European policy makers after having been pushed around in earlier crises. As we shall see, the depiction of an IMF finally emerging triumphant in intra-Troika wrangling is valid to some degree. But this version of events is overstated because it fails to account for some vital and little-known information.

The approach the Fund favoured for Cyprus was to restore the health of the nation's banks by using the ESM's powers to inject capital into banks directly. This would allow the country to maintain the banking-based economic model on which it had prospered, without saddling Cypriot taxpayers with the cost of saving the banks. Despite persistent prodding by Fund staffers in late 2012 to adopt this solution, European policy makers rejected it. Using a new regional bailout fund to save a nation's banking system from past errors was an unsaleable proposition to many European electorates; national parliaments would never bestow the necessary approval, European officials argued. The political difficulties were all the worse because of the perception — perhaps unfairly exaggerated in the media — of Cypriot banks as havens for money launderers, tax evaders and mobsters.

In any event, nearly nine months were to pass between the June 2012 formal request for Troika talks until the final deal. The Communist leadership spurned Troika-style austerity as a cure worse than the disease, and it managed to keep the government afloat thanks to a loan obtained from Russia, to the immense irritation of European officialdom.

Salvation looked as if it might come in early 2013 with the election of a centre-right president, Nicos Anastasiades, who got an enthusiastic welcome from Brussels because of his readiness to launch substantive negotiations with the Troika. Profound disillusionment was soon to set in on both sides.

Looking back on the night they spent in the EU's Justus Lipsius Building on March 15-16, 2013, a number of participants confess chagrin at the boneheadedness of the deal that was struck to "rescue" the Cypriot economy. It was one of the starkest examples in financial-crisis history of how highly intelligent people can make decisions under pressure in the middle of the night that look appallingly unwise in the light of day.

Perhaps its greatest saving grace was that it could be revised before any irrevocable steps were taken.[22]

If the pattern set by previous Troika rescues had been followed, Cyprus would receive a big enough loan to ensure that it could pay all of its obligations over the next three years. The government needed money to continue funding its operations while it undertook measures aimed at regaining access to private financial markets, plus extra billions to recapitalize the nation's crippled banks so they could be assured of solvency and avoid going bust. To fund such a conventional bailout, about €17 billion would be required from the IMF and the ESM, with the latter providing the vast bulk of the money.

In talks leading up to the March 15 meeting, it became clear that this approach wouldn't fly — and its most vehement detractor was the IMF, which had sound reasons for its stance. Cyprus's debt had already swelled to 86 percent of GDP by the end of 2012, so piling another €17 billion (an amount close to GDP) on top of that would drive the ratio well above sustainable levels, Fund staffers argued. Most offensively of all, it would burden Cypriot taxpayers with the cost of ensuring that government bondholders and bank creditors would be made whole. Public debt would replace private debt, in other words, as it had in Greece — an outcome that the Fund was simply unwilling to sign onto again.

The IMF's preferred option of a direct ESM bank recapitalization was off the table, as noted above. As a result, the Fund insisted that

22 Some of the information in this section is based on my own interviews, in particular concerning the revelation that the IMF preferred a direct ESM injection of capital. But much is derived from detailed published accounts about the March 15-16 meeting, including the following: Peter Spiegel, 2013, "Cyprus depositors' fate sealed in Berlin," *Financial Times*, March 17; Gabriele Steinhauser, Matina Stevis and Marcus Walker, 2013, "Cyprus Rescue Risks Backlash," *The Wall Street Journal*, March 18; James Kanter, Nicholas Kulish and Andrew Higgins, 2013, "Cyprus Bailout Incites Turmoil as Blame Flies," *The New York Times*, March 18; Peter Spiegel, 2013, "The Cyprus bailout blame game begins," *Financial Times*, Brussels Blog, March 19; Peter Spiegel, Kerin Hope and Quentin Peel, 2013, "Cyprus: A poor diagnosis, a bitter pill," *Financial Times*, March 22; and Peter Ludlow, 2013, "Cyprus: Chefsache after all: The making of the settlement on 24-25 March, 2013," EuroComment, Preliminary Evaluation 2013/2b.

the cost of shoring up the banks would have to come mainly from bank depositors. As shocking as that sounded — and it would be unprecedented for the euro-zone crisis — imposing losses on deposits was by no means unthinkable. Corporations and individuals who entrust their money to banks, after all, are not guaranteed that their funds will be lent so profitably as to ensure return of full principal and interest — unless, of course, their deposits are modest enough to be covered by government deposit-insurance schemes, which in Europe meant deposits below €100,000.

The IMF plan became known as the "full bail-in," because it would involve imposing losses not only on big depositors, but also on bondholders of the nation's two most problem-plagued banks, Laiki and the Bank of Cyprus. Under the full bail-in, those banks would be drastically shrunk, their loss-generating and troubled assets transferred into a new "bad bank." Small depositors would be spared, but big depositors would become depositors in the bad bank, implying losses for them of around 40 percent or even more. One unfortunate aspect of the full bail-in was that Cypriot banks, unlike Irish banks, had raised a relatively small portion of their funding by issuing bonds — about €2 billion worth. Consequently, the hit to depositors would be all the greater.

Convinced that the full bail-in entailed unacceptably high risks, European Commission staffers were doing everything in their power to block it. For Cyprus, the downside was obvious — it would devastate the nation's banking-based economic model — but the Commission contended that financial contagion would spread the damage far wider. Capital controls would clearly be necessary in Cyprus to keep depositors from moving their money out of danger, and once that happened, there was no telling how many more countries would have to impose similar bans as terrified depositors took flight.

Personal relations between Reza Moghadam and Marco Buti — the two top staffers at the IMF and the Commission, respectively — were already poor; the conflict over Cyprus deepened their animus to the point that some of their colleagues wondered whether it was affecting policy. Buti even tried to rid Europe of the Fund during this episode, making the case to several key players for pursuing a rescue without any IMF involvement. His quest soon proved futile. If the Fund were excluded from a Cyprus program, he was told, there was no way parliaments in several northern European countries would vote in favour, and the lack of rescue funds would doom Cyprus to bankruptcy, probably followed by departure from the euro zone.

The battle with the Commission was one the IMF was bound to win, because the Fund had the most powerful ally — Germany, whose policy makers were not about to put up taxpayer money to bail out rich Russian depositors. Schäuble insisted on limiting the size of the loan package to €10 billion; the remaining €7 billion needed for the banks would have to come from their depositors and other Cypriot sources. But as the March 15 meeting got under way a little after 5:00 p.m. on the Justus Lipsius Building's fifth floor, with Lagarde and Moghadam in attendance, the Fund's plan for an economically elegant rescue went haywire. A common-sense notion — that Europeans of modest means with a few thousand euros in the bank should feel secure about their accounts' security — was about to be transgressed.

The first proposal tabled at the meeting came from the European Commission's Rehn. It included a modest levy on deposits — not because the Commission liked the idea; rather, the strategy was to head off the more radical approach that the Commission knew the IMF would push. The biggest deposits, over €500,000, would be taxed at seven percent; those between €100,000 and €500,000 at five percent; insured deposits would pay three percent. That didn't raise the full €7 billion needed, so Rehn proposed that Cyprus also be obliged to enact a passel of other revenue-raising measures, including privatization.

A version of the Commission approach won reluctant support around 10:00 p.m. from President Anastasiades, who was ensconced in the Cypriot delegation office on the building's seventh floor. (The fifth-floor meeting was the Eurogroup, which consists of finance ministers, so Cypriot Finance Minister Michael Sarris was representing his country in the meeting.) But the hard-liners, notably Schäuble, were unsatisfied that the necessary revenue would be forthcoming, and they insisted on much higher rates. Under one plan developed later in the evening and put forward by Eurogroup president Jeroen Dijsselbloem, the Dutch finance minister, large deposits would be taxed at 12.5 percent and smaller ones less than half that amount.

Remarkably little concern was expressed about the supposed inviolability of deposits under €100,000 that, in accord with EU practice, were covered by governmental deposit insurance and were thus popularly assumed to be 100 percent safe. Some proposals advanced that night left those deposits untouched, including the IMF's original one. But the main options under debate drew no distinction between insured and uninsured deposits, except to hit the smaller ones more lightly.

Tension reached its peak at around 1:00 a.m. when Anastasiades flatly rejected the higher-rate plan in a meeting with a small group including Lagarde. "My country is not going to commit suicide," he declared.

At that point, the Cypriot president heard the same threat from the ECB that had been delivered previously to Greek and Irish officials — that is, a declaration of intention to cut off emergency funding for cash-strapped banks, which would lead to the banks' closure and, ultimately, the necessity to adopt a new currency. This ultimatum came from Jörg Asmussen, who was representing the central bank and phoned Draghi to make sure Anastasiades understood it was no bluff. It is important to recognize a key difference between the prior cases and this one, however: whereas the ECB's threats to Athens and Dublin were aimed at forcing governments to bail out private creditors, this time the central bank was using its clout to force a bail-*in*.

Furious as he was at this arm-twisting, Anastasiades capitulated. But he insisted on one principle: the maximum rate of tax, no matter how big the deposit, must be under 10 percent. To a number of those present, this clearly evinced that the president was focused mainly on protecting wealthy friends and associates who had banking-related interests at stake, with scant sympathy for the pain ordinary Cypriots would suffer. If big (uninsured) deposits were to be taxed at just under

10 percent, a simple mathematical exercise showed that insured deposits would have to be taxed at 6.75 percent.

According to nearly all recollections, this assault on small deposits encountered no objections on grounds of principle. The hour was so late, and participants were so relieved to have struck a deal, that nobody paid much attention to the likely political reaction. As long as the plan added up and the loan package was capped at €10 billion, the Cypriot authorities would be allowed to decide which depositors would bear the burden of deposit taxes and how to spread the pain. Lagarde and Moghadam also refrained from speaking up on that issue. On the issues that they most deeply cared about, they were satisfied: Cyprus's debt could be plausibly deemed sustainable, and the IMF's contribution to the program would be limited to just €1 billion, about 500 percent of the country's quota. (Since Cyprus was such a tiny country, it would be hard to justify providing an exceptionally large Fund loan on the grounds of preventing financial spillovers.) Lagarde promptly issued a statement saying "I welcome the agreement reached today….The IMF has always said that we would support a solution that is sustainable, that is fully financed, and that appropriately allocates the burden sharing. I believe that the agreed package meets these three objectives."[23]

Only in the immediate aftermath of the plan's announcement, when gasps of horror emanated from both the economic commentariat and the European public, did those involved in crafting it recognize the error of their ways in undermining the deposit-insurance system. Another, related aspect of the plan that drew condemnation was its failure to haircut senior bondholders of Cypriot banks; even though the amounts at stake were low, the unfairness of soaking small savers while exempting big bondholders sent a poisonous signal. But that flaw paled in significance amid the broader uproar over the envisioned tampering with insured deposits.

23 IMF, 2013, "Statement on Cyprus at the Eurogroup Meeting," Press Release No. 13/80, March 16, www.imf.org/external/np/sec/pr/2013/pr1380.htm.

"My mother-in-law called me the next day, to ask whether her bank deposits were safe," recalled Klaus Regling, the ESM's managing director, who attended the March 15-16 meeting. "This was happening throughout Germany. People said, 'Deposits below €100,000 should never be touched.'" In terms of substance, Regling added, the deal had some merit: "Small haircuts [on deposits] would have been like a wealth tax, spread widely, and six to seven percent is not devastating. We probably could have avoided capital controls. But it's a really interesting question, why we got it so politically wrong."

And the wrong would be righted. On Tuesday, March 19, with Cypriot banks closed and streets full of angry depositors clamouring for their cash, the nation's Parliament rejected the plan. Not a single "yes" vote was cast, despite pleas from the nation's leaders that failure to approve the legislation would put the country's membership in the euro zone at risk. That risk now loomed more menacingly than ever.

Hunkered down in the offices of the Cypriot central bank two days after the parliamentary vote, Delia Velculescu, the IMF's mission chief for Cyprus, and her counterparts from other Troika institutions, were hoping for productive meetings with Cypriot officials that might afford a way out of the country's predicament. To their frustration, many of their calls and emails were going unanswered, indicating that the government was paralyzed.

The ECB decided it could not wait much longer. That day, a Thursday, the central bank's Governing Council delivered a new ultimatum: either Cyprus would strike a new agreement with the Troika by the following Monday, March 25, or emergency funding for the nation's banks would cease.

Negotiations proceeded, albeit in disjointed fashion between Brussels and Nicosia, based on the principle that insured deposits would henceforth be treated as sacrosanct — but not necessarily uninsured ones. The IMF was forcefully demanding that the sickest banks, Laiki and the Bank of Cyprus, must be wound up. Anastasiades continued to balk, turning down one proposal after another, with a final rejection coming at 1:00 a.m. on Sunday, March 24. A European summit, scheduled for that day in Brussels, offered what appeared to be the last chance for averting a rupture in the monetary union.[24]

On the morning of the 24th, a Belgian government plane was sent to Nicosia to fly Anastasiades to the summit. While the Cypriot president was en route to Brussels, a meeting in the Justus Lipsius building reached a common position on what to tell him, with attendees including Lagarde, Draghi, Rehn, van Rompuy and Dijsselbloem. The IMF and ECB were winning support, even from the European Commission, for the full bail-in. The only major question was whether the Cypriots would be required to shutter both of the two big banks, or just one.

Discouragement set in during a working lunch that began after Anastasiades' arrival. The menu of lamb and baby potatoes did not prevent tempers from flaring or the discussion from dragging on for roughly three hours, with the Cypriot president adamantly maintaining that bank closures, if they happened, could only be voluntary rather than mandatory. Afterwards he retreated together with other Cypriot officials to their seventh-floor offices, and a sort of shuttle diplomacy ensued with policy makers coming up from the fifth floor to negotiate. Although around 8:00 p.m. it appeared that a text might be agreed, Troika officials came back downstairs reporting that Anastasiades refused to sign. The talks were at a hopeless impasse, they declared — but von Rompuy thought it was worth one more try to make Anastasiades see the light, and he met with the Cypriot president for almost an hour and a half, joined only by Barroso. As she often does at long meetings to keep rancor from getting out of hand, Lagarde passed out M&Ms.

24 Information about these events, in particular the summit meeting, can be found in: Peter Ludlow, 2013, "Cyprus: Chefsache after all" (see footnote 22 in this chapter); and Gabriele Steinhauser, Marcus Walker and Matina Stevis, 2013, "Bailout Strains European Ties," *The Wall Street Journal*, March 26.

Faced again with the prospect of his country plunging into economic chaos, Anastasiades finally buckled, agreeing to terms that were very close to the IMF's full bail-in, one exception being that the Bank of Cyprus would survive. A bad bank would be established for Laiki's bad assets and large deposits; the rest would go into a restructured Bank of Cyprus. Deposit insurance would be fully honoured for the amounts insured — but beyond that, depositors would have to take their lumps, which were bound to be huge. Bank shareholders would be fully wiped out; both junior and senior bondholders would be obliged to exchange their claims for equity.

The euro zone remained intact. Cyprus was still a member. To be sure, the Cypriot authorities had to impose capital controls, limiting cash withdrawals and transfers of bank deposits abroad, to prevent a flood of money from pouring out of the country. One of the fundamental principles of monetary union had been violated — the right to move unrestricted amounts of money from any part of the union to another. A euro in Nicosia was not as widely usable as a euro in, say, Munich or Marseilles, either for purchasing goods or lending or investing.

But a salutary advance had also been made, toward a preference for bail-ins over bailouts. Investors and depositors who made bad bets by extending credit to failing European banks could be compelled, even amid crises, to take losses rather than rely on taxpayer money to make them whole; the only exceptions would be small savers with deposit insurance. This was a gratifying outcome for the IMF, especially for Moghadam and others on the staff who had chafed at the bailouts of Greek government bondholders and Irish bank bondholders. In this context, it is important to note that the Fund did not get its way entirely in Cyprus, its first-choice solution (the ESM bank recapitalization) having failed to get traction. Another blot on the Fund's role in Cyprus is the fact that it went along with the March 15-16 deal involving the tax on insured deposits. Still, the final result reflected the Fund using its leverage to mobilize consensus behind its second-choice solution and block much worse possibilities.

A few weeks later, when the IMF board met to approve the Cyprus program, fears were widespread that the nation's economy had been pitched into depression, and a number of directors echoed those concerns. Even though the staff report forecast that GDP would contract by 8.7 percent in 2013 and another 3.9 percent the following year, that struck some members of the board as too rosy. "It is difficult to avoid a feeling of déjà vu with the Greek experience still vivid in mind," said Jafar Mojarrad, who represented Iran, Pakistan and five other countries. "The key question going forward is what options would be available if growth and debt scenarios follow the pattern of the initial Greek program." Brazil's Nogueira Batista was even more caustic. "Every program needs a pinch of optimism but in this one the required dose of goodwill — or suspension of disbelief, if you will — goes way beyond the average," he stated, noting that Cyprus "needs to find a new business model in the midst of the deepest crisis it has ever had, in an unfavorable international environment." He acknowledged that the program was better than the initial deal on March 15, but "that is not a difficult mark to meet…It should have never been endorsed by Management."[25]

In this case, however, the surprise was on the upside. The Cypriot economy declined by 5.4 percent in 2013 and 2.3 percent in 2014 — and as anguishing as that was for many of the nation's citizens, it was not nearly as bad as the forecast. The worries expressed by European Commission economists about the bail-in proved overblown. Financial contagion was minimal, thanks perhaps to market respect for Draghi's OMT. As for capital controls, no other country was obliged to impose them, and even in Cyprus their effects were milder than many expected.

In Greece, meanwhile, surprises would continue on both the upside and downside, first with a preponderance of the former, then an increasing preponderance of the latter.

25 In an unusual leak of IMF board documents, an online site, "Stockwatch," obtained copies of the directors' written submissions. They are available at: www.stockwatch.com.cy/media/announce_pdf/May15_2013_IMF.pdf.

17

MAKING NUMBERS ADD UP

As with many Greek tragedies, the one that has befallen modern Greece in recent years is full of plot twists that start promisingly. One important example is the January 2013 appointment of a man named Haris Theoharis to a new and powerful position in the Greek government aimed at improving the nation's collection of taxes.

This move, taken by the government of Antonis Samaras, appeared to herald a long-overdue, decisive assault against the flouting of tax law by Greek citizens. The deleteriousness of the problem, and lack of progress in tackling it, made it one of the IMF's chief sources of exasperation, as evinced in the report submitted to the board after the November 2012 agreement.

"Losses to the state from tax evasion are enormous," the Fund report said in a special box on the subject, adding that under-reporting of income was "particularly common among the self-employed — doctors, lawyers, engineers, accountants." The report's authors cited a newly published academic study indicating that in Greece, such taxpayers were earning between 1¼ and 2½ times as much as they were declaring on their tax returns. "VAT fraud is also widespread, with 450,000 fictitious invoices detected since 2009," the report continued, and it complained that implementation of legislation aimed at improving tax collection "has been stalled for most of [2012]."[1]

Theoharis's appointment came after previous efforts to fix the system's woes had encountered discouraging setbacks. When Papandreou became prime minister in late 2009, he appointed a renowned professor of software engineering named Diomedes Spinellis to head the finance ministry's General Secretariat of Information Systems. As legendarily disorganized as Greek tax collection was, Spinellis was stunned to discover that an expensive computerized data-gathering network purchased several years earlier had gone virtually unused by a bureaucracy steeped in old-fashioned methods for amassing and checking information. His efforts to instill the system with a semblance of modernity ran into a series of obstacles, chief among them being opposition from the union representing tax officials. Citing "personal reasons," Spinellis resigned in October 2011, asserting soon thereafter that the pervasiveness of kickbacks and other crooked conniving by tax officials had made his job impossible. (The union, which maintains that its poorly paid and beleaguered members are scapegoats for the actions of higher-ups, sued him for slander.)[2]

In the hope of overcoming such barriers, the Troika secured a pledge as a condition of the March 2012 rescue program that Greece would name a new revenue-collection czar endowed with extraordinary authority and independence. Months passed, but in November of that year the nation's Parliament finally approved legislation creating a new post — permanent general secretary for revenue — whose holder would wield clout that reflected the deep-rootedness of the nation's tax-collection problems. The general secretary would be in office for a five-year term, renewable only once, during which he or she could take measures against corruption within the tax agency, and set targets for tax offices that could result in the dismissal of officials for failing to meet their goals. To protect against interference from

1 IMF, 2013, "Greece: First and Second Reviews under the Extended Arrangement Under the Extended Fund Facility" (see footnote 17 in chapter 16).

2 Palaiologos, *The 13th Labour of Hercules* (see footnote 3 in chapter 5), provides a detailed account of the Greek tax-collection system and the efforts to reform it.

powerful politicians, information about the identities of individuals and businesses undergoing tax audits would be kept strictly within the general secretary's office — no sharing of information allowed, not even with the finance minister.

It was cause for cheer, therefore, that the Samaras government not only established the job but appointed Theoharis to fill it. A 42-year-old graduate of London's Imperial College, Theoharis had been one of Spinellis's most trusted and zealous lieutenants. Theoharis took to the airwaves, Facebook and Twitter to preach the cause of compliance, and in an effort to dispel the impression that only small businesses and middle-class people were being targeted, he stepped up enforcement against large companies and the rich. Threats on his life provided evidence that he was in pursuit of big money. "My office was getting phone calls saying, 'Tell him it would only cost €5,000 to break his legs,'" he recalled later, adding that he was given bodyguards.[3]

Alas, the flush of enthusiasm that the Theoharis appointment engendered among Troika officials was destined to fade, and eventually to go kaput — along with relations between Samaras and the IMF, as this chapter will reveal. Waiting in the wings, and eager to capitalize on Samaras's misfortune, were the prime minister's foes on the radical left.

The Theoharis appointment was not the only sign by the Samaras government of readiness to turn a reformist leaf. For a substantial stretch of time continuing into the first half of 2014, the conservative prime minister and this team were fulfilling, and in some cases exceeding, many of Greece's commitments under the terms of its bailout program.

In June 2013 the government shut ERT, the state radio and TV broadcaster. Howls erupted from the left that political motivations were involved, but ERT's workforce of 2,600 was notoriously inefficient

3 Nick Squires, 2015, "Death threats forced me to quit my job, says Greece's top tax man," *The Telegraph*, January 31.

and overstaffed, due in no small part to patronage and nepotism.[4] This action marked the first time since the start of the crisis that public employees were actually laid off; up until then, the government payroll had shrunk only because tens of thousands of civil servants took early retirement to avoid pay cuts and protect their pension rights. New property taxes and pension reforms instituted under Samaras's stewardship also won plaudits from Troika officials.

Then in September came the eye-popping news that the Greek government had run a primary budget surplus for the previous six months. For the full year, the primary surplus would exceed €800 million, according to finance ministry projections released soon thereafter.[5] This achievement materialized a year ahead of schedule, much to the surprise of many, including the IMF — and it came as vindication for Stournaras and his finance ministry team, who had been more optimistic in their expectations about budget and tax trends. It was all the more impressive considering the effect of the recession's length and depth on revenue. To offset the shrinkage in tax receipts, Athens had genuinely cut spending — even in politically sensitive areas. The €38.4 billion in outlays Greece was making in 2013 for social benefits, for example, was 27 percent below the level of four years earlier.[6]

The attainment of a primary budget surplus, even just a narrow one, evoked excitement in Athens, because under the November 2012 agreement this was the key benchmark for determining whether Greece should get additional debt relief from its European creditors. In his meetings with fellow finance ministers, Stournaras raised this point at almost every opportunity. When, he asked, would concessions on debt be forthcoming now that Greece's primary balance had swung into the black?

4 James Angelos, 2015, *The Full Catastrophe: Travels Among the New Greek Ruins*, New York, NY: Crown Publishers, chapter 4.

5 The budget itself was not in surplus; it must be recalled that a primary budget surplus does not include outlays for interest payments.

6 Yiannis Mouzakis and Nick Malkoutzis, 2015, "You've heard the Greek crisis myths, now here are some truths," macropolis.gr, February 20.

The retort from Europe was that to qualify for additional debt relief, Greece was also obliged under the November 2012 deal to fulfill all conditions of its program — and on a number of counts, it was still falling short, especially on structural reforms. The IMF concurred; Thomsen was as hawkish as ever on structural measures, citing as an example of continued lapses the government's half-hearted liberalization of product and service markets.

Sympathy at the Fund for the cause of Greek debt relief at this point was also attenuated by recollections of the November 2012 meeting. Instead of siding with the IMF, which was aiming for a debt haircut, Stournaras had accepted the European approach. He may have reasonably believed there was no other choice, but he had agreed that Greece would maintain its earlier pledge to run even bigger primary surpluses years into the future, thereby helping to pay down its debt. Admirable as this commitment might be, it was seen by many at the Fund as beyond the reach of the nation's political system. But the dotted lines were signed. Everyone would have to live with the consequences.

Meanwhile, another perspective on Greek debt was taking hold in European policy circles, and it would throw a spanner in the works for both Athens and the IMF.

Having spent more than a decade of his career on the IMF staff, Klaus Regling was not intimidated by his former Fund colleagues. Indeed, he took satisfaction from pointing out mistakes they had made, for example their insistence in 2008 that Latvia must depreciate its currency. He believed the Fund lacked a good grasp of the way European Monetary Union worked, especially concerning the rules that were supposed to prevent mutualization and monetization of member states' debt. When Fund economists argued that European policy makers should bend the rules of monetary union for the sake of containing the crisis, Regling pushed back, pointing out that respect for the rules was critical to making the system function properly in the long run. Emboldening him to speak his mind was the size of the institutions he headed, the EFSF and ESM, which were substantially bigger than the IMF as measured by the amounts of international loans outstanding.

In the fall of 2013, Regling went public with a new line of analysis, arguing that concern held by the IMF and others about Greece's debt burden was misplaced — or at least outdated. The money Athens owed was payable over very long periods, and at very low interest rates, since the debt owed both to private bondholders and to official lenders in Europe had been restructured. Under the terms of the November 2012 agreement, the debt owed to Regling's institutions — which were now Greece's biggest creditors — had an average maturity of over 30 years, with interest charges slashed below the rates paid by a number of euro area governments. As a result, Regling contended, the amounts Greece had to pay each year were hardly of a magnitude that should prevent the economy from recovering, even though the debt-to-GDP ratio remained well above 170 percent. Put another way, the stock of debt might appear unsustainable, but the flow of debt was not. The emphasis on shrinking the debt-to-GDP ratio that the Fund championed was therefore "meaningless," Regling said in an interview with *The Wall Street Journal* published September 26, 2013. "I'm surprised some people say there has to be a debt reduction."[7]

Anybody with a house mortgage could grasp the point. If the amount borrowed for a typical home has to be paid off in the near future — say, in five years — then generating the income to make the monthly principal and interest payments is almost impossible for any middle-class person. But if the payments are stretched out over decades, then the monthly payments may be much more bearable, all the more so if in addition the interest rate has been lowered. Nobody thinks of such a person as hopelessly indebted simply because the principal amount of the mortgage is greatly in excess of income. And if the homeowner proves unable to make the monthly payments, it isn't necessary to cut

7 Matina Stevis and Gabriele Steinhauser, 2013, "Bailout Boss Says Current Greek Debt Analysis 'Meaningless,'" *The Wall Street Journal*, "Real Time Brussels" blog, September 26.

the amount of principal owed; it may well be better to stretch out the payments and lower interest rates further. For the lender, there should be no difference in financial terms which form of debt relief is given.

IMF economists readily understood Regling's logic; earlier in 2013, the Fund staff had adopted a new approach for assessing a country's debt sustainability that included as a key criterion "gross financing needs" (essentially the money that must be raised annually to cover its budget deficit, interest payments and maturing debt).[8] But the IMF was unpersuaded that Greece's debt-to-GDP ratio was as inconsequential as Regling claimed. The Fund's greatest worry was that with such a huge debt "overhang," the country would likely have problems attracting badly needed private investment, including companies looking for places to build and expand business operations. "Debt will remain exceptionally high well into the next decade. This could raise concerns on the part of investors...and the assumed recovery may not take hold," the Fund warned in its 2013 Article IV report on Greece.[9] Moreover, how would the Greek government ever return to the point where it could raise enough money in financial markets to fund its operations — which was supposedly the objective of any IMF rescue? Fund officials believed that investors would be understandably nervous about the amounts owed to European official creditors like Regling's institution, even if the payments did not come due until well into the future. Greece might be able to borrow for short periods, but not sustainably or affordably over a long period of time as long as investors knew that a major crunch point loomed down the road, when Athens must make big debt payments to official creditors.

This was, at bottom, a ratcheting-up of the debate about whether Greece should get a haircut on its official debt — a debate that would intensify in the future. Regling's argument bolstered the German government's forceful position that when it came to official debt, a haircut was unacceptable under any circumstances. By this reasoning, even if

8 IMF, 2013, "Staff Guidance Note for Public Debt Sustainability Analysis in Market-Access Countries," May 9, www.imf.org/external/np/pp/eng/2013/050913.pdf.

9 IMF, 2013, "Greece: 2013 Article IV Consultation," Country Report No. 13/154, June, www.imf.org/external/pubs/ft/scr/2013/cr13154.pdf.

Greece faced difficulties servicing its flow of debt, that problem could be addressed by offering Athens additional concessions on maturities and interest payments.

But was that the best outcome for Greece, compared with a haircut that would shrink the debt-to-GDP ratio in one fell swoop? And if a haircut was better for Greece, why not do it? The answer was chiefly political, not economic: Merkel and company could get away with extending maturities and reducing interest payments, based on the claim that this didn't constitute formal debt forgiveness (even though, in financial terms, it was completely equivalent). A haircut, by contrast, could not be disguised as anything other than debt forgiveness — and was therefore anathema in Berlin. Legal considerations were also involved; the German government feared being found in violation of treaty rules prohibiting outright bailouts of one euro-zone member by others.

Whatever the merits of the IMF's argument, this was a debate it was bound to lose, because in contrast with the Cyprus case, the Fund had no powerful allies like Germany; indeed, Berlin was the Fund's main opposition. German officials shared Regling's conclusion that Greece's debt had undergone an adequate amount of reduction in November 2012 — and if some further easing of repayment terms proved necessary, that should come after much more progress on reforms. When Samaras visited Merkel in the spring of 2014 to seek her help on the issue, the chancellor seized on his use of the term "debt relief," and asked an interpreter for a translation. "It doesn't sound as good in German," she told Samaras.[10]

"Graduation time" was arriving for some European crisis countries in late 2013. Even as recession continued to batter Greece, economic rebounds were under way elsewhere, making exit possible from rescue programs. Ireland liberated itself from the Troika in December, having

10 Marcus Walker and Marianna Kakaounaki, 2015, "How Greece and Germany Brought Europe's Long-Simmering Crisis Back to a Boil," *The Wall Street Journal*, January 21.

dutifully implemented its program; Portugal was to follow in the spring of 2014, and Spain also exited its banking bailout. Amid these signs of crisis abatement, the region's leaders were patting themselves on the back. "This shows that our policy of stabilization of the European currency is successful and right," Schäuble proclaimed.

Effects of the crisis were still much in evidence. Unemployment in the euro zone was about 12 percent overall, with highest jobless rates in the periphery. The economies of Ireland, Spain and Portugal might have been growing lustily, but only after falling far and shedding tens of thousands of jobs. In the big core countries — Germany, France and Italy — economic growth was stagnant at best, prompting the IMF to push the ECB hard for pumping up the money supply in new and innovative ways. Still, European Monetary Union was not only surviving, it was gaining new members. Latvia became the eighteenth country to adopt the euro on January 1, 2014, capping its recovery from the turmoil of 2008-2009 — a development that the IMF surely had failed to envision. Lithuania was on track to join next, in 2015.

The odium of Troika oversight weighed all the heavier on Greece, the only euro-zone country besides Cyprus that would remain subject to quarterly inspections, demands for "prior actions" and the like. Athens and its taskmasters were still locked in battles over issues such as whether two loss-making defence companies could stay open (as the government wanted) or shut down (as the Troika insisted).

Samaras made no secret of his desire to be the prime minister who would put an end to this humiliation. Indeed, he considered it politically imperative, and became increasingly resolved to do it in 2014. He was getting hammered by opposition parties, whose leaders were demanding to know why Greece, having endured so much sacrifice, was not getting the debt relief it had been promised — nor any turnaround in still-depressed living standards. The national unemployment rate was still well above 20 percent.

The Troika member that Samaras most fervently wanted banished from Athens was the IMF. Although the Fund had reaped some goodwill for its well-known views on debt restructuring in the past, it had shown itself to be the toughest stickler for Greek adherence to program conditions, and was heartily despised in many quarters as a result. With the aim of demonstrating that the country could manage on its own in the future, Samaras's government pulled off a surprising coup.

Buoyed by the improvement in the budget numbers, and by an environment of generally low interest rates, Greece sold bonds to private investors on April 9 for the first time in four years — €3 billion worth of five-year bonds at a yield of 4.95 percent. Given the relatively small amount, the bond sale was hardly sufficient to put the country on independent financial footing. Still, it provided a symbolic political boost to Samaras's plans for untethering Athens from the Troika.

Unfortunately for Samaras, large swaths of the Greek populace did not share the elite's appreciation for budget surpluses and bond sales, as an election on May 25 would show. The purpose of the election — choosing members of the European Parliament — had little practical implications for Greek policy, given the relative powerlessness of the European body. But the result would transform the nation's political landscape.

As he campaigned for New Democracy candidates in the election, the prime minister's mantra was "no new measures" — meaning no further concessions to demands by the Troika for austerity. The nation's voters, however, wanted to send Europe a much more rebellious message. Finishing first was Syriza, which rallied 26.5 percent of the electorate based on Tsipras's vow to rip up the "barbarous" bailout agreement. New Democracy finished four percentage points behind Syriza, and in a particularly disturbing sign of rising extremist sentiment, the neo-Nazi Golden Dawn party came in third, ahead of PASOK.

Tsipras's strong popular appeal threw a huge scare into Samaras and his colleagues in the New Democracy leadership, who became more skittish than ever about taking actions that might offend powerful blocs of the citizenry. To bolster his narrow parliamentary majority, the prime minister reshuffled his cabinet, appointing populists to replace reformers in ministries such as development and health. And then, on

June 5, came the news that may be seen in retrospect as the point of no return between the Samaras government and its Troika overseers.

Only 17 months into his supposedly guaranteed five-year term, Haris Theoharis resigned as general secretary for revenue, citing "personal reasons" (as Spinellis had). Lack of support — if not open antagonism — from the prime minister's office was clearly a factor. Adversaries in the government had been sniping at Theoharis almost from the beginning, and they had prevented his office from getting certain powers that it sought, such as control over the tax police.

The European Commission responded with a statement that "this development gives cause for deep concern."[11] The IMF maintained a lofty no-comment stance, but by many accounts the dismay among Fund officials, Thomsen in particular, was profound; undermining Theoharis was not just a failure to reform, but an unmistakable case of backtracking on an issue of major significance. For Greece's creditors, the departure of Theoharis was the grimmest signal yet that the old guard in Athens would never fundamentally change the way the country was run.

When finance ministers attending the spring and fall meetings of the IMF and World Bank seek private audiences with the Fund managing director, the get-togethers usually take the form of courtesy calls aimed at establishing acquaintanceship or deepening personal bonds. Gikas Hardouvelis, who was appointed Greece's finance minister in June 2014, was nevertheless interested in discussing some substantive points with Lagarde when he met her, along with Thomsen and a couple of other people, on October 12 during the 2014 annual conclave. After spending a few minutes on pleasantries, Hardouvelis attempted to raise the issue of Greece's IMF program, only to be gently rebuffed. "Minister, I am not here to negotiate," Lagarde said, according to a participant. "A mission is scheduled to arrive in Athens soon, and you

11 Kerin Hope, 2014, "Greece's top tax collector leaves under pressure," *Financial Times*, June 5.

should take up all the issues you have on your mind with Mr. Thomsen and his team."

Take up issues with Thomsen? This was akin to an invitation for Greek officials to bang their heads against a wall, as far as Samaras and his inner circle were concerned. Thomsen had been named acting director of the European Department in July after the previous department head, Reza Moghadam, left to join Morgan Stanley. Although a new mission chief, Rishi Goyal, had assumed direct responsibility for negotiations with Athens, Thomsen was Goyal's boss, and there was no doubt about which of them was really running the show. The Danish economist was refusing to confer his blessing on the government's policies; whatever they did, the Greeks concluded, it never seemed to be enough.[12]

More urgently than ever, the Samaras team was trying, in the fall of 2014, to detach Greece from Troika control. With the economy having finally sputtered to life at mid-year, their idea was to end the bailout program earlier than initially envisioned, or at least change it in ways that would drastically curtail the role of international authorities, especially the IMF. "Greece has emerged from its crisis and won't be dragged back in," the prime minister told Parliament, adding that since the country "went to the markets and borrowed at reasonable rates," it "doesn't need another bailout program or another forced loan."[13]

The alternative, Samaras feared, would lead to Syriza taking the reins of government. Convoluted though this logic was, it was based on the indisputable fact that a momentous political deadline was looming. Early in 2015, Parliament had to choose a new president of the

12 Much of the material in this section is based on my own interviews, but a substantial amount of information also comes from Marcus Walker and Marianna Kakaounaki, 2015, "How Greece and Germany Brought Europe's Long-Simmering Crisis Back to a Boil," *The Wall Street Journal*, (see footnote 10 in this chapter); Eleni Varvitsioti and Tasos Telloglou, 2015, "The Saga of the Greek Review that Never Ended," *Kathimerini*, June 13; Matthew Karnitschnig, 2015, "How Merkel may have bungled Greek rescue," *Politico*, June 15; and Yannis Palaiologos, "The Greek-German breakthrough that didn't come," *Kathimerini* (see footnote 2 in chapter 16).

13 Kerin Hope, 2014, "Greece coalition survives confidence vote," *Financial Times*, October 11.

Hellenic Republic — that is, head of state — and although the post was mostly ceremonial, failure to muster the necessary parliamentary supermajority would automatically trigger a general election. Polls showed that Syriza would very likely win such an election. The only way to avoid this outcome was for Samaras to show that the Troika was history; he could then secure enough parliamentary votes to avert a general election, which would enable his ruling coalition to remain in power. If he failed at ending Troika control, or if he had to break his "no new measures" promise, the parliamentary vote would probably go against him, followed by a general election with the odds heavily in favour of Tsipras winning the prime ministership.

One big hurdle remained — a quarterly review of the program by the Troika, which Greece had to "pass" in order to get another €7.2 billion disbursement, needed for paying a number of obligations coming due. The Samaras pitch was that if Greece could get that dollop of aid, it would be the last one Athens would request. A "follow-up arrangement" could be negotiated, providing a precautionary line of credit that Greece could quickly tap in an emergency, but with much lighter conditionality than before and no Troika enforcers.

To help minimize political embarrassment to Samaras as talks began over this review in early September, Troika representatives met in Paris rather than Athens with their Greek interlocutors. But for all the City of Light's charms — the negotiators from the two sides sometimes went out together for dinner — there was no escaping the vast gulf in negotiating positions.

A large number of program conditions had been postponed from previous reviews, involving matters such as sales taxes, pensions, union bargaining and liberalization of markets. The Troika was not willing to simply waive these issues; they saw all too much evidence that Samaras was abandoning any reform efforts now that his political strength was ebbing. The Greeks protested that Samaras had secured enactment of some privatizations of power companies and airports in the summer, bulldozing passionate Syriza opposition. Surely other measures could be deferred, they implored, because trying to get parliamentary support at that point for much of anything that smacked of austerity would be both an exercise in futility and a political gift to Tsipras.

For Goyal, this was a baptism by fire as IMF mission chief. The shouting to which he was subjected by Stavros Papastavrou, a top Samaras aide, induced cringing even among some on the Greek side. Goyal's stiff mode of communication did not sit well with the team from Athens, but far more important was the growing realization that the Fund was the most immovable among the creditor institutions, especially by comparison to the Commission. Papastavrou and his colleagues couldn't help but suspect that an underlying problem was Thomsen's accumulated mistrust of Greek officialdom, which inflamed their resentment and conviction that ridding themselves of the Fund was crucial. "You're not even going to be here in a month," Papastravrou snarled at Goyal, according to participants' recollections. Such talk, needless to say, was not conducive to the softening of IMF hearts.

Nor was it based in reality. In an effort to cut a deal without the IMF, Samaras appealed to higher authorities — Regling, US Treasury Secretary Jacob Lew and other top policy makers — by calling them directly. But he met with the same response that others had: Fund approval was essential to obtaining the assent of Germany and several other European countries.

On September 23, Samaras flew to Berlin, where he sought to get Merkel's backing for loosening the Troika's grip and easing conditions for the review. The Greek economy was recovering snappily — third-quarter growth would prove to be the fastest in the euro zone — and Samaras argued that this near-miraculous turnaround gave Europe a perfect opportunity to take its bows for completing a successful rescue. "We want to declare victory," he explained. But Merkel was dubious about Greece's ability to finance itself over a sustained period; so was the IMF — and the same went for financial markets. In mid-October, after Samaras expressed some of his clearest hopes for sending the Troika packing, investors drove yields on Greek government bonds above nine percent. That market rout showed that Samaras had misjudged Greece's capacity for financial independence.

Using Syriza as a bogeyman wasn't working either, because European policy makers were not convinced that Tsipras would be quite the catastrophe that Samaras and his allies were claiming. Although the leftist leader was vowing to reverse cuts in the minimum wage, restore social benefits and re-nationalize privatized enterprises, he had distanced himself from some of Syriza's most extreme elements, who favoured suspending Greece's debt payments and abandoning the euro. According to some sanguine assessments, Tsipras might even prove more willing than previous leaders to take on special interests; he showed no sign of corruptibility, and was promising a crackdown on tax evasion by the plutocracy.

Wrangling continued apace in November between the Troika and Athens over a host of issues concerning the requirements to pass the review. But one dispute above all was leading the two sides toward irreconcilable divergence, and again it was the IMF that was cracking the whip.

The bone of contention concerned the target for the Greek government to run a primary budget surplus of three percent of GDP in 2015. To generate such a surplus, Athens needed to enact more than €2 billion in new budget savings, according to IMF calculations. The Greeks countered that the Fund was using overly pessimistic projections, which would result in needlessly excessive pain being inflicted on the still-fragile economy. A substantially smaller package of budget measures would suffice to meet the target, they pleaded, noting that their fiscal estimates had often proven more accurate in 2013 and 2014 than the IMF's downbeat ones. But they got nowhere with Goyal, who repeatedly stated, "We have a major gap."

This was a classic example of Thomsen tenaciously applying the dictum that "the numbers must add up." Within the Fund, there was recognition that binding Greece rigidly to its primary surplus targets year after year would be doctrinal overkill. As Moghadam, Thomsen's predecessor, wrote in an op-ed in early 2015, "Current plans call for the primary fiscal surplus...to rise from 1.5 percent of gross domestic product in 2014 to 4.5 percent in 2016 and beyond. This would threaten social cohesion and wreck any prospect of economic recovery.

Politically, it is out of reach."[14] But in the closing months of 2014, the Fund was brooking no slippage in the target for the coming year, nor in the amount of measures it deemed necessary, even if that entailed demands for action beyond Samaras's political capacity to produce.

The IMF was keeping the bar raised very high for approval of the review — impossibly high, in the view of the Greeks, as well as some of the Europeans involved, to whom it appeared that the Fund had resolved to block approval, period. Theories abound in Athens and Brussels about the reasons why. One hypothesis is that IMF officials were upset about the efforts by the Samaras team to push the Fund out of the picture. Another is that IMF officials were writing Greece off as non-reformable, at least under regimes such as that of Samaras. Another is that the Fund wanted to halt all disbursement of loans to Greece until the political outlook cleared up, because that way international lenders could ensure they could maintain maximum leverage if Syriza came to power.

It is crucial to bear in mind that in addition to the issue of the 2015 fiscal balance, the IMF had numerous other grounds for complaint against the Samaras government, most of them concerning the continued non-delivery or incomplete implementation of structural reforms. Tax evasion remained a major irritant in the fall of 2014. Even as anger simmered over the Theoharis episode, Athens proposed a law allowing people in arrears on their taxes to pay off tax debts in 100 monthly installments — an approach that, in the Troika's view, was antithetical to fostering a culture of compliance.

Moreover, the IMF was not alone in taking a hard line on Greece, as would become distressingly apparent to Samaras.

14 Reza Moghadam, 2015, "Halve Greek debt and keep the eurozone together," *Financial Times,* January 26. Moghadam was no longer an IMF official at that time, and he was writing in the context of the Syriza election victory, which had occurred the day before the article's publication. But the point he was making about the surplus targets was equally applicable to the period a couple of months earlier. And his view was hardly unique among economists still at the Fund.

On December 2, the prime minister learned from Hardouvelis that hopes were dimming fast for a favourable decision on the review in an upcoming Eurogroup meeting. That evening, he delivered a dinner speech to an international audience where he lashed out at what he called "absurd and unjustifiable pressure," and declared: "Nobody has the right to treat us like two and a half or five years ago, when everything was collapsing. Greece has turned a page. We have a duty to defend this country's dignity and everyone must respect it."[15]

The prime minister was at the end of his tether. He wanted to try again at changing Troika minds, and after the speech he called his former finance minister, Yannis Stournaras, who was now governor of the Bank of Greece. He could not get Parliament to approve €2 billion worth of measures as the IMF was insisting, but he wanted Stournaras to press the case for a compromise. The government's projections indicated that only about €1 billion in savings was required to achieve the primary surplus target — a view which Stournaras wholeheartedly shared — so the proposed compromise would work as follows: if by the middle of 2015 that projection was proving to be too optimistic, the government would enact additional savings.

Get me a good deal with the Troika, the prime minister told Stournaras, and I'll be able to obtain what is needed from Parliament to forestall an election. Even though Stournaras was no longer involved in the negotiations, he was an ideal choice to seek such a pact, given his forceful personality, stature as an economist and reputation as a straight shooter whose projections had often been on the mark.

First Stournaras called the top people at the ECB (Draghi and Benoit Coeuré, an influential member of the central bank's board) and at the European Commission (Pierre Moscovici, the newly installed European commissioner for economic and monetary affairs). Their reaction, according to Stournaras, was that they could go along with a consensus if the IMF agreed too. Then — at about 1:00 a.m. in Athens — Stournaras called Thomsen in Washington, where it was early evening.

15 *To Vima* (English edition), 2014, "Samaras to troika: 'I will not accept absurd and unjustifiable pressure," December 3, www.tovima.gr/en/article/?aid=655938.

The two men spoke for more than an hour, to no avail; Thomsen said the IMF could not accept what the Greeks were proposing. It was after 2:00 a.m. when Stournaras called Samaras to give him the bad news.

The final verdict was rendered by the Eurogroup on December 8. The broad question at issue was whether Samaras should be given a smidgen of hope, in the form of a favorable Troika gesture, that he might avoid elections. The narrow question was whether Greece had gone far enough to merit the dispatch of another mission to Athens. Moscovici maintained that the answer was yes — not that the Commission believed the review ought to be approved and the €7.2 billion disbursed, but a mission should at least go and try for a deal. "The Greek authorities have moved significantly in a number of areas," he said, according to notes of the meeting taken by a participant. "We consider there is a critical mass of reforms on the table."

Draghi, however, threw his considerable weight against this. "Progress is not enough to send a team without risk of failure," he said, and he also indicated his discomfort over the prospect of an end to the Greek program: "We should avoid having Greece without an umbrella."

Thomsen then chimed in: "I agree with Mario Draghi." With both the ECB and the IMF viewing another mission as fruitless, the assembled finance ministers decided that instead, Greece would get an extension of its rescue program until the end of February, on the assumption that the political situation would have been resolved one way or the other by then. The country would remain a ward of the Troika.

Samaras's government was now in its death throes. The next day the prime minister called for Parliament to vote promptly on the selection of a president, but as he had feared, the necessary supermajority was not forthcoming, and he had no choice but to submit to the will of the voters in a general election, which would take place on January 25, 2015.

18

HOW DO YOU SOLVE A PROBLEM LIKE SYRIZA?

The caller to Poul Thomsen's phone on the morning of Saturday, January 31, 2015, was a man whose shaved head, flashing dark eyes and defiant mien were fast gaining global fame. It was Yanis Varoufakis, Greece's new finance minister, who had an urgent request for Thomsen: could they meet in Paris that afternoon? Thomsen replied that he was in Washington, so a meeting couldn't take place that quickly, but he would catch a flight as soon as possible. The next day, the two men came face to face in a Paris hotel. The 53-year-old Greek minister wore an electric-blue shirt, untucked at the waist, with no tie.

The contrast with interlocutors to which IMF staffers are accustomed could arguably be described as just desserts for the position the Fund had taken on Greece the previous year. The New Democracy government was gone; as Samaras and his henchmen had predicted, the refusal of the Troika to accommodate them had led to the January 25 elections in which Syriza won the most parliamentary seats, enough to form a coalition government with a small right-wing, anti-bailout party. Now, therefore, the Fund and Greece's European creditors would have to deal with Varoufakis, a former academic economist of self-described "Marxist disposition" who comported himself with a swashbuckling aura — he rode a motorcycle to his office, and favoured black leather jackets — that inflamed his downtrodden compatriots' sense of pride.

Citing the democratic mandate their citizens had given them, Syriza leaders were demanding an end to the current rescue program, which Varoufakis called "a toxic mistake" that had inflicted "fiscal waterboarding" on the Greek economy. In its place must come a "new contract" that would foster growth and social justice with a combination of debt relief and greatly relaxed budget targets, thereby generating jobs for the unemployed and restoring proper care for vulnerable segments of the population. And there would be no more negotiating with the Troika — "a rottenly constructed committee," in Varoufakis's words, that had insulted the nation's dignity by dictating policies to government ministries.[1]

The international media was in thrall to the spectacle of Varoufakis and the charismatic 40-year-old who had appointed him, Prime Minister Alexis Tsipras, jetting around European capitals in their initial forays to press their radical agenda. Public interest worldwide was intense, and would remain so for months as a confrontation unfolded that was redolent of both David and Goliath and the "Perils of Pauline." Could this band of leftist ideologues face down the mighty powers of Berlin, Frankfurt, Brussels and Washington, by forcing a drastic turnabout from austerity for the sake of keeping monetary union intact? Or would the lenders use financial pressure to crush the new leaders' revolutionary zeal, compelling the continuation of the same policies as before? Or would the clashing positions of the two sides prove impossible to bridge, with the ultimate result a huge default and plunge into the burning pits of Grexit?

Thomsen's meeting with Varoufakis came a couple of days after an early episode indicating that events were hurtling toward Grexit faster than either side wanted. On January 30, Jeroen Dijsselbloem, the president of the Eurogroup, had come to Athens, and at a joint press conference with Varoufakis the Dutchman had become visibly enraged at the Greek finance minister's denunciation of the Troika. Photos of the frosty, awkward handshake as they parted adorned the front pages of newspapers the world over.[2]

1 Kerin Hope and Stefan Wagstyl, 2015, "Greece will no longer deal with 'troika,' Yanis Varoufakis says," *Financial Times*, January 30.

2 See, for example, www.wsj.com/articles/as-greece-and-eu-clash-clues-on-deal-emerge-1422663008.

Given the rockiness of that start to his international financial diplomacy, Varoufakis's eagerness to meet Thomsen was understandable. No press conference followed the Thomsen-Varoufakis meeting, the occurrence of which was disclosed a few days later by an IMF spokesman who said its purpose was "to get acquainted."[3] In fact, the discussion between the two men was considerably more substantive than that. Thomsen "appeared even keener than I was to press for a debt writeoff," according to Varoufakis, who quoted the IMF European Department director as saying, "At a minimum, €54 billion of Greece's debt left over from the first bailout should be written off immediately in exchange for serious reforms." That, Varoufakis added, "was music to my ears."[4] Thomsen's account differs. He told me that he didn't mention any particular amount and didn't propose or endorse any particular debt scheme, since he believed a variety of them would work. But he didn't dispute having indicated approval for substantial debt relief in one form or another.

Whatever specific words were spoken, it is clear that both men favoured — in broad outline at least — a deal involving the exchange of debt relief for reform, with some easing of fiscal austerity. As a guiding principle, this made eminent sense; savvy experts were advocating similar overall approaches.[5] Greece's economy had been beaten down too much and for too long, and had to be given a chance to recover, but Athens still had far to go in addressing the structural rigidities and clientelistic practices, both in the public and private sectors, that limited the country's potential. If the new government could deliver truly transformative results on the structural side where previous regimes had failed, why not make the quid pro quo an alleviation of Greek debt and the accompanying demands for ever-greater fiscal discipline? And why shouldn't Greece's official creditors take significant losses on their loans, as the private sector had? Even if Greece bore primary responsibility for the mess it was in, didn't

3 IMF, 2015, "Transcript of a Press Briefing by Gerry Rice, Director, Communications Department," February 5, www.imf.org/external/np/tr/2015/tr020515.htm.

4 Yanis Varoufakis, 2016, "Endgame for the IMF-EU Feud Over Greece's Debt," Spiegel Online International, April 3, www.spiegel.de/international/europe/op-ed-yanis-varoufakis-imf-eu-quarrel-over-greece-s-debt-a-1085203.html.

5 Reza Moghadam, 2015, "Halve Greek debt and keep the eurozone together" (see footnote 14 in chapter 17); Martin Wolf, 2015, "A deal to bring modernity to Greece," *Financial Times*, February 3.

the creditors share blame for having foisted bailouts that were clearly based on questionable assumptions?

Before pursuing such grand bargains, however, it was first necessary to address Greece's need for the cash required to make debt payments falling due in the coming months. Under the existing program, Athens was still slated to receive €7.2 billion from European institutions and the IMF in early 2015, and disbursal was contingent upon compliance with the conditions that had remained unmet under the previous government's tenure. Without receiving that money, the Greek government would be at high risk of defaulting on at least some of its looming debt. Complicating matters further was the fact that the European portion of the program was due to expire at the end of February, after which time no more loans could be furnished under the existing accord. The Europeans were willing to extend the program for another few months, which would give all parties time to consider and negotiate their major differences calmly. But the creditor countries insisted that Greece would have to ask for such an extension, and it would have to follow the program's basic rules.

The Greek response was to double down on audacity. Varoufakis said Athens didn't want the €7.2 billion, because for too long "we have resembled drug addicts craving the next dose. What this government is all about is ending the addiction."[6] To ensure that Greece had the necessary financing to continue paying its bills, he expected the creditors to agree on a "bridging program" for several months, with the ECB continuing to provide the Greek banking system with euros needed to remain in operation — after which time Athens and its partners would reach their "new contract."

But simply jettisoning the program and ignoring its major strictures was not going to fly. Leaders in creditor Europe rebutted pieties about respecting Greek popular will by pointing out that they too were accountable to electorates with entirely different views of how aid to Athens ought to work. On February 4, the cause of Greek militancy

6 Anne-Sylvaine Chassany and Peter Spiegel, 2015, "Eurozone alarm grows over Greek bailout brinkmanship," *Financial Times*, February 1.

suffered a setback when the ECB shut off its main source of lending to the country's banks, which had been losing deposits during the previous month at a rate of about €400 million a day. In a statement, the central bank said its decision was "based on the fact that it is currently not possible to assume" Athens would continue to meet its bailout requirements. Accordingly, the ECB would no longer accept Greek government bonds, or government-guaranteed private bonds, as collateral for cheap loans. Greek banks could continue receiving euros via the more expensive channel of Emergency Liquidity Assistance (which involved borrowing from the Bank of Greece), but the ECB had the power to withdraw that source of supply too — as it had threatened, to great effect, in Ireland and Cyprus.[7]

With the Greek banking system now at the ECB's mercy, the country was one big step closer to Grexit — and although some of the most extreme Syriza cadres were eager to cut the bonds of monetary union, those in high policy-making positions abhorred the prospect on both political and economic grounds. Tsipras had campaigned on a pledge to stay in the euro zone; polls showed a wide majority of Greeks still wanted to keep the common currency. Varoufakis himself, who had lamented adoption of the euro as a historic error, likened it to the line from "Hotel California" of rock music fame: "You can check out anytime you like, but you can never leave" — a sardonic acknowledgement that the costs of returning to the drachma would be unacceptably high.[8]

European finance ministers believed, therefore, that they held the upper hand as they prepared to begin jousting with their Greek counterpart. Their confidence was justified.

7 European Central Bank, 2015, "Eligibility of Greek bonds used as collateral in Eurosystem monetary policy operations," Press Release, February 4, www.ecb.europa.eu/press/pr/date/2015/html/pr150204.en.html.

8 Liz Alderman, 2015, "Greece's Feisty Finance Minister Tries a More Moderate Message," *The New York Times*, January 29.

First impressions are important. So at his initial Eurogroup meeting on February 11, Varoufakis struck an emollient tone in his opening statement. "Some of you, I know, were displeased by the victory of a radical leftwing party," he told his fellow finance ministers. "To them I have this to say: It would be a lost opportunity to see us as adversaries. We are dedicated Europeanists." Although the Troika as formerly constituted belonged in the dustbin of history, "our government will however maintain dialogue and continue to cooperate fully with the European Commission, the ECB and the IMF," Varoufakis averred.[9]

He was facing a united group, whose 18 members delivered a similar message, one after the other: before any revamped program could be negotiated, Athens must ask to extend the current bailout beyond its February 28 expiration, and adhere to the conditions in the meantime — which Syriza leaders had vowed never to do. For his part, Varoufakis seemed ready to yield, provided he could obtain concessions giving his government some leeway in substituting its own preferred reforms for ones set previously by the Troika. First, he wanted to lay out some broader guideposts for the negotiations that would take place over the next few months.

The new regime in Athens, Varoufakis said, "will be the most reform-oriented government in Greek modern history.…Why? Simply because we are not tied to any interest groups." On issues such as fighting tax evasion and corruption, "We stand ready to support structural reforms previously agreed with our Eurogroup partners….we will even accelerate them." As for the debt, he reminded the Eurogroup that in 2012, Greece had been promised more relief provided certain conditions were met. "This discussion should be reopened when we will discuss our new contract."

But some aspects of the prior approach must change, he said, most notably conditions requiring the government to turn the fiscal screws

9 Although comments made in Eurogroup meetings are supposed to be kept confidential, Varoufakis posted his statement on his blog in late 2015, after leaving office, in rebuttal to critics. It is available at: https://yanisvaroufakis.eu/2015/11/02/judge-for-yourself-the-speech-with-which-i-antagonised-the-eurogroup/.

yet again and keep them tightly fastened. "A primary surplus target of 4.5 percent of GDP year-in-year-out has no historical precedent in any situation resembling that of Greece today," he asserted, referring to the primary surpluses in the 4–4.5 percent range that Athens was expected to continue generating into the 2020s under the terms of the old program. "It will simply not be possible for our country to grow if we remain on the growth sapping austerity path imposed on our economy."

Varoufakis's claim about the singularly excessive nature of the surplus targets was soundly based. A 2014 study by Barry Eichengreen and Ugo Panizza found that it was "extremely rare" for countries to generate primary surpluses as large as four percent of GDP over as long as a decade. And close examination of five countries that had managed to do so — Belgium starting in 1995, Ireland starting in 1991, Norway starting in 1999, Singapore starting in 1990 and New Zealand starting in 1994 — indicated that "their circumstances [were] special," according to the study (Norway's oil boom being one example). As Eichengreen and Panizza noted, Greece exemplified the more typical case of countries where, "when tax revenues rise, legislators and their constituents apply pressure to spend them." That was exactly what had happened when the Greek primary budget balance first went into the black in 2013; "after years of deficits and fiscal austerity...the government immediately came under pressure to disburse a 'social dividend' of €525 million to 500,000 low-income households."[10]

Amid all the shrillness emanating from Syriza, therefore, Varoufakis was making a convincing case — utterly lacking in detail, to be sure — for a deal in which reform would be exchanged for debt relief and a minimization of further austerity. And he wasn't insisting on outright debt forgiveness; he urged that Greece's creditors accept GDP-linked bonds — that is, securities that would pay interest depending on the

10 Barry Eichengreen and Ugo Panizza, 2014, "Can large primary surpluses solve Europe's debt problem?" July 30, VOX, Centre for Economic Policy Research, http://voxeu.org/article/can-large-primary-surpluses-solve-europe-s-debt-problem.

economy's rate of growth. That idea, long favoured by the IMF itself, could hardly be dismissed out of hand.

The forces working against such a deal, however, were manifold. Europe's power elite didn't want to offer political succour to leftist parties elsewhere, such as the increasingly popular Podemos in Spain. The governments that had already undergone austerity, and fulfilled most of their promises — Ireland's, for example — objected to allowing Greece to get away with less. Debt relief that looked anything like a haircut of principal would draw a *nein* from Germany.

As for the Greeks, their behaviour inspired little confidence that they would embrace far-reaching reform with true ownership, much less enthusiasm. Therein lay the biggest obstacle of all to a mutually beneficial deal — mistrust. Syriza had been elected on a platform, and its leaders embraced an ideology, that amounted to *disownership* of the existing program; who could believe they were capable of owning anything resembling it now? Varoufakis liked to declare that the new government could readily accept 70 percent of the program's reforms — but that figure was unaccompanied by any specifics regarding which reforms were included. The real purpose of such gauzy assurances, European officials suspected, was to obtain both the time and money to start reversing many of the measures taken by previous governments, in accord with promises made to Syriza's own constituencies — by rehiring laid-off public workers, for example. The Greeks, meanwhile, feared that the Europeans had no intention of fundamentally changing the rescue's approach, either in February or later.

Indeed, trust took a battering at the February 11 Eurogroup meeting later in the evening after Varoufakis's remarks. A deal for extending the program first appeared to be agreed — Schäuble and other ministers left the building on that assumption — then fell part amid discord over what each side had accepted. Varoufakis stood accused of having initially endorsed a communiqué, then backing away after calling Athens for approval and hearing objections from other ranking Syriza officials. The Greeks vehemently disputed this version of events, asserting that the deal's terms had been changed without their consent. A few days later, another Eurogroup meeting broke down when Greek officials claimed they had reached an understanding with Jean-Claude Juncker, who was now the European Commission president, only to be confronted shortly thereafter with a terse draft communiqué requiring them to "successfully conclude the [current] programme" before progressing to talks on a "follow-up arrangement."

Regardless of where the truth lay, ill will was poisoning interactions between Varoufakis and the rest of the Eurogroup, a problem that would worsen as time went on. Relations were particularly tense between Varoufakis and Dijsselbloem, whose rimless spectacles accentuated his Calvinist demeanor. The group's lack of legally sanctioned standing, and tradition of confidentiality regarding its internal proceedings, struck Varoufakis as anti-democratic, and he made little effort to conceal his disdain. At one of his early meetings, the group was 20 minutes into its discussion when, to collective astonishment, Varoufakis — shirt untucked and tieless as usual — strode in trailed by a television cameraman, whom a furious Dijsselbloem ordered out.[11]

The Greeks swallowed their pride and struck an agreement on February 20 for a four-month extension of the program. In recounting the sequence of events shortly thereafter, Dijsselbloem was not shy about highlighting how he had circumvented Varoufakis by negotiating directly with Tsipras over the phone. "I didn't see Varoufakis at all that morning," he told the *Financial Times*, and he also candidly cited another reason for Greek acquiescence — the increasing flight of deposits from the nation's banks, which had nearly doubled by late February from the €400 million-a-day rate of the previous month. "That was the biggest driver" causing Athens to soften its position, Dijsselbloem said.[12]

He might have added that another financial phenomenon working in his favour was the virtual absence of contagion spreading to European

11 Matthew Dalton, 2015, "Greek Minister Yanis Varoufakis's Style Irks His Eurozone Peers," *The Wall Street Journal*, February 18.

12 Peter Spiegel, 2015, "How Jeroen Dijsselbloem did the deal to extend the Greece bailout," *Financial Times*, March 1.

securities markets; the bonds of other weak European countries were rallying despite mounting fears of Grexit. The buoyancy in European markets was in turn attributable in large part to the ECB's announcement on January 22 that it would join other major central banks in "quantitative easing." This action, an unorthodox form of money creation involving massive bond purchases, was effectively insulating the rest of the region from Greece's troubles. As a result, pressure on the Europeans to make concessions was lessened.

Under the February 20 pact, the expiration of the previous rescue program would be postponed until the end of June, which would come shortly before the due date on some large Greek debt repayments. To get the €7.2 billion still eligible for disbursement, the Syriza leaders could submit proposals of their own as substitutes for the reform measures that the Troika had been demanding since 2014. But that didn't mean the Syriza proposals would be accepted; they would have to pass muster with essentially the same monitors as before—who would now be called "the institutions" rather than the Troika, in deference to Greek sensibilities. And the new government would have to refrain from taking measures that contravened the program's rules.

This episode was not a total rout from the Greek perspective. Athens got some flexibility regarding its primary surplus targets, which meant that at least in the immediate future, fiscal "consolidation" wouldn't be as drastic as had been envisioned under the previous accord. And time was gained for a government full of senior officials who were just becoming acquainted with their new job duties after careers spent as academics or activists — in some cases with little experience outside Greece other than attendance at demonstrations or conferences. Although Varoufakis later rued signing the extension arrangement, "I thought, we might as well have the additional four months to negotiate," he said.[13]

But Greece's financial future was still tenuous, and the IMF promptly made clear that it was going to hold the Greek authorities' feet to the

13 Interview with Paul Mason of Britain's Channel 4 News, for the documentary *#ThisIsACoup*, available at: www.youtube.com/watch?v=l14C7TCX_8A.

fire in upcoming months, as it had with the Samaras regime. A letter from Lagarde to Dijsselbloem, dated February 23, expressed a strong demurral about a six-page list of reforms that Varoufakis submitted to demonstrate the new government's willingness to deliver sufficient measures for disbursement of the €7.2 billion. The list may be "a valid starting point," Lagarde wrote, but it is "not very specific.…In quite a few areas, including perhaps the most important ones, [Varoufakis's list] is not conveying clear assurances" that Athens will go far enough. The managing director voiced particular disappointment about the lack of clarity regarding pensions, value-added taxes, the opening of closed sectors and labour market liberalization, among others.[14]

Lagarde's letter bespoke the role that the IMF saw for itself as this new act in the Greek drama unfolded — that of an honest broker, more prepared than ever to speak out, publicly as well as privately, about shortcomings in the approach being taken by both the Greek and European sides. The Europeans would undergo an uncomfortably harsh measure of IMF candour later in the year. In the process, both sides would complain, with some justification, that the Fund was going overboard in its rigour. That is what sometimes happens when an institution like the Fund is compelled to compensate for its past laxity.

The hackles that Varoufakis raised with his early behaviour in the Eurogroup were nothing compared to the antagonism that was to erupt as the two sides began discussing what would be required for disbursal of the €7.2 billion. Once the agreement to extend the program was struck, the institutions wanted to send missions to Athens as usual, so that they could conduct talks with individual Greek ministry officials as well as ministers such as Varoufakis. But the new government, which had mocked its opponents during the election campaign for taking orders from unelected civil servants, was determined to avoid such procedures. For about two weeks, Greece and its creditors were at loggerheads over whether meetings would take place in Athens

14 Lagarde's letter is available at: http://im.ft-static.com/content/images/30862706-bc33-11e4-b6ec-00144feab7de.pdf.

or Brussels. Even after a decision was made to hold talks in both cities, Greek authorities made visiting staffers from the IMF, ECB and European Commission conduct business only in their Athens hotels, and Varoufakis himself refused to meet mission chiefs as his predecessors had done. "The idea of Troika visits comprising cabals of technocrats from the three institutions in lockstep walking to our ministries and trying to implement a program which has failed, at least in the estimation of our government and I think of our people, that is a thing of the past," he said.[15]

Communication was often pointless, if it occurred at all. When staffers from the creditor side arrived at meetings in Athens, they sometimes found the room full of journalists. The Brussels gatherings, too, were often unproductive to the point of absurdity. Members of the Euro Working Group, a body consisting of finance ministry deputies from countries belonging to the monetary union, recall being subjected to a lecture about basic Keynesian economics by a Greek official who didn't seem to know, or care, that many of those present had received advanced training in the subject. At meetings where data was to be reviewed, the Greek side would sometimes show up without anyone who could use spreadsheets, even though their ministries had people who were perfectly competent at it. Although Varoufakis sent "reform" proposals to Brussels, they included ideas ranging from dreamy-eyed to outlandish, such as a plan to improve tax collection by recruiting tourists, students and housekeepers as undercover agents armed with video and audio recording devices, on the theory that this would frighten businesses into complying with the law.[16] Most galling of all to the creditor side were Greek officials who acted as if the details of conditionality were unimportant — because of their certainty that the money would be forthcoming in the end no matter what.

15 Peter Spiegel, 2015, "Greek talks with creditors finally to start," *Financial Times*, March 9.

16 The list of proposed reforms in which this tax-collection measure was included is available at: http://im.ft-static.com/content/images/4e4b2122-c40f-11e4-a02e-00144feab7de.pdf.

There was some measure of method to this madness, at least from Varoufakis's perspective, because he was among those who believed that the creditors would cave in rather than allow Grexit to occur. Although his confidence was not shared by all high-ranking Syriza officials, the finance minister had good reason to surmise that most of his European counterparts were anxious to avoid such a scenario. Even if Grexit would have little immediate impact on their economies, the solidarity of the euro zone — and of Europe itself — would be gravely fractured. The geopolitical implications of Greece becoming a "rogue state" in the Balkans were far greater in 2015 than in earlier years, following the Russian invasion of Ukraine in 2014.

But a strong preference in Europe for avoiding Grexit did not connote a willingness to prevent it at all costs, and negotiators from the creditor side gave Athens no grounds for hope that the Varoufakian approach would work. The Troika's unity may have cracked in late 2014, when the European Commission was markedly more conciliatory than the IMF, "but during the first few months of 2015, those institutional differences dissipated," a Brussels policy maker recalled. "And the reason for that was that the Greeks were taking such a crazy position."

The Syriza government was thrown further on the defensive as it underwent the same torture-by-cash-shortage that its predecessors had. To pay pensions and civil service salaries, while also honouring an obligation to repay €1.5 billion to the IMF in March, the finance ministry was raiding reserves of cash squirreled away in various government and quasi-government coffers. Examples included €600 million held by state-owned corporations including power utilities and the Athens metro. The government even withheld €150 million that had been budgeted for hospital supplies.[17]

In part to seek respite for the government from its cash pressures, Varoufakis flew to Washington on Easter weekend for meetings at the IMF, which he hoped would allow some postponement in payments coming due in coming months. It was a moment fraught

17 Kerin Hope, Peter Spiegel and Claire Jones, 2015, "Athens raids public health coffers in hunt for cash," *Financial Times,* March 24.

with portentous symbolism, because many in Syriza held typically leftist views of the Fund — that is, as a malign agent of international capitalism, responsible for oppression of the poor in large swaths of the world. Before coming to power, Syriza leaders had denounced the Fund's presence in Greece; the deputy prime minister, Yannis Dragasakis, was the author of a book arguing that the Greek crisis should be resolved between Athens and its European partners, without IMF involvement. But the Fund's efforts to promote debt relief had been duly noted by the new government's inner circle, who regarded the institution with ambivalence rather than hostility.

At 6:00 p.m. on Easter Sunday, Lagarde met Varoufakis in her twelfth-floor office, where she made clear that she couldn't agree to a postponement of payments to the IMF. To safeguard its preferred-creditor status, the Fund is loath to even consider any restructuring of its loans, and since the Fund wasn't granting such favours to its poorest borrowers in Africa and other parts of the developing world, it wasn't about to do so for Greece. For his part, Varoufakis told the managing director that the Greek government "intends" to honour its obligations to the Fund — an assuring-sounding statement, though using a deliberately ambiguous word that left open the possibility of default under certain circumstances.[18]

Another meeting, between Varoufakis and Lipton, focused on more fundamental questions about how the Fund might be of help. Like Lagarde, the IMF's no. 2 official had a message that wasn't what his Greek visitor was hoping to hear. But it was an excellent guide to the Fund's mindset throughout this phase of the crisis.

Lipton's central point was this: the Fund doesn't do one-sided programs. Both policy and financing are necessary, and they need to match. By this he meant that the IMF could not assist Greece simply by mobilizing loans or debt relief unless the government was willing to adopt a corresponding set of policies. The Fund cared as much as

18 Chris Giles, Sam Fleming and Peter Spiegel, 2015, "Christine Lagarde dashes Greek hopes on loan respite," *Financial Times*, April 16; and Landon Thomas Jr., 2015, "Greece Flashes Warning Signals About Its Debt," *The New York Times*, April 19.

ever about the general principle that Greek debt must be genuinely sustainable, Lipton assured Varoufakis. But the Fund could only work with Greece on a two-sided program, in which Athens would take enough action on the policy front to generate surpluses large enough to service whatever debt it owed. So far, the Syriza regime had shown little willingness to put forward such a package of policies that could credibly replace the ones in the old program. Lipton sympathized, to some extent, with the dilemma Varoufakis faced; the Europeans wanted to talk only about policies, and there was a risk that once such a discussion started they would simply ask for more and more without offering anything significant in return. But by the same token, the Europeans had legitimate grounds to fear what might happen once talks started on finance and debt. To get IMF help, Varoufakis and his colleagues would have to seriously engage on policy, and commit to measures sufficient to keeping their country from going broke in the long run.

It was not only the Greeks who were on the receiving end of IMF admonitions. The Fund was ready to start applying pressure on the Europeans, too. That would become evident when the Eurogroup assembled in Riga, Latvia, on April 24, with Thomsen representing the Fund.

Media coverage of the Riga meeting depicted it as a massive ganging up on Varoufakis by his fellow finance ministers — and that was indeed the most attention-grabbing development.[19] Even outside the meeting room, the Greek was conspicuous by his isolation. He didn't join his colleagues at a gala dinner, and at breakfast the next morning, he ate alone in the dining room of the hotel where other ministers were staying. The meeting itself led to a rift surpassing in its vitriol anything that long-time attendees at such sessions could remember.

Thomsen was among the first to speak, reporting that Greek engagement with missions from "the institutions" remained minimal.

19 Robin Emmett and Ingrid Melander, 2015, "Isolated in debt talks, Greek finance rebel gets the cold shoulder," Reuters, April 25.

"We are still in a situation where we cannot go to ministries," the IMF official said, according to notes taken by a participant. "We have not had a single meeting with ministers."

When Varoufakis took the floor, he asserted nonetheless that "there is convergence" causing him to feel "optimism that we will reach an agreement." Sufficient progress had been made on a few key issues, he argued, that the Eurogroup should soon convene a conference call to approve a distribution of funds.

An icy silence followed, finally interrupted by Peter Kažmir of Slovakia. "Unbelievable," said Kažmir, and he urged his colleagues to "start to discuss serious consequences," by which he clearly meant the need to plan for Grexit. Others chimed in, using similarly somber language. "The discussion is going nowhere. I'm very worried" said the minister from Luxembourg. "The agreements of February are not going anywhere — they've collapsed," echoed the Italian. "I agree, we need to start talking Plan B," said his Slovenian counterpart. Even Michel Sapin of France, a country that had almost always been one of the most indulgent toward Greek sins, referred to Plan B as a real possibility if the talks did not start becoming more fruitful. As news circulated about the criticism heaped on Varoufakis, he posted an insouciant tweet using the response of President Franklin Roosevelt to the barons of capitalism during the fight over the New Deal: "They are unanimous in their hatred for me and I welcome their hatred."

But amid all this mudslinging and fist shaking, there was another disconcerting blast from Thomsen for the Eurogroup to consider. Greece's debt outlook was deteriorating sharply, because the upheaval associated with Syriza's victory was causing a fall-off in tax revenue and a fresh downturn in the economy, partially due to the flight of deposits from banks. Although IMF calculations had indicated at the end of 2014 that the country's debt would be sustainable if Athens fully implemented its program, that was no longer the case now that the recovery had aborted.

"I want to caution you, ministers," Thomsen said, according to the meeting notes. "There will be a need for very large new [financing], contrary to expectations of six months ago....Very significant debt relief from Europe will be necessary. Do not be surprised when this will come."

On May 14, the IMF executive board met for a briefing on the latest developments in the Greek crisis. There was a lot of news to discuss. Varoufakis had been sidelined shortly after the Riga Eurogroup meeting; although he was still finance minister, he would play less of a direct role in negotiations with interlocutors, based on Tsipras's recognition that the alienation Varoufakis was engendering might destroy any chance of an agreement. Another important development was a May 12 payment by Greece to the IMF of €750 million — a sum the cash-strapped government had barely managed to cough up. Athens had resorted to an accounting gimmick of sorts, drawing from a reserve account of SDRs that it held at the IMF (as do all IMF member countries). This ploy could only be used once, because there was not enough left in Greece's account for payments that were coming due in June and July.

The board heard a few encouraging tidbits from Thomsen and other staffers about how the negotiations were proceeding, according to a memo summarizing the meeting.[20] The Greek government was no longer insisting on meeting separately with each of the three institutions, and was now willing to meet with representatives of all three together. On the other hand, Greek negotiators "appear to have limited room of maneuver," the memo said, and Athens still wasn't allowing staffers from the institutions to meet ministers. As for substantive matters, Greek officials were indicating some readiness to consider reforms favoured by the IMF and the other institutions, such as curtailing certain tax breaks in the VAT system that were limiting the amount of revenue the government collected. But the two sides

20 The memo was first disclosed by Paul Mason of Britain's Channel 4 News. IMF, Office of the Executive Director for Italy, Greece [and other countries], 2015, "Informal meeting to brief the Executive Board on recent developments in Greece," May 14.

"are still away from reaching an agreement," and, if anything, the Greeks were moving away from a deal by reversing or planning to reverse measures that previous governments had taken. Syriza leaders had ordered the re-hiring of most civil servants that had been laid off in the recent past, for example. Another area where Athens was trying to reverse previous actions concerned the pension system.

Pensions were the most explosive issue dividing Greece and its creditors. A system that had once provided some of the most extravagant retirement benefits in Europe had become much stingier, thanks to a series of cuts starting in 2010 that eliminated annual bonuses and reduced monthly payouts by nearly 50 percent for some retirees and by about one-third for many others. By 2015, tales were legion of Greeks in their seventies and eighties scrimping to pay their water and power bills, even as they had to support adult offspring who had lost their jobs. The amounts they were receiving were still much greater than their counterparts were receiving in poorer euro-zone countries such as Slovenia, Slovakia, Latvia and Lithuania — a point often raised in Eurogroup meetings by those countries' finance ministers, who saw little fairness in their taxpayers helping to subsidize a wealthier country's seniors. But with more than half of Greek households heavily dependent on pension income (because of job losses), and about 45 percent of Greek pensioners receiving monthly payments below the official poverty line of €665, Syriza leaders were proclaiming further cuts in benefits to be a "red line" that they couldn't possibly cross.

Hardship and fairness issues aside, the problem the IMF refused to ignore was that projections showed the Greek system was still unsustainable, even after the previous benefit cuts. To subsidize payments, the government was transferring a sum close to 10 percent of GDP — a huge drain on a national budget that had already been slashed in other areas. The system's financial woes were not entirely due to pension costs; one reason was that several billion dollars of reserves — which were invested in government bonds — were wiped out in the 2012 debt restructuring. Another reason was the fall-off in contributions to the system resulting from rising joblessness and shrinking incomes. Even so, the system had to be put on a more viable footing for the Greek state to have a decent prospect of solvency in future years.

The pension issue was one in which differences among the institutions were starting to become apparent in May 2015, with the sternest line taken by the IMF. On May 4, Panos Skourletis, the labour minister, told a Greek TV network that the Fund "is the most inflexible…the most extreme voice" that Greek negotiators were encountering, citing not only pensions, but labour market rules.[21]

At the May 14 board meeting, Thomsen told the directors that the staff stands "ready to be flexible" on Greek policies, according to the memo. But predictably, this was combined with the message that "numbers need to add up" and that the same principle would apply to financing and debt. In other words, the more Greece could do to make its economy more competitive and more fiscally sound, the greater the chance that the financial concessions offered by the nation's creditors would suffice to meet the Fund's standards for debt sustainability. Lagarde backed Thomsen to the hilt; the memo quoted her as emphasizing that "the Fund cannot complete a 'quick and dirty' review, and that the staff has to play by the rules and not obscure the Fund's mandate."

As on previous occasions, the IMF's stiff-necked stance was inducing efforts to forge an agreement with no Fund involvement. The Greeks mooted this idea, as did the European Commission in the form of a proposition from Juncker. But German officials and their northern European allies were as dubious as ever about the Commission, whose leadership they saw as too prone to play "good cop" for the sake of fostering regional unity. At a European summit on May 21, Merkel told Tsipras that whatever deal emerged would have to pass muster with the Fund.

Just a little over a month remained before the end-of-June deadline when Greece's current program would expire. It was beginning to look as if a miracle would be required to stitch together an agreement in time for the Greek government to get the €7.2 billion it needed to replenish its coffers and pay obligations coming due before mid-year — especially since a number of European parliaments would

21 Renee Maltezou and Jan Strupczewski, 2015, "Pension, labour disputes dog Greek talks as cash dwindles," Reuters, May 4.

have to bestow approval first. And after that would presumably come the necessity of thrashing out another deal — bigger yet, and almost certainly more contentious — for a new bailout ensuring that Athens would have the financial resources to pay larger amounts falling due later in 2015 and beyond. Absent such pacts, Greece wouldn't get the euros it needed to avoid default. Nor would its banks get the euros needed from the ECB to continue functioning and keep the country in the monetary union.

When Olivier Blanchard joined the IMF as chief economist in 2008, he resisted requests to write blog items for the Fund's website, telling staffers from the Communications Department: "I do not blog." But he relented, and started posting items that, owing to his towering academic reputation, drew considerable interest from colleagues in the field. On June 14, 2015, he publicly sallied into the fray over the Greek crisis by posting a blog entry spelling out the Fund's determination that a solution would require not only painful changes in Greek policy, but substantial sacrifice on the part of European lenders in the form of debt relief. His opening paragraph identified, with crystal clarity, the knotty question that made compromise so difficult: "How much of an adjustment has to be made by Greece, and how much has to be made by its official creditors?"[22] Using that question as a starting point provided an illuminating conceptual framework for assessing a rapidly evolving state of play.

Blanchard focused chiefly on the long-term target for Greece's primary budget surplus, a crucial number because it was a proxy of sorts for how the burden would be divided between Athens and the creditors. At one extreme, if Greece were to generate a huge surplus well into the future — say, 10 percent of GDP — the country could pay off its debt, and fund its government operations, with no additional help

22 Olivier Blanchard, 2015, "Greece: A Credible Deal Will Require Difficult Decisions By All Sides," *iMFdirect*, https://blog-imfdirect.imf.org/2015/06/14/greece-a-credible-deal-will-require-difficult-decisions-by-all-sides/.

from its creditors — albeit at the cost of inflicting severe distress on its citizens, who would be receiving far less in government benefits than they were paying in taxes. At the other extreme, if Greece were allowed to run substantial deficits far into the long term, it could provide its citizens with a generous welfare state of the sort Syriza had promised during the election campaign. But Athens would be making little if any contribution to reducing its debt, and would be depending on its creditors to forgive some huge portion of their loans, or lend vast new sums to enable the Greek government to cover its expenses, or some combination of the two.

Blanchard reminded readers that under the bailout deals of 2012, Greece and its creditors had agreed that the primary surplus over the long term would be 4.5 percent of GDP. "Economic and political developments have made this an unattainable goal, and the target clearly must be decreased," he wrote — which was little surprise to the IMF, since as noted previously Fund staffers strongly doubted that Greece could generate such large surpluses over a sustained period.

Now that the old target was scrapped, "how much should the primary surplus be reduced?" Blanchard asked. "A lower target leads to a less painful fiscal and economic adjustment for Greece. But it also leads to a need for more external official financing, and a commitment to more debt relief on the part of the European creditor countries. Just as there is a limit to what Greece can do, there is a limit to how much financing and debt relief official creditors are willing and realistically able to provide given that they have their own taxpayers to consider."

In fact, a new target for the primary surplus was one of the few points of agreement emerging from the negotiations. Two weeks before Blanchard's blog post, at a meeting in Berlin, leaders including Merkel, Hollande, Lagarde and Draghi had gathered to draft the outline of a comprehensive deal — not a take-it-or-leave-it proposal, but a plan they could present to Athens with the aim of breaking the stalemate and finally moving talks into high gear. Once word got out that the creditors had prepared a plan, the Greeks responded with papers of their own, including one laying out a scheme for debt relief. Tsipras flew to Brussels on June 3, issuing a statement declaring, "I am going to discuss the proposal of the Greek government," while making no mention of the institutions' plan.[23]

It was at this point when Greek officials accepted the new target for the long-term primary surplus — a perplexingly high 3.5 percent of GDP, only one percentage point lower than before. This was yet another "what were they thinking?" moment in the Greek crisis. Varoufakis has asserted that the decision was taken without his consent, and coincided with "a major turnaround in spirit" among his Syriza colleagues following his sidelining after the Riga meeting of the Eurogroup. "The rationale was…we will do this in exchange for debt restructuring," he recalled later in an interview for a TV documentary. "I said, 'This to me sounds completely nonsensical. If you give them high primary surpluses, why should they give you debt restructuring? It is like admitting that your debt does not need restructuring.'"

Many IMF staffers viewed the 3.5 percent of GDP target with only slightly less skepticism than the old one. Their doubts would be revealed in the fine print of a soon-to-be published Fund document,[24] and more forthrightly by Lagarde in 2016.[25] But for the time being, the Fund was suppressing its reservations about the target. Greece was going along with the target European officials favoured, so the Fund was going along too. Instead of denouncing the target as exorbitant, the Fund would do little more in June 2015 than warn about the pain involved — and insist anew that the numbers add up.

23 Hellenic Republic, 2015, "Prime Minister Alexis Tsipras' statement prior to his departure to Brussels in order to meet with the President of the European Commission Jean-Claude Juncker," www.primeminister.gov.gr/english/2015/06/03/prime-minister-alexis-tsipras-statement-prior-to-his-departure-for-brussels-in-order-to-meet-with-the-president-of-the-european-commission-jean-claude-juncker/.

24 This document will be discussed in the next chapter. IMF, 2015, "Greece: An Update of IMF Staff's Preliminary Public Debt Sustainability Analysis," July 14, www.imf.org/external/pubs/ft/scr/2015/cr15186.pdf.

25 IMF, 2016, "Press Briefing of the Managing Director," April 14, www.imf.org/external/np/tr/2016/tr041416.htm.

Agreement by Greece and its creditors on the surplus target, after all, did not imply agreement on the steps that would be necessary to achieve it. Shortly after Tsipras's arrival in Brussels, details of the rival positions began to leak,[26] and, as expected, one big sticking point was pensions. The institutions wanted savings squeezed out of the system, starting in 2016, to the tune of one percent of GDP (about €1.8 billion per year). The Greeks were willing to gradually phase-out rules allowing early retirements, but little more. Another issue on which the two sides were crossing swords was the VAT, where the creditors wanted to raise about €1.8 billion — far more than the Greek counter-proposal, by eliminating a host of loopholes such as lower rates that applied on Aegean islands. On labour markets, Syriza was aiming to fulfill its campaign promise to restore the pre-crisis minimum wage and reinstate collective-bargaining procedures that unions favoured, which would violate the institutions' demand to refrain from reversing measures adopted during the crisis. To the disgruntlement of Greek policy makers, the institutions' proposal contained no word on debt relief, the idea being that this issue would be discussed only after a deal was struck on the policies Athens would implement.

No sooner had the prime minister returned to Athens than the mood darkened amid renewed signs that the negotiations were headed toward breakdown. The IMF recalled its mission in Brussels back to Washington on June 11 in a public display of pique; spokesman Gerry Rice cited "major differences between us in most key areas" and said "the ball is very much in Greece's court right now."[27] Greek officials hotly blamed the discord on "maximalist IMF proposals" that they couldn't possibly accept.[28] But even Juncker and his European Commission underlings — the strongest advocates of leniency toward Athens — threw up their hands and declared an impasse on June 14, after receiving what they called "vague and repetitive" proposals from

26 Viktoria Dendrinou and Nektaria Stamouli, 2015, "Greece's Creditors Make Some Concessions as Showdown Approaches," *The Wall Street Journal,* June 3.

27 IMF, 2015, "Transcript of a Press Briefing by Gerry Rice, Director, Communications Department," June 11, www.imf.org/external/np/tr/2015/tr061115.htm.

28 Liz Alderman and Landon Thomas Jr., 2015, "I.M.F. Recalls Negotiators as Deadline Looms for Greek Deal," *The New York Times,* June 11.

the Greek team, including a promise to achieve €2.4 billion in savings using "administrative measures" and another €700 million by cracking down on VAT fraud. Such brazen use of smoke and mirrors indicated that while the Greeks were consenting to ambitious budget and revenue targets, they had no real intention of meeting them.[29]

What did all this thrusting and parrying add up to? Blanchard's blog post helped educe the implications. "[T]he Greek government has to offer truly credible measures" to meet the new primary surplus target, "and it has to show its commitment to…reforms" that would instill competitiveness, he wrote. "We believe that even the lower new target cannot be credibly achieved without comprehensive reform of the value-added tax (VAT)…and further adjustment of pensions." The IMF couldn't accept fakery like "administrative measures," which was why the Fund was pushing Athens so aggressively.

At the same time, the target implied that "the European creditors would have to agree to significant additional financing, and to debt relief sufficient to maintain debt sustainability," Blanchard continued. What sort of debt relief? Provided the target was held at 3.5 percent of GDP, "debt relief could be achieved through a long rescheduling of debt payments at low interest rates. Any further decrease in the primary surplus…would probably require, however, haircuts."

Aye, there was the rub. Should the target for the surplus be decreased further, in Greece's favour — to, say, two percent of GDP, or even lower? Was Greece being asked to bear a disproportionate share of the burden of adjustment so that the haircut-hating Germans and other European governments could continue assuring their voters that Athens would someday pay back all the money it had borrowed?

These questions — variations on Blanchard's initial question about how much adjustment each side should make — are ultimately political, of course. On the one hand, it didn't seem fair to ask Europeans, especially those from countries poorer than Greece, to make greater

29 Gabriele Steinhauser, 2015, "EU_Greece Talks on Bailout Break Down, Setting Up Showdown," *The Wall Street Journal,* June 14.

sacrifices so that Greek retirees could avoid further cuts in their pensions. On the other hand, Greece had already undergone six years of recession, the disastrousness of which was attributable in no small part to misjudgments by the creditors. Was it fair, or even sensible, to ask the Greek people to endure significantly more belt-tightening?

Fairly or not, sensibly or not, the further significant tightening of Greek belts was going to be demanded, with the primary surplus target of 3.5 percent of GDP maintained as the goal, and the IMF making sure that the numbers added up. The great unknown, in the days leading up to the June 30 expiration of the country's program, was whether Athens would submit. Unsurprisingly, as the end of the month drew closer, Greeks were pulling money out of their bank accounts at an accelerated rate.

19

A TASTE OF GREXIT

The wrong draft of Greece's proposal was accidentally transmitted from Athens to Brussels on Sunday night, June 21, 2015. The correct version arrived the next morning. It was a fitting start to one of the most frenzied periods of the Greek crisis. Never were the news media's favourite clichés — "make or break," "do or die," "last ditch," "final stretch," "true endgame," "eleventh hour," "drop-dead moment," "on the edge of the abyss" — more apt for Greece's membership in the euro zone than during the three weeks starting on June 22.[1]

Almost the entire four months granted for extension of the program had passed with Syriza leaders showing scant willingness to deviate from the populist manifesto on which they were elected, and the creditors displaying equal resolve to cut off funding in the absence of an accord that would essentially amount to betrayal of that manifesto. Large debt payments by Greece were coming due in July and in the months thereafter. Rejection of the terms necessary to make those

1 Some of the material in this section is derived from my own interviews, but much also comes from published retrospectives, including: Landon Thomas Jr., 2015, "Hopeful Start to Greek Debt Negotiations Quickly Soured," July 2; Nektaria Stamouli and Marcus Walker, 2015, "How Alexis Tsipras's Greek Referendum Call Came After Creditors Covered His Proposals in Red Ink," *The Wall Street Journal,* June 28; and Peter Spiegel, 2015, "A bewildering week in the Greece crisis when trust evaporated," *The Financial Times*, July 3.

payments would signal Tsipras's readiness to abandon another main element in his electoral mandate — keeping the euro as the country's currency. The odds in favour of such an outcome appeared to be rising fast as the number of days dwindled before the June 30 expiration of the program.

One faction in the prime minister's camp, led by Deputy Prime Minister Dragasakis, was urging compromise. Another camp, led by Varoufakis, was urging an escalation in confrontation, based on his belief that this would not lead to a full Grexit but rather capitulation by the creditors. Varoufakis had secretly mobilized a small team of experts to prepare a plan for how Greece could cope, at least temporarily, in the event that European authorities deprived Greek banks of euros; the idea was to create a "parallel currency" that would enable the country's payments system to continue functioning. Under Varoufakis's plan, the government should default — even to the ECB, the ultimate source of euros — and the economy would survive the disruption while negotiations proceeded toward an accord satisfactory to Athens, including full resumption of euro-zone membership.[2]

Greece had taken a tentative step in the default direction on June 4, when it notified the IMF that it would not make a €300 million loan repayment due that day. Instead, the government would invoke a rare procedure allowing it to "bundle" all of the €1.5 billion it owed in June into one payment, which would be transferred to Washington at

2 Varoufakis explained some elements of this strategy in October 2015 in an interview with Norbert Häring, an economics correspondent for Germany's *Handeslblatt.* An English version is posted on Varoufakis's blog, available at: http://yanisvaroufakis.eu/2015/10/30/europe-is-our-home-we-need-to-fix-it-in-handelsblatt-30-oct-2015/. The secret group, which Varoufakis dubbed a "war cabinet" of about five people, was also preparing a contingency plan in the event that Greece was obliged to abandon the euro entirely. One of the members, Professor James Galbraith of the University of Texas, has written about the issues the group considered in a book, *Welcome to the Poisoned Chalice: The Destruction of Greece and the Future of Europe,* New Haven, CT: Yale University Press, 2016, chapters 30, 31 and appendix.

the end of the month. This stopped well short of a major breach of obligations to the Fund, although it did not bode well for the payment due on June 30.[3]

But the Varoufakis camp lost out, at least initially, to the moderates. An 11-page submission by the government on June 22 contained by far the largest amount of substantive proposals for tax increases and spending cuts that the Syriza leadership had ever offered. Donald Tusk, the European Council president, said Athens had produced "its first real proposals in many weeks," and Dijsselbloem called it "a positive step." The apparent breakthrough ignited a nine percent rally in Greek stocks.[4]

The euphoria quickly faded as details of the proposal came under scrutiny and others weighed in during a series of meetings at EU buildings in Brussels. Most critical of all, to the surprise of no one, was the IMF, although the European Commission staff shared many of the Fund's concerns.

Too many tax increases that would crimp the businesses Greece needed for growth, not enough spending cuts — that was the Fund's overarching complaint about the Greek proposal. On pensions, for example, Greek officials were willing to go further than before in discouraging early retirement, but instead of curtailing benefits their main proposal for improving the system's solvency was a hefty boost in contributions by employers and employees. The Fund was also unhappy about a Greek plan to impose a one-time levy of 12 percent on corporate profits above €500,000. Beyond dissatisfaction with the budgetary items, Fund staffers thought there was a distinct absence of structural measures that would boost productivity.

3 Kerin Hope and Peter Spiegel, 2015, "Greece to delay IMF repayment as Tsipras faces backlash," *Financial Times*, June 4.

4 Peter Spiegel, Anne-Sylvaine Chassany and Claire Jones, 2015, "Concessions from Athens keep hopes of Greece bailout deal alive," *Financial Times*, June 23.

To the consternation of the Greek negotiators, their proposal was handed back to them on the morning of Wednesday, June 24, marked up in red type and strike-throughs indicating precisely where the institutions wanted additions, subtractions and deletions.[5] Some of the institutions' changes seemed almost picayune, an example being the substitution of an increase in the corporate tax rate to 28 percent instead of the 29 percent the Greeks proposed. A number of others, especially regarding pensions, were considerably more contentious, such as one regarding the "solidarity grant," a supplementary benefit given to poor retirees. Whereas the Greek proposal was to "gradually replace the solidarity grant," the institutions struck those words and inserted "phase out the solidarity grant…by December 2017."

The Greek proposal could be fairly deemed austerity, left-wing style — a soak-the-rich, soak-the-corporations approach to budgetary discipline, which Syriza leaders thought they could persuade their supporters to accept. Put another way, it stood a chance of meeting the test of ownership. It may have come too late in the game for careful consideration, and it may have been excessively populistic economic policy, so the IMF may have been right to dismiss much of it as bad medicine for the Greek economy. But a more important issue, which wasn't being addressed at all, was the target for the long-term primary budget surplus. Easing it significantly from 3.5 percent of GDP could have had a much greater impact on Greece's growth prospects than modifying the Greek plan in accordance with the red marks inserted by the institutions. Also left off the negotiating table at that stage was debt relief; Greek officials sought the inclusion of a provision on debt that would help them win votes in Parliament, but by firm agreement among the creditors the debt issue could be tackled only after Greece had taken policy action first.

The moderate approach having been dealt a severe setback, the confrontation camp among Tsipras's counsellors gained in influence accordingly. On the afternoon and evening of the 24th, the prime minister spent hours with Juncker, Draghi, Lagarde and other European

5 The marked-up version, which was obtained by Kerin Hope of the *Financial Times*, is available at: http://blogs.ft.com/brusselsblog/files/2015/06/Greek-crediors.pdf.

officials. On at least one point during the evening he appeared to agree on a package of terms, but reversed himself after excusing himself to consult with his advisers. As one participant recalls:

> We all sat in this increasingly smoke-filled room on the thirteenth floor of Berlaymont (the Commission headquarters). There was constant haggling. Tsipras said, "I think I'm in agreement now, but let me go and check." There were a couple of mundane things — taxation of farmers, and the VAT on [Aegean] islands. So Juncker lit up another cigarette, and Lagarde passed around M&Ms and complained about the smoke. Then he didn't come back, and didn't come back — it was two or three hours. Finally he came back and said, "I totally disagree with everything we've done this evening." Obviously his delegation had whipped him back into form.

Tsipras's irritated interlocutors set a deadline of 11:00 a.m. the next day for a final decision. A similar drama unfolded that morning; by some accounts the two sides were only €600 million apart, only to see hopes dashed when Tsipras left for consultations and came back insisting on a new list of concessions, the result being that the talks were disbanded shortly before the 11:00 a.m. deadline. The mood became uglier still at a Eurogroup meeting that afternoon, where Schäuble declared that even the deal presented earlier to Tsipras was too soft and wouldn't have passed muster in the German Parliament. The German finance minister also accused the Commission of trying to circumvent the IMF, and reiterated Berlin's admonition that the Fund would have to be involved in any final accord.

Varoufakis, despite having withdrawn from most face-to-face negotiations with the creditors, was representing Greece at this meeting, and he delivered one of his customary provocations. Here is his account, published on his blog:

> During that Eurogroup meeting, I posed a question to Christine Lagarde: "Is it the view of the IMF that Greece's debt is sustainable under the proposed agreement?" Ms

> Lagarde, when her turn came to speak, tried to skirt the issue but, in the end, conceded that Greece's public debt "had to be looked at again". At that point, the Eurogroup President Dijsselbloem interrupted the proceedings and addressed me with the express threat that, if the Greek government insisted on discussing a debt restructure, there would be no deal.[6]

In fact, a detailed answer to Varoufakis's question was already contained in an IMF document. Although still secret, it had been discussed by lower-level officials that morning.

It was time to stop being delusional about Greece. The Greek economy would not eventually outperform nearly every country in the euro zone in one of the crucial measures of economic dynamism; nor would the Greek government privatize several billions of euros worth of assets annually. Once reality was taken into account on those scores, and further adjustments made for the deterioration in the nation's economic fortunes during the first half of 2015, the depth of Greece's debt woes was impossible to gloss over. Even if the country received a new bailout, "debt would remain very high for decades and highly vulnerable to shocks." Sustainability would entail many tens of billions of euros in new loans and debt relief from Europe.

Those were some of the main conclusions from an IMF debt sustainability analysis that Poul Thomsen presented to the finance ministry deputies of the Euro Working Group on Thursday, June 25.[7] European policy makers wanted it kept private. Their reasons were not difficult to discern.

6 Varoufakis's blog post is available at: http://yanisvaroufakis.eu/2015/08/17/my-question-to-christine-lagarde-eurogroup-25th-june-2015-as-narrated-by-landon-thomas-in-the-nyt/.

7 IMF, 2015, "Greece: Preliminary Draft Debt Sustainability Analysis," Country Report 15/165, June 26, www.imf.org/external/pubs/ft/scr/2015/cr15165.pdf.

The document showed how badly the situation in mid-2015 compared with the second half of 2014. It started off noting that by the closing months of the Samaras regime, Greece's debt dynamics stood some chance of becoming sustainable, with debt projected to fall as low as 104 percent of GDP in 2022 provided that the government fully implemented the conditions of its bailout. Heroic though that assumption might be — it was premised on adoption of all structural reforms, privatization and attainment of a very high primary budget surplus — it meant that "no further debt relief would have been needed," at least based on the framework agreed in November 2012.

Look at current circumstances, the authors of the IMF analysis said, and it should be clear that the old assumptions had become either inapplicable or non-credible. One of these assumptions, for example, was that the Greek economy would grow at two percent a year over the long term. That, in turn, was premised on some optimistic expectations, including Greece's dramatic rise from the lowest in the euro zone to almost the highest in growth of total factor productivity (a yardstick for measuring an economy's long-term technological change and efficiency improvements). The only basis for projecting such an outcome was the assumption that Athens would wholeheartedly embrace structural reform, but if anything, "there is a substantial weakening in the delivery of structural reforms and in the reform commitments," the authors wrote. Using a "slightly more modest, yet still ambitious" projection about Greek productivity, the Fund concluded that it would be reasonable to assume GDP growth averaging about 1.5 percent annually in coming years.

As for privatization, the analysis took note of what had happened since the announcement in the spring of 2011 that Greece would aim to generate €50 billion in revenue by the end of 2015. "Actual receipts through the first quarter of 2015 were €3.2 billion," the authors wrote, and they tacitly acknowledged that the original initiative was simply naive: "Experience has shown that there is deep-seated political resistance to privatization in Greece....The sale of real estate assets faces well-known obstacles including lack of a good database, disputed property rights, and problems securing needed permits for land development." Based on these inconvenient truths, "it is critical for a realistic and robust [debt sustainability analysis] to assume reduced privatization revenues…totaling about €500 million per year."

Then there was the fact that the new long-term target for Greece's primary budget surplus was lower for Syriza than for Samaras's government. Combining all the changes in the outlook "render[s] the debt dynamics unsustainable," the analysis concluded, noting that by 2022 the debt-to-GDP ratio would remain close to 140 percent — and easily a lot higher than that if events took new turns for the worse.

The IMF was making one major concession to Europe in this document: it was switching its debt sustainability methodology for Greece to the approach favoured by Klaus Regling, who as noted in chapter 17 argued that the most relevant metric was Greece's low annual payments of principal and interest. "Given the extraordinarily concessional terms that now apply to the bulk of Greece's debt, the debt/GDP ratio is not a very meaningful proxy for the forward-looking debt burden," the document said. But even using a more Regling-like system of projecting "gross financing needs" as a percent of GDP, Greek debt was shaping up as unsustainable, according to the analysis.

Coming on top of the aggravation involved in the negotiations with the Greeks, this fresh offensive by the IMF went over poorly with European officials. Cynicism was already running high in Brussels about debt sustainability analyses in general, and the IMF's in particular — which European policy makers suspected were being massaged to fit the agendas of the analyzers. The Fund's new analysis suggested to them that their cynicism was amply justified. For one thing, the Fund was no longer assuming that Greece would adhere to its program; in contrast to previous analyses, the Fund seemed to be taking for granted that Athens *would not* honour commitments to implement many structural reforms or privatizations. And what was really motivating the new, worse assumptions about long-term growth and privatization? "Many of us thought, this was artificially depressed, to prove that debt relief was needed," said one of the Europeans involved in the discussions.

Thomsen and his colleagues had strong rebuttals to these criticisms. The analysis was simply adjusting for new realities as they had unfolded, IMF officials argued. Furthermore, the Fund wasn't assuming Greek failure to adopt the whole program; crucially, the calculations incorporated full achievement, long into the future, of the 3.5 percent of GDP target for the primary budget surplus.

There lay the IMF's full answer to Varoufakis's question. Even assuming that Greece generated large enough surpluses to meet the target over a long period, remedying its debt problem would require Europe to consider options such as extending the grace period on repayments to 20 years and doubling the maturities on debt owed to European governments and institutions, according to the Fund's analysis. And the analysis contained yet another unwelcome message for Europe, concerning what would happen if Athens couldn't muster as much fiscal self-control as was being demanded of it. Suppose, the Fund asked, "the surplus target were to be reduced to 2½ percent of GDP, say because this is all that the Greek authorities could credibly commit to.…In such a case, a haircut would be needed."

The 23-page IMF analysis was not intended for publication; it was labelled "preliminary draft." But Fund officials were indignant when they saw the short shrift their gloomy assessment got from their European counterparts. A few of the Fund's figures were incorporated into a two-page document labelled "Preliminary Debt Sustainability Analysis for Greece," which was circulated to finance ministers and other European policy makers. It showed three scenarios, two of which — "Scenario A" and "Scenario B," prepared by staffers from European institutions — used assumptions considerably more optimistic than the Fund's. Under A and B, Greece would not need additional debt relief. Under "Scenario C," which was identified as the IMF's, "significant reprofiling of the stock of debt and concessional lending terms would improve sustainability."[8]

In any event, even more wholesale revision of Greece's debt outlook would soon be necessary.

8 This document, which was obtained by *The Wall Street Journal*, is available at: http://online.wsj.com/public/resources/documents/eurogroupdebtanalysis.pdf.

On the evening of Thursday, June 25, a few hours after the IMF presented its debt analysis to the Euro Working Group, Tsipras excoriated the Fund during a summit of European leaders, fulminating about its "extreme opinion." The Greek prime minister was unaware of the Fund document making the case for debt relief, and perhaps he would have been just as angry at the Fund anyway. The only concession Athens was being offered on the debt issue at that stage was a vague promise to consider relief in the future. All Tsipras knew was that the Fund was the institution giving him the hardest time about the necessity of cutting pension benefits and other such measures.

His one big hope for a deal he could swallow — persuading Merkel to broker a compromise using her clout over the institutions and other creditors — wasn't panning out. The German chancellor refused to intervene at the summit, and Tsipras endured stern lectures from the prime ministers of other countries that had undergone crises — Ireland, Portugal and Spain — about the necessity of hewing to his country's bailout terms. The next day, Merkel told reporters that she and Hollande had "asked and urged" Tsipras to accept the "extraordinarily generous" terms on offer from the three institutions.[9]

After conferring with his advisers in his hotel room on that Friday morning, Tsipras emerged to issue a brief statement deploring the use of "blackmail and ultimatums," and he then flew back to Athens. News reached Brussels that the Greek cabinet was on standby for an urgent meeting after his arrival, but the prime minister's intentions were unknown. Negotiations were still under way in EU buildings, with the media quoting European officials expressing hope that a breakthrough might still be possible, although contingency plans were also reportedly being readied to minimize the impact of Grexit on other European economies.

Late that evening, a group of Greek negotiators was meeting with European and IMF counterparts in the EU's Charlemagne Building when news flashes from Athens suddenly rendered their efforts

9 Stefan Wagstyl, Peter Spiegel and Kerin Hope, 2015, "Merkel tells Tsipras no alternative to creditors' offer," *Financial Times*, June 26.

irrelevant. Tsipras was calling a national referendum on whether to accept the institutions' proposal. As far as the Europeans could tell, the Greeks were just as shocked as anyone else at the meeting, which promptly adjourned.

Tsipras called Merkel and Hollande to inform them of the referendum, which would take place on Sunday, July 5. To their dismay, he said his government would campaign for a "no" vote, although he would respect the result. In a nationally televised speech beginning at around 1:00 a.m., he said: "I call on you to decide — with sovereignty and dignity as Greek history demands — whether we should accept the extortionate ultimatum that calls for strict and humiliating austerity without end, and without the prospect of ever standing on our own two feet, socially and financially."

Efforts to persuade European policy makers for financial lifelines pending the vote were in vain. In an emergency meeting on Sunday, the ECB Governing Council decided to hold the line against any increase in the loans of euros that had been keeping Greek banks afloat while depositors pulled their money out. Long lines at ATMs throughout Greece soon drained supplies of cash, and withdrawals were capped at €60 a day per account. The government ordered the banks shut for six days starting Monday, as the nation's central bank imposed capital controls to keep the flood of money abroad to a minimum.[10]

Would the banks reopen with euros in the accounts? Or would it be necessary for the system to dispense some new currency? Amid enormous uncertainty, Greeks were getting a foretaste of what Grexit would be like.

And so was the IMF.

10 Brian Blackstone, Nektaria Stamouli and Charles Forelle, 2015, "Greece Orders Banks Closed, Imposes Capital Controls to Stem Deposit Flight," *The Wall Street Journal,* June 28.

A long-dreaded moment for the IMF came shortly after 6:00 p.m. — the Fund's official close of business — on Tuesday, June 30, when Greece failed to make a €1.5 billion payment to the Fund due by that time. A statement by Gerry Rice, the Fund's director of communications, promptly conveyed to the media that the money was not received, and therefore "Greece is now in arrears"[11] — although most news stories and commentators used the less polite term: default.

This development came as no surprise, and did not cause any immediate financial perturbations. The Greek government barely had the cash to pay pensions and other benefits, and the failure to pay the IMF on June 30 was well-anticipated since Athens had been using a special procedure allowing the postponement of its June payments until the end of the month, as previously noted. Moreover, the missed payment to the Fund was not a formal default as defined by the three major private credit rating agencies; nor did it trigger "cross-default" provisions on other Greek government obligations; nor did it have any direct bearing on Greece's membership in the euro zone.

Still, in the annals of the IMF, June 30, 2015, will go down as an infamous date. Whatever the legal terminology, this clear case of non-repayment was on the largest loan the Fund had ever made — and the borrower was not some famine-stricken or war-torn nation in the tropics, but a member state of the European Union. For an institution that depends on its members to provide financing based on the principle that it always gets repaid, the Greek default will be hard to erase from the memories of the international community.

Befitting the solemnity of the occasion, the board was convened, partly for the purpose of formally notifying the IMF's membership and also to explain the institution's complex procedures for dealing with such cases. Although the IMF is the world's senior-most creditor, with the

11 IMF, 2015, "Statement by the IMF on Greece," Press Release No. 15/310, June 30, www.imf.org/external/np/sec/pr/2015/pr15310.htm.

uber-preferred status that comes with being a lender of last resort, it treats delinquent borrowers with a fair degree of forbearance. The use of the term "arrears" is suggestive of its approach. The assumption is that countries in arrears to the Fund will want to clear the arrears as soon as possible, because they will become virtually ineligible to obtain new loans from any source abroad. The Fund itself is prohibited under its rules from providing financial resources to a country in arrears to it; the only Fund aid such a country can receive is technical assistance. It is no coincidence that most of the countries that have landed in this predicament for extended periods were "failed states" or regimes that were essentially cutting themselves off from the rest of the world. They include Sudan, Somalia, Zimbabwe, Afghanistan and Cambodia under the Khmer Rouge. Even those countries were never subjected to the ultimate penalty that IMF members can impose in cases of "extreme and protracted" arrears by countries deemed to be "non-cooperative" — being expelled from the Fund.

Reassurances that the sky wasn't falling, and that many previous cases of arrears had been satisfactorily handled, and that Greece would surely want to clear its arrears quickly, were among the main messages conveyed by top IMF officials at the June 30 board meeting. Beneath their calm exteriors, however, they were very worried, and with good reason. Although numerous countries had fallen into arrears during the Fund's 70-year history, the amounts involved were relatively small, never exceeding $1.4 billion. Greece's arrears at the end of June 2015 were slightly larger than that, and Greek obligations to the IMF over the coming 10 years totalled $26 billion.[12] Thus a prolonged default by Athens would severely undercut the Fund's status as a super-safe repository of its members' money. The implications would not be favourable for the Fund's long-term ability to continue providing global public goods.

12 Benn Steil and Dinah Walker, 2015, "A Full Greek IMF-Debt Default Would Be Four Times All Previous Defaults Combined," Council on Foreign Relations, Geo-Graphics blog, June 24, http://blogs.cfr.org/geographics/2015/06/24/greekdefault/.

Why should anyone have been concerned that Greece might fall into prolonged default to the IMF? It was a distinct possibility if the country returned to the drachma. Its debts to all of its foreign creditors — which were denominated in hard currency — would become unbearably burdensome, and although Athens would have an incentive to make sure that at least the IMF got paid, the country might conceivably plunge into such chaos that it would renege on all of its foreign obligations for a long time. This would have presented the IMF with another predicament, in addition to the hit to its finances: it would not have been able to fulfill its duty to help a member country in profound distress, because it would remain legally prohibited from providing loans as long as Greece was in arrears.

At the time of the default, the chances for Grexit appeared as high as ever, as the battle over the referendum was generating an impassioned debate both within Greece and outside. Polls showed the Greek public sharply divided, but the forces favouring rejection of the institutions' proposal were gaining momentum, spurred on by massive rallies of people bearing signs emblazoned *Oxi* (No). Tsipras and his ministers, including Varoufakis, were assuring the populace that an *Oxi* vote was not a vote for Grexit; rather, they said, the government needed a powerful democratic mandate to extract better terms from the creditors. A number of European leaders were warning that the opposite was true — that a majority "no" vote wouldn't improve Greek leverage and would be tantamount to casting the country adrift from the common currency.

Meanwhile, the economic squeeze on the country was growing more visible by the day. Lines at ATMs remained long; throngs of elderly besieged bank entrances pleading for shuttered vaults to be opened; importers reported orders withheld from shipment, or blocked from delivery, because of their inability to pay foreign suppliers. (Some importers, to be sure, had prepared for such problems by setting up bank accounts abroad.) Rumours spread that bank deposits would be haircut as they had been in Cyprus, and although government officials dismissed those worries as groundless, many businesses and individuals were doing everything possible to drain funds from their accounts — paying tax and utility bills in advance, for example.

Amid this tumult came a bolt from the IMF. On July 2, three days before the referendum, the Fund publicly released the full debt sustainability analysis that Thomsen had presented to the Euro Working Group. Aside from the document's substance, its issuance — like Blanchard's blog post — evinced the Fund's determination to act independently of Europe and to be seen doing so.

Greek officials exulted that on this issue at least, their arguments were getting high-level validation. "[T]his latest DSA (debt sustainability analysis) by the IMF could not be blunter," Varoufakis wrote on his blog. "In fact, it is even 'ruder' to official Europe, that remains in denial of the need for any debt relief, than we — the SYRIZA government — would imagine being."[13]

It was unusual, if not unprecedented, for the Fund to disclose a preliminary draft of such a document, and the move came only after a behind-the-scenes tussle. European members of the Fund's board strenuously objected, arguing that the analysis would obviously give aid and comfort to the *Oxi* forces. But Lagarde, Lipton and others retorted that the Fund's integrity would be compromised if the analysis remained secret. The aforementioned European document with the three scenarios — which, in the Fund's view, mischaracterized its analysis — had been published on the Greek government's website. How would it look if, after the referendum, Greek voters found out that the IMF analysis was much more dire than they had been led to believe? This was the case that came before the full board — and with strong backing from the US director, Mark Sobel, the decision to release the analysis was approved.

Not only was the IMF barred from lending to Greece while the country was in arrears. The debt analysis implied that the Fund's role in Greece might be curtailed for even more fundamental reasons, according to a senior IMF official who briefed reporters in a conference call on the

13 This blog post of Varoufakis's, titled "IMF backs (ever so peculiarly) the SYRIZA government's debt assessment," is available at: http://yanisvaroufakis.eu/2015/07/03/imf-backs-ever-so-peculiarly-the-syriza-governments-debt-assessment/.

day the document was disclosed. (The official's identity was protected under the ground rules of the call.[14]) "We cannot go to our board… unless we have a comprehensive program" that includes significant debt relief, this official said. "A program that is sustainable in a medium-term context…requires, on the one hand, that Greece adopts reforms that credibly deliver the targets to be set for [themselves]. And two, on the other hand, that the Europeans agree to a debt operation that helps bring debt on a sustainable path. So before we have both of these things in place, we would not be able to go to our board and say we have a program" that meets Fund standards.

Imagine — the IMF might walk away from any new rescues of Greece and leave the job to Europe. This was an idea that had been bruited around for some time, both inside and outside the Fund. Various formulations were suggested; under one option, the IMF would reduce its role to providing only advice and technical support, while the ESM could assume the Fund's Greek exposure.

The growing appeal that such ideas had for many of the people working at IMF headquarters showed how the institution had come full circle since the spring of 2010, when active involvement in the Greek crisis was a top priority for Strauss-Kahn. But the Fund was not going to extricate itself so easily. It could not ignore the demands of Germany and the other northern Europeans for the continuation of a major Fund role. Nor could the Fund simply shirk its responsibility to help clean up a mess that it had some hand in making. Greece was the IMF's proverbial tar baby.

By 7:00 p.m. on July 5, when polls for the referendum closed, crowds were already starting to assemble in Syntagma Square and other city centres throughout Greece. As the result became clear — 61.3 percent for *Oxi,* an unexpected landslide — the swelling mass of celebrants erupted in a carnival of dancing and singing, strumming of bouzoukis,

14 I was given a transcript of the conference call, but am also obliged to honour the confidentiality of the senior official.

chanting of anti-austerity slogans and waving of Greek flags. Tsipras hailed the vote, telling his compatriots, "You made a very brave choice. The mandate you gave me is not a mandate for rupture with Europe, but a mandate to strengthen our negotiating position to seek a viable solution." European leaders, although taken aback, maintained their position that Athens would gain nothing from the referendum and might well lose all. "This result is very regrettable for the future of Greece," Dijsselbloem said in a statement, and Slovakia's Peter Kažmir tweeted: "The nightmare of the 'euro-architects' that a country could leave the club seems like a realistic scenario after Greece voted No today."

For all their outward jubilation, Tsipras and his team were already scrambling that evening to tamp down Grexit risks. The Greek prime minister called Hollande in Paris, saying, "I want to stay in Europe and in the euro," to which the French President replied: "Help me help you." Hollande urged Tsipras to submit ambitious proposals as soon as possible; Tsipras said he would do so.[15]

An even more unmistakable sign of the chastened mood that was taking hold among the Greek leadership was the departure of Varoufakis. The finance minister has recalled that he was "elated" at the referendum result, and revelled in the "electric atmosphere" of the huge demonstration in the streets, but upon joining the rest of the cabinet at the Maximos (the prime minister's office), "the whole sensation simply vanished....the sensation I got was one of terror: 'What do we do *now?*'"[16]

It was a good question. Greece needed money very soon if it was to avoid a default that would dramatically heighten the danger to the

15 The exchange between Tsipras and Hollande was reported in Matthew Dalton, William Horobin and Stacy Meichtry, 2015, "France Intercedes on Greece's Behalf to Try to Hold Eurozone Together," *The Wall Street Journal,* July 9. That article provides some of the information on which this section is based, as does Peter Ludlow, 2015, "Dealing with Greece: Tusk's ultimatum and its consequences," EuroComment, Preliminary Evaluation 2015/6 and 7, which is particularly illuminating on events during the Eurogroup and summit meetings.

16 Christos Tsiolkas, 2015, "Greek Tragedy," *Monthly* (Australia).

country's membership in the monetary union. Specifically, a payment of €3.5 billion to the ECB was due on July 20. Falling into arrears to the IMF was one thing; defaulting to the ultimate supplier of euros was something else entirely, because the authorities in Frankfurt had the power to withdraw all of the emergency liquidity provided to Greek banks. Varoufakis had been making the case, both publicly and within the high councils of government, that Greece could win a settlement on its terms by squarely confronting Europe with the prospect of default on the hundreds of billions of euros of debt that Athens owed. But as he later acknowledged, he was "a minority of one"[17] in the cabinet; his colleagues saw such an approach as foolhardy.

Varoufakis therefore stepped down in the early morning hours of July 6, although it might be more accurate to say that he was sacked.[18] "Soon after the announcement of the referendum results, I was made aware of a certain preference by some Eurogroup participants, and assorted 'partners,' for my 'absence' from its meetings, an idea that the Prime Minister judged to be potentially helpful to him in reaching an agreement," he wrote in his blog that morning. "For this reason I am leaving the Ministry of Finance today. I shall wear the creditors' loathing with pride." His replacement was Euclid Tsakalotos, a long-time Syriza stalwart but much more modest and low-key in personality, as European and IMF officials had already discovered since he took charge of the Greek negotiating team in late April. The 55-year-old Tsakalotos spoke with a mellifluous British accent, having spent much of his childhood in the United Kingdom, where he got his Ph.D. from Oxford before moving back to Greece with his family in 1993.

The IMF did not play a particularly noteworthy role in the events of the week that followed the referendum, partly because of the arrears

17 This comment of Varoufakis's came in his interview for the *#ThisIsACoup* documentary (see footnote 13 in chapter 18).

18 It is worth noting that Varoufakis had previously committed to resigning if the outcome of the referendum was a "yes" vote — that is, the opposite of the actual outcome.

issue. But those events are important to this book's narrative because of how close the situation came to a breakdown that could have badly shaken the Fund's financial foundations.

At the centre of the action that week was Donald Tusk, the former Polish prime minister who was in his eighth month at the presidency of the European Council. At Tusk's behest, leaders of the 19 euro-zone countries met in Brussels for an emergency summit on Tuesday, July 7, with plans for a second summit on Sunday the 12th that would represent the truly final chance for striking an accord that would keep Greece in the euro — or, if no such deal was forthcoming, a discussion of how to cope with Grexit.

At the Tuesday summit, Tsipras came under a barrage of complaints from his peers that the referendum had made it more difficult for them to reach an accommodation with him. "They were very, very critical to the Greek prime minister, basically saying, 'What basis is there to work together for the future? You've gone to a referendum on the basis of an agreement that wasn't even an agreement, proposals that weren't basically agreed, you tell your people to vote no and you promise them there will be a better deal; it's impossible,'" Dijsselbloem told *The Wall Street Journal* a few days later.[19]

Tsipras emphasized that the "no" vote was not aimed at the euro, but rather as a message about the Greek people's desire for an end to their suffering — and although he got assurances from the others that they shared his desire for Greece to keep the common currency, he also heard warnings that Grexit should be considered an imminent threat. He agreed to submit proposals no later than Thursday, which would be evaluated as usual by the three institutions formerly known as the Troika. This posed an extraordinary challenge, because as Tsipras was repeatedly reminded, his government was no longer seeking a mere €7.2 billion disbursement from the old bailout; that program had expired. Greece would be applying for an entirely new, multi-

19 Gabriele Steinhauser, 2015, "Eurogroup Head Dijsselbloem on the Race to Find a Plan for Greece," *The Wall Street Journal*, July 17.

year bailout, under the strict policy conditions required by the ESM. Normally such a process would take place over the course of weeks or even months rather than a few days. And Athens would have to accept at least as tough terms as the Greek people had just rejected, if not tougher — or so Tsipras was admonished, as was Tsakalotos at a Eurogroup meeting earlier in the day.

After the summit, Tusk told the media: "The stark reality is that we have only five days left to find the ultimate agreement. Until now, I have avoided talking about deadlines. But tonight I have to say loud and clear that the final deadline ends this week."

As promised, Greek officials did send a package of proposed actions by Thursday — and it provided indisputable evidence that Tsipras was hoisting the white flag. This package was much more polished and comprehensive than previous submissions, in part because the Greeks were getting drafting help from a senior policy maker in the French Treasury as well as Commission staffers. More important, it contained a 13-page list of "prior actions" (measures that Parliament would enact before any aid was granted) that was very similar to the last proposal the creditors had offered before the referendum. Athens essentially conceded to the creditors' demands on divisive issues such as raising the effective retirement age to 67 by 2022 and phasing out the solidarity grant for low-income pensioners. The proposal also set the same target for the long-term primary budget surplus, 3.5 percent of GDP starting in 2018, although with the caveat that the targets for the intervening years might have to be eased "given the deteriorating economic circumstances."

The next day, the three institutions pronounced the package a satisfactory basis on which to proceed in discussions scheduled for the weekend. Prospects for keeping Greece from crashing out of the euro zone appeared to be improving. Then, however, came a much more negative verdict from one player whose judgment could not be ignored — Schäuble.

The German finance minister was still of the view that the euro zone would be better off without a non-reformable Greece, and he saw

Grexit as arguably the least-bad option for the Greek economy as well. A debt haircut, not permissible for Greece if it stayed in the monetary union, could be arranged once Athens left; so could large-scale humanitarian aid. He was understandably dubious about the idea that the Syriza government, which was elected on an anti-bailout platform and had now gone further by securing the "no" vote in the referendum, would faithfully implement a package of measures like the ones it was proposing.

Mistrust of the Greek state, in other words, remained a huge problem, as became painfully clear when the Eurogroup assembled on Saturday, July 11. Before them was an estimate, prepared by the three institutions, showing that the new bailout would require approximately €85 billion in loans over three years — money that would have to be lent at highly concessional terms, with repayments put off until far in the future.

Schäuble tabled two provocative proposals, which garnered support from several of Germany's northern European allies. First, Greek assets worth up to €50 billion would be transferred to an "external and independent fund" — a Luxembourg-based institution that Schäuble himself chaired was cited as a good candidate — and the assets would be privatized over time, with the proceeds used to decrease Greek debt. But if Greece did not want to accept the terms creditors were demanding, Greece would be offered terms for a "time out from the euro area" of five years or more.

These proposals had all the hallmarks of a Grexit-forcing ploy. Since the notion that Greece could reap a large amount from privatization had been shown to be fanciful, the motivation driving supporters of the first proposal is open to question. One justification was to compel Athens in a highly visible way to make more concessions for the sake of getting a new bailout; a widely shared sentiment was that the Greeks had worsened their mess by calling the referendum, and they ought to pay for it somehow. Or perhaps, as some theorize, the supporters were conniving to present Tsipras with a demand so offensive that he could never accept, which in turn would lead to the second of Schäuble's proposals — Grexit. French officials strove mightily to quash any official endorsement of the time-out plan, but to their horror they realized that even Merkel, who had overruled Schäuble regarding Grexit in the past, might be warming to his plan. "We knew Germany could go far to exert pressure on Greece, but maybe not this far," French Finance Minister Michel Sapin later told the *Financial Times*,[20] and Hollande observed: "There was in Germany a rather strong pressure for Grexit."[21]

For nine hours of often ill-tempered debate, the finance ministers grappled over the wording of a draft text that would be presented to the leaders at their climactic Sunday summit. Although they commended Tsakalotos as vastly preferable to Varoufakis as an interlocutor, the hawks — with Schäuble in the lead — insisted that the text needed tightening to counteract the lack of trustworthiness in Athens. Sapin was in the fore of rebutting such accusations against the Greeks. "They're taking huge risks. Maybe it's time to start having confidence," the Frenchman contended. When tempers started to fray late in the evening, with Schäuble snapping at Draghi, Dijsselbloem adjourned the meeting shortly before midnight and suggested everyone get some sleep. A group of top-level officials stayed up to draft a new text reflecting the input of Schäuble and others, with a number of passages — including the privatization fund and the time-out offer — in square brackets to denote that they were in dispute.

The summit, which commenced at 4:00 p.m. Sunday, July 12, was thus bound to take a long time, and it did — until almost 9:00 a.m. the next morning. Still, few could have foreseen the odd way in which the majority of that time would be spent. For nearly 10 of the 17 hours, five people — Tusk, Merkel, Hollande, Tsipras and Tsakalotos — met separately in the Salon du Président on the eighth floor of the Council building to handle the most contentious issues, leaving 16 other national leaders and the heads of the IMF, ECB, European Commission and Eurogroup to cool their heels.

20 Anne-Sylvaine Chassany, James Politi and Peter Spiegel, 2015, "Greece clash sparks fears over German power," *Financial Times*, July 17.

21 Anne-Sylvaine Chassany, Alex Barker and Duncan Robinson, 2015, "Greece talks: 'Sorry, but there is no way you are leaving this room,'" *Financial Times*, July 13.

Tsipras was in no position at that point to contest most of the substantive economic measures that his government was committing to take; Greece's own proposal earlier in the week had settled most of those. But there was only so far he could go in bending to the will of the creditors, especially on matters where Greek national pride was at stake. Anguish among Syriza cadres over the government's U-turn after the referendum was palpable, and the prime minister needed to salvage as many shreds of dignity as he could, while standing firm against egregious affronts.

Even after seven hours, therefore, Tsipras was refusing to yield on several key points, and at 11:30 p.m. Tusk adjourned the main summit pending the results of a breakout session in his office among the aforementioned group of five. For another four-and-a-half hours the small group continued wrangling, and although Tusk emerged at around 4:00 a.m. to inform the rest of the summiteers that an agreement was close, Tsipras left to make some phone calls to Athens. When he returned, the deal was off, and starting at 5:45 a.m. another breakout round — which would drag on for three hours — commenced among Tusk, Merkel, Hollande, Tsipras and Tsakalotos.

The IMF's role in the new bailout was one of the main sticking points. Tsipras wanted to omit any requirement for Greece to request Fund involvement. His anti-IMF position confounded a number of European policy makers, given the Fund's outspokenness on the necessity of debt relief, but fury was still running high in Athens (especially on the left) over the Fund's insistence on pension cuts and labour market reforms. Lagarde herself made little effort to preserve an IMF role; she noted that she could not engage in negotiations in any case until arrears were cleared. But she didn't have to stand up for her institution, because Merkel and her allies were as adamant as ever on the issue. "It's nice to be in the middle of so many desires," Lagarde joked, according to notes of the meeting taken by a participant, and in the end the Greeks settled for wording on a request for IMF involvement that sounded slightly less imperative.

The privatization fund was a much more combustible subject — and here was where the summit came to the brink of failure. Merkel conceded that the fund could be located in Greece and managed by Greek officials; the idea of putting it in Luxembourg was so blatant an insult to Greek sovereignty that a number of other European leaders rallied to Tsipras's side. But that still left open the hotly disputed question of how the €50 billion in revenue would be used. The German chancellor wanted it earmarked for paying down Greek debt, as per Schäuble's plan; Tsipras was willing to accept the creation of such a new fund only if the money could be invested in the Greek economy. They were able to move a little closer to agreement by stipulating that €25 billion would go toward recapitalizing Greek banks, and under prodding from Tusk they edged a little closer still on how the remaining €25 billion could be used. But then both leaders said they could go no further, asked for a halt and got up to leave — which Tusk refused to allow.

It was then about 7:00 a.m., and Tusk believed that a complete rift was "really possible or probable." As he put it later in an interview with the *Financial Times:*

> For me, it was absolutely clear this was the end of the negotiation. In fact, they wanted to stop this summit, but they were not ready to say "this is the end," and it was an excuse. But it was very spontaneous. It's also why it was so dangerous, because it was an authentic reaction, fatigue, also irritation. Both of them were absolutely sure they compromised too much.[22]

The difference between Merkel and Tsipras was relatively inconsequential at that point — essentially a matter of about €2.5 billion. The German chancellor wanted €10 billion from the privatization fund earmarked for investment, while the Greek prime minister was holding out for €15 billion. Neither of them would move to a compromise of €12.5 billion, Tusk continued, so "I told them, 'If you stop this negotiation, I'm ready to say publicly: Europe is close to catastrophe because of €2.5 billion.'"

It should come as no surprise that the difference between the two figures was split. The summit could therefore conclude with Greece

22 Peter Spiegel, 2015, "Donald Tusk interview: the annotated transcript," *Financial Times*, Brussels blog, July 16.

still in the euro zone; the Schäuble time-out plan was excised from the final summit communiqué, much to the relief of the French.

Readers may well wonder what Greek leaders say about why they surrendered so much — not just on the privatization fund, but on many other matters, accepting terms so similar to those rejected in the referendum. Despite having swept into office on promises to end austerity, secure debt relief and banish the Troika, Tsipras was effectively submitting to another major dose of austerity, more debt and continued foreign domination over his country's sovereignty.

The alternative — Grexit — would have been worse for the very people whose cause Syriza championed, Tsakalotos explained in an interview for a TV documentary. "The banks would have failed," he said. "That would have had the biggest impact on the poorest of the poor. The rich and middle class had already taken their money out….So the biggest impact would be on those who had only 1,000, 2,000, 5,000 euros."[23]

Tsipras gave a similar answer, asserting that he feared "the collapse of the banks first and then the collapse of the economy." Pressed on why he didn't just walk away from the summit, he replied:

> If I walked away on this night, probably I would have become a hero for one night, maybe two or three, but it would have been a true disaster for the next days and nights, not only for me but for the majority of the Greek people. So it was a very difficult dilemma: My heart and soul told me to leave, but my mind told me I had to find a solution, even though I knew this solution was very difficult and tough.[24]

23 Interview for the *#ThisIsACoup* documentary, episode 3"Testimonies: Euclid Tsakalotos," available at: www.youtube.com/watch?v=L6YNlI8T4RE.

24 Interview for the *#ThisIsACoup* documentary, episode 4, "Surrender or Die," available at: www.youtube.com/watch?v=lWjRyq7KIR4.

It may seem petty, in view of the momentous events of July 13, 2015, to devote attention to another development, relatively trivial by comparison, involving the IMF that day. But note of it must be taken in a book that focuses on the Fund.

By coincidence, another payment owed by Greece to the IMF fell due on July 13, and for a second time Greece failed to pay the amount, which was €456 million, bringing its arrears to a total of about €2 billion. To make matters worse, Greece honoured a payment of about $95 million due that day to foreign holders of private bonds — specifically, some of the bondholders who, like billionaire Kenneth Dart, had declined to submit to the debt restructuring of 2012.[25] This was a rational decision on the part of the Greek finance ministry, since failure to pay the bondholders would have triggered immediate default claims, while the IMF was willing to wait. But what inference might be drawn from the fact that Greece gave priority to paying holdout private creditors? The Fund's preferred-creditor status was still intact, to be sure. The episode was nevertheless emblematic of the battering the Greek crisis has dealt to the Fund's standing as a scrupulously prudent steward of its members' money.

The far more important question, of course, was whether the new bailout — Greece's third — would succeed or whether it would go the way of the previous two. And for the IMF, the related question was whether, and how, it ought to be involved in this undertaking or whether it could find some way to dissociate itself.

On July 14, the IMF released a three-page document that provided discouraging insights about what would be required for the program's success. It was a memo updating the previous debt sustainability analysis, based on recent developments.[26] "The events of the past two weeks — the closure of banks and imposition of capital controls — are exacting a heavy toll on the banking system and the economy, leading to a further significant deterioration in debt sustainability," the IMF memo said.

25 Finbarr Flynn and Tesun Oh, 2015, "Greece Repays Samurai Bonds as Deal Reached with Creditors," Bloomberg News, July 13.

26 IMF, 2015, "Greece: An Update of IMF Staff's Preliminary Public Debt Sustainability Analysis," Country Report 15/186, July 14, www.imf.org/external/pubs/ft/scr/2015/cr15186.pdf.

"Greece's debt can only be made sustainable through debt relief measures that go far beyond what Europe has been willing to consider so far."

It was still too early to assess the economic damage with much precision, the memo's authors wrote, but it was possible to adjust the previous analysis "mechanically" using rough calculations, including the estimate that the new bailout would require about €85 billion in loans through 2018. Under those assumptions, "Debt would peak at close to 200 percent of GDP in the next two years," and it would still be about 170 percent of GDP in 2022, the memo said. Even using the gross financing needs approach favoured by Regling and other European officials, the debt burden would be well above the level deemed safe.

If Europe continued to eschew haircuts in favour of giving debt relief in other ways, the memo said, "there would have to be a very dramatic extension" of repayment dates, "with grace periods of say, 30 years" — meaning Greece would not make any payments of interest or principal for several decades.

The release of the memo was an unmistakable rebuke to the tepid promise on debt relief that Greece received in the July 13 summit statement. Using wording that reiterated previous pledges, the summit statement said the euro area "stands ready to consider, if necessary, possible additional measures (possible longer grace and payment periods) aiming at ensuring that gross financing needs remain at a sustainable level." Even that "consideration" would come only after "full implementation" of Greece's commitments, as assessed in the first review of the program.[27]

One damning passage in the IMF's memo caught the eye of Peter Doyle, an ex-Fund economist who had left the institution three years earlier in a blaze of recrimination, accusing his former employer of "European bias" and a multitude of other sins that had led to failings in the euro zone and elsewhere.[28]

27 European Council, 2015, "Euro Summit statement," July 12, www.consilium.europa.eu/en/press/press-releases/2015/07/12-euro-summit-statement-greece/.

28 Nina Dos Santos, 2012, "Departing IMF economist blasts fund for eurozone 'failure'; Lagarde is 'tainted,'" cnn.com, July 20, http://edition.cnn.com/2012/07/19/business/imf-economist-letter/.

Doyle was amused to see the Fund revealing its skepticism that the Greek government could exercise exceptional fiscal discipline over a long period. In a section on "downside risks," the memo said: "Greece is expected to maintain primary surpluses for the next several decades of 3.5 percent of GDP. Few countries have managed to do so."

The thing was, the IMF had blithely gone along with even bigger primary surplus targets in prior years, ranging between 4.5 and 6.5 percent of GDP, as Doyle noted in a guest blog post for the *Financial Times*.[29] The Fund's debt analyses — and its programs — "presumed that Greece would rapidly attain and secure unprecedented primary balance surpluses, implying sustained expenditure cuts and taxes rises which would make what the UK has been through since 2010 look like a cakewalk," Doyle wrote. By admitting that the new 3.5 percent target was almost certainly unattainable, he concluded, the Fund "thereby acknowledges the complete nonsense of all its prior DSA's" — indeed, the complete nonsense of Greece's prior programs.

In any event, the IMF was not going to join in the third rescue, at least not right away and not without major modifications. On July 29, Lagarde told the board that the bailout did not meet the Fund's standards for new lending, although Fund staffers would join their European counterparts in negotiations with the Greeks.

Arrears were no longer a reason for the IMF to refrain from lending; Greece had gotten a quick infusion of cash from European institutions and repaid its outstanding delinquencies to the Fund on July 20. Rather, the problem was "very large" differences with Europe over debt relief, and a lack of faith in Greece's ability to implement reforms, according to a confidential summary of the meeting that was disclosed in the *Financial Times*.[30]

29 Peter Doyle, 2015, "IMF Debt Sustainability Assessments of Greece (and others)," *Financial Times*, FT Alphaville, July 15.

30 Peter Spiegel, 2015, "Greece disqualified from new IMF bailout, board told," *Financial Times*, July 30.

The IMF staff concluded that the program did not meet two of the criteria in the No More Argentinas rule. The staff wasn't persuaded that Greece had the "institutional and political capacity" for broad-scale reforms of the kind required under the program. Nor could the staff certify a "high probability" that Greece's debt was sustainable.

"Greece wants to decide on some important reforms only in the fall and the Europeans only want to deal with the debt issue after the first review because they first want to rebuild trust," stated the confidential summary. "The differences between the IMF's thinking about the debt issue and what the Europeans are currently discussing are very large."

As a result, the IMF would decide whether to participate in the program only during a "stage two" phase, after Greece had agreed on comprehensive reforms and the Europeans had offered an adequate amount of debt relief. When directors from Asia, Brazil and Canada admonished Lagarde about the need to "protect the reputation of the Fund," she essentially echoed their concerns, according to the summary, which quoted Lagarde as "stress[ing] that in their engagement they have to be mindful about the reputation of the Fund."

As this book went into the final stages of preparation in May 2016, Greece was in the throes of yet another unsettling round of brinkmanship over its finances. Nearly every element of the previous five years' dramas was recurring, with one big exception — the IMF's truth telling, the ruthlessness of which was greater than ever.

Once again, the Greeks needed the disbursement of several billion euros from their creditors so that default could be averted on pending debt payments in the summer. Once again, the government was ramming a package of spending cuts and tax increases through Parliament in an effort to satisfy the terms of its latest bailout, while trade unions called a general strike and protesters tangled with police on Syntagma Square. (The irony of anti-austerity protests against a radical left government was lost on no one.) And once again, the IMF was at odds with European policy makers over what sort of measures Greece should be required to adopt and how much debt relief should be provided. Germany and its northern European allies were simultaneously rejecting the Fund's demands for debt relief while insisting that it remain involved in the program. Greek officials were denouncing the IMF as the main obstacle to the kind of deal they wanted, even though the Fund's preferred approach would ease the overall degree of austerity in the long run. The economy remained stagnant, well over 20 percent of the workforce remained unemployed, and debt still stood at €321 billion.

This time, however, the IMF was specifying with greater precision, openness and resolution what would be necessary for its participation in the program. In an April 14 news conference at the spring 2016 meetings of the Fund and the World Bank, Lagarde said the primary budget surplus that Greece was expected to generate in the future would have to be lowered to a reasonable level. The Fund could reluctantly go along with demands for Athens to attain a 3.5 percent of GDP surplus in 2018, as the program envisioned, provided the Greek government took credible budget and tax measures to get there. "What we find highly unrealistic, on the other hand, is the assumption that this primary surplus of 3.5 percent can be maintained over decades. That just will not happen," she said.[31]

A couple of weeks later, Lagarde sent a letter to European finance ministers on the eve of a Eurogroup meeting, making her case even more forcefully. In this letter, which was promptly leaked,[32] she dismissed as "not very credible [and] also undesirable" the budget and tax actions Greece was taking to reach the surplus target for 2018. (This was why the Tsipras government was upset with the Fund.) More important, she set forth the IMF's idea of an achievable target for the long-term primary surplus — 1.5 percent of GDP; the 3.5 percent figure was "higher than what we consider economically and socially

31 IMF, 2016, "Press Briefing of the Managing Director," April 14, www.imf.org/external/np/tr/2016/tr041416.htm.

32 Peter Spiegel, 2016, "IMF tells eurozone to start Greek debt talks," *Financial Times*, May 6.

sustainable," the managing director wrote. The much more modest surplus target, of course, implied the need for much greater amounts of debt restructuring.

Then Lagarde came as close as possible to threatening that the IMF would pull out of the Greek rescue. "For us to support Greece with a new IMF arrangement, it is essential that the financing and debt relief from Greece's European partners are based on fiscal targets that are realistic," she wrote. "We insist on such assurances in all our programs, and we cannot deviate from this basic principle in the case of Greece."

All of this IMF huffing and puffing resulted in nothing more than another deal to buy time. Trumping all other considerations was the need to minimize financial turbulence during a period when the region was beset by new afflictions. Greece was undergoing severe travails coping with an influx of migrants from conflicts in the Islamic world, and Europe was struggling with myriad political strains, notably the pending vote in the United Kingdom on "Brexit" from the European Union.

Accordingly, an 11-hour meeting of the Eurogroup on May 24 ended with Greece assured of receiving a €10.3 billion disbursement from the ESM, enough to make its summer debt payments. European officials agreed to start discussing debt relief, and to consider revising Greece's long-term primary surplus targets, but they limited themselves to vague promises about actions that might be taken many months or years down the road. For its part, the IMF gave lukewarm approval, asserting that it would put up money only if an analysis to be conducted later in 2016 indicated that Athens was enacting sufficient measures and Europe was providing adequate debt relief to generate sustainability.

It is unclear how this matter will be resolved. Whatever the outcome, Lagarde's words raised some obvious questions: why had the IMF waited until this point to stake out such a tough stance? And why was the Fund only now deeming Greece's long-term primary budget surplus targets to be economically and socially unsustainable? Why had it acceded in the past to much larger surplus targets?

A charitable answer would go as follows: in the early stages of the crisis, the Fund felt that if the Greek authorities expressed confidence in their ability to meet the targets, they should be given a chance to try. And only later, when experience with the Greek political system showed how misplaced that confidence was, could the Fund act resolutely in the face of European resistance.

A less charitable answer would be that the IMF took too long — both for Greece's sake and its own — to muster sufficient pluck.

20

TIME TO RECTIFY TRAVESTY

"My guest tonight: the managing director of the International Monetary Fund!" Jon Stewart, the host of *The Daily Show*, announced on the February 23, 2015, episode, eliciting boisterous cheers from the studio audience as Lagarde emerged, clad in a black leather jacket, dark slacks and a brightly coloured scarf. When she settled into her chair at Stewart's desk, a shout of "We love you, Christine!" rang out, prompting Stewart to crack, "You find that, I imagine, everywhere. Anytime the International Monetary Fund is out there." To appreciative gales of laughter, Lagarde and Stewart bantered briefly before launching into a discussion of legal and cultural impediments to women's economic advancement, an issue that the managing director has put on the IMF's agenda on the grounds that it is inextricably linked to the prosperity of nations. Her appearance on the famously edgy program was a PR tour de force that would have boggled the minds of Fund press officers back in the day of Lagarde's staid predecessors.[1]

Such rock-star treatment has become almost standard for Lagarde, who hopscotches around the globe to laudatory media coverage, lending authority to her pronouncements large and small. Her commanding aura, leavened with femininity and the élan with which she makes her points, are by no means the only reasons for this phenomenon; also fuelling her

1 Available at: www.cc.com/episodes/tplmmj/the-daily-show-with-jon-stewart-february-23--2015---christine-lagarde-season-20-ep-20064.

popularity are her initiatives for the IMF to focus more on gender disparity and other issues, including income inequality and climate change. Some at IMF headquarters, while agreeing with her basic positions, believe that such matters belong under the purview of other international institutions (the United Nations, World Bank, and the Organization for Economic Cooperation and Development, among others), and should not be allowed to distract the Fund from its challenging core mission of global macroeconomic and financial stability. Lagarde has overcome the naysayers, who cannot help but admit that the IMF reaps benefits from her punchy discourse, such as this line on the gender issue: "Women's empowerment is not just a fundamentally moral cause, it is also an absolute economic no-brainer." Unsurprisingly, she was a shoo-in for a second term as managing director. Within seconds after the formal selection process opened in January 2016, the British Treasury nominated her, followed swiftly by endorsements from a host of other capitals, including many in emerging markets.

At a time when the managing director enjoys such adulation, concern about the IMF's place in the world might appear incongruous. Without doubt, Lagarde's leadership style has enhanced the Fund's public profile. Whatever stain was left by the May 2011 events at the New York Sofitel has long since vanished. But all the bon mots in the world cannot erase the more substantive developments involving the Fund's role in Europe both before and after Strauss-Kahn's departure, nor the harm that resulted.

A more meaningful gauge of the IMF's institutional potency is the criticism it has undergone from economists who previously worked there regarding its policies in the euro-zone crisis. For an organization that puts a high premium on staff maintaining policy cohesion when communicating with outsiders, the intensity of this denunciation is remarkable, and is a testament to the impact the crisis has had on the Fund.

"The IMF...has been dragged along in an unprecedented set-up as a junior partner within Europe, used as a cover for the continent's policy makers and its independence lost," Ousmene Mandeng, an ex-Fund staffer, wrote in a

Financial Times op-ed.[2] Both of the economists who headed the mission to Ireland in 2010 have also levelled blasts at their former employer; Ashoka Mody was quoted in a *Financial Times* article saying, "The crisis has brought out the worst in the Fund. The Fund has been subservient to its major shareholders,"[3] while Ajai Chopra told *The Wall Street Journal* that "the entire Greek saga since 2010 has been hugely damaging to the IMF's reputation."[4] James Boughton, who retired in 2012 as the Fund's official historian (and is now a colleague of mine at the Centre for International Governance Innovation [CIGI]), lamented in a CIGI paper that the Fund "ceded its role as the primary arbiter of policy conditions" in Europe, the result being that its "authority and credibility have been...diminished."[5]

Perhaps the most damning reproof has come from Susan Schadler,[6] the European Department's former deputy director, who authored a series of articles and papers drawing attention to the breach of the Fund's rules in May 2010 that enabled the first rescue of Greece to proceed. In one article, Schadler accused the Fund of "bowing to the exigencies of European politics," the result being that "it cobbled together low-probability assumptions about future growth, how quickly tax systems could be reformed, how rapidly government spending could be cut and when markets would re-engage in heavily indebted countries."[7]

Any suspicion that such negative commentary might stem from resentment by disgruntled ex-employees should be put aside. These are people who care passionately about the IMF and believe it ought to be empowered

2 Ousmène Mandeng, 2013, "The IMF must quit the troika to survive," *Financial Times*, April 17.

3 Shawn Donnan, 2015, "IMF: Lagarde eyes new act in Greek drama," *Financial Times*, August 13.

4 Ian Talley, 2015, "Greek default deals blow to IMF," *The Wall Street Journal*, June 30.

5 James Boughton, 2015, *The IMF as Just One Creditor: Who's in Charge When a Country Can't Pay?*, CIGI Papers No. 66, April.

6 Schadler, like Boughton, is a CIGI senior fellow, as well as a nonresident senior fellow with the Atlantic Council.

7 Susan Schadler, 2012, "The IMF has been cut adrift," *Economics Blog* (*The Guardian*), November 7, www.theguardian.com/business/economics-blog/2012/nov/07/imf-cut-adrift-eurozone-crisis.

to succeed at its mission of providing the global public good of financial stability. Having become disillusioned at seeing the Fund fall short, they decided that as knowledgeable insiders they have a duty to speak out in the hope of fostering progress toward the ideal. Although some IMF officials bridle at seeing their institution taken to task so harshly by ex-colleagues, many see the criticism for what it is — an effort at prodding the Fund to live up to the principles that led to its founding in 1944.

This book has been written in a similar spirit. As should be obvious from preceding chapters, the research I conducted led me to conclude that the criticisms by Mandeng, Schadler et al. were, by and large, on the mark, and that it was essential to convey the story in all its good, bad and ugly detail to inform a wide audience of the need for action by the international community. To repeat a point made at the outset, the euro-zone crisis — the biggest the IMF has ever faced — showed that a strong and effective Fund is more critical than ever before. By seeing how and why the Fund failed and was undermined at certain crucial junctures during this crisis, those who recognize the value of the Fund's multilateral mission will be better equipped to offer the right kind of support. The events I have chronicled may lead to many conclusions; the following are the major points I believe deserve highlighting in a recapitulation of what went wrong, how things might have gone better and how the system ought to be fixed.

One word aptly describes the IMF's role as junior partner in the Troika: travesty.

The arrangement struck in the spring of 2010, when the Troika was established, was an original sin that led to many others. Even though the Fund was putting up a minority share of the loan package for Greece, it should have participated as senior partner, with the power to determine the terms and conditions of the rescue, based on an understanding that it would consult European policy makers without being obliged to defer to them or reach compromises with them. This is not to say that compromise between the IMF and major shareholders is necessarily bad; as an institution with political masters the Fund has been obliged to reach some sort of accommodation with them in virtually every crisis it has confronted. But when it came to the euro zone, the Europeans should not have been "the leaders," as Strauss-Kahn put it in his meetings with them in the spring of 2010; the working assumption all along should have been the opposite.[8]

8 In late July 2016, shortly before this book was to be sent to the printer, the IMF's Independent Evaluation Office (IEO) published a lengthy report that, although blistering in its criticism of the Fund's role in the euro-zone crisis, took issue with the phrase "junior partner" in characterizing the Fund's status in the Troika. The report's scope did not encompass the entire crisis through 2015; it covered the first Greek program and the programs for Ireland and Portugal, as well as surveillance issues. Its publication came too late for its insights to be reflected in this book, but most of the material and arguments were already familiar to me.

The report stated: "[T]he IMF was not a junior partner in the troika if the troika is defined as a device for inter-agency coordination. The IMF was not a senior partner, either — which contrasted with the IMF's customary sole or lead role in its lending to emerging markets and developing countries. It is the consensus view of all interviewed for this evaluation that each member of the troika had a veto power. Thus, the troika arrangement was effectively viewed as consisting of coequal partners."

I found this conclusion somewhat perplexing. It is true that some of the officials involved in managing the crisis dispute the term "junior partner," and as repeatedly noted in this book the IMF gained substantially greater leverage in the latter stages of the crisis. But a number of Fund staffers involved in the crisis viewed their institution's role as effectively junior — see, for example, Mody's use of the term "subservient" above. Also illuminating in this regard is Strauss-Kahn's account of his 2010 conversation with EU officials, in which he acknowledged assuring the Europeans that they would be "the leaders."

To some extent, this issue may be a matter of semantics. It is fair to say that the IMF could have exercised a veto over Troika decisions, even in the early stages of the crisis, if it had threatened to withhold its support. In that sense, the Fund was coequal to the other institutions. But as I hope this book has made clear, abundant evidence shows that the Fund generally gave way when confronted with strongly held positions among top European policy makers — Trichet, Merkel and Schäuble in particular. On one occasion when Strauss-Kahn threatened an IMF withdrawal from the Troika — with regard to Portugal — his bluff was called, as noted at the end of chapter 9. In any event, the Fund's role was not nearly as senior as it ought to have been.

The IEO did agree that the Fund's handling of the crisis "helped create the perception that the IMF treated Europe differently" from other members. In particular, according to the IEO, the Fund's board was accorded only a "perfunctory role in key decisions," which muted the voice of non-European member countries (such as Brazil and India) whose officials were skeptical of the approach taken.

See IMF IEO, 2016, "The IMF and the Crises in Greece, Ireland and Portugal: An Evaluation by the Independent Evaluation Office," July, www.ieo-imf.org/ieo/pages/EvaluationImages267.aspx. A number of background papers, written by individual authors, provide excellent insights on specific issues covered in the main report.

Ideally, the Fund should have gotten even more clout, in the form of what I will call a "super-senior" partnership — that is, the authority to set terms and conditions for the entire euro zone, as per the argument made by Ted Truman that was mentioned in chapter 2. Rather than sitting on the same side of the negotiating table as the ECB, the Fund should have been on the opposite side, and it should have had the power to require action from all of the member countries, not just the ones urgently in need of international assistance. The Fund was coming to the rescue of the euro; if the countries using that currency were not willing to take the steps that the Fund believed necessary, they of course had the right to refuse. But the Fund had the right, and arguably the duty, to tell the Europeans they would then be left to their own devices.

Fully recognizing that the preceding paragraph may have stretched the boundaries of geopolitical reality, I believe one more demand by the IMF to the member countries of the euro zone would have been in order. The Fund should have extracted a guarantee that every cent of its loan to Greece would be paid back. Above and beyond assurance that the IMF's preferred-creditor status would be respected, in other words, the countries belonging to European Monetary Union should have protected the Fund against any financial loss. By putting its imprimatur on such a dicey program, the IMF was taking a huge reputational risk. Under such circumstances, it should not have been expected to put its financial integrity at risk too. The countries that were the main beneficiaries of the IMF's action — whose currency was being saved — should have been required to provide safeguards against such an eventuality. The logic behind this argument became even more compelling as the likelihood of Grexit rose in 2012 and thereafter.

To some readers, the argument that the IMF should have had so much power relative to European governments may sound suspiciously akin to advocacy of world government. Let me stress, therefore, that I am not proposing to put a fleet of black helicopters at the disposal of Madame Lagarde or her successors; given the current state of human evolution, the sovereignty of nation-states appears to be desirable and durable — unassailable, even. Under such a system, any country can reject the terms that an international lender seeks to impose if its government concludes that the aid on offer isn't worth the cost. But where problems are global in nature — as in the case of volatile international capital flows — the world needs robust multilateral institutions to respond. And such institutions can only be effective in the long run if member countries properly nurture them. Their effectiveness will atrophy if member countries exploit them for narrow purposes of national self-interest.

Strauss-Kahn bears almost sole responsibility for the terms under which the IMF joined the Troika. Lest he be condemned too harshly, it is worth recalling the circumstances he was facing at the time. He was heading an institution that was still recuperating from its existential crisis, and remained in some danger of falling back into perceived irrelevancy. Moreover, having played a second-fiddle role to Europe in the rescue of Latvia, the Fund could not easily draw the line against doing the same in the case of Greece. If Strauss-Kahn had taken a "my way or the highway" stance regarding the Greek program, European policy makers might very well have rejected IMF involvement. He took a gamble that keeping the Fund at the table would guide management of the crisis in a favourable direction and improve chances for a good outcome, while at the same time avoiding another marginalization for his institution.

My reasons for using the term "Faustian bargain" in my initial reference to this arrangement are hopefully now apparent. As with many such bargains, the hope at the time was that the costs to the IMF — and the global financial system it oversees — would be less oppressive than they eventually proved to be.

The first big price the Fund paid was the legal acrobatics it had to perform in the process of facilitating the first Greek rescue in May 2010. The change in the No More Argentinas rule may have been unavoidable amid the frenzy to make sure the program was approved in time to prevent a default. But an opportunity was squandered to arrange a solution early on that could have rendered Greece's debt load sustainable. And the Fund was set up for castigation as a toady of Europe's big powers, especially once the unsustainability of that debt became glaringly obvious.

How much better would Greece have fared if a restructuring had taken place well before March 2012? That is impossible to say, but with a less burdensome debt load, Athens would have had more leeway to manage its fiscal affairs, and although painful budget cuts and tax increases would have been required in any event, the degree of austerity could have been substantially mitigated. The Greek body politic might have responded more positively to structural reforms if citizens had seen that creditors were sharing in the national sacrifice by taking major losses. Economists will probably continue debating this counterfactual scenario for decades. Whatever it might have meant for Greece, it could have absolved the IMF from complicity in lending to an over-indebted borrower.

The IMF's own verdict on this question is admirably self-critical. It came in the form of a mid-2013 report on the first Greek program that was popularly dubbed "the mea culpa paper" and was written by a staff team (without the official endorsement of the board).[9] The term "mea culpa" is a bit of a misnomer, because the report did not actually say the Fund erred in approving the May 2010 rescue; it said there was little choice given "the considerable dangers for the euro area and the global economy should Greece have been allowed to default." But the authors, pointing out the grossly over-optimistic economic assumptions underlying the program, argued that the country's bondholders should have been forced to take haircuts much sooner than they did — a mistake the report pinned on European policy makers. "[N]ot tackling the public debt problem decisively at the outset or early in the program created uncertainty about the euro area's capacity to resolve the crisis and likely aggravated the contraction in output," the report said. "An upfront debt restructuring would have been

9 IMF, 2013, "Greece: Ex Post Evaluation of Exceptional Access under the 2010 Stand-By Arrangement," Country Report No. 13/156, June, www.imf.org/external/pubs/ft/scr/2013/cr13156.pdf.

better for Greece although this was not acceptable to the euro partners[10]... [it] could have eased the burden of adjustment on Greece and contributed to a less dramatic" recession in that country. Furthermore, "The delay provided a window for private creditors to reduce exposures and shift debt into official hands...leaving taxpayers and the official sector on the hook."

Regarding Ireland, too, a similar staff report published four years after the 2010 rescue took the view that the IMF had been wrong to go along with the decision to bail out senior bondholders of Irish banks.[11] The authors observed that in retrospect, burning the bondholders would have saved Irish taxpayers billions of euros, and the report argued that doing so would have sparked less contagion than was feared at the time. "Spillovers should have been limited if markets and bondholders of Irish senior unsecured banks debt were expecting a bail-in," the report said. "Indeed, Irish (senior unsecured) bank bonds traded at the time at levels consistent with clear anticipations of a principal haircut....Moreover, even if...contagion risks were considered important, steps could have been taken to ring fence these through appropriate policy responses." Several years after the fact, the authors added, "adverse legacy effects" remain, "relat[ing] principally to issues of perceived fairness and burden sharing."[12]

---

10 European officials have raised doubts about the report's suggestion that the IMF was ahead of the curve in the spring of 2010. "I have absolutely no recollection that the IMF called for anything that would be stronger" on Greek debt, Trichet told Reuters in an interview shortly after the report's publication. "It seems to me that there is some kind of reconstruction of what has happened." Olli Rehn agreed, saying, "I don't recall Dominique Strauss-Kahn proposing early debt restructuring, but I do recall that Christine Lagarde was opposed to it" when she was French finance minister. These statements are no doubt honest, but they do not contradict the revelations in previous chapters, such as the material in chapter 6 about the secret talks that Fund staffers held to make the case for a debt restructuring, since the Europeans invited to those talks did not include either the ECB or the Commission.

11 IMF, 2015, "Ireland: Ex Post Evaluation of Exceptional Access under the 2010 Extended Arrangement," Country Report 15/20, January, www.imf.org/external/pubs/ft/scr/2015/cr1520.pdf.

12 EU policy has been changed so that when a bank needs a government bailout, both junior and senior bondholders must be bailed in first, by imposing haircuts on their claims. But this policy was undergoing a severe challenge in mid-2016, when the Italian government vigorously resisted imposing haircuts on such bondholders because many of them were individual savers of relatively modest means; political pressure to spare them was intense.

As will be recalled from chapter 9, the IMF gave in on the bondholder issue after the G7 had held a conference call. The Fund's "mea culpa" paper on Ireland therefore contains only vague hints of the differences that arose within the Troika. With regard to this episode, it is instructive to spin a small fantasy how events might have gone differently. If the IMF had held super-senior status instead of mere junior partnership, might not the Fund's initial view have prevailed, making it possible to resolve the Irish crisis a lot less messily and more fairly? The answer is unknowable; fortunately, Ireland's crisis has had a much happier ending than Greece's.

How refreshing it was when, in late 2011, the IMF began stiffening its spine vis-à-vis Europe. Lagarde's speech daring to state the truth about European banks' capital shortfalls was an early sign of a new and more resolute institutional mindset. The Fund began insisting on more realistic growth forecasts and debt sustainability analyses for Greece; Blanchard issued his analyses on fiscal multipliers; the Fund's demands that the program for Cyprus include creditor bail-ins won the day. During 2015, the IMF was at its boldest yet in facing down both Greece and its European creditors, as witnessed most clearly in the public release of its debt sustainability analyses over European objections.

Better late than never, the IMF's assertiveness during this period helped improve the management of the crisis. But it did not come in time for Greece, and the Fund could not turn back the clock on its own major lapses. The reasons for the change are also important to bear in mind. Tempting as it is to conclude that the dauntless Lagarde showed more gumption than Strauss-Kahn, the crucial factor was the different position the IMF found itself in during the months after Lagarde's arrival. This was the period when Europe's need for Fund involvement — both its money and its credibility — was at its peak.

Commendable as the IMF's frankness was in 2015 regarding Greek debt sustainability, the Fund should have been tougher regarding the country's official debt — and acted sooner. Imagine, for example, if Fund officials had forcefully exercised their influence to obtain a HIPC-type debt-relief plan for Greece, of the sort advanced in late 2012 by

French officials (as noted in chapter 16). Such an approach might have envisioned cutting Greek debt in half after six years of demonstrated, root-and-branch reform of the country's clientelistic system, including a painful overhaul of pensions, but using substantially lower targets for the long-term primary budget surplus than 3.5 percent of GDP so that the degree of fiscal contraction would be lessened. Athens would have had ample incentive to deliver in the form of both carrot (major debt relief in the future) and stick (no debt relief, even the implied threat of Grexit, if the reforms didn't materialize). What a pity that instead, the IMF ended up supporting an approach that prolonged austerity, with Greek officials making hollow promises to meet stringent fiscal targets and then being held to account when they fell short. It would have been preferable for the IMF to extract itself from the Greek morass than associate itself with this folly.

Moreover, the IMF never went so far as to demand a super-senior partnership in the Troika, not even during the Lagarde era, when the Fund's leverage was far greater than before. To fully appreciate why the Fund should have been bestowed with power to set euro-zone-wide conditionality, readers should cast their minds back to 2012. A host of measures were in motion that would finally quell the crisis, at least in the virulent form it had taken starting in 2010. The orderly restructuring of Greek private debt was completed early in the year. European banks were bolstering their capital under pressure from regulators, making them less vulnerable to a possible default and thus reducing the danger of contagion. Banking union was in the process of initiation, which helped ease concerns that in some countries (Spain, in particular), governments might lack the financial wherewithal to bail out their fragile banking systems. Fiscal disciplines were being strengthened. Most important of all, Draghi was marshalling support for OMT, meaning that at last a credible firewall was being erected.

Why did it take so long — both to restructure Greek debt and do these other things? One big reason is that various steps had to be taken more or less in concert. Dealing with Greece's debt, which was essential to minimize constant worries of the monetary union being shattered by disorderly default, was hard to tackle until the problem of contagion looked like it could be contained. A credible anti-contagion firewall had to wait because of concerns of the German government and the ECB — the entities that controlled large amounts of euros. They were reluctant to commit massive resources to a firewall because they feared that doing so would ease pressure for resolving other fundamental weaknesses in Europe, both at the individual country level and at the monetary union level. In other words, nobody wanted to move, even on measures that were clearly essential and desirable, unless others did too, and building political consensus for all these actions took time.

The only way to overcome this problem was for an outside actor to tell all the European actors what to do — to knock a lot of heads together, so to speak — and the only outsider with any legitimate credentials for playing such a role was the IMF. Instead, the opposite occurred. The Europeans would be "the leaders," the problem being that nobody in Europe was fully capable of leading the others. At one turning point after another, European policy makers took just enough action to avoid the worst, perpetuating stalemate and setting the stage for the next blow-up. In the end, Europe accomplished a great deal — considerably more than could have been imagined in 2010 — reaching agreement on new rules, establishing new institutions, creating new firefighting mechanisms, and reducing many vulnerabilities. Given the institutional and political constraints, perhaps a faster pace of reform would have been impossible. But under pressure from an international institution with super-senior authority, Europe might have done all those things much more efficiently, and at less cost to millions of people.

Much remains undone in Europe. New chapters in the euro-zone crisis may yet unfold; the Italian banking system was beset by jitters in mid-2016, and serious doubts were arising over the durability of Portugal's recovery. Only in the first quarter of 2016 did GDP in the 19-nation bloc finally recover to the pre-crisis level of early 2008. (The US economy had bounced back by 2011.) Amid persistent deflationary pressures, unemployment for the full euro area was still stuck above 10 percent in the spring of 2016, and although some countries were enjoying healthy expansions — notably Germany, the Netherlands and Ireland — joblessness continued to plague Spain (20 percent), Italy (11.4 percent) and of course Greece (24 percent). The region has been drawing attention mostly because of the migration crush, terrorist attacks, rise of extremist movements and other political forces that are widening social divisions and threatening to undermine the European experiment. But economic woes may prove even more destabilizing. Fresh financial shocks may materialize as a result of policy shortcomings such as the failure to complete banking union and fully break the doom loop between sovereigns and banks. If so, Europeans may regret having spurned the idea of according the IMF more influence over region-wide matters.

This is not to imply that the IMF is endowed with such brilliant insight that it can be assured of diagnosing every international economic and financial problem accurately and prescribing optimal policies. Quite the contrary, this book has provided extensive evidence showing how the Fund often makes faulty assessments, some of the most embarrassing examples including its failure to foresee vulnerabilities in Europe and its appraisal regarding the viability of Latvia's currency. The Fund's erroneous analyses, which afflict both its surveillance and crisis management, stem inevitably from the bewildering complexity of modern financial markets. But the case for the Fund exercising supreme authority in financial crisis situations should be based not on its infallibility (which it clearly does not have), but on its independence, objectivity and global perspective. In other words, although the Fund cannot credibly claim to have superior wisdom regarding each and every crisis that comes along, it should be in a position to assert that its analysis must take priority by dint of its status as a multilateral institution entrusted by the international community to exercise neutral, objective judgment about the best possible resolution. The Fund ought to listen closely to the opinions of outsiders, especially other institutions that may be joining it in rescues. There should be no doubt, however, about which institution gets to call the shots on the terms and conditions for the assistance involved.

Should Strauss-Kahn have taken a more aggressive stance by demanding a senior partnership role in the Troika, or maybe even super-senior? Should Lagarde have taken advantage of the IMF's enhanced leverage to insist on super-senior status? These matters of hindsight, although well worth debate, are not as crucial as the question of what the IMF ought to do now to undo, or at least mitigate, the damage done to its credibility and effectiveness in future crises.

Perhaps it will be Asia, perhaps it will be Latin America — nobody can predict with certainty where the next financial crisis will be centred. But when it happens, powerful countries may insist that the IMF play a junior partner role again, based on the precedent set in Europe. They may wish to use the IMF to endorse their view of how matters should be handled, possibly for narrow reasons of national interest (protecting their big banks from taking severe losses, for example). Although the euro zone is *sui generis* to some extent, as the only major region of the world with a currency union, that does not mean the problem that arose there with regard to the IMF's role could not happen elsewhere.

Regional financial institutions and ad hoc arrangements among countries are on the rise, one motive being to create alternatives to the IMF or at least influential adjuncts to it. The most recent of these is the BRICS countries' $100 billion Contingency Reserve Arrangement (CRA), a pool of currencies intended "to forestall short-term balance of payments pressures, provide mutual support and further strengthen financial stability."[13] The CRA, the establishment of which was agreed in July 2014, is modelled on a similar currency-pooling arrangement called the Chiang Mai Initiative that was launched some years ago among Asian countries. Although these entities will never supplant the IMF, it is not hard to imagine that, in a crisis, they could be used to help tilt the terms of rescue packages in directions that suited major countries' governments, against the Fund's best judgment.

Such an approach would erode the IMF's value as a global public goods provider, which would be to the long-term detriment of all. The Fund needs to reclaim its historic role as the ultimate arbiter in financial crises, based (as noted above) on its independence and neutrality.

13 People's Bank of China, 2014, "Treaty for the Establishment of a BRICS Contingent Reserve Arrangement," June 21, www.pbc.gov.cn/english/130721/2882232/index.html.

Unfortunately, the IMF cannot command sufficient respect for either its independence or neutrality to stake out such a position. It has acquired too much baggage, in particular during the euro-zone crisis, that calls its independence into question. Considerable efforts should be made, both at the Fund and among its shareholders, to shed that baggage.

First on the list of essential steps is governance reform. The IMF's member countries agreed to a redistribution of quota shares in 2010, along with an accord to double permanent quota contributions, as noted in chapter 12. Europe's surfeit of power on the executive board relative to its share of world GDP was reduced, but only modestly; an imbalance remains. Moreover, the deal was stymied for five years because of a stalemate in the US Congress, where Republican lawmakers balked at approving the necessary legislation. The good news is that in December 2015, Congress finally approved the legislation, so IMF quotas are now both larger (about $660 billion) and a bit more fairly apportioned than before.[14] Although the IMF won't change meaningfully as a result, and the accord does not boost the Fund's overall firepower (arrangements to borrow from member countries are shrinking in proportion), the institution's legitimacy has been enhanced somewhat. One worry is that because of the congressional delay, chances are bleak for securing further initiatives to beef up Fund finances or shift quotas anytime in the near future, even if the need arises.

Just as important for IMF governance, if not more so, would be an end to the European monopoly over the IMF managing directorship — which will, in turn, require an end to the American monopoly over the World Bank presidency. Despite repeated promises by US and European officials to eliminate this problem, political pressures to maintain the current system are strong on both sides of the Atlantic. Lagarde is just starting her second five-year term in mid-2016, so a long time will pass before any non-European candidate can even get a

14 For example, China gained 2.3 percentage points in voting share, putting it in third place behind the United States and Japan. Brazil also gained, so it is at least ahead of Belgium. EU countries lost about 1.6 percentage points; the bloc's votes now account for 29.4 percent of the total.

crack at the IMF job. She has re-emphasized her independence from Europe, and to a significant extent her actions have spoken as loudly as her words, but she ought to go further. She should take what I have called an "oath of objectivity" — swearing that she will neither seek nor accept any public office, elected or appointed, in France or any European agency or institution, for at least two years after leaving the IMF. She has been mentioned as a possible future president of France, a job for which she may well be brilliantly suited. But the crisis in the euro zone is not entirely extinguished, and the Fund's biggest exposure is still to a euro-zone country; Lagarde therefore continues to face a potential conflict of interest. For the sake of the institution, she should do everything in her power to eliminate doubts about where her loyalties lie.

Second, the IMF board should formally adopt a "never again" position regarding the Fund's assumption of junior partner status in rescues. This would understandably draw objections from non-European countries that it is akin to closing the barn door long after the cow's escape, because it would come after the Fund had already taken junior partnership during the euro-zone crisis. The Fund cannot undo the past in Europe, but it can rectify at least some of the institutional damage that was inflicted. The board could state that if IMF assistance is required for any euro-zone member in the future — hardly an implausible scenario — members of the board representing the bloc's countries would be expected to refrain from voting, as Jim Flaherty, Canada's late finance minister, suggested in the spring of 2012.[15] Flaherty's proposal should be resurrected and approved. Furthermore, IMF aid for a euro-zone country would entail conditions for the entire bloc, not just the individual member nation.

Third, the IMF should go further toward making sure that its judgments are as technocratic as possible — and seen to be so. One good way to do this is to borrow a leaf from the World Trade Organization (WTO) by using independent tribunals to adjudicate contentious issues. The WTO's system, for good reason, is widely recognized as one of the few

15 Robin Harding, Claire Jones and Joe Leahy, 2012, "IMF secures $430 bn to boost firepower," *Financial Times*, April 20.

successful innovations in international governance. When countries accuse each other of violating the rules of international trade, panels of outside experts weigh the evidence and render judgments, which command impressive respect and compliance because of their perceived fairness and objectivity. As I have suggested previously,[16] the IMF could use tribunals of this kind to render verdicts on complaints that countries are guilty of fomenting external instability or maintaining fundamentally misaligned exchange rates. Emerging-market countries are understandably skeptical that such issues will receive a fair hearing if the judge and jury consists of the IMF staff, management and board; they would probably be more willing to abide by rules if the allegations were to be judged by neutral parties according to objective criteria. The Fund ought to look for ways of incorporating this kind of mechanism into all manner of important decisions.[17] Although crises such as Greece's may be too fast-moving to allow for the deliberation that would be required, the idea should not be dismissed out of hand. Susan Schadler has raised an interesting example of how this might work in such cases:

> Does the IMF have sufficient independence from political influences to make efficient and timely decisions on the balance between financing, adjustment and restructuring? Should a separate, independent body, charged with assessing the nature of crises — specifically whether a crisis stems from illiquidity or an inability/unwillingness to repay — be set up? Would such a body, serving its judgment in advance of decisions on financing and adjustment made by the IMF itself, help to offset political interference?[18]

16 Blustein, 2013, *Off Balance: The Travails of Institutions That Govern the Global Financial System,* Waterloo, ON: CIGI, chapter 9.

17 I acknowledge that trade rules are precise and legally binding, whereas issues such as fundamental misalignment of currencies are judgment calls on which views can reasonably differ. Even so, independent tribunals may be the best way to resolve disputes.

18 Schadler, 2012, *Sovereign Debtors in Distress: Are Our Institutions Up to the Challenge?* CIGI and Institute for New Economic Thinking. CIGI Papers No. 6. August, www.cigionline.org/sites/default/files/no.6.pdf.

Fourth, the IMF should finally demand indemnification from Europe against loss on its loans to Greece. Lagarde should have sought such a guarantee sooner, but it is not too late, and as long as danger of Grexit remains, so does the need for the Fund to protect its finances. One argument against such a move is that it would create a kind of moral hazard for the Fund; reducing the Fund's financial risk may make it prone to lend too recklessly if similar cases arise in the future. What is to keep the Fund from joining in dodgy rescues of over-indebted countries such as Greece if it doesn't stand to lose money? This problem can, and should, be addressed by altering the Fund's rules about lending to countries with questionable debt sustainability.

That last point about countries with questionable debt sustainability raises another issue where policy change is sorely needed. The case for a better approach to sovereign debt problems is even stronger in the wake of the euro-zone crisis than it was before.

When people borrow lots of money and fall into financial distress, one of the first solutions that usually comes to their minds is to seek some kind of debt relief from their creditors, or perhaps even walk away from their obligations. It stands to reason that the same goes for countries. Governments that have gotten into debt trouble will naturally look for ways to reduce their burdens — indeed, they will be all too prone to negotiate more favourable repayment terms as soon as they can possibly do so, and maybe even default if they can get away with it. This is one justification for rejecting international bankruptcy schemes such as the one the IMF proposed in 2001; countries must be discouraged from pursuing the easy path of debt relief.

Logical as that line of argumentation may seem, an IMF paper published in April 2013 offered a powerful rebuttal. Experience showed, the paper said, that the biggest problem with over-indebted countries was not excessive eagerness to seek relief but excessive reluctance. Policy makers typically wait too long to face the reality of debt unsustainability, and when they finally do, they do not go far enough in addressing it. As a result, the paper said, "[D]ebt restructurings have often been too little and too late."[19]

This was no ordinary IMF paper. It was based on input from a wide range of staff, and it was aimed at sparking a fundamental rethink by the international community about how to handle countries that are struggling with debt — a problem that was no longer limited to emerging markets, as Greece had shown. Like all IMF documents, it was technical and jargon-filled, but its underlying reasoning was comprehensible to anyone with a rudimentary grasp of how economies work: sometimes because of their own irresponsibility, sometimes because of bad luck, countries find themselves owing more to creditors than they can reasonably afford to pay, and as desirable as it normally is to honour the sanctity of contractual obligations, circumstances may arise in which abrogating that principle is necessary. Domestic bankruptcy laws properly recognize this necessity by giving debtors — both individuals and companies — a second chance while ensuring that creditors receive equitable treatment. At the international level, too, the system should provide ways for countries to reduce overly onerous debts to levels proportionate to their ability to pay — and with as little costly delay as possible.

Just as it had after Argentina's default, the Fund was undertaking to learn from its mistakes. "In hindsight, the Fund's assessments of debt sustainability and market access may sometimes have been too sanguine," the paper said, adding that this was partly attributable to powerful outsiders who "may have an interest in accepting, and pressuring the Fund to accept" such assessments. Beyond that, the paper noted, "there have been important developments in sovereign debt restructuring" that would make future cases more difficult to manage successfully. For shorthand purposes, those untoward developments can be defined as "Greece" and "Griesa."

19 IMF, 2013, "Sovereign Debt Restructuring—Recent Developments and Implications for the Fund's Legal and Policy Framework," April 26, www.imf.org/external/np/pp/eng/2013/042613.pdf.

Greece was the most obvious case of "too little, too late," and the paper tacitly acknowledged it had been poorly handled. By modifying the No More Argentinas rule, "the Fund lowered the bar" for making big loans, leaving itself more vulnerable to pressure for delay on the debt issue. This had been done largely because of fear of contagion; even so, "the official bailout strategy did not prove sufficient...and did not avert a spreading of the crisis beyond Greece." In retrospect, the paper said that in cases involving overly indebted countries belonging to currency unions, "the appropriate response" would be to restructure the country's debt sooner and "deal with contagion effects of restructuring head-on by...requiring that currency union authorities establish adequate safeguards promptly and decisively," for example, by establishing firewalls and recapitalizing banks.[20] Even after debt restructuring became unavoidable and an enormous haircut was imposed on bondholders in March 2012, Athens still could not recover growth or debt sustainability, and had to stagger back for more restructuring.

The very enormity of the haircut, and the orderly way in which it was conducted, might lead one to believe that the Greek case at least provided a useful precedent for other debt-strapped countries to follow if they need a restructuring. Not so; several unusual factors were at work in making Greece's restructuring proceed smoothly, as noted in chapter 14. Worse yet, certain aspects of the Greek debt odyssey portend serious adversity for other countries down the road.

Recall what happened after the 2012 restructuring when billionaire "vulture investor" Kenneth Dart earned a bonanza by holding out against the deal. Because the Greek government feared being sued by Dart, and figured that it had better pay him and a number of other holdouts the full amount they were owed (about €6.4 billion), the world's investors have learned that they have a big incentive to follow Dart's lead by holding out when similar circumstances arise. That severely complicates the future ability of sovereign debtors to

20 As those words suggest, the IMF would have liked the power to "require" action on the part of the entire euro zone, not just the individual countries seeking Fund assistance.

restructure, as does a maddening legal quirk that made it possible for Dart to reap his windfall.

The quirk stems from the way CACs usually work — namely, without full collective action. The bonds Dart bought had CACs, but that didn't mean he could be forced by a supermajority vote of all Greek bondholders into joining them in the restructuring. Like most bonds with CACs, the clauses applied only to the individual series of bonds that he bought rather than all Greek bonds as a group. His investment strategy was a masterpiece of lawful profiteering: he could buy just enough bonds in a single series to ensure that he could block a supermajority vote in favour of restructuring that series. Moreover, his bonds had been issued under foreign law, so they were not affected by the legislation enacted by the Greek Parliament that made it possible to haircut so many other bonds. That legislation applied to bonds issued under Greek law, which constituted the vast majority of the government's private debt, and the CACs that were inserted retroactively applied to all Greek-law bonds in the aggregate rather than individual series. Being legally unencumbered by that parliamentary act, Dart was free to hold out — and again, to teach the world an instructive lesson, namely that the CACs currently contained in most sovereign bonds may be ineffective the way they are formulated.

The other "important development" in sovereign debt — Griesa — refers to a 2012 ruling by Judge Thomas Griesa of the US Court for the Southern District of New York. The decision came in the long-running case that bondholders have brought against Argentina for its default and debt restructuring. The judge (whose name is pronounced Gri-SAY) handed a resounding victory to vulture investors, transforming the balance of power between sovereign governments and their creditors. For the first time since the era of gunboat diplomacy, when militaries were dispatched to enforce financial claims overseas, lenders were getting a useful remedy against the traditional rights of sovereigns to protect their assets from seizure.

In this litigation, as noted in chapter 7, the main plaintiff, investor Paul Singer, was demanding full payment of principal and interest on the Argentine bonds he had bought even though the vast majority of bondholders had accepted a deal in which they received new Argentine bonds worth about 33 cents on the dollar. After years of ruling that the Argentine government must pay Singer — to little effect, because Buenos Aires exercised its sovereign right to refuse — Judge Griesa finally gave the vultures legal means to obtain the riches they were seeking. Based on legal wording in bond contracts known in Latin as *pari passu* (equal footing), Griesa decreed that as long as Argentina continued to deny Singer payment on his claims, it would be forbidden to continue making payments of principal and interest on its new (restructured) bonds. Not only that, the judge put teeth into his ruling, by issuing an injunction prohibiting any financial institution from violating it. This meant sanctions for contempt of court could be slapped on the New York bank that was administratively processing Argentina's distribution of payments, if the bank — or any other financial institution — continued to perform that duty. It further meant that if Argentine government funds were transmitted to New York for the purpose of paying other bondholders, those funds would be vulnerable to attachment by Singer.

Many legal experts expressed astonishment at the peculiar reasoning in Griesa's ruling, not least because it threatened the rights of bondholders who had accepted Argentina's restructuring deal to collect what they were owed. What sane bondholder would go along with a debt-restructuring offer in the future, given the risk that a single holdout might be able to block payments under the new terms? At the IMF, anguish was profound, enough so that Fund officials planned to enter an amicus curiae (friend of the court) brief urging the Supreme Court to overturn the decision. But the high court declined to even consider the appeal, and the pro-creditor fundamentalism of Griesa's ruling now infuses the case law governing billions of dollars worth of sovereign bonds that many countries have issued in the world's biggest financial market.[21]

Then, in the spring of 2016, came a final, iniquitous turn in this story. Recognizing that Argentina was playing a losing hand, the country's

21 Floyd Norris, 2014, "The Muddled Case of Argentine Bonds," *The New York Times*, June 24.

newly elected president, Mauricio Macri, reached a settlement with the vultures on very generous terms — enough so that Singer could collect approximately $2.4 billion, a gain of somewhere between 10 and 15 times his firm's original investment, according to an estimate by *The Wall Street Journal.*[22] (Dart also cashed in big on his Argentine bond holdings.) Not that Macri should be blamed; he rightly took action that was necessary for his country's economic revival and reintegration with the global economy. But an appalling precedent was set. Investors holding bonds of countries that seek debt restructuring are now aware of the potential to rake in fortunes by pursuing aggressive strategies similar to the approach taken by Singer and Dart. The odds have greatly increased that future Argentine- and Greek-style crises will be even harder to resolve and more prolonged than they are already.

To anyone who isn't a wild-eyed zealot for bondholder rights, a nostalgia buff for debtors' prisons or an investor in a vulture fund, it should be clear that the international framework for sovereign debt is imbalanced way too far in favour of the Darts and Singers of the world, and against countries that genuinely need debt restructuring. The only question is the extent to which power should be rebalanced.

Nobody would suggest going so far as to make debt restructurings the norm when countries undergo financial crises. In many cases, perhaps most, the IMF can manage crises with its traditional combination of loans plus an agreed list of policy adjustments by the stricken country. When that formula looks like it will succeed at putting the country back on solid footing, it should be used. Often, a mild form of PSI may be necessary in addition — a good example being South Korea's 1997 crisis, where the IMF rescue was supplemented by a well-coordinated arrangement for international banks to stop pulling their money out. If there is no need to include PSI, full respect should be accorded the contractual obligations that debtors owe their creditors.

22 Gregory Zuckerman, Julie Wernau and Rob Copeland, 2016, "After 15 Years, a Bond Trade Now Pays Off," *The Wall Street Journal,* March 2. To Judge Griesa's credit, he helped nudge the deals along so that the holdouts settled for somewhat less than they were demanding. The judge threatened to lift his injunction if the holdouts failed to negotiate in good faith.

But when a country has dug itself into such a deep hole that even a big financing package and painful adjustment appear unlikely to work, debt restructuring may be the only way out — the sooner the better. Although it may be too much to hope that the world's powers could agree to establish an international bankruptcy mechanism such as the one the IMF's Anne Krueger nobly proposed in 2001, some major institutional and legal reforms would help restore a balance that is both fair to all parties and beneficial to the world economy.

The era of Greece and Griesa has generated an abundance of good ideas, ranging from the sensibly practical to the daringly ambitious. My favourite is the proposed creation of a new type of IMF lending instrument called a Sovereign Debt Adjustment Facility (SDAF).[23] A country with high debt of doubtful sustainability could apply to the Fund for aid under the SDAF rather than seeking a traditional crisis loan. If the Fund determined that the country qualified (which would be based on a set of specified criteria), a debt-restructuring plan would be drafted, using a debt sustainability analysis that would be posted on a publicly available website for any interested parties (creditors, civil society groups) to offer comments and criticism. The debtor country would then negotiate terms with each creditor group, with the IMF reviewing the terms to ensure that burdens were being shared equitably. The restructuring would be subject to approval by a supermajority of creditors. And to deal with litigious holdouts, the IMF would amend its articles so that the assets and revenues of a country undergoing an SDAF would be protected against attachment — which, in turn, would be legally binding in courts of all member countries. (The Fund's membership would have to ratify any such amendment to the articles, of course.)

The IMF hasn't gone so far as to adopt the SDAF, but it hasn't been idle either on the sovereign debt front. One sensible innovation, proposed

23 Committee on International Economic Policy and Reform, 2013, "Revisiting Sovereign Bankruptcy," Brookings Institution, October, www.brookings.edu/~/media/research/files/reports/2013/10/sovereign-bankruptcy/ciepr_2013_revisitingsovereignbankruptcyreport.pdf.

in a staff paper in 2014,[24] would create a new type of rescue for countries that fall into a sort of grey zone between definite liquidity crises and definite solvency crises. Suppose the Fund believes a country to have a decent chance at debt sustainability but cannot be sure "with high probability." Should the Fund follow the course it took with Greece in May 2010, and mobilize a large official loan package? To that question, the Fund staff gave a firm "no." Better to take a different approach, which would work as follows: the IMF would provide a loan on condition that the country re-profiles its debt — not a haircut, but an extension of maturities, in a voluntary accord with creditors. That would give time to determine whether the program was likely to work and whether the debt was proving to be sustainable or not. If the program went off track, and the debt was shaping up as too burdensome for the country to bear, a haircut could be administered. If the opposite occurred — if the country emerged from crisis and regained investor confidence — then little harm would have been done by a mere debt reprofiling.

Moreover, this approach would be followed even in crises where contagion posed risks to the financial system. The hastily crafted May 2010 compromise would be reversed; the No More Argentinas rule would again apply in all decisions involving large loans. IMF General Counsel Sean Hagan offered a compelling response to those who argue that the Fund ought to hold off from any form of debt restructuring in crises that might affect other countries. "Delaying a restructuring because of concerns about contagion is not only ineffective, it's actually counterproductive," Hagan said at a May 2015 conference on sovereign debt. "Contagion is generated by uncertainty. If the market feels that even with [a] bailout the [country's] debt is still unsustainable, you haven't really addressed contagion."[25]

Opposition to the staff proposal was fierce — and potent, since some of it came from the US Treasury. Critics contended that the Fund staff

24 IMF, 2014, The Fund's Lending Framework and Sovereign Debt—Preliminary Considerations," June, www.imf.org/external/np/pp/eng/2014/052214.pdf.

25 Atlantic Council, 2015, "Reforming the Future: Lessons from Sovereign Debt Restructuring," May 14, www.atlanticcouncil.org/news/transcripts/reforming-the-future-lessons-from-sovereign-debt-restructuring.

was much too focused on rectifying the errors made in Greece, while ignoring the wider ramifications of its scheme. Consider the fact that Ireland and Portugal, like Greece, were deemed by the Fund to fall short of debt sustainability with "high probability," yet the Irish and Portuguese emerged from Troika programs in relatively good shape, without having restructured or reprofiled their debts. In years past, Brazil and Turkey also successfully turned their economies around with the help of fairly standard IMF rescues, overcoming widespread doubts about their debt sustainability. Requiring those countries to reprofile their debts might have impaired their recoveries, according to critics of the IMF staff's proposals. Moreover, won't investors rush to dump their holdings at the first sign of financial turmoil in a country if they think a debt reprofiling is almost certainly in the offing? Might not the result be more frequent crises, precisely the outcome the IMF is supposed to help prevent? And regarding contagion — shouldn't the Fund have *some* flexibility to provide the sort of rescue loans that Greece received in May 2010, in cases where tampering with a country's debt might pose a serious threat to the global financial system?

The critics won — unfortunately. In late January 2016, the IMF board approved a new policy regarding large rescues that watered down the initial staff proposal considerably.[26] The new policy keeps some good elements from the staff proposal. It restored the No More Argentinas rule, reversing the exception adopted in 2010 for cases of "systemic risk."[27] In grey-zone cases like Greece, reprofiling of debt will be a strong option. But the new policy envisions allowing a lot of flexibility and case-by-case decision making — too much, in my opinion. As desirable as flexibility may be in principle, it ought to be weighed against the fact that the Fund, and other official actors in the international community, are too prone to opt for piling debt atop debt when crises erupt. Rules constraining the Fund's flexibility, and requiring it to take certain action based on careful evaluation of a crisis-stricken country's debt sustainability, would force all policy makers to squarely face reality and move more expeditiously to optimal solutions.

26 IMF, 2016, "IMF Reforms Policy for Exceptional Access Lending," IMF Survey, January 29, www.imf.org/external/pubs/ft/survey/so/2016/POL012916A.htm.

27 Eliminating that exception was mandated by US Congress when it approved the quota reform legislation. So, on that score, the IMF had little choice.

Less controversially, the IMF has also thrown its weight behind an initiative to improve CACs — the new versions have been called "Super-CACs" — so that countries can restructure debts more easily when necessary.[28] The idea is to insert Super-CACs in all sovereign bonds issued henceforth, to make them as Dart-proof, Singer-proof and Griesa-proof as possible. Under model language for Super-CACs that was drafted in consultation with market participants, votes on restructuring would be taken by all of a country's bondholders in aggregate, rather than bond issue by bond issue. Moreover, the model language defines *pari passu* in a different way from that used by Judge Griesa in his 2012 decision. A number of countries have issued bonds containing Super-CACs, including Kazakhstan, Mexico and Vietnam.

Significant benefits will result from Super-CACs in the long run. But they are no panacea, because global markets are still full of old-style bonds with old-style CACs, which give the vultures continued opportunities to foment mischief. More than a decade will have to pass before the world's supply of sovereign bonds is dominated by Super-CACs.

The question about these recent IMF-endorsed reforms, therefore, is not whether they are good or bad; they will improve the system compared to what existed before. The question is whether they go far enough: they don't. To truly rebalance the international framework for sovereign debt against the vultures, and in favour of countries that genuinely need restructuring, a great deal more — the SDAF or something with the same order of ambition — is required.

Having gotten on a soapbox and made an argument for the policy measures I favour, I will now step down and acknowledge that this portion of the book is the one I think is least valuable. Many people with greater expertise than I have on these issues are more qualified

28 IMF, 2014, "Strengthening the Contractual Framework to Address Collective Action Problems in Sovereign Debt Restructuring," October, www.imf.org/external/np/pp/eng/2014/090214.pdf.

to mount soapboxes, and many, if not all, would offer different policy recommendations. Where I hope I have added value is in the previous chapters' accounts of momentous developments in recent financial history. As a journalist whose competitive advantage lies in reporting and writing a narrative rather than evaluating policy, I like to fancy that I have provided information that will be useful to the public debate.

The euro-zone crisis taught economists and policy makers many lessons — about excessive austerity, excessive profligacy, excessively tight money, excessively *loose* money, moral hazard, contagion, the pitfalls of incomplete currency unions, banking regulation, sovereign debt and much more. The next financial crisis, wherever it comes, could result from any one or combination of those factors. That is one reason why this book has stayed focused on the one constant we can always be sure of for the foreseeable future — namely, the benefits and costs of a strong and effective IMF.

There should be no need to worry about the IMF undergoing another existential crisis of the sort that occurred in the years leading up to 2008. Even if tranquility reigns for a prolonged period in global financial markets, memories of what happened in 2009 and thereafter will presumably suffice to squelch any suggestions that the world can get by without a crisis-fighting multilateral institution. But the deeper lessons of the IMF's misadventures in the euro-zone crisis must also be fully taken on board, and appropriate remedies adopted. Only then will the Fund stand a decent chance of providing global public goods of the sort the world needs.

NAME GUIDE

To help readers keep track of the large number of people introduced in this book, below is a list of individuals whose names appear more than once, with the job titles/responsibilities they held at the time of the events in question.

Josef Ackermann, chief executive, Deutsche Bank; chairman, Institute of International Finance

Nicos Anastasiades, president of Cyprus since February 2013

Jörg Asmussen, state secretary (deputy minister) at German Ministry of Finance, 2008–2011; member of the ECB executive board, with responsibility for international and European relations, 2012-2013

Bas Bakker, IMF economist

José Manuel Barroso, president of the European Commission until October 2014

Marek Belka, director of IMF European Department, November 2008 to May 2010

Silvio Berlusconi, prime minister of Italy until November 2011

Lorenzo Bini Smaghi, member of the ECB executive board until November 2011

Olivier Blanchard, IMF chief economist and director of the Research Department

Antonio Borges, director of IMF European Department, November 2010 to November 2011

Lee Buchheit, attorney specializing in sovereign debt management

Marco Buti, director-general for economic and financial affairs, European Commission since 2008

Kevin Cardiff, secretary general, Ireland Department of Finance

Ajai Chopra, deputy director, IMF European Department; head of mission to Ireland during the November 2010 rescue

Charles Collyns, assistant secretary of the US Treasury for international finance

Carlo Cottarelli, director, IMF Fiscal Affairs Department

Brian Cowen, prime minister of Ireland until March 2011

Charles Dallara, managing director, Institute of International Finance

Kenneth Dart, investor, "holdout" in Greek and Argentine bonds after restructuring

Rodrigo De Rato, managing director of the IMF from mid-2004 to late 2007; chairman of Bankia (Spanish financial institution) from its inception in December 2010 until its nationalization in May 2012

Michael Deppler, director of the IMF's European Department until mid-2008

Servaas Deroose, European Commission mission chief for Greece; deputy director-general, European Commission's Directorate for Economic and Financial Affairs

Jeroen Dijsselbloem, finance minister of the Netherlands since November 2012; president of the Eurogroup since January 2013

Yannis Dragasakis, deputy prime minister of Greece since January 2015

Mario Draghi, governor, Bank of Italy until November 2011; thereafter, president, ECB

Sean FitzPatrick, CEO, Anglo Irish Bank

Timothy Geithner, Secretary of the US Treasury in the Obama administration until January 2013

Alex Gibbs, member of IMF executive board for the United Kingdom

Lorenzo Giorgianni, deputy director, IMF SPR Department

Rishi Goyal, IMF mission chief for Greece, August 2014 to July 2015

Vittorio Grilli, director-general, Italian Treasury; chairman of Economic and Financial Committee of the European Union; deputy finance minister of Italy, November 2011 to July 2012; finance minister of Italy, July 2012 to April 2013

Mitu Gulati, law professor, co-author with Lee Buchheit of papers on sovereign debt

Sean Hagan, general counsel of the IMF

Gikas Hardouvelis, adviser to Greek prime minister Lucas Papademos, November 2011 to May 2012; finance minister of Greece, June 2014 to January 2015

Thomas Hockin, member of IMF executive board for Canada and other countries

François Hollande, president of France since May 2012

Patrick Honohan, governor of the Central Bank of Ireland

Jean-Claude Juncker, Luxembourgish politician; president of the Eurogroup until 2013; president of the European Commission as of November 2014

Peter Kažmir, finance minister of Slovakia

Mervyn King, governor of the Bank of England until 2013

Desmond Lachman, economist at the American Enterprise Institute

Christine Lagarde, finance minister of France until May 2011; then managing director of the IMF

Christopher Legg, member of IMF executive board for Australia and other countries

Jean Lemierre, senior adviser to chairman of BNP Paribas; top negotiator for creditors in Greek debt restructuring

Brian Lenihan, finance minister of Ireland until March 2011

Jacob Lew, US secretary of the Treasury since February 2013

John Lipsky, first deputy managing director of the IMF from September 2006 to September 2011

David Lipton, first deputy managing director of the IMF since September 2011

Meg Lundsager, member of IMF executive board for the United States until May 2014

Klaus Masuch, ECB representative to the Troika for Greece and Ireland

Angela Merkel, chancellor of Germany

Ashoka Mody, IMF mission chief for Ireland for Article IV missions in 2009 and 2010; no. 2 official in IMF mission during the November 2010 rescue

Reza Moghadam, director of the IMF's Strategy, Policy and Review Department until November 2011; then director of the European Department until mid-2014

Mario Monti, prime minister of Italy, November 2011 to April 2013

Pierre Moscovici, European commissioner for economic and financial aaffairs since November 2014

Alexei Mozhin, member of IMF executive board for Russia

Paulo Nogueira Batista, member of IMF executive board for Brazil and other countries

Michael Noonan, finance minister of Ireland since March 2011

George Papaconstantinou, finance minister of Greece, October 2009 to June 2011

Lucas Papademos, prime minister of Greece, November 2011 to May 2012

George Papandreou, prime minister of Greece, October 2009 to November 2011

Henry Paulson, secretary of the Treasury in the George W. Bush administration

Ceyla Pazarbasioglu, chief of IMF FSAP mission to Spain in 2012

Mariano Rajoy, prime minister of Spain since November 2011

Klaus Regling, top international policy maker at the German Finance Ministry until 1998; director-general, European Commission's Economic and Financial Affairs Directorate, 2001–2008; managing director, European Financial Stability Facility starting in July 2010, and of the European Stability Mechanism upon its inauguration in 2012

Olli Rehn, European commissioner for economic and monetary affairs until July 2014

Gerry Rice, director, IMF Communications Department

Panagiotis Roumeliotis, alternate IMF executive director, representing Greece

Robert Rubin, secretary of the US Treasury in the Bill Clinton administration

Philippos Sachinidis, finance minister of Greece, March 2012 to May 2012

Antonis Samaras, prime minister of Greece, July 2012 to January 2015

Michel Sapin, finance minister of France since April 2014

Nicolas Sarkozy, president of France until mid-2012

Susan Schadler, deputy director of the IMF's European Department until 2007; senior fellow at CIGI

Wolfgang Schäuble, finance minister of Germany

Shakour Shaalan, "dean" of the IMF executive board, representing Egypt and other countries

Paul Singer, hedge fund manager, "holdout" investor in Argentine bonds after restructuring

Jürgen Stark, member of ECB executive board, announced resignation September 2011

Yannis Stournaras, finance minister of Greece, July 2012 to June 2014

Dominique Strauss-Kahn, managing director of the IMF from November 2007 to May 2011

Lawrence Summers, chairman of the US National Economic Council in the Obama administration; secretary of the Treasury in the Bill Clinton administration

Haris Theoharis, permanent general secretary for revenue, Greece, January 2013 to June 2014

Poul Thomsen, IMF mission chief for Greece from 2010 to mid-2014; director of European Department since July 2014

Siddharth Tiwari, secretary of the IMF executive board until late 2011, then director of the Strategy, Policy and Review Department

Giulio Tremonti, finance minister of Italy until November 2011

Jean-Claude Trichet, president of the European Central Bank until October 2011

Euclid Tsakalotos, finance minister of Greece since July 2015

Alexis Tsipras, prime minister of Greece since January 2015

Donald Tusk, president of the European Council since December 2014

Herman Van Rompuy, president of the European Council until November 2014

Yanis Varoufakis, finance minister of Greece, January 2015 to July 2015

Delia Velculescu, economist in the IMF European Department; author of 2009 study on Greek structural reform; responsible for Cyprus program

Evangelos Venizelos, Greek minister of finance, June 2011 to March 2012; deputy prime minister, June 2013 to January 2015

Arvind Virmani, member of IMF executive board for India and other countries

René Weber, member of IMF executive board for Switzerland and other countries

Jens Weidmann, president of German Bundesbank since May 2011

Thomas Wieser, president of the Euro Working Group since January 2012

José Luis Zapatero, prime minister of Spain until December 2011